# Greek and Latin Literature

## A Comparative Study

Edited by John Higginbotham

METHUEN & CO LTD
11 NEW FETTER LANE LONDON EC4

*First published 1969 by Methuen & Co Ltd*
*11 New Fetter Lane, London EC4*
© *1969 by John Higginbotham*
*Printed in Great Britain by*
*Richard Clay (The Chaucer Press), Ltd.,*
*Bungay, Suffolk*
SBN 416 11480 6/31 (HB)
SBN 416 12020 2/49 (UP)

*Distributed in the U.S.A. by*
*Barnes & Noble Inc*

# Contents

# CONTENTS

# *Preface*

A fact of education long recognized, but only recently in prominence, is that subject barriers are artificial. The realization of this has two implications for the classic: not only must he beware of studying in isolated compartments two languages like Greek and Latin, between which so many interesting parallels and analogies exist, but he must beware of the view, never openly stated but too often tacitly assumed, that the humanities end with Tacitus. A similar, or rather converse, sin besets the modern linguist or historian when he is tempted to study the medieval or modern worlds without any reference to the mighty influences that shaped them; European history, literature, and thought should be seen as a continuum, in which to cut off any product from its source deprives us of complete understanding and hence of true scholarly study.

The gap has, of course, been bridged, for example in the study of philosophy in Greats, but such bridges have in the past been few and narrow. More recently there have been encouraging signs in the development of inter-curricular discipline in the schools and more broadly based courses (like the European Studies courses at Sussex) in the universities. More and more students of the contemporary scene are spurred to look for classical origins, and the classic is, one hopes, more and more inclined to look for echoes, influences, and results in the medieval and modern worlds. The new Oxford and Cambridge School Examining Board's classical syllabuses have given a useful lead in broadening the student's outlook away from 'Set Books' to the study of 'Topics', in which reference is to be made to later literatures wherever possible.

This book has a twofold function: to serve the classic by indicating the lines along which study of a given genre (tragedy, comedy, lyric poetry, etc.) may take place by giving an account of the development of that genre in Greek and

Latin, pointing to where the influences of Greek on Latin (and both on later literature, where relevant) are apparent, and presenting material for further study in the form of a bibliography; but it is to be hoped that it will also serve the student of Milton who wishes to know something of the development of the classical epic, the student of Racine or Anouilh or T. S. Eliot who needs to know about themes and structure in classical drama, the historian and the philosopher who also need to know about the earliest origins of their subject. It is in the hope that the book may have something to say to the non-specialist that quotations from Latin and Greek (except for a few where the stress is solely on the language and style of the original) have been translated, and the bibliographies include works of general interest as well as those necessary for scholarly study.

It is equally important to make clear what the book is not. It is not a history of classical literature. *Outlines of Classical Literature*, as well as handbooks on the individual languages, we already owe to the learned pen of Dr Rose.[1-3] Nor is the book meant to be comprehensive; considerations of space have induced a strict **selectivity of passages** in chapters such as *Lyric Poetry*, where no attempt has been made to survey the whole field but rather to compare a few well-chosen individual passages, **selectivity of authors** in chapters such as *Epic Poetry*, in which Statius and Silius Italicus give place, as representatives of Silver Latin Epic, to Lucan and Valerius Flaccus, and **selectivity of the genres** themselves: one may well ask, 'Why omit *Letter-writing*? Why omit *Literary Criticism*?' and so one could go on. The choice has not been easy; it has to some extent been determined by the importance and influence of the genre, by the specialist interests of the contributors available, and by the existence of some of the material already, for

1. H. J. Rose, *Outlines of Classical Literature*, Methuen University Paperbacks, 1959.

2. H. J. Rose, *A Handbook of Greek Literature: From Homer to the Age of Lucian*, Methuen, 1934.

3. H. J. Rose, *A Handbook of Latin Literature*, Methuen, 1936.

example, Levens on *Letter-writing*.[4] *Literary Criticism* is a huge and diverse subject; ancient, as well as modern, criticism inevitably makes its appearence *passim* in a book of this nature, but those who require more concentrated treatment could not do better than read Professor Grube's recent scholarly analysis of the ancient critics.[5] Such omissions, I regret, are necessary, if such a volume is not to evolve to inordinate lengths, or to prove intolerably and quite uselessly superficial in its treatment.

As one would expect in a book of this scope, most contributors have found the conciseness required of them their greatest challenge; but brevity is a salutary disciplinarian as well for precluding prolixity in the writer as for stimulating research in the reader, who will not offend us if he feels that the book has raised more questions than it answers. The student who looks here for quick essay material will be disappointed; but he will find the way charted. Here is a map and a compass, not a vehicle on which he simply has to step.

It cannot be claimed, however, that this book will do more than plug a glaring gap until such time as a university school is established which will do for literature what Greats has done for philosophy. If this volume, for all its blemishes, directs a little light in that direction it will not have been in vain.

J.E.H.

*March* 1969

4. R. G. C. Levens, Introduction to *A Book of Latin Letters*, Methuen, 1938.
5. G. M. A. Grube, *The Greek and Roman Critics*, Methuen University Paperbacks, 1965.

# List of Abbreviations

| | |
|---|---|
| A.J.Ph. | American Journal of Philology. |
| C.Q. | Classical Quarterly. |
| C.J. | Classical Journal. |
| Cl.Ph. | Classical Philology. |
| C.R. | Classical Review. |
| Cl.W. | Classical Weekly, later Classical World. |
| G. & R. | Greece & Rome. |
| G.R.B.S. | Greek, Roman & Byzantine Studies. |
| H.G.L. | H. J. Rose, *A Handbook of Greek Literature: From Homer to the Age of Lucian.* |
| H.L.L. | H. J. Rose, *A Handbook of Latin Literature.* |
| H.S.C.P. | Harvard Studies in Classical Philology. |
| J.R.S. | Journal of Roman Studies |
| Mus. Helv. | Museum Helveticum. |
| O.B.G.V. | *Oxford Book of Greek Verse.* |
| O.B.L.V. | *Oxford Book of Latin Verse.* |
| O.C.D. | *Oxford Classical Dictionary.* |
| O.C.T. | Oxford Classical Text. |
| Proc. Virg. Soc. | Proceedings of the Virgil Society. |
| R.E.L. | Revue des Etudes Latines. |
| T.A.P.A. | Transactions of the American Philological Association. |
| V.S.L. | Virgil Society Lecture. |
| V.S.L.S. | Virgil Society Lecture Summary. |
| Y.C.S. | Yale Classical Studies. |

# *Acknowledgements*

Acknowledgements are due for the following passages quoted in the text: excerpts from C. Bailey's translation of Lucretius, A. S. L. Farquharson's translation of Marcus Aurelius, H. T. Stewart's translation of Boethius and translations from *The Pre-Socratic Philosophers* by G. S. Kirk and J. E. Raven in Chapter I; C. M. Bowra's translation of Pindar and a passage from Fraenkel's *Horace* in Chapter II; a number of passages from *The Oxford Book of Greek Verse* in Chapter III; fragments of Ennius from *The Oxford Book of Latin Verse* and E. H. Warmington's *Fragments of Old Latin* (Loeb) and the quotation from C. S. Lewis about Charles Williams' *Arthurian Torso* in Chapter VI; translations of fragments of Attic comedy by J. M. Edmonds and P. Vellacott, D. Barrett's translation of Aristophanes' *Frogs*, E. W. Handley's of Menander's *Dyscolos*, E. F. Watling's of Plautus' *Aulularia*, and an excerpt from W. Beare's *The Roman Stage* in Chapter VII; a quotation from Gilbert Highet's *Juvenal the Satirist* in Chapter VIII; the Loeb translations of Plutarch's *Moralia* (F. C. Babbitt), Dio (E. Cary), Hippocrates' *Airs, Waters, Places* (W. H. S. Jones), Polybius (W. R. Paton) in Chapter X; the Loeb translations of Cato the Elder (W. D. Hooper) and of Cicero's *Pro Archia* (N. H. Watts) in Chapter XI.

# I

# Philosophy
## *Hilary Armstrong*

1 There are two special difficulties in composing a chapter on ancient philosophical writing for a comparative history of classical literature. The first is that philosophers are never exclusively or primarily concerned, and in some cases are not concerned at all, with producing works of literary art. A great deal of what was written by philosophers and about philosophy in the ancient world is pretty well unreadable except by those passionately interested in the thought of the authors. So one must select: and the selection will be bound to leave out a great deal which is of major philosophical importance. The mature works of Aristotle (the only ones of which we possess more than fragments) are the foundations of much of European philosophy; but they have no place in a history of literature. One help to selection is that philosophers in writing had different kinds of readers in view. Some of their works were written for circulation among small groups of people seriously interested in the subject. Others were intended for a much wider readership of cultivated people whom they wished, not simply to interest in, but to convert to philosophy. 'Convert' is the right word. Most of the ancient philosophers did not think of philosophy as nothing more than the solution of interesting intellectual problems or detached speculation with a view to constructing a logically coherent system of concepts. It was an all-embracing activity, engaging the whole energies of man in an effort to reach a living apprehension of the truth

about the universe, the Divine, and ourselves, and to live by that truth the only sort of life which could bring real and lasting happiness. It was a universal way of knowledge which was also a way of life, including physical science at one end and religion and morality at the other. It is necessary to understand this in order to appreciate fully the intelligent passion and power of the greatest ancient philosophical writing. Most of the works of great literary merit written by philosophers, though not all, fall into this class of works addressed to a wide circle of readers to stimulate them to turn to philosophy; though of course not all the works written with this purpose are of great literary merit.

2 The second difficulty in writing a chapter on ancient philosophy in a book whose main purpose is to compare Greek and Latin literature is that there is really no such thing as Roman Philosophy. There is only one philosophical tradition in the ancient world, the Greek. This had a wide, though generally rather superficial, influence. Most educated men in the Graeco-Roman world had some tincture of philosophy, but not enough to give them any deep understanding of it or desire to write about it. Some non-Greeks, however, were thoroughly well educated philosophically and full of a genuine enthusiasm for philosophy. Cicero and Lucretius are notable examples. But it was, of course, Greek philosophy in which they had been educated, and when they were moved by their knowledge of and enthusiasm for philosophy to write about it, it was Greek philosophy they wrote about, whether in Latin or, like the Emperor Marcus Aurelius, in Greek. We are not dealing with two distinct traditions or kinds of philosophical literature but with one, including works written in Greek by Greeks, works written in Latin by Romans, and works written in Greek by Romans. And at every period from the first century B.C., when Romans first began to write about philosophy, onwards the works written in Greek by Greeks were more numerous and more philosophically important than those written in Latin by Romans. A certain 'Romanity' is sometimes apparent in

these last, notably in the philosophical works of Cicero, but it is not so strong as to amount to philosophical originality. It is in Cicero no more than the distinctive accent of a Roman statesman, for whom philosophy was a subsidiary study, though an engrossing one, and a help and support for his main concerns and activities.

3 In view of these difficulties, the best thing to do in this chapter seems to be to survey some forms of philosophical writing in which works of high literary merit were produced in both Greek and Latin, noting resemblances and differences when there are any. There will be no attempt to mention everything written by the ancient philosophers; and it must always be remembered that a very great many works which are not readable enough to find a place in a history of literature are of great philosophical interest. Nor will there be any attempt to pair Greek and Latin works off tidily, or give the false impression that there are two distinct philosophical literatures.

4 PHILOSOPHICAL POETRY. Poetry in the epic metre is the oldest genre in Greek literature, but philosophical poetry is not the oldest kind of Greek philosophical literature. The first philosophers, the Milesians of the sixth century B.C., Thales (if he wrote anything at all), Anaximander, and Anaximenes, wrote in prose. The first Greek to write anything which could be described as philosophical poetry, as distinct from moral advice or story-telling about the gods, was Xenophanes of Colophon, probably a younger contemporary of Anaximenes (the dating of these early philosophers is very uncertain). Xenophanes was a poet and sage who after the capture of his native city, Colophon, by the Medes in 546/5 B.C. wandered for the rest of his long life (he died, perhaps, about 475) over the Greek world singing or reciting his own poems: he was not a professional Homeric reciter or rhapsode. Xenophanes was a man of wide interests, particularly concerned about religion and the gods. He was the originator of the criticism of the traditional stories about the gods told by the older poets which had so great an influence on the fifth century and later. He attacked these

stories on grounds both of morality and reason, and was the
first Greek to assert that there was one god, whom he probably
thought of as either identical with or pervading the universe.
He is the founder of Greek philosophical theology. His fragments show him to have been a master of clear, vigorous
expression of ideas, both critical and positive, in verse. He has
the epic dignity where it is required, but is capable of a touch of
humour where necessary and desirable. Two short fragments
will give some idea of his quality. The first is critical of Homeric
anthropomorphism:

ἀλλ' εἰ χεῖρας ἔχον βόες ἵπποι τ'ἠὲ λέοντες,
ἢ γράψαι χείρεσσι καὶ ἔργα τελεῖν ἅπερ ἄνδρες
ἵπποι μέν θ' ἵπποισι βόες δέ τε βουσὶν ὁμοίας
καὶ κε θεῶν ἰδέας ἔγραφον καὶ σώματ' ἐποίουν
τοιαῦθ' οἷόν περ καὐτοὶ δέμας εἶχον ἕκαστοι.

*But if cattle and horses or lions had hands, and could draw with their
hands and make works of art like men, horses would draw the shapes of
the gods like horses and cattle like cattle, and they would make their bodies
of the kind that each had themselves.*     1. Fr. 15, tr. G. S. Kirk

The second is his great statement about the One God.

εἷς θεός, ἕν τε θεοῖσι καὶ ἀνθρώποισι μέγιστος
οὔτι δέμας θνητοῖσιν ὁμοίιος οὐδὲ νόημα.

*One god, greatest among gods and men, in no way like mortals in body or
in thought.*     Fr. 23, tr. G. S. Kirk

5 It may have been the success of the philosophical poetry of
Xenophanes which led Parmenides of Elea (born about 515–
510 B.C.) to take the rather surprising decision to express
his passionately held logical convictions in hexameter verse.
Parmenides is not a great poet. There is a genuine religious
fervour (his logical discovery seems to have struck him with
the force of a divine revelation) expressed in quite impressive
poetic imagery in his Prologue. But the prosaic and rather
bumpy hexameters of the main part of his poem which has

4

been preserved, in which he expresses his conviction of the unity and changelessness of Being, suggest that he might have done better to write in plain prose like the Milesians; though the scanty fragments of the second part, in which he dealt with the unreal world of perceptible appearances, again show traces of some poetic power. It may well, however, have been the example of Parmenides which led a much greater philosophical poet of the Greek West, Empedocles of Acragas (about 492–432 B.C.) to write in hexameter verse, though poetry seems to come so naturally to him that it is possible that he would have chosen this medium even if there had been no earlier examples. Empedocles wrote two poems, the Περὶ Φύσεως (On Nature) and the Καθαρμοί (Purifications), of which we have considerable fragments. The two poems have quite different subject-matter, and the relationship between the thought of the two is a problem which our evidence will perhaps never allow us to solve completely. The first describes his physical system, an amazing work of philosophical imagination in which two great opposing immanent active forces, Love and Strife, for ever arrange and rearrange the changeless and passive four elements, fire, air, earth, and water, into an endless cyclic succession of organized universes, with periods between in which there is no universe because one or other of the two powers is totally dominant. The second sets forth the Orphic–Pythagorean doctrine that men's souls, or some of them, are divine beings who have been punished for a primal sin by falling into the cycle of reincarnation, and after a long series of lives with periods of purgatory between, can hope to return again to the company of the gods. Empedocles in his poem presents himself as one 'no longer a mortal but a god', one who has gone through the whole cycle of reincarnation and purged his original sin, and now walks the earth for the last time as 'seer and singer and healer and leader of men' (and he seems really to have been all of these) before going back to his heavenly home. This second poem gives more obvious opportunities for fine writing than the first. But Empedocles is as skilled in explaining the complexities of his physical system clearly, interestingly, and at times excitingly in hexameter verse as he is in giving us a sense of sin and of glory, of the beauties of unfallen and the horrors of fallen life. Here are two examples of his art from the fragments of the two poems; the first is part of his account of the formation of organic substances from the four elements (from *On Nature*):

ἡ δὲ χθὼν τούτοισιν ἴση συνέκυρσε μάλιστα,
Ἡφαίστῳ τ' ὄμβρῳ τε καὶ αἰθέρι παμφανόωντι,
Κύπριδος ὁρμισθεῖσα τελείοις ἐν λιμένεσσιν,
εἴτ' ὀλίγον μείζων, εἴτε πλεόνεσσιν ἐλάσσων·
ἐκ τῶν αἷμά τε γέντο καὶ ἄλλης εἴδεα σαρκός.

*And the earth came together with these in almost equal proportions, with Hephaestus, with moisture and with brilliant aither, and so it anchored in the perfect harbours of Kupris, either a little more of it or less of it with more of the others. From these did blood arise, and the forms of flesh besides.*　　　　　　　　　　　　　　　　　　　　*Fr.* 98, tr. J. E. Raven

The second is from his description of the golden age of primal innocence before the fall due to the sin of flesh-eating (from *Purifications*):

οὐδέ τις ἦν κείνοισιν Ἄρης θεὸς οὐδὲ Κυδοιμὸς
οὐδὲ Ζεὺς βασιλεὺς οὐδὲ Κρόνος οὐδὲ Ποσειδῶν,
ἀλλὰ Κύπρις βασίλεια.
τὴν οἵ γ' εὐσεβέεσσιν ἀγάλμασιν ἱλάσκοντο
γραπτοῖς τε ζῴοισι μύροισί τε δαιδαλεόδμοις
σμύρνης τ' ἀκρήτου θυσίαις λιβάνου τε θυώδους,
ξανθῶν τε σπονδὰς μελίτων ῥίπτοντες ἐς οὖδας.

*They had no god Ares nor Kudoimos, nor king Zeus nor Kronos nor Poseidon, but Kupris as queen. Her did they propitiate with holy images, with paintings of living creatures, with perfumes of varied fragrance and with sacrifice of pure myrrh and sweet-scented frankincense, casting to the ground libations of golden honey.*　　　　　　*Fr.* 128, tr. J. E. Raven

6 Xenophanes, Parmenides, and Empedocles established philosophical poetry as a proper literary form, and in the early Hellenistic period (third century B.C.) two Stoic poets, Cleanthes

and Aratus, practised it with considerable distinction. The *Hymn to Zeus* by Cleanthes achieves real splendour in the celebration in Homeric language and mythological symbolism of the very un-Homeric Stoic God, the Divine Fire who permeates the world and made it out of his substance, and the passionate prayer to him to deliver men from the ignorance which keeps them from living according to his law, the law of nature and reason. And Aratus, in the prologue to his astronomical poem, the *Phaenomena*, echoes Cleanthes and expounds Stoic theology in clear and dignified epic language. (Astronomy for a Stoic was part of theology; it was the study of the structure and behaviour of God, for the universe, and especially its bright, fiery upper and outer part, the region of the heavenly bodies, was divine.) Aratus' astronomical poem was a great success; its reputation among both Greeks and Romans lasted till the end of antiquity. Latin translations of it were made by Varro Atacinus (perhaps), Cicero, Germanicus, and Avienus. But the greatest philosophical poet of the Hellenistic thought-world, and indeed the greatest philosophical poet in European literature, is not a Greek but a Roman, Lucretius (*c.* 94–55 B.C.). Lucretius was an Epicurean, and for Epicureans, even more than for other ancient philosophers, philosophy was a faith and a way of life, the only way of life which could bring true happiness. Epicurus was venerated by his followers as a prophet and saviour, and had transmitted to them his passionate belief that the imperturbable peace of mind which was the only thing worth living for could only be secured by complete acceptance of, and life according to, the great truths of which he had become certain: that the universe was a chance concatenation of atoms which had come together in the void (a doctrine taken over from earlier Greek philosophers, the Atomists); that the gods, though they exist and the contemplation of them can increase the peace and joy of philosophers, did not form and do not govern the universe and do not interfere in any way with human life, and so are not to be feared; that death is the end, the complete dissolution of the atomic structures of our bodies and souls, and so nothing to

7

be afraid of; that the natural needs of man are few and simple, and complete content and the maximum security from outside disturbances can be secured by cutting our desires down to the natural minimum and living a quiet life withdrawn from the world in the company of like-minded friends. These doctrines Lucretius preaches in his poem, the *De Rerum Natura*, to his friend Memmius, to all others who will listen, and (it is difficult not to feel) to himself, in Latin hexameters of great magnificence and sonority, with all the passionate devotion of a true Epicurean and with an imaginative power even greater than that of Empedocles (whom he greatly admired). The beauty of sound and the force and speed of the rhythm of his verses are secured by a highly individual choice of words and forms, with sometimes a touch of deliberate archaism, a choice of words or forms which were already old fashioned in his time; though we must always remember in reading Lucretius that he seems to us more archaic, more primitively solemn and rugged, than he would have seemed to his contemporaries, because we compare him instinctively to the great Augustans, and above all to Virgil. His imaginative power is particularly shown in the way he brings the rather dry abstractions of the physical theory of Epicurus to life by clothing them in concrete imagery taken from the Roman world of his day. His passionate devotion to the teachings of his master appears everywhere, but especially when he is preaching on the great Epicurean religious and moral themes and trying to deliver others (and perhaps himself) from the terror and misery generated by both popular and non-Epicurean philosophical religion or by fantasies about consciousness surviving the dissolution of our atomic structure at death. The following passage may give some idea of his skill in explaining atomic theory and making it come alive by poetic imagery:

Illud in his rebus non est mirabile, quare,
omnia cum rerum primordia sint in motu,
summa tamen summa videatur stare quiete,
praeterquam siquid proprio dat corpore motus.
omnis enim longe nostris ab sensibus infra

8

primorum natura iacet: quapropter, ubi ipsa
cernere iam nequeas, motus quoque surpere debent;
praesertim cum, quae possimus cernere, celent
saepe tamen motus spatio diducta locorum.
nam saepe in colli tondentes pabula laeta
lanigerae reptant pecudes quo quamque vocantes
invitant herbae gemmantes rore recenti,
et satiati agni ludunt blandeque coruscant;
omnia quae nobis longe confusa videntur
et velut in viridi candor consistere colli.

*Herein we need not wonder why it is that, when all the first beginnings of
things are in motion, yet the whole seems to stand wholly at rest, except
when anything starts moving with its own body. For all the nature of the
first-bodies lies far away from our senses, below their purview; wherefore,
since you cannot reach to look upon them, they must needs steal away their
motions from you too: above all since such things as we can look upon, yet
often hide their motions, when withdrawn from us upon some distant spot.
For often the fleecy flocks cropping the glad pasture on a hill creep on
whither each is called and tempted by the grass bejewelled with fresh dew,
and the lambs fed full gambol and butt playfully; yet all this seems blurred
to us from afar, and to lie like a white mass on a green hill.*

Lucretius II. 308–21, tr. C. Bailey

(There follows an equally brilliant word-picture of distant
army manoeuvres.)

And here is a great and famous passage from the demonstration that death is nothing to us, which shows with what power
and passion and splendour of language Lucretius could preach
one of the fundamental doctrines of Epicurus:

Denique si vocem rerum natura repente
mittat et hoc alicui nostrum sic increpet ipsa
'quid tibi tanto operest, mortalis, quod nimis aegris
luctibus indulges? quid mortem congemis ac fles?
nam si grata fuit tibi vita anteacta priorque
et non omnia pertusum congesta quasi in vas
commoda perfluxere atque ingrata interiere,
cur non ut plenus vitae conviva recedis
aequo animoque capis securam, stulte, quietem?
sin ea quae fructus cumque es periere profusa

vitaque in offensast, cur amplius addere quaeris,
rursum quod pereat male et ingratum occidat omne,
non potius vitae finem facis atque laboris?
nam tibi praeterea quod machiner inveniamque,
quod placeat, nil est: eadem sunt omnia semper.

*Again, suppose that the nature of things should of a sudden lift up her
voice, and thus in these words herself rebuke some of us: 'Why is death
so great a thing to thee, mortal, that thou dost give way overmuch to
sickly lamentation? why groan and weep at death? For if the life that is
past and gone has been pleasant to thee, nor have all its blessings, as though
heaped in a vessel full of holes, run through and perished unenjoyed, why
dost thou not retire like a guest sated with the banquet of life, and with
calm mind embrace, thou fool, a rest that knows no care? But if all thou
hast reaped hath been wasted and lost, and life is a stumbling-block, why
seek to add more, all to be lost again foolishly and pass away unenjoyed:
why not rather make an end of life and trouble? For there is nought more
which I can devise or discover to please thee: all things are ever as they
were.*                                     Lucretius III. 931–45, tr. C. Bailey

7 After Lucretius little philosophical poetry was written in the
Graeco-Roman world. Right at the end of antiquity Boethius
(of whom I shall say something in the last section of this
chapter) wrote some great philosophical poems; but there is
nothing worth mentioning between. The later Greek philosophers wrote in prose (except for the philosophical hymns of
Proclus, which are not of great literary merit), most of which
is not very attractive reading except for the specialist, though
there are exceptions, as we shall see.

8 THE DIALOGUE. All Greek philosophy began from conversation. It was in the endless conversations of Greek men,
sitting about, generally in the open air, talking about anything
and everything, as men still do all over the Mediterranean
world, that all serious European thinking had its origin. But
the philosophical dialogue as a literary form originated from
one particular set of conversations, those which his friends had
towards the end of the fifth century B.C. with the greatest
conversationalist in European history, Socrates. He himself
wrote nothing, but his way of talking to his friends stimulated

them, after his execution, to produce during the first part of the fourth century B.C. a large and varied collection of literary works of a new and unique kind, the Socratic Conversations (recognized by Aristotle as a distinct kind of literature). Socrates claimed that he knew nothing, and was wiser than others only because he knew that he did not know, though he was sure enough of his principles to die for them. He seems to have seen his mission in life as trying to find out and help others to find out, by a process of polite but rigorous cross-questioning and discussion, the great truths about human life and how men ought to live it, because he believed that once they had really found out, had attained that clear immediate certainty which was what he meant by knowledge, they would infallibly live by them, and to live rightly was the only thing that mattered. He was no sceptic; he believed that the truth was there to be found, and that it was supremely important to find it, even if he was never quite sure that he had done so; and he seems to have been a man of deep religion as well as absolute moral integrity. An important part of the questioning process was to expose the pretensions of those who claimed to be experts without sufficient reason, those who thought, and wished others to think, that they knew when they did not know; and this naturally made him unpopular. But he talked to every-body in Athens wherever he could find them, and some of those he talked to fell so completely under his spell that after his death it seemed to them supremely worth while to write some-thing that would bring Socrates as they had known him before later generations, and have something of the effect that real conversations with him had had upon them, his friends. None of these writings are historical or biographical in the modern sense: they are not attempts at verbatim reports of actual conversations in the fifth century, though some of them, notably the conversations in Xenophon's *Memorabilia*, are probably based on someone's (not necessarily the writer's) memories of such conversations. The man who, probably, originated the form was also its supreme master, Plato (about 429–347 B.C.), incomparably the greatest philosophical writer in the whole history of European literature. In comparison with the great *corpus* of his Dialogues which we fortunately possess, the other Socratic Conversations which we have are of minor importance. We have a few fragments of the dialogues of Aeschines of Sphettus. Their style was highly esteemed in ancient times, but the fragments are not very interesting or distinguished. And we have a good deal of Socratic writing by Xenophon (about 430–354 B.C.): besides the *Memorabilia* (Memoirs of Socrates) already mentioned, there are a couple of dialogues and a very inferior (especially when compared to Plato's) version of Socrates' speech at his trial. Xenophon presents, in his pleasant and lucid Greek (it is easy to underrate Xenophon as a stylist because he writes so straightforwardly and has no obvious tricks) a very respectable Socrates, no doubt the man he thought he knew and wished others to remember, a down-to-earth moralist, not very profound or original, with nothing in his teaching to alarm an intelligent conservative. Besides Aeschines and Xenophon, it is worth mentioning that in the Platonic *corpus*, as well as some dialogues which everyone from ancient times onwards has recognized as spurious, there are others which modern scholars generally think are not by Plato, but which appear to be fourth-century work, and not forgeries but Socratic Conversations written by members of Plato's philosophical college, the Academy, and naturally enough preserved in the manuscripts along with the master's own works; which indicates that the fashion of writing Socratic Conversations persisted beyond the generation of those who had known Socrates personally. (Aristotle's dialogues will be mentioned later.)

9 But the Socratic Conversations which really matter are the Dialogues of Plato, and we must now consider them in rather more detail. If Plato was, as seems likely, the inventor of the dialogue form, then he probably used it, and went on using it throughout his life, not only to keep the memory of Socrates and his methods alive but because it suited his philosophical purposes. For Plato all other considerations, of artistic form or

piety towards his master, were strictly subordinated to his
aims as a philosopher. Why, then, did Plato write at all? He
wrote, as he founded the Academy and made his unsuccessful
expeditions to Sicily, with the one purpose of reforming
individuals and society, of persuading men to order their
lives, individually and collectively, on the basis of the truth
about themselves and the nature of things discovered by right
reason. His earlier dialogues at least, therefore (the ones written
towards the end of his life will be considered later), are to be
taken as addressed very much to the sort of people who appear
in them, educated Athenians of good family and possible
influence in the city, but without philosophical training or, at
present, ambition to acquire it. The purpose of the dialogues
was to influence their minds in the right direction, and for this
purpose the Socratic Conversation was well suited, and Plato
would know its effectiveness from his own memories of
Socrates. And of course Plato's great secondary aim, that of
defending and justifying his master and his master's life-work,
fits in admirably with the use of Socratic conversations for his
main philosophical purpose.

10 How, then, precisely does the dialogue as used by Plato
aim to produce its effect on the minds of its intended readers,
and what, more exactly, is the effect aimed at? The dialogue is
not at all a suitable form for the systematic exposition of a
philosophy. If Plato had believed that philosophy was something which could be set out tidily in finished, orderly form,
and that all the pupil had to do was to learn off the arguments
and conclusions of the master, he would have written text-
books or treatises like later philosophers. But where the attainment of real philosophical wisdom, a living grasp of the whole
truth, was concerned, Plato had little faith in the power of
books of any sort. For this, he thought, oral teaching was
needed, and teaching which would not be just passing on a
system or a set of propositions but the stimulation of the pupil
to think things out for himself and grasp the truth with his own
mind. Plato saw more clearly than many that a real philosophy

must always be one's own philosophy, and however much one learns from others, one must think it through and see it for oneself. However, he obviously thought it was worth writing dialogues, in spite of his disbelief in written philosophy, and their purpose is to stimulate people to think for themselves and come to the right conclusions on particular subjects; an essential, and very Socratic, part of this process is to destroy any false confidence which they may have that they, and most ordinary people, are already thinking rightly about the subjects under discussion: and some of the earliest dialogues go no further than this. G. C. Field has described the dialogues as 'occasional essays written at different periods, and dealing with different special problems of thought. Each is a dramatic whole with an order and unity of its own.' Perhaps they are really more like philosophical short stories or novels than essays (the *Republic* might be described as the world's greatest philosophical novel), and certainly, till we come to the latest period, very readable ones. They are written in a superbly quick-moving, conversational but not colloquial Attic, enriched with a good deal of poetic vocabulary, and full of allusions to and quotations from the poets whom Plato passionately disapproved of and passionately loved. There are some superbly presented scenes, above all that of the death of Socrates in the *Phaedo*, which is one of the greatest things in European literature. The speakers, real people, many of whom Plato had known, are vividly characterized, with many touches of humour. The figure of Socrates, of course, dominates, and Plato's Socrates has haunted the minds and imaginations of Europe ever since the Dialogues were published.

11 The latest dialogues, though of great interest to philosophers, are less attractive to the ordinary reader. They are much less like real conversations. They tend to take the form of sustained expositions by the principal speaker, interspersed with formal questions and ejaculations by the secondary personages. Socrates retreats very much into the background, when he is there at all, and his place as the principal speaker is

taken by others, a visitor from Elea, Timaeus, or in Plato's last work, the *Laws*, perhaps Plato himself disguised as a visitor from Athens to Crete – normally Plato is very careful to keep himself out of his own dialogues. The subject-matter is more technical and abstruse: the subjects discussed are often the sort of things which interest professional philosophers rather than the generality of educated men. They were probably written either for philosophical correspondents of Plato or as occasional treatises for members of the Academy designed in some way to supplement Plato's lectures. The change of style is due partly to the nature of the subject-matter, partly to Plato's advancing age and the fact that he was now a regular lecturer. The withdrawal of Socrates, except in the one late dialogue which is on an ethical subject which would have interested him, the *Philebus*, is probably due to the fact that Plato knew that he was now discussing matters which were beyond Socrates' sphere of interest.

12 To end this account of Plato's dialogues something must be said about the great symbolic stories or myths which adorn some of them, in which that intense poetic imagination which Plato kept under such stringent philosophical control becomes evident. For Plato the truth about the nature of things is attained not by mythical imagination but by philosophical reason, and should be expounded as far as possible in strictly rational form. But he is well aware that poetic imagery can help to impress rational truth more vividly on the mind; and there are some things which are important for him which cannot be reached by purely rational intuition or argued about and expounded in a strictly rational way. These are: (1) the details of the life after death – most of the myths are stories about this: we can be rationally sure that the soul is immortal and that the good are rewarded and the wicked are punished after death, but anything more must be left to the poetic imagination, which is magnificently displayed in the great stories about the after-world and what happens to the soul in it in the *Phaedo* and the *Republic*; and (2) the nature of the physical world, which is not

a proper object for reason because it is always changing, though we can be rationally sure that it is formed and governed by a perfectly good and wise divine reason. This is the subject of the vast and elaborate myth which forms the main body of the *Timaeus*. Plato, then, resorts to myth and poetic imagery either to bring rationally certain truths more vividly home to us (as in the unforgettable picture of the three-part soul as a Charioteer with his two horses in the *Phaedrus*) or to give the best possible account of what cannot be the object of pure reason. His myths are poetry, not allegory. They cannot be translated image by image into rational terms. But it is poetry under strict philosophical control, 'the product of the play of an imagination responsible to the philosophic reason' (Guardini). The great basic truths are never lost sight of.

Short extracts from the Dialogues can give no idea of their literary quality. The whole of a dialogue, or at least a very substantial portion, must be read if Plato's art is to be appreciated (some of the earlier dialogues are quite short). Therefore no quotations will be given in this section.

13 Plato's greatest pupil, Aristotle (384–322 B.C.), also wrote dialogues in his earlier years. Their style was greatly admired in antiquity; but only fragments of them remain. At least in the most famous of these dialogues, that entitled *On Philosophy*, and perhaps in others, he abandoned the lively and natural form of the Socratic Conversation for that of a more formal debate in a series of set speeches; and he introduced himself as one of the characters taking part in the discussion. It was this Aristotelian model, rather than the dialogues of Plato, which was followed by Cicero (106–43 B.C.) in his dialogues on philosophy and rhetoric. Another literary influence was that of the dialogues of another of Plato's pupils, the brilliant, eccentric, and superstitious Heraclides Ponticus (about 390–310 B.C.); these were much admired by Cicero and others in ancient times, but almost nothing of them remains. Cicero's philosophical dialogues are, like too many academic conversations, each a series of monologues. He himself is one of the principal speakers in those

which follow the example of Aristotle rather than that of Heraclides, who apparently tended to make his speakers famous characters of the past, as Cicero does in his *De Republica*. They expound at length, in smooth, lucid, and beautiful Latin, the divergent opinions of the Greek philosophical schools and individual philosophers of the recent past, and are of great value as a source for reconstructing the thought of important Hellenistic philosophers whose works are lost. In his rendering of Greek philosophy into Latin Cicero laid the foundations of the Western European philosophical vocabulary: we owe to him the philosophical use of *materia* and the word *qualitas* (for the Greek ποιότης). One of the most successful of his dialogues (unfortunately it has not survived complete) is the *De Republica*, which is on a subject, the ideal constitution as exemplified at Rome, congenial to the great Roman statesman who was its author, and consequently has a more distinctively Roman flavour than the rest. It ends with a very fine Romanized version of a Platonic myth, the *Somnium Scipionis*, which is one of the most impressive expositions of the cosmic or astral theology of late antiquity, with its picture of the souls of those who have deserved well of their country enjoying a blessed immortality in the Milky Way among the divine stars from whom the fiery reason of men derives. The dialogue form, it must be admitted, never really comes alive in Cicero's hands, and seems to have been adopted by him more out of admiration for his Greek models than because of its intrinsic suitability for what he wants to do. The most influential, though not the most interesting, of his philosophical works, the *De Officiis*, is not a dialogue.

14 LITERATURE OF EDIFICATION. This rather forbidding title does not refer to a distinct genre of literature with an easily recognizable form like those of the two preceding sections – much of the literature discussed in them would, of course, come under this heading from the point of view of its content. But I have chosen it as a convenient title under which to group a good deal of work of considerable literary merit

written by philosophers in prose in the Roman Imperial period. This was a time when philosophy was more than ever before a way of life, when philosophers were more and more passionately concerned to win moral perfection and the vision of God through their philosophy: and they consequently wrote a great deal designed to urge themselves and others to seek after God and goodness. Much of this is tedious stuff, as sermons so often are; but some of it is of great power and beauty. Many of the very varied writings on religious, philosophical, literary, and antiquarian topics of Plutarch (about 47 – after A.D. 120) which are collected under the general title of *Moralia* can be classed as 'literature of edification'. They include both essays and dialogues, and express, in a readable, if somewhat artificial and self-conscious Greek, the wide-ranging interests, sane morality, and sincere and sensible piety of a cultivated and charming Platonist. The Stoics of the early Roman Empire produced a great deal of this literature. Another eminent Roman statesman addicted to philosophy, Seneca (about 4 B.C.–A.D. 65) wrote reams of moral exhortation in the epigrammatic, staccato, rhetorical Latin of his period. Though they have been greatly admired in the past, most of us nowadays find his works exhaustingly boring to read in any quantity, but they have flashes of real power and eloquence. The discourses (Διατριβαί, informal seminars and conversations) of the great Stoic moralist Epictetus (about 50–between A.D. 125 and 130), taken down in the simple and vigorous Greek in which they were spoken by his disciple Arrian, have no literary pretensions, but make a far more vivid impression and seem far more readable nowadays than the laboured moralizings of Seneca. Arrian's notes were intended primarily for himself and his friends, and not for publication, which goes far to account for the impression of freshness and authenticity which they make, though Arrian was no self-conscious rhetorical stylist even when he wrote for publication, as his history of Alexander the Great shows.

15 The finest work in all this Stoic literature of edification,

and one of the great books of the world, is the collection of meditations which the philosopher Emperor, Marcus Aurelius Antoninus (A.D. 121–80), addressed to himself. Though it has the form of a personal spiritual diary or meditation book, it is not so certain as has generally been assumed that it is an entirely private work, intended to be read by the Emperor alone. Though some of it is in the barest note form, the greater part is carefully written, and may have been intended for some sort of publication. Even the most carefully written and composed parts, however, are in an intensely concentrated, stripped, austere Greek, without self-conscious artifice and rhetorical tricks. This makes it all the more impressive. The following quotation will give some idea of the power of this Stoic writing at its best:

Πᾶν μοι συναρμόζει ὃ σοὶ εὐάρμοστόν ἐστιν, ὦ κόσμε· οὐδέν μοι πρόωρον οὐδὲ ὄψιμον ὃ σοὶ εὔκαιρον. πᾶν μοι καρπὸς ὃ φέρουσιν αἱ σαὶ ὧραι, ὦ φύσις· ἐκ σοῦ πάντα, ἐν σοὶ πάντα, εἰς σὲ πάντα. ἐκεῖνος μέν φησιν· 'ὦ πόλι φίλη Κέκροπος' σὺ δὲ οὐκ ἐρεῖς· 'ὦ πόλι φίλη Διός;'

*Everything is fitting for me, my Universe, which fits thy purpose. Nothing in thy good time is too early or too late for me; everything is fruit for me which thy seasons, Nature, bear; from thee, in thee, to thee are all things. The poet sings: 'Dear city of Cecrops' and will you not say 'Dear city of God'?*                IV. 23, tr. A. S. L. Farquharson

16 But the two greatest masters of this kind of writing designed to turn men to God and goodness were not Stoics but Platonists, one a pagan Greek philosopher of the third century A.D., Plotinus, and the other a Christian Roman statesman at the very end of the ancient world, Boethius. (The great Christian preachers like Gregory Nazianzen, John Chrysostom, Ambrose, and Augustine fall outside the scope of this chapter.) Plotinus (A.D. 204/5–270), one of the greatest philosophers of antiquity, was not by any means a popular writer. His treatises, collected by his disciple and editor Porphyry into six sets of nine (the *Enneads*), were not intended for a wide circle of readers. Some of them, dealing with highly technical philosophical

problems, can only have been meant for his closest associates, men as deeply concerned with philosophy as himself. But he had a wider group of friends, admirers, and regular attendants at his lectures in Rome, many of them members of the Roman senatorial aristocracy, and some of his treatises seem to have been intended for them, still a restricted audience, but not one of professional philosophers. And in these (and sometimes in the others) there are passages of such power and imaginative quality that they rank with the greatest philosophical writing of any period. Plotinus wrote very much as he spoke, informally and without rhetorical artifice. His Greek is individualistic and can be extremely difficult, though often because he is trying to express something obscure or inexpressible rather than by reason of any defect in the language. He can write moral exhortation as powerful as anything in Stoic literature, but his greatest literary achievements are the passages in which he presents the spiritual realities in which he believed in imaginative terms, with a power of controlled imagery of the most original kind which is unsurpassed in philosophical literature. Two quotations will give some idea of the quality of his writing. The first is from a famous chapter in the treatise *On Beauty*. which is the earliest and one of the most generally intelligible and attractive of his works.

Πατρὶς δὴ ἡμῖν, ὅθεν παρήλθομεν, καὶ πατὴρ ἐκεῖ. τίς οὖν ὁ στόλος καὶ ἡ φυγή; οὐ ποσὶ δεῖ διανύσαι· πανταχοῦ γὰρ φέρουσι πόδες ἐπὶ γῆν ἄλλην ἀπ' ἄλλης· οὐδέ σε δεῖ ἵππων ὄχημα ἤ τι θαλάττιον παρασκευάσαι, ἀλλὰ ταῦτα πάντα ἀφεῖναι δεῖ καὶ μὴ βλέπειν, ἀλλ' οἷον μύσαντα ὄψιν ἄλλην ἀλλάξασθαι καὶ ἀνεγεῖραι ἣν ἔχει μὲν πᾶς, χρῶνται δὲ ὀλίγοι.

*Our country from which we came is there, our Father is there. How shall we travel to it, where is our way of escape? We cannot get there on foot; for our feet only carry us everywhere in this world, from one country to another. You must not get ready a carriage, either, or a boat. Let all these things go, and do not look. Shut your eyes, and change to and wake another way of seeing, which everyone has but few use.*

I. 6(1)8, tr. A. H. Armstrong

The other, from one of his greatest metaphysical treatises, *How the Multitude of the Ideas Came into Being and on the Good*, will show how he continually illuminates his philosophical discussions with the most vivid imagery, and also how aware he is of the inadequacy of this sort of imaging. The subject is the living unity-in-diversity of the intelligible world.

διὸ καὶ εἴ τις αὐτὸν ἀπεικάζοι σφαίρᾳ ζώσῃ ποικίλῃ, εἴτε παμπρόσωπόν τι χρῆμα λάμπον ζῶσι προσώποις, εἴτε ψυχὰς τὰς καθαρὰς πάσας εἰς τὸ αὐτὸ συνδραμούσας φαντάζοιτο οὐκ ἐνδέεις, ἀλλὰ πάντα τὰ αὑτῶν ἐχούσας, καὶ νοῦν τὸν πάντα ἐπ᾽ ἄκραις αὐταῖς ἱδρυμένον, ὡς φέγγει νοερῷ καταλάμπεσθαι τὸν τόπον—φανταζόμενος μὲν οὕτως ἔξω πως ἄλλος ὢν ὁρῴη ἂν ἄλλον· δεῖ δὲ ἑαυτὸν ἐκεῖνο γενόμενον τὴν θέαν ἑαυτὸν ποιήσασθαι.

*So one might compare it to a living sphere of varied colour and pattern or something all faces, shining with living faces, or imagine all the pure souls gathered together, with no defect but complete in all their parts, and universal Intellect set at their highest point, illumining the region with intellectual light. If one imagined it like this one would be seeing it from outside, as something different from oneself. But we have to become it ourselves and make ourselves that which we contemplate.*

VI. 7(38)15, tr. A. H. Armstrong

17 In the sixth century A.D. the last of the great Roman philosopher-statesmen, Anicius Manlius Severinus Boethius (about A.D. 480–524) was imprisoned and executed on a charge of high treason by Theodoric, the Gothic king of Italy whom he served. While in prison awaiting death he turned for strength and comfort to his philosophy, a simple and straightforward Platonism which he seems to have felt was perfectly compatible with the Christianity which he sincerely professed, and to have found of more help at the end than any specifically Christian piety. The book which he wrote in prison, the *De Consolatione Philosophiae*, had an immense influence in succeeding centuries. It is one of the formative books of the Middle Ages and the noblest example of the ancient 'literature of edification'. It is written in the stately and somewhat artificial and self-conscious

literary Latin of the last centuries of antiquity, a language already very remote from that which was actually spoken. In form it is a dialogue between Boethius and the allegorical figure of Philosophy: the dialogue is somewhat stilted and formal, and made even less like a real conversation by the regular interpolation of passages in verse, in a variety of metres, in the manner of the philosophical satires of the Cynic Menippus which were imitated by the great Roman antiquarian and philologist Varro, a contemporary of Cicero's. It will be appropriate to end this chapter with part of one of the finest of these verse interludes; the famous *O qui perpetua*, on which many commentaries were written in the early Middle Ages.

O qui perpetua mundum ratione gubernas
Terrarum caelique sator qui tempus ab aeuo
Ire iubes stabilisque manens das cuncta moueri,
Quem non externae pepulerunt fingere causae
Materiae fluitantis opus, uerum insita summi
Forma boni liuore carens, tu cuncta superno
Ducis ab exemplo: pulchrum pulcherrimus ipse
Mundum mente gerens similique in imagine formans
Perfectasque iubens perfectum absoluere partes. . . .

Da pater augustam menti conscendere sedem,
Da fontem lustrare boni, da luce reperta
In te conspicuos animi defigere uisus.
Dissice terrenae nebulas et pondera molis
Atque tuo splendore mica: tu namque serenum
Tu requies tranquilla piis, te cernere finis
Principium uector dux semita terminus idem.

*O thou, that does the world in lasting order guide,*
*Father of heaven and earth, Who makest time swiftly slide,*
*And standing still thyself, yet fram'st all moving laws,*
*Who to Thy work wert moved by no external cause:*
*But by a sweet desire, where envy hath no place,*
*Thy goodness moving Thee to give each thing his grace,*
*Thou dost all creatures' forms from highest patterns take,*
*From thy fair mind the world fair like Thyself doth make,*
*Thus thou perfect the whole perfect each part dost frame. . . .*

22

*Dear Father, let my mind Thy hallowed seat ascend,*
*Let me behold the spring of grace and find Thy light,*
*That I on thee may fix my soul's well cleared sight.*
*Cast off the earthly weight wherewith I am opprest,*
*Shine as thou art most bright, Thou only calm and rest*
*To pious men whose end is to behold Thy ray,*
*Who their beginning art, their guide, their bound and way.*

III. 9b, tr. 'I.T.' (1609) revised by
H. F. Stewart in *Boethius*, Loeb Classical Library

# Bibliography

ARMSTRONG, A. H. *An Introduction to Ancient Philosophy*, 4th edition with Critical Introduction by the author, London, 1965.

ARMSTRONG, A. H. (ED.) *The Cambridge History of Later Greek and Early Mediaeval Philosophy*, Cambridge, 1967.

GUTHRIE, W. K. C. *A History of Greek Philosophy*, Cambridge, 1962, 2 volumes so far published.

MASSON, J. *Lucretius, Epicurean and Poet*, 2 vols., London, 1908–9.

CROMBIE, I. M. *Plato, the Midwife's Apprentice*, London, 1964.

FIELD, G. C. *Plato and his Contemporaries*, London, 1930.

RIST, J. M. *Plotinus: The Road to Reality*, Cambridge, 1967.

STEWART, H. T. *Boethius*, Edinburgh, 1891.

# II

# Lyric Poetry

## *Maurice Balme*

1 The term 'lyric' does not seem to have been used to describe poetry until the Hellenistic age, when Alexandrian scholars looking back on the Greek literary tradition distinguished different genres of poetry, each with its own style and characteristics. By 'lyric' they meant poetry sung to the lyre, and their canon included nine poets of this genre: Alcman, Sappho, Alcaeus, Stesichorus, Anacreon, Ibycus, Simonides, Pindar, Bacchylides.[1] These spanned a period from about 610, Alcman's *floruit*, until 438, the death of Pindar. Others wrote lyric poetry before, during, and after this period, but these were reckoned in antiquity to be the masters.

2 The Alexandrians further distinguished two main types of lyric poetry – choral and monody. Choral lyric was performed by a choir with dancing or gesture and was accompanied by the lyre or by the lyre and flute. It belonged to social and public occasions, especially to the celebration of religious

1. For this list, see *A.P.* IX, 184, quoted by Edmonds, *L. G. I.*; it is not certain that it is the authentic Alexandrian canon. Alcman's date is discussed by M. L. West, *Classical Quarterly* XV (1965) pp. 188 ff., and F. D. Harvey, *Journal of Hellenic Studies* LXXXVII (1967). They conclude, on the evidence of Oxyrhynchus Papyrus 2390, that Alcman lived in the reign of Leotychidas I, i.e. at the end of the seventh century. Harvey accepts as approximately correct Eusebius' second *floruit* of 609; West, who supports his argument by evidence drawn from other fragments, would place him even a little later. The evidence seems strong, but the new dating raises unresolved problems about the social and economic conditions reflected in Alcman's poems in relation to the Lycurgan reforms.

cult. It was called *molpê* (dance-song). Monody, often called simply *melos* (song), was closer to what we mean by lyric poetry today; it was solo song accompanied by the lyre, usually giving expressions to personal feelings and performed on private occasions, to a group of friends or at a dinner party. But these distinctions should not be pressed too far. They were clearly unknown to Homer and would have meant little to the poets themselves. The poets wrote within a certain tradition and for certain occasions; they were not concerned with classifying their poetry. It is therefore not surprising to find Alcaeus writing hymns for public performance predominantly in the style of 'monody', and Ibycus writing love songs, presumably for private performance without dancing, in the style of 'choral lyric'.

3 The origins of lyric poetry are lost in antiquity. If the Greeks did not bring song and dance with them when they entered Greece, they certainly took them over from the Cretans together with other features of Minoan civilization. According to the Greeks, Crete was the original home of the dance; on Mount Dikte, Rhea, wife of Kronos, taught the Kouretes to dance, and it was their noisy dancing which saved the infant Zeus from destruction at the hands of his father. The archaeological evidence shows that music certainly played a prominent part in the social and religious life of Bronze Age Crete; dancers and musicians are represented on seal-stones, rings, and frescos, in bronzes and terra-cottas. In the Late Helladic period in Mycenaean works of art we find portrayed among other features of Minoan religion worshippers dancing, and the lyre is pictured in a fresco from Pylos. Towards the end of the dark age, when the human figure reappears in pottery and other artefacts, dancers and musicians are again portrayed. This evidence, and the continuity of cult at sites like Eleusis and Delos, suggest that there was an unbroken tradition of dance and song from the Bronze Age until Homer's time.

4 In the Homeric poems we find a world in which almost every important occasion in life is celebrated with music. It is signifi-

cant that on the Shield of Achilles, where the scenes depicted
are an epitome of life in the poet's time, dance-song occurs
three times: at weddings (*Iliad* 18, 491–6); at the vintage (569–
72); and in a scene entirely devoted to dancing (590–606).
In the *Odyssey* the suitors of Penelope, after they have feasted,
again and again turn their minds to other things,

μολπή τ' ὀρχηστύς τε· τὰ γάρ τ' ἀνθήματα δαιτός.

*song and dance; for these are the glory of the feast.*

On more serious occasions we twice find the Achaeans singing
a *paean* to Apollo. On the first occasion (*Iliad* 1, 472–5), after
they have taken Chryseis back to her father, they sacrifice and
feast; then

οἱ δὲ πανημέριοι μολπῇ θεὸν ἱλάσκοντο
καλὸν ἀείδοντες παιήονα κοῦροι Ἀχαιῶν,
μέλποντες ἑκάεργον· ὁ δὲ φρένα τέρπετ' ἀκούων.

*All day long the young Achaean warriors appeased the god with dance-
song singing a lovely paean, honouring the Archer in dance and song;
and he rejoiced at heart when he heard it.*

At every funeral the dirge (*threnos*) is performed, as when
Hector is laid upon the bier,

παρὰ δ' εἷσαν ἀοιδοὺς
θρήνων ἐξάρχους, οἵ τε στονόεσσαν ἀοιδὴν
οἱ μὲν ἄρ' ἐθρήνεον, ἐπὶ δὲ στενάχοντο γυναῖκες.

*And they set singers by the bier to lead the dirge, and they sang a song of
mourning while the women lamented in chorus.*     Iliad 24, 720–2.

5 Homer's descriptions show dance and song, solo and choral,
in every possible combination on secular and religious occasions, grave and gay. Apart from the communal *molpê*, we sometimes find individuals singing alone, as when Calypso sings at
her loom (*Odyssey* 5, 61), and we may suppose that a people so

deeply imbued with music had a tradition of personal song. One would expect such songs to be composed in simple rhythms not necessarily suited to dancing, and this speculation is supported by a few fragments of popular song from Lesbos and elsewhere (cf. *O.B.G.V.* 124–7).

6 By Homer's time song and dance permeated Greek life. They continued to do so throughout the archaic and classical ages. If we are now to speak of the development of literary monody and *molpê*, it should not be supposed that these were divorced from life. Almost all lyric until the fourth century was in a sense occasional; it arose from or was composed for a particular situation. Monody was not limited to any particular sphere of life; its themes were co-extensive with the poet's experience, but, as the dinner party and symposium were the commonest occasions for solo song, they provide a frequent theme or background. Choral lyric, of which the Alexandrians named twenty-one types, was always composed for a specific celebration. The works of the six masters must have been a minute proportion of the choral lyrics continually being written throughout all the cities of Greece; for every city had its cycle of religious festivals, and a vital part of these festivals was the performance of *molpai* in honour of the gods. Dancing and singing and lyre-playing were important in the aristocratic education. At dinner parties every educated man was expected to be able to play his part, whether in singing solo or in impromptu *molpê*. To be chosen for the choruses which performed at the great festivals was an honour, to be overlooked was an insult.

7 A chronological survey of lyric must begin with Archilochus of Paros (*fl.* 660?). The surviving fragments are mainly in elegiacs or iambic metres, but we know that he wrote lyrics also, and as he writes in the vernacular poetry which gives expression to his own feelings, he may be considered the founder of literary monody and indeed of the central tradition of European lyric poetry. But these are not fumbling beginnings in a new medium; Archilochus speaks with an amazing

directness, facility, and confidence. Although it is true that social and political conditions of seventh-century Ionia were likely to foster individualism and so the lyric, as the expression of individual feelings, it is impossible to believe that he was not building on past achievements. But Archilochus was an outstanding poet, mentioned by ancient critics in the same breath as Homer, so that he or his admirers thought it worth while to write down his poetry, while that of his unknown predecessors and contemporaries is lost.

8 The next generation but one saw Sappho and Alcaeus (*fl.* 600) bring the personal lyric to perfection. Sappho I ² is the only complete poem surviving from the nine books into which the Alexandrians arranged her lyrics:

ποικιλόθρον' ἀθανάτ' 'Αφρόδιτα,
παῖ Δίος δολόπλοκε, λίσσομαί σε,
μή μ' ἄσαισι μηδ' ὀνίαισι δάμνα,
πότνια, θῦμον,

ἀλλὰ τυίδ' ἔλθ', αἴ ποτα κἀτέρωτα
τὰς ἔμας αὔδας ἀίοισα πήλοι
ἔκλυες, πάτρος δὲ δόμον λίποισα
χρύσιον ἦλθες

ἄρμ' ὑπασδεύξαισα· κάλοι δέ σ' ἆγον
ὤκεες στροῦθοι περὶ γᾶς μελαίνας
πύκνα δίννεντες πτέρ' ἀπ' ὠρανωἴθε-
ρος διὰ μέσσω,

αἶψα δ' ἐξίκοντο· σὺ δ' ὦ μάκαιρα,
μειδιαίσαισ' ἀθανάτωι προσώπωι
ἤρε' ὄττι δηὖτε πέπονθα κὤττι
δηὖτε κάλημμι,

κὤττι μοι μάλιστα θέλω γένεσθαι
μαινόλαι θύμωι· τίνα δηὖτε πείθω
ἀψ† σάγην† ἐς σὰν φιλότητα; τίς σ' ὦ
Ψάπφ' ἀδικήει;

2. In numbering the lyric poets I have used for Bacchylides Snell's numbers; for the rest the marginal numbers of Page, *Lyrica Graeca Selecta* (O. C. T., 1968), which are the same as those of Lobel and Page, *Poetarum Lesbiorum Fragmenta*, Page, *Poetae Melici Graeci*, and Campbell, *Greek Lyric Poetry*. I have also given *O.B.G.V.* numbers for convenience but have not used that text.

καὶ γὰρ αἰ φεύγει, ταχέως διώξει·
αἰ δὲ δῶρα μὴ δέκετ᾽, ἀλλὰ δώσει·
αἰ δὲ μὴ φίλει, ταχέως φιλήσει
κοὐκ ἐθέλοισα.

ἔλθε μοι καὶ νῦν, χαλέπαν δὲ λῦσον
ἐκ μερίμναν, ὅσσα δέ μοι τέλεσσαι
θῦμος ἰμέρρει, τέλεσον· σὺ δ᾽ αὔτα
σύμμαχος ἔσσο.

*Immortal Aphrodite of the richly-wrought throne, daughter of Zeus,
weaver of wiles, I beseech you, do not with distress and anguish, lady,
break my heart, but come here, if ever before you heard my voice and
listened to me from afar; and you left your father's house and came, yoking
your golden chariot; and the beautiful, swift sparrows bore you over the
black earth through the middle of the sky beating their rapid wings, and
quickly they were come. And you, blessed lady, with a smile on your immortal face, asked what had happened to me now, and why I was calling
on you now, and what in the madness of my heart I most wanted to happen.
'Whom am I now to persuade to join your love? Who is wronging you,
Sappho? For even if she flees, she shall soon pursue; and if she refuses
gifts, yet she shall give; and if she loves not, soon she shall love even against
her will.' Come to me now too, and free me from my heavy cares, and
fulfil what my heart desires to have fulfilled; and do you your self fight at
my side.*

The poem is in the form of a ritual prayer, of which we have
many examples in ancient literature. It falls into three parts:
the invocation to Aphrodite (ll. 1–4); the sanction, here a
remembrance of past benefits received (ll. 5–20); and the
entreaty (ll. 21–4). The structure is carefully balanced. The
invocation occupies the first stanza, the entreaty the last; in
the intervening stanzas the sanction is developed. The beginning and end are serious, indeed passionate. The tone of the
opening lines is set by the accumulation of epithets, recalling
in form, but not in content, the cult epithets of ritual prayer;
two, ποικιλόθρονος (of the richly-wrought throne) and δολόπλ-
οκος (weaver of wiles), are highly poetic and perhaps coined by
Sappho; they stand out in contrast with the diction of the rest
of the poem, which can scarcely contain a word or arrangement
of words which would not have been natural in the spoken

language of her time. The tone of earnest supplication is sustained in the third and fourth lines, where every word is significant, and ἄσαισι and ὀνίαισι are pointed by assonance. The sanction begins in forms of language which were traditional in ritual prayer, but the tone changes as Sappho paints the picture of Aphrodite flying down from heaven in her chariot drawn by sparrows. The picture is clearly visualized, elegant, and fresh, but surely not to be taken seriously as an epiphany; it is a flight of fancy, which prepares the way for the fourth stanza, where Aphrodite addresses Sappho with a smile, in a tone of gentle irony, made clear by the thrice repeated δηῦτε (again), and by the implications of διώξει[3] in the sixth stanza ('for even if she is running away from you now, she will soon pursue, and it will be you who are running away'). The entreaty begins with an echo of line 5 and so re-establishes the mood of the opening. The request itself is stated in three crisp imperatives, the first recalling lines 3 and 4, the last perhaps δολόπλοκε (weaver of wiles) of line 2 (Aphrodite will fight at Sappho's side with cunning). The poem illustrates Sappho's ability to be detached even when she is deeply involved in her theme and to observe herself (cf. *Fr.* 31). For all its simplicity of thought and diction this is a sophisticated poem, in which every word carries weight, and in which a traditional form has been adapted to give expression to personal feelings.

9 Literary *molpê* or choral lyric developed in Sparta. Sparta in the early seventh century was not the grim military academy of later times, but a centre of the arts, which attracted poets and craftsmen from the whole Greek world. Pottery, bronze, and ivory work reached a peak of excellence, and there were many religious festivals in which song and dance flourished:

ῥέπει γὰρ ἄντα τῶ σιδάρω τὸ καλῶς κιθαρίσδην.

*beautiful lyre playing weighs as heavy as the sword.*     Alcman *Fr.* 41

3. I here follow Page, *Sappho and Alcaeus*, p. 15, who argues that διώκειν in early and classical Greek meant 'not merely to run after somebody, but to run after somebody who is running away'. This seems consistent with the tone of the passage as a whole.

Apart from the spread of literacy, survival of lyric from this period may be accounted for by the musical inventions of Terpander of Lesbos, who worked at Sparta in the first half of the seventh century; he is said to have fitted the musical scale to the lyre, which made it possible to give a fixed and permanent form to the songs he wrote.

10 Alcman (*fl.* 610) was thus the inheritor of an established tradition when he came to Sparta from Lydia. He is the earliest lyric poet of whom considerable fragments survive. He was especially famous for his maiden-songs (*partheneia*); these were performed by choirs of girls in honour of Artemis and other goddesses. Alcman *Fr.* 1 (*O.B.G.V.* 114) is from such a song. Despite the mutilated state of the text and the difficulties of interpretation, it is important for an understanding of the development of choral lyric and has a unique charm. Our text begins in the middle of a myth, from which a moral is drawn, ll. 34–5:

$$ἄλαστα \ δὲ$$
$$Ƒέργα \ πάσον \ κακὰ \ μησάμενοι.$$

*for their evil machinations they suffered things not to be forgotten.*

The moral is at once universalized:

$$ἔστι \ τις \ σιῶν \ τίσις$$

*there is vengeance from the gods.*                              l. 36

and the fate of the sinners is contrasted with the happiness of the wise, 'who weaves the web of life to its end without tears'; this leads straight to the present scene. The choir is taking part in a ritual, perhaps in honour of Artemis Ortheia and in rivalry with another choir. Through our ignorance of the ritual and the personalities with which this part of the poem is concerned there shines an unmistakable warmth and brilliance. It is filled with bright imagery (the sun, silver, gold, purple). The language is rich and expressive, drawing from epic[4] as well as from the Doric vernacular; for instance, ll. 47–9:

$$\ddot{\iota}\pi\pi\text{o}\nu$$
$$\pi\acute{\alpha}\gamma\text{o}\nu\ \dot{\alpha}\epsilon\theta\lambda\text{o}\phi\acute{\text{o}}\rho\text{o}\nu\ \kappa\alpha\nu\alpha\chi\acute{\alpha}\pi\text{o}\delta\alpha$$
$$\tau\hat{\omega}\nu\ \dot{\upsilon}\pi\text{o}\pi\epsilon\tau\rho\iota\delta\acute{\iota}\omega\nu\ \dot{\text{o}}\nu\epsilon\acute{\iota}\rho\omega\nu$$

*a mighty horse, a prize-winner with ringing hooves, of the race of winged dreams.*[4]

The mood is predominantly gay, no doubt in contrast with the sternness of the myth, and even when the purpose of the ritual is touched on in tones of grave piety, this is interrupted by mock self-depreciation in a homely and humorous simile:

$$\dot{\alpha}\lambda\lambda\dot{\alpha}\ \tau\hat{\alpha}\nu\ \epsilon\dot{\upsilon}\chi\acute{\alpha}\varsigma,\ \sigma\iota\text{o}\acute{\iota},$$
$$\delta\acute{\epsilon}\xi\alpha\sigma\theta\epsilon\cdot\ \sigma\iota\hat{\omega}\nu\ \gamma\grave{\alpha}\rho\ \ddot{\alpha}\nu\alpha$$
$$\kappa\alpha\grave{\iota}\ \tau\acute{\epsilon}\lambda\text{o}\varsigma\cdot\ \chi\text{o}\rho\text{o}\sigma\tau\acute{\alpha}\tau\iota\varsigma,$$
$$\digamma\epsilon\acute{\iota}\pi\text{o}\iota\mu\acute{\iota}\ \kappa',\ \dot{\epsilon}\gamma\grave{\omega}\nu\ \mu\grave{\epsilon}\nu\ \alpha\dot{\upsilon}\tau\grave{\alpha}$$
$$\pi\alpha\rho\sigma\acute{\epsilon}\nu\text{o}\varsigma\ \mu\acute{\alpha}\tau\alpha\nu\ \dot{\alpha}\pi\grave{\text{o}}\ \theta\rho\acute{\alpha}\nu\omega\ \lambda\acute{\epsilon}\lambda\alpha\kappa\alpha$$
$$\gamma\lambda\alpha\acute{\upsilon}\xi\cdot\ \dot{\epsilon}\gamma\grave{\omega}\nu\ \delta\grave{\epsilon}\ \tau\alpha\hat{\iota}\ \mu\grave{\epsilon}\nu\ \text{'}A\acute{\omega}\tau\iota\ \mu\acute{\alpha}\lambda\iota\sigma\tau\alpha$$
$$\digamma\alpha\nu\delta\acute{\alpha}\nu\eta\nu\ \dot{\epsilon}\rho\hat{\omega}\cdot\ \pi\acute{\text{o}}\nu\omega\nu\ \gamma\grave{\alpha}\rho$$
$$\ddot{\alpha}\mu\iota\nu\ \dot{\iota}\acute{\alpha}\tau\omega\rho\ \ddot{\epsilon}\gamma\epsilon\nu\tau\text{o}\cdot$$
$$\dot{\epsilon}\xi\ \text{'}A\gamma\eta\sigma\iota\chi\acute{\text{o}}\rho\alpha\varsigma\ \delta\grave{\epsilon}\ \nu\epsilon\acute{\alpha}\nu\iota\delta\epsilon\varsigma$$
$$\dot{\iota}\rho\acute{\eta}\nu\alpha\varsigma\ \dot{\epsilon}\rho\alpha\tau\hat{\alpha}\varsigma\ \dot{\epsilon}\pi\acute{\epsilon}\beta\alpha\nu.$$

*O gods, accept their prayers. For to the gods belong the accomplishment and the fulfilment. Teacher of the choir, I shall say, I, who am myself a maiden, have screeched in vain like an owl from the roof-beam. But I wish most of all to please the Lady of the Dawn. For she has been the healer of our pains, and because of Hagesichora the maidens have found the peace which they desired.* ll. 82–91, tr. C. M. Bowra

11 The Alcman fragment has several characteristics in common with the odes of Bacchylides and Pindar; most notably the use of myth and morals drawn from myth; secondly, the sudden transitions, in which the audience is left to supply the links in thought; thirdly, the abundant use of imagery, both in metaphor and simile (not usually so striking in Bacchylides);

4. Cf. *Iliad* 9, 123–4, ἵππους πηγοὺς ἀθλοφόρους. *Certamen*, 100, κανα\χήποδες ἵπποι.

fourthly, the dialect, which is predominantly the Doric vernacular with borrowings from epic. From its Dorian beginnings
choral lyric gradually developed an artificial literary dialect,
which retained a Doric colouring even when it became pan-
hellenic in character; its conventions were observed by Pindar,
who speaks of his Dorian lyre, and to some extent by the Attic
tragedians in their lyrics. Lastly, although the fragment is
usually divided into fourteen-line stanzas of identical metrical
form, each stanza can be subdivided into strophe (ll. 1–4),
antistrophe (ll. 5–8), and epode (ll. 9–14); the triad form, said
to have been invented by Stesichorus, is nearly always used by
Pindar and is sometimes found in Attic tragedy.

12 Alcman's other fragments suggest that he was a highly
individual poet with a wide range. The description of nature
asleep (*Fr.* 89, *O.B.G.V.* 117), which has influenced poets
directly or indirectly from Virgil to Goethe, may set the scene
in another maiden-song. The metre and content of *Fr.* 26
(*O.B.G.V.* 115), in which he regrets that he is too old to join the
dance, make it likely that the lines come from a solo prelude
to a choral song. *Fr.* 59a, according to tradition, comes from a
personal love song:

> Ἔρως με δαῦτε Κύπριδος Ϝέκατι
> γλυκὺς κατείβων καρδίαν ἰαίνει.

> *Love again by the will of Cyprian Aphrodite pours down and melts my*
> *heart.*

In 58, on the other hand, he seems to be expressing dramatically the feelings of a girl from his choir:

> Ἀφροδίτα μὲν οὐκ ἔστι, μάργος δ' Ἔρως οἷα παῖς παίσδει,
> ἄκρ' ἐπ' ἄνθη καβαίνων, ἃ μή μοι θίγῃς, τῶ κυπαιρίσκω.

> *It is not Aphrodite, but wild Love playing like a boy, as he comes down*
> *over the topmost flowers of the galingale – touch them not, I pray.*

13 The next developments in choral lyric are attributed to
Stesichorus (*c.* 630–553). He came from Himera, an outpost of

Hellenism on the north coast of Sicily, which had already developed a poetic tradition and connections with Sparta. He is said to have increased the narrative element, and he seems to have drawn heavily on epic as well as on local legends. He may have been influenced by Arion, who visited Sicily from Corinth. Arion, according to Herodotus (1, 23), first established the *dithyramb* as a literary form, at the court of Periander. The *dithyramb* was a choral hymn in honour of Dionysus; it is first mentioned by Archilochus (*Fr.* 77):

ὡς Διωνύσοι᾽ ἄνακτος καλὸν ἐξάρξαι μέλος
οἶδα διθύραμβον οἴνῳ συγκεραυνωθεὶς φρένας.

*For I know how to lead the fair song of lord Dionysus, the dithyramb, when my wits are smitten with wine.*

At this stage it seems to have been an extempore song led off by one of the company at dinner; perhaps the *exarchos* improvised on traditional words while the rest sang a refrain, as in the dirges described by Homer. If Herodotus' statement is true, it appears that as the worship of Dionysus became more prominent the dithyramb was made part of his regular cult. It was introduced into Athens under the tyrants, where dithyrambic contests were a feature of the reformed Greater Dionysia. These 'cyclic choruses', five of men and five of boys, were one of the most long-lived forms of choral lyric and were still being performed in the second century after Christ. The form has particular interest, since Aristotle says that tragedy originated in improvisation by the leader of the dithyramb (Poetics, 1449a).

The high proportion of lyrics in the earlier tragedies (about two-thirds of the *Supplices* and a half of the *Persae* and *Agamemnon*) confirms the theory which Aristotle gives here on the origin of tragedy, and the lyric choruses remain an integral part of the drama until some of the later plays of Euripides, in which they tend to become no more than interludes. The choruses of tragedy often show the traditional features of choral lyric proper – didactic myth, abundant imagery, and a Doric

34

colouring (e.g. Aeschylus, *Choephori* 585–687, Sophocles, *Antigone* 944–87, Euripides, *Hippolytus* 525–64), and although they fall outside the scope of this chapter, they in fact provide some of the finest examples of choral lyric.

14 Ibycus (*fl.* 522) also came from the west, from Rhegium in south Italy, and his earlier poems seem to have resembled Stesichorus' in theme. But when he left Rhegium for the court of Polycrates of Samos he abandoned the serious heroic manner and adopted a tone more suitable to the luxurious and sceptical society in which he was working. It was here that his contemporary Anacreon, asked why he wrote hymns not to the gods but to boys, replied, 'Because they are our gods.' It is not surprising to find that in this milieu Ibycus wrote secular songs in the style and form of choral lyric. A comparison of Ibycus *Fr.* 286 with Anacreon 358 (a complete poem) illustrates some of the differences between the styles of choral lyric and monody.

> ἦρι μὲν αἵ τε Κυδώνιαι
> μηλίδες ἀρδόμεναι ῥοᾶν
> ἐκ ποταμῶν, ἵνα Παρθένων
> κῆπος ἀκήρατος, αἵ τ' οἰνανθίδες
> αὐξόμεναι σκιεροῖσιν ὑφ' ἔρνεσιν
> οἰναρέοις θαλέθοισιν· ἐμοὶ δ' ἔρος
> οὐδεμίαν κατάκοιτος ὥραν.
> ἀλλ' ἄθ' ὑπὸ στεροπᾶς φλέγων
> Θρηίκιος Βορέας
> ἀίσσων παρὰ Κύπριδος ἀζαλέ-
>   αις μανίαισιν ἐρεμνὸς ἀθαμβὴς
> ἐγκρατέως πεδόθεν τινάσσει
> ἡμετέρας φρένας.

*In the spring the Cydonian quinces bloom, watered from the flowing rivers where is the maidens' inviolate garden, and the vine blossoms swell to strength under the shady sprays of the vine; but for me Love sleeps at no season. But like the North Wind from Thrace, aflame with lightning, it comes with a rush from the Cyprian, dark and shameless with shrivelling madness, and masterfully shakes my heart from the roots.*[5]

5. Translated by C. M. Bowra, whose discussion of this poem in *Greek Lyric Poetry*, pp. 260 ff., I have followed closely.

D                                              35

σφαίρῃ δηὖτέ με πορφυρῇ
βάλλων χρυσοκόμης Ἔρως
νήνι ποικιλοσαμβάλῳ
  συμπαίζειν προκαλεῖται·
ἡ δ', ἐστὶν γὰρ ἀπ' εὐκτίτου
Λέσβου, τὴν μὲν ἐμὴν κόμην,
λευκὴ γάρ, καταμέμφεται,
  πρὸς δ' ἄλλην τινὰ χάσκει.

*Again golden-haired Love hits me with his brightly-coloured ball and
challenges me to play with the girl of the motley sandal; but she – for she
comes from well-established Lesbos – despises my hair – for it is white –
and gapes after another (girl).*

15 The metre of the Ibycus fragment is complex; it must be part
of a system with strophic responsion, perhaps in triadic form.
The metre of Anacreon's poem is extremely simple.[6] Ibycus
writes in the literary dialect of choral lyric, with Doric colouring (cf. ῥοᾶν, στεροπᾶς) and epic borrowings or reminiscences
(cf. Θρηίκιος Βορέας, ἀζαλέαις). His language is exotic (οἰνάνθιδες
and κατάκοιτος occur nowhere else) and rich; epithets tend to
accumulate. Anacreon writes in the Ionic vernacular and his
language is simple. He does not eschew the poetic word;
χρυσοκόμης (golden-haired) perhaps raises romantic expectations
which will be belied, just as the epic εὐκτίτου (well-established)
gives a mock solemnity, but the overall impression is of
natural diction in a natural order. The Ibycus fragment consists
of a series of images from nature contrasting the innocence of
girls growing in the spring-time of their lives towards a natural
love, with his own unseasonable and destructive passion; the
Cydonian quince was a familiar symbol of love – here the trees
grow by the fertilizing rivers, showing promise of their fruit
(ἦρι – in the spring – suggests blossom); the inviolate garden
of the maidens symbolizes the innocence of girlhood (cf.
Euripides, *Hippolytus* 73–8); and the grapes swelling to fullness

6. Each stanza consists of three *glyconics* – –/– ∪ ∪ –/∪ – followed by a
*pherecratean* – ∪/– ∪ ∪ –/–. The *glyconic* consists of a *choriamb* – ∪ ∪ –, the
nucleus of all Aeolic verse, preceded by the Aeolic base, which is normally ∪ ∪,
and followed by a clausula ∪ –; the *pherecratean* is an abbreviated line of the same
form.

suggest the ripening of girlhood towards love. Anacreon starts with an image from everyday life, Love's challenge; a colour epithet lights up each of the first three lines, and the fourth is given point by the ambivalent συμπαίζειν (to play with), which is found elsewhere in erotic contexts. The second verse conceals its point until the last line, where ἄλλην (another girl)[7] is clinched by the derogatory χάσκει (gapes). While Ibycus takes our emotions by storm, Anacreon is a poet of wit, who achieves his effects by careful positioning and balance. The different treatment of their themes no doubt stems from differences in their situations and temperaments, but each treatment is appropriate to its genre.

16 Simonides (556–468), his nephew Bacchylides (born 518 or 507), and Pindar (518–438) were not only contemporaries but were all working at the same time in Sicily; some passages in Bacchylides and Pindar reflect their rivalry. Simonides began composing for the boys' choirs which sang in Ceos and Delos in honour of Apollo. When his reputation was established he was invited, like Anacreon, by Hipparchus to Athens. On the latter's death he moved to the courts of the Aleuadae and Scopadae in Thessaly. He returned to Athens during the Persian Wars and ended his life in Sicily, where he was the friend of Hieron of Syracuse. He had a long and outstandingly successful career; in choral lyric he was probably the first to write epinician odes, celebrating victories in the great athletic games, and is said to have won fifty-six prizes in dithyrambic contests.

17 Ceos was a strangely austere Ionian island, where no flute girls were allowed and men were compelled to commit suicide at the age of sixty. Much of Simonides' poetry seems to show something of the character of his homeland. It is clear, simple, and economical. *Fr.* 531 (*O.B.G.V.* 203), from a hymn in honour of the Spartans who died at Thermopylae, well illustrates this sinewy style. But the *Danae* fragment, 543 (*O.B.G.V.*

---

7. It should be remembered that the poem was composed to be sung aloud and that ἄλλην differs from the expected ἄλλον (another man) only in one vowel sound.

206), shows him a master of narrative lyric, writing in a richer vein, with epic borrowing, accumulated epithets and exotic words. But the fragment is memorable not so much for the diction as for the dramatic power with which he envisages the scene and re-creates the feelings of the mother set adrift with her sleeping baby.

18 Pindar compares Simonides and Bacchylides to a pair of chattering crows and himself to an eagle of song:

$$\sigma o \phi \grave{o} s \; \acute{o} \; \pi o \lambda \lambda \grave{a} \; \epsilon \acute{i} \delta \grave{\omega} s \; \phi \upsilon \hat{a} \cdot$$
$$\mu a \theta \acute{o} \nu \tau \epsilon s \; \delta \grave{\epsilon} \; \lambda \acute{a} \beta \rho o \iota$$
$$\pi a \gamma \gamma \lambda \omega \sigma \sigma \acute{\iota} a \; \kappa \acute{o} \rho a \kappa \epsilon s \; \grave{\omega} s \; \acute{a} \kappa \rho a \nu \tau o \iota \; \gamma a \rho \acute{\upsilon} \epsilon \tau o \nu$$
$$\varDelta \iota \grave{o} s \; \pi \rho \grave{o} s \; \check{o} \rho \nu \iota \chi a \; \theta \epsilon \hat{\iota} o \nu.$$

*wise is he who knows much by nature; but those who have only learnt, turbulent in their garrulity, chatter fruitlessly, like a pair of crows in competition with the heavenly bird of Zeus.*      Ol. II, 86–8

Bacchylides has often had the misfortune to be ranked as a second-rate Pindar, but if we do not look for Pindaric qualities in a poet who is not generally aiming at them, we may feel that he has been underrated. When Hieron achieved his greatest athletic triumph, victory in the chariot race at Olympia in 468, he commissioned Bacchylides, not Pindar, to write the victory ode.

19 The structure of this poem (Bacchylides 3, of which *O.B.G.V.* 306 gives ll. 15–62) is close knit. It opens with an invocation to Clio and a statement of the occasion – Hieron's chariot victory at Olympia, where the throng admired him for his power, his wealth, and his generosity; to this his dedications at Delphi bear witness (ll. 1–22). There follows the 'myth' of Croesus, who is linked to Hieron by his wealth, his horses, and above all by his gifts to Delphi; because of his piety and generosity Apollo saved him from the pyre (ll. 23–62). The praise of Hieron is then expanded, as one who has given more to Delphi than any of his generation. This section ends on a note of consolation (Hieron was old and sick), culminating in Apollo's advice to

Admetus – to think at once that tomorrow was his last day and that he would live in prosperity for fifty years (ll. 63–84). In the concluding section Bacchylides says that, although man cannot recover his lost youth, the Muse confers immortality and that with the true glories of Hieron shall be celebrated the charm of the honey-tongued nightingale of Ceos (ll. 85–97).

20 The poem moves fast. In the first sections a series of scenes is presented dramatically: the scene of the victory at Olympia; Delphi in full festival (the abruptness of the transition is striking); Croesus on the pyre. The myth is told in the lyric manner, concentrating on the significant episode and re-creating the incidents which illustrate the moral – that despite all appearances piety is rewarded. The relevance of the myth is made explicit both at the beginning and the end.

21 The least successful lines are those which imitate Pindar (ll. 85–8)

> φρονέοντι συνετὰ γαρύω· βαθὺς μὲν
> αἰθὴρ ἀμίαντος· ὕδωρ δὲ πόντου
> οὐ σάπεται· εὐφροσύνη δ' ὁ χρύσος·
> ἀνδρὶ δ' οὐ θέμις. . . .

*I speak what the wise may understand; the deep sky is undefiled; the water of the sea rots not; gold is a delight; but to man it is not granted . . .*

The first clause clearly echoes Pindar *Olympian* II, 83–5:

> πολλά μοι ὑπ'
> ἀγκῶνος ὠκέα βέλη
> ἔνδον ἐντὶ φαρέτρας
> φωνάεντα συνετοῖσιν.

*I have many swift arrows in my quiver under my arm which speak to the wise.*

As this passage is followed immediately by the lines quoted above, in which Pindar compares Simonides and Bacchylides to a pair of crows, the latter seems to be hitting back. But his choice of ground is unfortunate, for where does this hieratic statement lead? The bold, bright images, hinting at some mystery, culminate in the irrelevant maxim that man cannot regain his lost youth, but the Muse confers immortality on his glory. The form in which he gives this thought is an old one; parallel cases are stated paratactically leading up to the main theme (the *priamel*); it is found in the last stanza of Alcman *Fr.* 1 and is common in Pindar. Pindar had used the same form and the same images of water and gold with supreme effect in the opening of Olympian 1.[8] It is hard to resist the conclusion that Bacchylides is attempting to imitate Pindar here too, and with singular lack of success. The ode illustrates both the strength and the weakness of Bacchylides. He can create a scene vividly (cf. ll. 15–20). He can carry us with him in an exciting narrative. The ode is skilfully and harmoniously constructed and contains memorable passages; for instance, (ll. 49–52):

$$\text{ἔκλαγον δὲ}$$
$$\text{παρθένοι, φίλας τ' ἀνὰ ματρὶ χεῖρας}$$
$$\text{ἔβαλλον· ὁ γὰρ προφανὴς θνα-}$$
$$\text{τοῖσιν ἔχθιστος φόνων.}$$

*and the girls shrieked aloud and threw up their hands to their mother; for the death foreseen is the most loathsome to mortals.*

But he cannot compete with Pindar when he goes beyond what his senses give him.

22 The ancient critics were agreed that Pindar was the greatest of the lyric poets; 'longe princeps,' says Quintilian (*Inst. Orat.* x, 61). The seventeen books of his collected works contained Hymns, Paeans, Dithyrambs, Processional Songs, Maiden Songs, Songs for Dancing (*Hyporchemata*), Encomia, Dirges, and Epinicia, written for festivals and patrons in most of the leading cities of mainland and western Greece. The four books of the Epinicians have survived because they were used in the

8. For a discussion of these passages see Bowra, *Pindar*, pp. 203 ff.

schools of the Roman Empire; of his other works there are fragments, some quite substantial, which do not seem to differ greatly in style from the Epinicians.

23 The Epinicians themselves vary considerably in length, structure, and conditions of performance. Some are short and simple in construction and were composed for performance at the athletic festival itself. *Pythian* VII well illustrates this type. It was written for the chariot victory of Megacles, uncle of Pericles, at Delphi in 486. The ode consists of one triad: Athens is the fairest prelude for laying a foundation of song in honour of the Alcmeonidae for their chariot victory. Athens is illustrious throughout Greece, for her citizens made Apollo's temple a marvel to behold (the Alcmeonidae in exile had faced the temple with marble). Megacles and his family have won seven victories at the games. Pindar rejoices at their good fortune, but is grieved at the return made by envy (Megacles' exile). But they say that a man's prosperity, though abiding, may bring some passing trouble. The ode is clearly constructed and perfectly fitted to the occasion. It contains all the usual elements of the epinician except for myth: praise of the victor's city, the achievements of the victor's family, including a victory list, an expression of the poet's own feeling, and an appropriate maxim at the end.

24 The longer odes were commissioned by a patron and performed at a celebration on the victor's homecoming, sometimes, as in *Pythian* II, in connection with a regular religious festival. *Pythian* I (of which *O.B.G.V.* 278 gives ll. 1–28) celebrates Hieron's victory in the chariot race at Delphi in 470. At this festival Hieron proclaimed the foundation of the city of Etna, in which he established his son, Deinomenes, as ruler. The ode seems to have been written for a ceremony celebrating both events.

25 It opens with an invocation to the golden lyre, 'which belongs of right to Apollo and the Muses'. This develops into a great hymn in praise of music: the lyre rules the dance and is

powerful in heaven, where it brings peace, soothing even the heart of Ares (ll. 1–12). But those whom Zeus has not received in friendship are appalled when they hear the sound of the Muses, all on land and sea and he who lies in Tartaros, Typhos, confined in his prison beneath Etna (ll. 13–28).

26 Pindar then prays that Zeus of Etna may bless the new city, named after the mountain, and claims that the chariot victory is a good omen for its future, that it shall be famous for its victories and for its harmonious festivals (εὐφώνοις θαλίαις). Apollo grant this prayer (ll. 28–40).

27 For it is from the gods that come all means to human excellence in wisdom, in strength, and in eloquence. Even so may I succeed in praising Hieron appropriately. May time give him continued prosperity and forgetfulness of sufferings (Hieron was sick at this time); then he would remember his great victories of the past (Himera, 480, where Hieron and his brothers defeated the Carthaginians) and of the present (probably the defeat of Thrasydaeus of Acragas, which left Hieron master of Sicily), when, though sick like Philoctetes, he forced a proud enemy to fawn (ll. 41–57).

28 With a new invocation to the Muses, Pindar turns to sing of Deinomenes, for whom his father has established a new city with god-built freedom following the Dorian rules. Like the Dorians of Sparta, grant, Zeus, that Etna may observe these rules. May father and son, honouring the people, bring the city to peace and harmony (σύμφωνον ἐς ἡσυχίαν) (ll. 58–71). And grant that the Carthaginians may stay quiet at home and the Etruscans, remembering their defeat at Cumae (where Hieron defeated the Etruscan fleet in 474), when Hieron saved Hellas from slavery. At Athens, Pindar says, I shall win reward by praise of Salamis, at Sparta by praise of Plataea, from the Deinomids by celebrating Himera (ll. 72–80).

29 Drawing together the strands of many themes, Pindar ends by advising Deinomenes on how to conduct himself as king:

be just, be truthful. . . . When men are dead, only their praise
lives on in song and story. The gentle goodness of Solon fades
not, but the lyre accompanies no songs in praise of Phaleris.

> Good fortune is the best and first of prizes,
> Good name is the second possession:
> The man who has found both and keeps them
> Has won the highest crown.[9]

30 The structure of the poem centres on the foundation of
Etna and is unified by the image of the lyre with which it
opens. This image is developed in two contrasting themes.
On the one hand are set order, peace, and harmony, at the
dance, in heaven, and in the city. Harmony in the city is first
hinted at in the hope expressed for Etna's future – that it may
be famous for its harmonious festivals (l. 37); this is developed
in the passage on the Dorian order with which Hieron has
established Etna (ll. 61 ff.) and the prayer that Hieron and
Deinomenes may turn the city towards peace and harmony
(l. 72). The sketch of ideal kingship shows how this harmony
may be achieved so that the ruler may win undying fame in a
new 'harmony' created by the poet in the world of art (ll. 88–
98).

31 On the other side are all those 'whom Zeus has not received
in friendship' (l. 13); these are confounded when they hear the
voice of the Muses, like Typhos, who tried to destroy the order
of the universe. Included in this class are the enemies whom
Hieron has overthrown – the Carthaginians and the Etruscans
with their discordant battle-cry (ἀλαλατός l. 72); and the Sicilian Greeks who have obstructed the order which Hieron is
trying to impose. All the diverse elements are thus welded together in the themes of the praise of Hieron and Pindar's hopes
for the new city.

32 In this ode Pindar speaks of drawing together the strands
of many themes (l. 80). Elsewhere he writes:

9. ll. 99–100 translated by C. M. Bowra, *Pindar*, p. 337.

εἴρειν στεφάνους ἐλαφρόν· ἀναβάλεο· Μοῖσά τοι
κολλᾷ χρυσὸν ἔν τε λευκὸν ἐλέφανθ' ἁμᾷ
καὶ λείριον ἄνθεμον ποντίας ὑφελοῖσ' ἐέρσας.

*To plait garlands is easy. Strike up! The Muse*
*Welds together gold and white ivory*
*And the lily-flower snatched from the sea's dew.*

Nemean VII, 77–9, tr. C. M. Bowra

This describes a composition in which brilliant imagery and
rich language cohere in a pattern which has an inner unity. The
ode does not move straight forward like a narrative but circles
round its themes and develops different aspects in succession.
Pindar sometimes proceeds in a series of images. Thus in line 5
we move abruptly from the scene of the festival to Olympus.
In this transition the thunderbolt might seem a universal
symbol, the instrument of Zeus' power. But images in Pindar
are seldom mere symbols, and if the lyre is visualized as 'quench-
ing the speared thunderbolt of ever-flowing fire', a scene is
suggested in which the fire of the thunderbolt burns low while
Apollo plays his lyre on Olympus. It is then natural to see also
the eagle sleeping on Zeus' sceptre. This picture is drawn precisely in language of concentrated power: 'you (the lyre) have
poured a cloud on his hooked head, a sweet seal to his eyes,
darkening his face; as he sleeps, he heaves his lithe back, bound
by your waves (i.e. by the sound-waves of your music).'
The images succeed each other in rapid succession, often
startling but each contributing to the visual picture or to the
tone.

33 In this ode the place of myth is taken by the description of
Typhos in his prison and Etna in eruption. The eruption,[10]
which had perhaps actually been seen by Pindar in 479, is
attributed to Typhos, shifting on his rocky bed as it scrapes
and spikes his back. Here myth and reality blend in an astonish-

10. The eruption is also described by Aeschylus, *P.V.* 369–74. To Prometheus,
Typhos is a fellow-sufferer, punished for seeking to overthrow the tyranny of
Zeus, but in Aeschylus' description of the eruption and its mythical cause there
is a close similarity to Pindar.

ing way. The full significance of the myth, even to the extension of the prison from Etna to Cumae, gradually becomes apparent as the ode proceeds.

34 Finally, a religious tone pervades the whole. This is not a secular encomium of Hieron, nor is the feeling conveyed merely by the grave invocations to Apollo and Zeus; we are given an interpretation of life in religious terms. The order which Pindar hymns is a divine order, and men share it by the grace of the gods; the lyre is the possession of Apollo and the Muses (l. 1, 2); from the gods come all means to human excellence (l. 41); political freedom is god-built (l. 60). For this reason, through the praise of Hieron and the hopes expressed for the new city may be heard a note of warning, sounded most clearly in lines 69–71 and in the closing lines.

35 From the death of Pindar little Greek lyric survives. Choral lyrics were still composed for festivals throughout the Greek world. In the late fifth century changes were introduced in Athens to which Aristophanes and Plato refer disparagingly; greater importance was attached to the music, and the different forms of choral lyric were confused. The lyrics of some of Euripides' later plays seem to reflect the new fashion. A number of choral songs survive in inscriptions, notably those from Delphi with much disputed musical notation, and the Hymn of the Kouretes from Palaiokastro in Crete (*O.B.G.V.* 496).

36 Personal lyrics were still written, although they were a minor form compared with the elegiac epigram, which had become the fashionable genre for self-expression since the fourth century. The *Anacreontea* may be typical of Hellenistic lyric (*O.B.G.V.* 178–80). Theocritus, *Idylls* 18, 29, 30 (O.C.T.) are written in Aeolic dialect and metre; 29 might be called a dramatic monologue, in which Theocritus shows the same power to project himself into a situation as we find in the *Pharmaceutria* and *Cyclops Idylls* (2 and 12). Both Theocritus and other Hellenistic poets use Aeolic metres stichically, i.e. in lines of the same pattern instead of writing in stanzas. In this they

were followed by Catullus, whose favourite lyric metre, the hendecasyllable, is found in Sappho and Anacreon, but was so much used by the fourth-century poet Phalaecus that it has been named the Phalaecian.

37 Catullus appears to be without predecessors in Latin literature, if we discount the experiments of Laevius' *Erotopaegnia*, and without successors; Horace pointedly ignores him in his claim to have been the first to introduce Aeolian song into Italian poetry (*Odes*, III, xxx). As we know so little about Hellenistic lyric, it is impossible to trace in detail the influences which helped to form Catullus' style, but we do know that he, like the other Neoterics, was revolting against the Ennian tradition of Roman poetry and that he studied carefully the Alexandrian masters, especially Callimachus. Their influence is clear enough in his longer poems and in some of the elegiac epigrams.

38 He uses lyric, iambic and elegiac verse almost indifferently to express his feelings on any topic from obscene invective to passionate love. Recent criticism has shown that a dichotomy between Catullus the child of nature, warbling native wood-notes wild, and Catullus the learned imitator of Alexandrian models, is false.[11] Even the short lyric poems which appear most spontaneous often show a high degree of art, and it is the tension between deep feeling and intellectual control that makes his best lyrics so remarkable.

39 Although we know little about the influences of Hellenistic lyric, we can sometimes see that elegiac epigram was a source of ideas and perhaps of language. Thus, of the sparrow poems, 3 has many predecessors in the Greek Anthology in the form of 'sepulchral' epigrams on pets and wild creatures (e.g. *O.B.G.V.* 575 and 577). For Catullus 2 we may have a model in Meleager (*A.P.* VII, 195, Mackail 1, 64). Meleager addresses a grasshopper, calling it 'the beguilement of my longings' and asking

11. See Quinn, *The Catullan Revolution*, ch. III.

it to sing a song of love 'to save me from the pain of sleepless care, playing a note that will send love wandering (φθόγγον ἐρωτόπλανον)'. So Catullus, ostensibly addressing Lesbia's sparrow, writes a love poem to her. Apart from the common idea that listening to the grasshopper or playing with the sparrow may bring relief from the pains of love, there are certain equivalences in language which may be significant: πόθων (l. 1) = desiderio (l. 5) (longing); μερίμνης (l. 5) = curae (l. 10) (care); πόνων (l. 5) = doloris (l. 8) (pain). But Catullus' handling of the theme is quite different. He writes, until the end, from Lesbia's point of view. In the first four lines he gives a precise picture, while Meleager speaks in generalities. The unexpected image of l. 5, 'desiderio meo nitenti' (the radiant object of my longing), lifts the poem on to a higher plane. The connection between Lesbia's playing with the sparrow and her love is delayed and then expressed as a hope rather than as a fact (cf. 'credo' I believe, l. 7). The whole poem is written in one long sentence culminating in the wish which is the declaration of his passion. It shows careful construction on a tiny scale and, if Catullus had Meleager's epigram in mind, he has written something new and with a different intention; Meleager intends primarily to amuse, Catullus' poem, for all its whimsicality, is serious.[12]

40 If the main influences on Catullus were Hellenistic, he, like every educated Roman of his time, was thoroughly familiar with classical Greek literature. 51 is sometimes assumed to be his first poem to Lesbia, just as his only other poem in Sapphics, 11, is said with more justification to be his last. The Lesbia poems can indeed be arranged in a dramatic sequence which shows first a period of happy and responsive love, then the beginnings of disillusionment, and lastly complete disillusionment. But how 51 fits into this sequence depends partly on its relationship to Sappho *Fr.* 31.

12. The text and meaning of lines 7–8 are disputed. I follow the Oxford text and take *et solaciolum sui doloris* as a second object of *iocari*. This is certainly difficult; but not, I think, impossible; see Gordon Williams, *Tradition and Originality in Roman Poetry*, p. 140.

41 φαίνεταί μοι κῆνος ἴσος θέοισιν
ἔμμεν᾽ ὤνηρ, ὄττις ἐνάντιός τοι
ἰσδάνει καὶ πλάσιον ἆδυ φωνεί-
σας ὑπακούει

καὶ γελαίσας ἰμέροεν, τό μ᾽ ἦ μὰν
καρδίαν ἐν στήθεσιν ἐπτόαισεν·
ὡς γὰρ ἔς σ᾽ ἴδω βρόχε᾽, ὥς με φώναι-
σ᾽ οὐδ᾽ ἒν ἔτ᾽ εἴκει,

ἀλλ᾽ ἄκαν μὲν γλῶσσα †ἔαγε†, λέπτον
δ᾽ αὔτικα χρῶι πῦρ ὑπαδεδρόμηκεν,
ὀππάτεσσι δ᾽ οὐδ᾽ ἒν ὄρημμ᾽, ἐπιρρόμ-
βεισι δ᾽ ἄκουαι,

κὰδ δέ μ᾽ ἴδρως ψῦχρος ἔχει, τρόμος δὲ
παῖσαν ἄγρει, χλωροτέρα δὲ ποίας
ἔμμι, τεθνάκην δ᾽ ὀλίγω 'πιδεύης
φαίνομ᾽ ἔμ᾽ αὔται·

ἀλλὰ πὰν τόλματον, ἐπεὶ †καὶ πένητα

*He seems to me to be the equal of the gods, the man who sits opposite you and hears from near your sweet voice and lovely laugh, which, truly, has made my heart flutter in my breast. For when I see you a moment, then I can no longer speak a word, but my tongue keeps silence; at once fine fire has run over my flesh, and I see nothing with my eyes, and my ears are humming, and a cold sweat covers me, and trembling takes hold of me all over, and I am paler than grass, and I seem to myself but a little way from death. . . . But all must be endured, since. . . .*

42 Sappho describes what she feels as she sees a girl whom she loves sitting and talking to a man. We are told nothing about the man (we have no reason to suppose, for instance, that he is the bridegroom at the girl's wedding), except that in Sappho's eyes he is like the gods in being so privileged; we may infer that the girl loved him. The first six lines make clear the intense passion which Sappho feels for the girl and the jealousy which at this moment is the predominant aspect of this passion; for surely it is seeing the girl and the man together which has made her heart flutter? The remainder of the fragment describes the physical symptoms of this passion. The description is extraordinarily simple and objective; Sappho observes herself

with a strange precision and detachment. 'The style is realistic, severely plain and candid, unadorned by literary artifice' (Page, *Sappho and Alcaeus*, p. 30). The very absence of embellishment and rhetoric increases the impact of these lines.

43 Only a superficial reading could lead to the view that Catullus 51 is a close translation. There are the following additions: the whole of l. 2; l. 3 'identidem' (again and again); l. 4 'spectat' (looks at); l. 5 'misero' (unhappy); l. 6 Lesbia. From l. 5 'and lovely laugh' is omitted, as is the entire sense of Sappho's fourth stanza and whatever followed it. For Sappho's 'which has made my heart flutter in my breast' (ll. 5, 6), Catullus has 'misero quod omnis / eripit sensus mihi' (which robs me in my misery of all my senses). For Sappho's 'I see nothing with my eyes' (l. 11), Catullus has 'gemina teguntur / lumina nocte' (the light of my eyes is covered with twin night).

44 The affect of these additions, omissions, and alterations is to make Catullus' an entirely different sort of poem. Where Sappho is simple and objective, Catullus is rhetorical, e.g. in l. 2 the repeated 'ille' and the exaggeration, in l. 11 the memorable hypallage (instead of his two eyes being covered by night – an image notably absent in Sappho – his eyes are covered by two nights); and subjective, cf. l. 5 'misero . . . mihi'. It is impossible to believe that, if Catullus had simply been intending to translate Sappho, he would not have made a better job of it; the difficulties of the metre will not account for the nature of the changes, and his translation of Callimachus' *Coma Berenices* (66) shows that he could translate accurately if he wanted to.

45 We should also consider whether the fourth stanza, attached to Catullus 51 by MS tradition, is not in fact a part of the poem. If it is, we have an abrupt change of tone. After addressing Lesbia in the first three stanzas, and describing the helpless misery to which his jealousy reduces him, Catullus suddenly rounds on himself and says, 'Your trouble, Catullus, is idle-

ness, and you revel in this idleness. Idleness has destroyed kings and rich cities before now.' This makes sense if we remember that 'otium' was often associated with love and that it means not 'doing nothing' but 'freedom from serious occupation'. This is well illustrated by Ovid, *Remedia Amoris*, 141-4:[13]

> Quam platanus vino gaudet, quam populus unda,
>   et quam limosa canna palustris humo,
> tam Venus otia amat: qui finem quaeris amoris,
>   (cedit amor rebus) res age: tutus eris.

> *As the plane tree rejoices in the vine, as the poplar in the water, and as the marsh reed in the muddy ground, so Venus loves idleness: you who seek an end of love (love yields to business), get busy: you will be safe.*

The kings and cities of ll. 15-16 recall Paris and the destruction of Troy. In this stanza Catullus is saying that unless he gets a job pretty quickly, e.g. in Bithynia, Lesbia will be the death of him. Such a change in tone and address is characteristic of Catullus; compare the plan of this poem with '*Miser Catulle . . .*' (8), in which he first addresses himself (ll. 1-11), then Lesbia (ll. 12-18), finally himself again.

46 If this interpretation is correct, far from being a translation of Sappho in which Catullus first makes his love known to Lesbia, it is a poem of disillusionment, in which he has taken Sappho's poem as a starting-point but in which the main effect is achieved by the differences from Sappho.

47 Horace tells us that in his *Epodes* he followed Archilochus:

>           Parios ego primus iambos
> ostendi Latio, numeros animosque secutus
> Archilochi.

> *I first showed to Latium Parian iambics, following the metre and spirit of Archilochus.*                                    *Ep.* I. 19, 23-5

An anonymous papyrus fragment, usually attributed to Archilochus (*Fr.* 79a), seems to give us the model for *Epode* x.[14]

13. For this quotation and the interpretation of the whole stanza, see D. A. Kidd, *AUMLA* No. 20, 1963, pp. 298 ff.

14. For a full discussion of these poems see Fraenkel, *Horace*, pp. 24-36.

48  κύμασι πλαζόμενος
    κἂν Σαλμυδησσῷ γυμνὸν εὐφρονέστατα
    Θρήικες ἀκρόκομοι
    λάβοιεν – ἔνθα πόλλ' ἀναπλήσει κακὰ
    δούλιον ἄρτον ἔδων –
    ῥίγει πεπηγότ' αὐτόν, ἐκ δὲ τοῦ χνόου
    φυκία πόλλ' ἐπέχοι,
    κροτέοι δ' ὀδόντας ὡς κύων ἐπὶ στόμα
    κείμενος ἀκρασίη
    ἄκρον παρὰ ῥηγμῖνα κυμαντῳ . . . . ι
    ταῦτ' ἐθέλοιμ' ἂν ἰδεῖν,
    ὅς μ' ἠδίκησε, λὰξ δ' ἐπ' ὁρκίοις ἔβη
    τὸ πρὶν ἑταῖρος ἐών.

*. . . washed along by the waves, and in Salmydessos may the top-knotted
Thracians seize him naked, in a kindly spirit, – there he will endure his
fill of troubles eating the bread of slavery – stiff with cold, and from the
scum may a heap of sea-weed cover him, and may he gnash his teeth like
a dog lying on his face in helplessness by the edge of the breakers in the
swelling . . . That's what I should like to see for him who wronged me
and trod our oaths underfoot, who was formerly my friend.*

49 The fragment is striking for the intense hatred which
makes Archilochus conjure up so vividly the fate he wishes
his enemy to suffer. The sequence of optatives – interrupted
by one future indicative of exultant prophecy – builds up with
ever more precision, appealing to the senses of touch ('stiff
with cold') and hearing ('may he gnash his teeth') as well as to
the eye. Irony ('in a kindly spirit') and contempt ('like a dog')
add to the bitterness. Suddenly the picture is complete and the
poem ends with the statement of the crime which merits such
a fate. The structure is extremely simple, but there is a masterly
control in the positioning of the words, and the passionate
feeling is conveyed partly by the speed with which the fragment moves owing to the absence of end-stops.

50 Mala soluta navis exit alite,
    ferens olentem Maevium:
ut horridis utrumque verberes latus,
    Auster, memento fluctibus.

niger rudentis Eurus inverso mari
  fractosque remos differat;
insurgat Aquilo, quantus altis montibus
  frangit trementis ilices;
nec sidus atra nocte amicum appareat,
  qua tristis Orion cadit;
quietiore nec feratur aequore
  quam Graia victorum manus,
cum Pallas usto vertit iram ab Ilio
  in impiam Aiacis ratem!
o quantus instat navitis sudor tuis
  tibique pallor luteus
et illa non virilis eiulatio,
  preces et aversum ad Iovem,
Ionius udo cum remugiens sinus
  Noto carinam ruperit!
opima quodsi praeda curvo litore
  porrecta mergos iuverit,
libidinosus immolabitur caper
  et agna Tempestatibus.

*With an evil omen the ship is unmoored and departs, carrying the stinking Maevius: South Wind, remember to lash each side with wild waves. May the black South-easter turn the sea upside down and break the stays and oars and scatter them; rise up the North Wind, as strong as that which on the high mountains breaks the trembling ilexes; and may no friendly star appear in the dark night when Orion sets in gloom; may he sail on a sea as rough as that which struck the victorious host of Greece, when Pallas turned her anger from Troy, now burnt, to the wicked ship of Ajax. Oh, what a sweat comes on your sailors and what a yellow paleness comes on you, and those unmanly shrieks and prayers to Jupiter who heeds them not, when the Ionian shore, bellowing with the wet south wind, shall split the hull. But if he is stretched on the curving beach, a fat prey to please the sea-birds, a playful goat shall be sacrificed and a lamb to the Spirits of Storm.*

51 If Archilochus provided the model for *Epode* x, it is clear that Horace has taken over little more than the idea of cursing an enemy who is going on a voyage. The poem is constructed with careful symmetry. The first two lines state the situation; the central section, lines 3–20, gives the curse; the last four form

an epilogue. Precisely in the middle is a mythological exemplum. In the first part of the curse the south, the south-east, and the north winds are called in succession to wreck the ship, each in a couplet (the west wind would have assisted Maevius on a voyage from Italy to Greece); at the conclusion of the curse – the moment of catastrophe – the south wind is again invoked, this time by its Greek name, Notus. The epilogue concludes with the name of the Storm Spirits, Tempestatibus, ringing in our ears.

52 Despite the formality of the structure, the poem is not lacking in force. It moves from the generalized to the more precise, rising to a climax at the wreck itself, when Maevius is directly addressed and the scene is vividly sketched. But it does not make the impact of the Archilochus fragment. Apart from the highly tactile quality of Archilochus' lines, what is missing is a real crime to evoke such a curse: we are told that Maevius smelt; 'that, if true, is certainly unpleasant, but this complaint is far too common, both in the ancient and in the modern world, to justify such a violent outburst' (Fraenkel).

53 But Horace is not merely writing a poem on a theme taken from Archilochus. A common poetic form in the ancient tradition was the *propempticon*,[15] defined by the rhetorician Menander as 'a farewell with words of good omen'. We find a prototype in the fragment by Sappho written to her brother returning from Egypt (*Fr.* 5). The form became popular in the Alexandrian period (cf. Theocritus VII, 52–70 and Callimachus *Fr.* 400 Pfeiffer) and was adopted by the Neoterics. Thereafter it was common in Latin literature. Horace wrote such a poem to Virgil on his voyage to Greece, *Odes* I, iii.

54 The ode begins by praying that the gods may grant Virgil a safe voyage, confining all but the west wind. The rest of the

15. For a discussion of some poems based on this form, see K. Quinn, *Latin Explorations*, ch. 9. Gordon Williams, *Tradition and Originality*, p. 159, questions whether the *propempticon* was a single traditional form, but in the passages referred to, and in others, certain themes recur with sufficient regularity to suggest that a literary convention was established.

poem developes the commonplace (*communis locus*) of the hardi-hood of the first mariners and the sinful enterprise of man, re-gular themes of the *propempticon*. The effect of the poem de-pends partly on the irony of this section, which is an exercise in rhetorical exaggeration, written with such skill that we are carried along by it while conscious that it is quite out of pro-portion to the actual situation, a short crossing on a regular sailing route.

55 In *Epode* x Horace takes the *propempticon* form and turns it inside out. Maevius' ship departs 'mala alite' (with a bad omen). He prays that far from being confined, the adverse winds may bring storm; the favourable wind is omitted. The customary encomium of the traveller – in *Odes* I, iii 'animae dimidium meae' (the half of my soul) – is represented with the single word 'olentem' (stinking). Instead of the promise of a sacrifice to the gods for a safe return (cf. Ovid, *Amores* II, xi, 46 'pro reditu victima vota cadet' (for your return the votive offering shall fall)), a goat and a lamb will be sacrificed to the Storm Spirits, if Maevius becomes a prey to the sea birds.

56 The effect of the poem depends upon recognizing the anti-propempticon form, the tension between what Horace is actually saying and what was usually said on such occasions. This is a highly literary poem (which is not a judgement on its merit). It is not intended like the Archilochus fragment to convey a feeling of bitter hatred. Its purpose is to amuse an educated public which shared the same background of reading. In this purpose it is surely successful.

57 In *Odes* I, ix Horace opens with a reminiscence of Alcaeus, which we may assume he intended his readers to recognize.

ὕει μὲν ὁ Ζεύς, ἐκ δ᾽ ὀράνω μέγας
χείμων, πεπάγαισιν δ᾽ ὑδάτων ῥόαι
. . . . . . . . . . . . . . . . . . .
κάββαλε τὸν χείμων᾽, ἐπὶ μὲν τίθεις
πῦρ, ἐν δὲ κέρναις οἶνον ἀφειδέως
μέλιχρον, αὐτὰρ ἀμφὶ κόρσᾳ
μόλθακον ἀμφιβάλων γνόφαλλον.

*Zeus is raining, and from heaven comes a great storm, and the water courses are frozen. . . . Defy the storm, laying on the fire and mixing the sweet wine unsparingly, and putting a soft cushion about your head.*

*Fr. 338*

Despite important differences in detail, the correspondence is close enough to be unmistakable. Horace's poem is a dramatic monologue; he creates or re-creates (whether the situation is biographically true is irrelevant) a scene and develops from this some reflections on life and death. Horace is dining with a younger friend near Mount Soracte, about twenty-five miles north of Rome, in winter; he can see the trees burdened with snow and the streams frozen in their beds. The wintry scene leads him to tell his host to heap up the fire and to be more generous with the wine, and to 'leave all else to the gods'. The packed snow and frozen streams of the first stanza are contrasted with the blazing hearth and flowing wine of the second.

58 The imagery of the third stanza does not seem to be connected with the present scene; 'once the gods have stilled the winds that battle on the seething ocean neither the cypresses nor the old ashes are shaken'. But the first stanza suggested a scene of winter stillness – 'stet Soracte' (Soracte stands), 'flumina constiterint' (the streams stand still). The calm which follows the storm seems to correspond to the winter stillness; the battling winds look back to the scene of human activity.

59 In the second half he tells his host not to worry about the future and not to despise sweet love while he is young. Now, i.e. in youth, is the time for lovers' trysts. The thought is developed in terms of another scene, visualized on a summer's evening in Rome, which becomes more particularized as it proceeds, so that the poem ends with a lively picture contrasted at every point with that of the opening stanza.

60 At first reading the poem seems rational enough but disconcerting. The opening scene is depicted with precision and economy. The tone of the third and fourth stanzas is avuncular;

Thaliarchus seems to be experiencing troubles which make him brood and reject the pleasures natural to youth. And why should not Horace, talking like this in winter, imagine a summer's scene to illustrate his point? Nevertheless, the imagery of the third stanza appears incongruous and the opening and closing scenes are so strongly contrasted that the reader is shocked. It has been suggested, e.g. by Fraenkel (p. 177), that Horace has failed to observe his own principle 'sit quodvis, simplex dumtaxat et unum' (whatever it, the work of art, may be, it must be uniform). But in fact the whole poem seems to be on one theme to which all the images contribute: winter cold and stillness are contrasted with the warmth of human activity; battling winds (emotional storms) are contrasted with stillness (of death, cf. cypresses, the trees especially associated with death, l. 11). In the fourth stanza the imminence of death is explicitly suggested (l. 14). 'Puer' (l. 16) is developed by

'donec virenti canities abest morosa.'

*while you are green in youth and peevish white hairs are far away.*

This would seem extravagant in an economical poem unless it had some point; perhaps there is an echo here of the white snow piled on the green branches of lines 2–3 (cf. Commager, p. 271).

61 Even if Alcaeus proceeded in his poem from drinking to reflections on the shortness of human life, as in *Fr.* 38a, it is hard to believe that his poem had much in common with Horace's ode. Horace has used an echo of some lines of Alcaeus to open a poem which is really on one of the Epicurean commonplaces he was so fond of. The thought is not profound, but its expression is striking and original; it is the images, not the overt philosophizing, which make the emotional impact, and the feelings these evoke cohere with the philosophical message.

62 *Odes* I, i, the preface to Books I–III, is a programme poem. After the dedication to Maecenas, Horace uses the priamel form

to say what he hopes to achieve in the Odes – to win a place among the Greek lyric poets; in the last ode of these books (III, xxx) he claims to have won this place. The first ambition mentioned is victory in the chariot race at Olympia. Juxtaposed is the ambition of the Roman politician, and there follows a series firmly set in the contemporary Roman world, e.g. the quietest drinks Massic (Campanian) wine (l. 19) and the hunter is waiting for a Marsian boar (l. 28) in Latium. In fact, no chariot race was run at Olympia in Horace's time, and in no period since Pindar could athletic victories rank with political success as a life's ambition. For an educated Roman victory in the Olympic chariot race could hardly fail to recall Pindar.

63 When we come to Horace's own ambition it is placed in an unambiguously Greek context; 'doctus' (learned l. 29) is the Greek σοφός, traditionally applied to poets, 'hederae' (l. 29) is the ivy of Dionysus, who inspired the poet. He hopes to sing not only to the Lesbian lyre (monody like that of Sappho and Alcaeus) but also to the flute (choral lyric), and the opening reference to the Olympic games suggests that his master in this genre is to be Pindar.

64 None of Horace's poems is in a metrical form remotely like that of choral lyric, none of them was meant to be performed with dancing or on occasions like those when Greek choral lyric was performed. Even if their first performance was given at a *recitatio*, the odes were published in book form and were intended primarily for a reading public. Horace's ambition to follow Pindar cannot have been fulfilled in any obvious sense.

65 *Odes* III, iv[16] is the longest and at first reading one of the most difficult of the odes. Horace invokes the Muse and calls on her to descend from heaven and to play him a lengthy song. In the second stanza he believes he hears her and wanders in her holy grove, i.e. he is inspired. He then claims to have been under the special protection of the Muses in childhood, when he was miraculously preserved; in the present, whether at his

16. For a discussion of this ode and its relation to Pindar, *Pythian* I, see Fraenkel, *Horace*, pp. 273–85, which I here follow closely.

Sabine farm or at Praeneste, Tibur, or Baiae; in manhood, when he was saved at Philippi and from the falling tree (*Odes* III, viii) and from shipwreck; and in the future, whatever wild countries he may visit (ll. 9–36).

66 The mention of these wild peoples leads to Augustus, who is responsible for keeping them at bay or in submission, and so in the central stanzas of the poem we reach its principal theme – Augustus and his new order and their relations to the Muses (ll. 41–2).

> vos lene consilium et datis et dato
> gaudetis almae.

> *you both give gentle counsel and rejoice, when it is given, with tender care.*

We are then lauched abruptly into the myth (ll. 42–64) of the rebellion of the Giants against Jupiter and the ordered government of the universe, and of their defeat, in which Apollo features prominently. From the myth a moral is drawn (ll. 65–8):

> vis consili expers mole ruit sua:
> vim temperatam di quoque provehunt
>   in maius; idem odere viris
>     omne nefas animo moventis.

> *force without wisdom collapses under its own weight: force (or strength) under control the very gods carry on to greatness; but they hate the force that conceives every kind of wickedness.*

There follow further mythical examples of those who used brute force to wicked ends (including Typhos, still spouting fire under Etna, ll. 75–6). The ode ends, by a sudden twist characteristic of Horace, on a note of sadness; Perithous, the lover, is among these sinners, but how different is his sin from that of the 'immanis turba' (inhuman mob) of the Giants.

67 Apart from the overt echoes of Pindar's first *Pythian*, most clear in the description of Apollo (ll. 61–4 cf. *Pythian* I, 39,

39b), the poem as a whole is inspired by Pindar's ode but profoundly changed and, so to speak, brought up to date. Both poems make their main theme the power of the Muses. Both start from this power working in a narrower sphere (music actually heard in Pindar, symbolically heard in Horace) and proceed from this to the power of music or harmony in the divine and in the political order. In both a great ruler, who is the founder of a new order, is represented as the agent of the divine order. Both rulers have been active against external and internal disorders and in both poems, through the encomium, there seems to sound a note of warning or appeal, to use their victories with moderation.

68 The striking difference is in the stanzas concerned with Horace's own relations with the Muses (ll. 9–36). Horace's personal reminiscences of miraculous intervention by the Muses are clearly not to be taken literally and are completely alien to Pindar. Pindar starts from the performance which was the occasion of his song. He wrote in a society in which music, especially choral song and dance, was an essential and ubiquitous feature.

> Horace had no such ground to stand on, and he was fully conscious of it. . . . His poetry, his music, was not the joint product of his individuality and of something which was there before he was born, that existed independently of him and had its roots in a supra-personal sphere. His poetry, though inspired by the Muses, was entirely the work of himself alone.
>
> (Fraenkel, *Horace*, p. 284)

In writing an ode which was intended to recall Pindar's, he devotes the first part to making this difference clear. His inspiration is the product of his own experiences, whether in the humble surroundings of his birth or in the prosperity of the present, or in the various crises of his life. But he claims that he, like Pindar, expresses in his poetry a harmony which is an aspect of a greater harmony.

69 In the concluding lines of Book III (xxx, ll. 13–14) Horace

claims 'to have made Aeolian song at home in Italian poetry' (princeps Aeolium carmen ad Italos / deduxisse modos). He does not here mention Pindar or choral lyric. In IV, ii he recognizes the difficulty of challenging Pindar (ll. 1–4):

> Pindarum quisquis studet aemulari,
> Iule, ceratis ope Daedalea
> nititur pennis vitreo daturus
>     nomina ponto.

*Whoever strives to rival Pindar, Iulus, puts his trust in wings joined by wax with Daedalus' skill, doomed to give a name to the glassy sea.*

He contrasts the lofty flight of the swan of Dirce (Pindar) with his own performance – a Matine (Apulian) bee, a humble craftsman (parvus l. 31) composing his laborious songs (operosa carmina). Though the praise of Pindar rings true enough, we may detect a note of irony in his self-depreciation. Horace was well enough aware of his achievement. He did not imitate Greek models but immersed himself so deeply in the Greek tradition that he was able to create from it something new, contemporary, and clearly stamped with his own personality, to which the influences of Aeolian monody, Pindar's choral odes, and Alexandrian 'art' (cf. especially *Odes* I, vi[17]) all contributed.

70 So completely did Horace succeed that he had no real followers; later poets did not care to challenge comparison with the master, who at one bound had brought the genre to perfection. Lyrics were still occasionally written; Statius' *Silvae* include an alcaic (IV, v) and a sapphic (IV, vii) ode. Hendecasyllables were commoner, not only in Martial; his contemporary, Pliny, published a book of hendecasyllables of which he was inordinately proud – the product of leisure moments in his

17. In this ode Horace refuses to attempt epic themes (*grandia*), on the grounds that he is too slight, or fine, a poet (*nos . . . tenues*). *Tenuis* is used by Virgil (*Ecl. VI*, 8) and Propertius (III, I, 8) to render the Greek λεπταλέος and implies adherence to Callimachus' principle of the Μοῦσα λεπταλέη. Like the young Virgil and Propertius, Horace accepts the artistic principles of the Prologue to the *Aetia*.

carriage, in the bath, and at dinner (*Ep.* IV, 14, 2). But for a real revival of lyric we have to wait until the fourth century, the time of Ausonius, Tiberianus, the *Pervigilium Veneris*, and Prudentius. By then Latin poetry was on the threshold of the revolution which replaced quantative metres with stress and rhyming verse. From this developed not only the great Christian hymns but also the wonderful secular lyrics, best known in the *Cambridge Songs* (eleventh century) and the *Carmina Burana* (thirteenth century).

## Bibliography

Greek Lyric

BURN, A. R. *The Lyric Age of Greece*, Arnold, 1960.

BOWRA, C. M. *Greek Lyric Poetry*, Oxford, 2nd edition, 1961.

BOWRA, C. M. *Pindar*, Oxford, 1964.

BURTON, R. W. B. *Pindar's Pythian Odes, Essays in Interpretation*, Oxford, 1962.

CAMPBELL, D. A. *Greek Lyric Poetry*, a selection of early Greek lyric, elegiac, and iambic poetry, Macmillan, 1967. (This contains an historical introduction, the text of most of the important fragments, including some Bacchylides but excluding Pindar; a metrical analysis of the lyric poems; a full commentary including bibliographical references, and a metrical appendix.)

EDMONDS, J. M. *Lyra Graeca*, 3 volumes, Loeb, 1922–7. (The text is now superseded.)

PAGE, D. L. *Alcman; the Partheneion*, Oxford, 1951.

PAGE, D. L. *Sappho and Alcaeus*, Oxford, 1955.

PAGE, D. L. *Lyrica Graeca Selecta*, Oxford Classical Texts, 1968.

Latin Lyric

COMMAGER, S. *The Odes of Horace, A Critical Study*, Yale, 1962.

FRAENKEL, E. F. *Horace*, Oxford, 1957.

QUINN, K. *Latin Explorations*, London, 1963.

QUINN, K. *The Catullan Revolution*, Melbourne, 1959.

SULLIVAN, J. P. (ed.) *Critical Essays on Roman Literature, Elegy and Lyric*, London, 1962.

WHEELER, A. L. *Catullus and the Traditions of Ancient Poetry*, California, 1934.

GORDON WILLIAMS, *Tradition and Originality in Roman Poetry*, Oxford, 1968. (This massive and scholarly work unfortunately appeared too late for me to do more than incorporate references in footnotes 12 and 15.)

## Translations

LATTIMORE, R. *Pindar*, Chicago, 1947.

LATTIMORE, R. *Greek Lyrics*, Chicago, 1960.

MICHIE, J. *The Odes of Horace* (with Latin text), Harmondsworth, 1967.

WHIGHAM, P. *The Poems of Catullus*, Harmondsworth, 1966.

BRITTAIN, F. *The Penguin Book of Latin Verse* (text and translation, about three-fifths of the poems post-classical), Harmondsworth. 1962.

# III

# Elegiac Poetry

## John Fancourt Bell

Quis tamen exiguos elegos emiserit auctor
Grammatici certant et adhuc sub iudice lis est

*Who first wrote slight elegies, scholars debate and the matter is still unsettled*

Horace, *Ars Poetica* 77, 78

1 All the earliest writers of elegy flourished some time in the seventh century B.C. Callinus of Ephesus lived at a time of great unheaval in Asia Minor, when Cimmerians from Southern Russia, in company with the Trerians from Thrace, were attacking Phrygia, Lydia, and Ionia and came in conflict with Assyrians, whose rulers, Sargon (722–705 B.C.) and Esarhaddon (who fought with them before his accession in 681), celebrated successes over them. Driven back by Assyria, they attacked Gyges, king of Lydia, who was slain in battle with them about 655 B.C. Established in Sinope and Heraclea, they continued to threaten Ionia and Lydia, until they gave way before the invasion of the Scythians about 628–626. The Greek cities of Ionia were inevitably involved in the great sweep of these events and in his one substantial surviving fragment Callinus summons the young men of Ephesus to action:

Μέχρις τεῦ κατάκεισθε; κότ' ἄλκιμον ἕξετε θυμόν,
  ὦ νέοι; οὐδ' αἰδεῖσθ' ἀμφιπερικτίονας,
ὧδε λίην μεθίεντες, ἐν εἰρήνῃ δὲ δοκεῖτε
  ἧσθαι, ἀτὰρ πόλεμος γαῖαν ἅπασαν ἔχει.

63

*How long are you going to lie about? When will you show a stout heart, young men? You fail to regard the scorn of neighbours round you for being so very slack, but are resolved to sit at home in peace, though all the land is in the grip of war.*

(O.B.G.V. 102)

He goes on to say that death will find them just as easily at home, whereas they will be feted as demi-gods if they fall in battle. It would be hard to find a clearer call across the centuries denouncing appeasement in the face of impending danger. Elegy is a vehicle here for a call to arms and reveals the ancient poet involved in public affairs and using poetry as a medium for political or social policies. In the same strain Tyrtaeus summoned the young Spartans to show similar courage in the face of the Messenian revolt and Argive power:

ἀνδράσι μὲν θηητὸς ἰδεῖν, ἐρατὸς δὲ γυναιξίν,
ζωὸς ἐών, καλὸς δ' ἐν προμάχοισι πεσών.
ἀλλά τις εὖ διαβὰς μενέτω ποσὶν ἀμφοτέροισιν
στηριχθεὶς ἐπὶ γῆς, χεῖλος ὀδοῦσι δακών.

*Warriors gaze with wonder at him, women desire him when alive. Fair is he, too, fallen in the thick of battle. Let a man remain steadfast, both feet astride and firmly placed, biting his lip with his teeth.*

(O.B.G.V. 97)

2 Later at the beginning of the sixth century, Solon, lawgiver of Athens, perhaps under the influence of Tyrtaeus, employed elegies to give expression to personal and political opinions. He summed up his compromise for an Athens distraught with political and social upheaval in these words:

Δήμῳ μὲν γὰρ ἔδωκα τόσον κράτος, ὅσσον ἀπαρκεῖ,
τιμῆς οὔτ' ἀφελὼν οὔτ' ἐπορεξάμενος·
οἳ δ' εἶχον δύναμιν καὶ χρήμασιν ἦσαν ἀγητοί,
καὶ τοῖς ἐφρασάμην μηδὲν ἀεικὲς ἔχειν·
ἔστην δ' ἀμφιβαλὼν κρατερὸν σάκος ἀμφοτέροισιν
νικᾶν δ' οὐκ εἴασ' οὐδετέρους ἀδίκως.

*To the people I gave just as much power as they needed without robbing them of their privileges or giving them too much: as for those who had*

64

*power and were wondered at for their wealth, I arranged that they should not lose face, and I stood protecting both sides with a strong shield and did not allow either side to gain an unjust victory.*

O.B.G.V. No. 159

In another fragment he analyses the political situation and attacks the ruling class for their hybris and praises the concept of *Eunomia* (good order), which alone can free Athens from social strife. Like Callinus and Tyrtaeus in an earlier poem, he exhorts Athens to war against Megara to win the island of Salamis:

ἴομεν εἰς Σαλαμῖνα, μαχησόμενοι περὶ νήσου
ἱμερτῆς, χαλεπὸν τ᾽ αἶσχος ἀπωσόμενοι.

*We shall go to Salamis to contend for the lovely isle and thrust aside a terrible disgrace.*

His verse has few flights of poetry in it, but is interesting as revealing that verse was in this period the medium for the expression of political thoughts and policies, and the elegiac couplet was eminently suitable for making gnomic utterances succinctly.

3 The poet, Archilochus of Paros, is variously dated by the ancients. A passage in Cicero (*Tusc. Disp.* 1, i. 3) makes him contemporary with Romulus, 753–716 B.C., while in Herodotus (1. 12) he is mentioned as alive in Gyges' time, who died in *c*. 652. He took part in the colonization of Thasos, which is dated *c*. 708. He could be the first of the writers of elegy. Here is a man who is conscious of his poetic power:

εἰμὶ δ᾽ ἐγὼ θεράπων μὲν Ἐνναλίοιο ἄνακτος
καὶ Μουσέων ἐρατὸν δῶρον ἐπιστάμενος.

*I am a servant of Mars and skilled in the lovely gift of the Muses.*

His poetry ranges over much more varied subjects, metres, and language, and he was regarded in the ancient world as an innovator. Here verse is not being used as an instrument of public policy but to reveal his own strong and personal reactions to places and events. When Horace says he threw away his shield in flight from the battle of Philippi in 42, he must have had in mind Archilochus' reaction to a similar event, expressed with an openness and humour as fresh as the day he wrote it.

'Ασπίδι μὲν Σαΐων τις ἀγάλλεται, ἣν παρὰ θάμνῳ
  ἔντος ἀμώμητον κάλλιπον οὐκ ἐθέλων·
αὐτὸς δ' ἐξέφυγον θανάτου τέλος· ἀσπὶς ἐκείνη
  ἐρρέτω· ἐξαῦτις κτήσομαι οὐ κακίω.

*Some Thracian is crowing over my shield. All against my will I left it in spotless condition in a bush, but I saved myself from death. As for that shield? Perish the thing! I will get another just as good again.*

O.B.G.V. 104

Wine, which can often unleash a poet's inspiration, is a constant theme among the fragments, whether he wants to quench his thirst after a hard fight or to keep at bay the numbing cold of a long watch during a hard row at sea:

'Αλλ' ἄγε σὺν κώθωνι θοῆς διὰ σέλματα νηὸς
  φοίτα καὶ κοίλων πώματ' ἄφελκε κάδων,
ἄγρει δ' οἶνον ἐρυθρὸν ἀπὸ τρυγός· οὐδὲ γὰρ ἡμεῖς
  νήφειν ἐν φυλακῇ τῇδε δυνησόμεθα.

*Come on, wander with the wine along the benches of our fast ship and take off the covers from the hollow casks. Drain the red wine to the dregs. We won't be able to stay sober through this watch.*

The sea and its perils, actual and metaphorical, are never long absent from Greek poetry. In another fragment Archilochus offers consolation and bracing advice to those like himself who have lost friends drowned at sea. At first glance this looks like a lament capturing the mood which many ancient writers thought was the original inspiration of elegy. But the tone of the whole poem bids men endure and put aside womanish tears and not spoil the enjoyment of the feast with too much brooding over their sorrows. So far, then, elegy appears spirited, martial, direct, and in Archilochus, almost lyrical in its subjective treatment.

4 Finally and most important of the Archaic Greek elegists for the development of elegy, there is Mimnermus, a poet and musician, and variously associated either with Colophon or Smyrna in Asia Minor. Of the fourteen elegiac fragments, five are said to be quotations from his *Nanno*, a book of poems addressed to a courtesan. It is tantalizing to possess such few fragments. If more had survived we would know more clearly the relationship between them and how it compared with that of Propertius and Cynthia, Tibullus and Delia, and Catullus and Lesbia. In Book I, elegies vii and ix, Propertius addresses Ponticus, an epic poet, who in the first poem is warned that he will fall in love and in the second is seen to have done so. The grand themes of the epic muse cannot help any victim of unreasoning Aphrodite.

> Quid tibi nunc misero prodest grave dicere carmen
> aut Amphioniae moenia flere lyrae?
> plus in amore valet Mimnermi versus Homero:
> carmina mansuetus lenia quaerit Amor.

> *What use is there, poor man, in your singing in solemn and tragic mood of the walls built by Amphion's lyre? In love the poems of Mimnermus outshine Homer: gentle love demands calm flowing poems.*

Propertius is conscious enough that he writes in the tradition of Mimnermus, whether or not Mimnermus bared his soul as much in his poems. One fragment suggests he may have:

> Ἀληθείη δὲ παρέστω
> σοὶ καὶ ἐμοί, πάντων χρῆμα δικαιότατον.

> *Let truth be present between you and me, the best possession of all.*

Not for nothing is he said to have been a musician, as his verses have a more musical quality than Archilochus' and capture the same freshness and spontaneity of experience. In the love poems he harps constantly on the fleeting and momentary nature of life, the rapture of youth, and the pleasures of love contrasted with the squalid decay of old age. It has become a commonplace in literature, but rarely more exquisitely expressed.

τίς δὲ βίος, τί δὲ τερπνὸν ἄτερ χρυσῆς Ἀφροδίτης;
τεθναίην, ὅτε μοι μηκέτι ταῦτα μέλοι,
κρυπταδίη φιλότης καὶ μείλιχα δῶρα καὶ εὐνή·
οἷ᾽ ἥβης ἄνθεα γίγνεται ἁρπαλέα
ἀνδράσιν ἠδὲ γυναιξίν· ἐπεὶ δ᾽ ὀδυνηρὸν ἐπέλθῃ
γῆρας, ὅ τ᾽ αἰσχρὸν ὁμῶς καὶ καλὸν ἄνδρα τιθεῖ,
αἰεί μιν φρένας ἀμφὶ κακαὶ τείρουσι μέριμναι,
οὐδ᾽ αὐγὰς προσορῶν τέρπεται ἠελίου,
ἀλλ᾽ ἐχθρὸς μὲν παισίν, ἀτίμαστος δὲ γυναιξίν·
οὕτως ἀργαλέον γῆρας ἔθηκε θεός.

*What life, what delight is there without golden Aphrodite? May I be dead, when I no longer care for these – secret affection, gifts of love and bed. Such are the flowers of youth alluring to men and women. But when pinching old age comes upon a man and casts both ugly and handsome in the same mould, constant nagging worries weary his heart, he enjoys no more to gaze at the sun's rays. No, he is hateful to boy and scorned by women. So painful has God made old age*

O.B.G.V. 118

There is the play on dentals and labials in the opening line and in the third line the harder consonants resolve into liquids. 'Secret affection . . .' it calls to mind the last stanza of Horace's poem 'Vides ut alta . . .' the love-play in the Piazza, and rarely can εὐνή have been used to such effect. Then there is the dominant position of γῆρας, αἰσχρὸν, κακαί, ἐχθρὸς, ἀργαλέον, and their hard guttural sounds pointing the ugliness of old age. Another fragment tells of the settlement of Colophon from Nestor's Pylos and from there the capture of Smyrna. It is a world but little removed from Homeric times, and the influence of Homer is apparent throughout in his use of language and well-known phrases such as ῥοδοδάκτυλος Ἠώς (rosy-fingered dawn). In yet another fragment, telling perhaps of the war between Gyges and Smyrna, Mimnermus is eloquent on courage, and regrets about old age give place to the virile tone of military elegies.

5 There is little sign yet that elegy would develop into the fully-fledged art form of the Latin love elegy, but Mimnermus at least, and to some extent Archilochus, contain the themes which later writers of elegy were going to expand with countless variations. There is the admiration of beauty, youth, and love and the power and freedom it conveys and the same pessimism and shadow of tragedy, because it can only be imagined, if experienced to the full, as in a transient moment of time, never to be recaptured.

6 There are varied suggestions about the original meaning of the word, elegy. To any English reader with little knowledge of the classics, it suggests the mournful grace of Gray's Elegy, and Ovid (*Amores* III 9.3) calls it 'Flebilis Elegia', and certainly successive poets treated it in this way, from Callimachus to Ovid; and further it was thought that this was suggested by its etymology, $\dot{\epsilon}$ $\dot{\epsilon}$ λέγειν (to cry woe! woe!). But the bulk of the early elegies carry no theme of lamentation, but, as has been observed, are martial in expression. Homeric verse, and for that matter all early poetry, was accompanied by some instrument, and it is generally accepted that the word ἔλεγος perhaps derives from some song accompanied by a pipe. There is an Armenian word for 'reed', *elegn*, and there may be a connection. So often people refer to Phrygian pipes as if they were flutes. It is much more likely they were reed instruments akin to an oboe or at worst the noise of a bag-pipe. Shepherd boys in Crete still fashion reeds to make that thin and penetrating wailing sound and then sell them to tourists. This is the sound of the traditional Phrygian *aulos* – 'the channel of all elegiac singing – all fugitive personal moods, delights and sorrows that ever the western world has sung' (Freya Stark).

Sex mihi surgat opus numeris, in quinque residat.

*Let my work rise in six feet and sink back in five.*

So wrote Ovid in *Amores* I. I. 27. It is this rhythm which dictated whether a poem was called elegy or not. In hexameters there are sixteen possible permutations, while in the pentameter which followed there are four. Moreover, the pentameter with its constant dactyls (– ∪ ∪) in the second half appears with this rigid form in the earliest elegy. The basic rhythm is confined to two feet, a dactyl (– ∪ ∪) and a spondee (– –). Ovid, as quoted above, suggests that the rhythm of the elegiac couplet is like the rise and fall of a fountain. This is fair enough, though the fountain is rather erratic in subsiding and falls back in two movements, the first and second half of the penta-meter, not unlike a waltz rhythm. The dactylic form of the pentameter influenced the hexameter, which in elegy tends to be more dactylic than otherwise. It is the abruptness of the pentameter and the element of surprise about it which made the elegaic couplet such a suitable vehicle for the pointed thrust of epigram. More than this, the pentameter fell into two divi-sions of two and a half feet and, if the endings of both halves rhymed, the effect is immediately obvious. In the hexameter the force of rhyme, if found there, is not so great owing to the un-even distribution of the caesura. The hexameter with its many permutations was ideal for the narrative power of epic, but the pentameter has more in common with personal expression of lyric. It is this blend of two opposites which gives the elegy as an art form its tension, its grace, and its wit.

7 From the second half of the sixth century B.C. there comes the unusually large corpus of works attributed to Theognis of Megara. There are difficulties about the authorship of much ascribed to him, but it was common in antiquity for poems in the style of a particular author to be attributed to him (cf. the Homeric hymns). The tone of his poetry is aristocratic in ex-pression and mood, and asserts the value of the traditional Greek morality of his day, and for this the elegiac couplet is shown to be eminently suitable for the gnomic utterances which express this view of life. The following is an example of the aristocrat's disdain of money and the preference for a wealthy to a well-bred wife.

Χρήματα γὰρ τιμῶσι· καὶ ἐκ κακοῦ ἐσθλὸς ἔγημεν,
καὶ κακὸς ἐξ ἀγαθοῦ· πλοῦτος ἔμιξε γένος.

*Money they worship: and noble marries plebeian and plebeian noble: wealth*
*brings mixed breeding.* O.B.G.V. 188

The whole passage is a bit repetitive, but speaking with feeling
the aristocrat reacts to the new-won power of the *nouveaux*
*riches*. In another passage there are echoes of Mimnermus:

"Ἄφρονες ἄνθρωποι καὶ νήπιοι, οἵτε θανόντας
κλαίουσ᾽, οὐδ᾽ ἥβης ἄνθος ἀπολλύμενον.

*Fools are men and childish, who weep for the dead, and not for the wilting*
*bloom of youth.* O.B.G.V. 196

The tone is more forthright and tough. Yet his work is not
without pathos, as when he experienced the bitterness of exile:

"Ὄρνιθος φωνήν, Πολυπαΐδη, ὀξὺ βοώσης
ἤκουσ᾽, ἥτε βροτοῖς ἄγγελος ἦλθ᾽ ἀρότου
ὡραίου· καί μοι κραδίην ἐπάταξε μέλαιναν,
ὅττι μοι εὐανθεῖς ἄλλοι ἔχουσιν ἀγρούς.

*I heard the sound of the bird's shrill cry, Polypaide, who came to mortals*
*as herald of the ploughing season. And my heart was smitten with gloom*
*that other men possess my fertile fields.* O.B.G.V. 199

This song expresses the particular experience of many nobles
amid the political upheavals of this period and the general
experience of all exiles from home. Elsewhere he upbraids his
friend Cyrnus for his faithlessness, when the songs he has
written in his praise have won him immortality, or cries out for
vengeance on his enemies with the same vigour as the Hebrew
psalmist denounces the ungodly – an eye for an eye. They had
stripped him of his property but:

ἐγὼ δὲ κύων ἐπέρησα χαράδρην,
χειμάρρῳ ποταμῷ πάντ᾽ ἀποσεισάμενος·
τῶν εἴη μέλαν αἷμα πιεῖν· ἐπί τ᾽ ἐσθλὸς ὄροιτο
δαίμων, ὃς κατ᾽ ἐμὸν νοῦν τελέσειε τάδε.

*I like a dog passed across the torrent, in its wintry flood shaken free of*
*all; let me drink their black blood: may some kind spirit rise against*
*them and fulfil all as I would like* O.B.G.V. 191

The hunted man has barely escaped with his life. This is strong and vigorous, with bold and suggestive use of images. Many of his couplets stand by themselves as epigrams, and this feeling that the elegaic couplet can contain within itself all that needed to be said finds expression in another warning to Cyrnus:

Ὕβρις καὶ Μάγνητας ἀπώλεσε καὶ Κολοφῶνα
καὶ Σμύρνην. πάντως, Κύρνε, καὶ ὑμμ' ἀπολεῖ.

*Pride has destroyed Magnesia and Colophon and Smyrna. It will utterly destroy you as well, Cyrnus.*                              O.B.G.V. 197

Echoes again of Mimnermus and Callinus. This capacity of the couplet to express thoughts so neatly made elegy inevitably the medium for epigrams, both epitaphs and dedications.

8 Few poets have written more moving epitaphs than Simonides (mid-sixth to mid-fifth century B.C.) who employed elegy for this (though it must be admitted that many may have been ascribed to him wrongly). His epitaph on the Spartan dead at Thermopylae is well known. The long wailing vowel sounds wring the heart:

Ὦ ξεῖν', ἀγγέλλειν Λακεδαιμονίοις ὅτι τῇδε
κείμεθα, τοῖς κείνων ῥήμασι πειθόμενοι.

*Oh stranger, tell the Spartans that we lie here, obedient to their orders.*
O.B.G.V. 212

'Stranger' – there is no one left to bring the news home, a present participle suggests the eternal worth of their sacrifice. Their obedience lasts beyond death itself. It is a bare and simple statement and yet contains an ocean of feeling, more deeply felt because of its disciplined expression.

9 In another he commemorates a shipwreck:

τούσδε ποτ' ἐκ Σπάρτας ἀκροθίνια Φοίβῳ ἄγοντας
ἓν πέλαγος, μία νύξ, εἷς τάφος ἐκτέρισεν.

72

*These men as they were bringing the first fruits from Sparta to Apollo, one sea, one night, one tomb has buried.*         *O.B.G.V.* 217

He expresses the suddenness of disaster at sea and points the unity of circumstance by the inversion of εἷς–μία–ἕν (masculine–feminine–neuter). They were carrying out their obligations to Apollo, yet what a weight of irony in the final word ἐκτέρισεν (bury with honour). The BBC reporters could learn something here in the coverage of disasters at sea from the sheer reticence of this couplet. The epigrams of Plato show a similar neatness:

Ἀστέρας εἰσαθρεῖς ἀστὴρ ἐμός. εἴθε γενοίμην
   οὐρανός, ὡς πολλοῖς ὄμμασιν εἰς σὲ βλέπω.

*You gaze upon the stars, my star. Would I were the heavens, to gaze on you with many eyes.*         *O.B.G.V.* 445

It speaks for itself. In another (*O.B.G.V.* 450) Plato seems to foreshadow Callimachus and Alexandrian writers in his power to evoke the atmosphere of natural surroundings:

Ὑψίκομον παρὰ τάνδε καθίζεο φωνήεσσαν
   φρίσσουσαν πυκινοῖς κῶνον ὑπὸ Ζεφύροις,
καί σοι καχλάζουσιν ἐμοῖς παρὰ νάμασι σύριγξ
   θελγομένων ἄξει κῶμα κατὰ βλεφάρων.

*Come, sit beneath this pine tree as its high foliage murmurs, rustling in the frequent gusts of the Zephyrs and my pipe accompanied by the babbling waters will lull your eyelids to a gentle sleep.*    *O.B.G.V.* 450

There is a whole world of beauty here and a sympathy with nature rarely found in the poetry of the classical period but developed later by the poets of the Hellenistic world. These are a few examples to show how the epigram in dedications, on tombs, as short love poems like exquisite graffiti or aphorisms on life, continued to develop and vary the original themes. In this way the elegiac couplet displayed the possibilities inherent in it for saying things pointedly and with restraint and became a natural vehicle for inscriptions.

10 Elegia quoque Graecos provocamus

> *In elegy also we challenge the Greeks.*          *Inst. Or.* 10. 1. 93

So wrote Quintilian after a mention of Philetas and Callimachus as the leading elegists of Alexandria. These two and
perhaps Meleager were the last significant writers of elegy
among the Greeks. Propertius, in Book III, i, acknowledges
both as a source of inspiration:

> Callimachi Manes et Coi sacra Philetae,
>     In vestrum, quaeso, me sinite ire nemus.
> Primus ego ingredior puro de fonte sacerdos
>     Itala per Graios orgia ferre choros.

> *Departed spirits of Callimachus and Philetas of Cos whom we worship,
> allow me entrance, I beg, into your wood. I am the first to attempt, a
> priest from a pure spring, to celebrate Italian mysteries in Greek measures.*

He is not claiming that either wrote elegies resembling the love
elegies of the Romans, but he summons them as masters of
elegaic style and metre. In *puro de fonte*, 'the purity of the
water symbolizes the refined perfection of the poetry'. The idea
is borrowed from Callimachus' *Hymn to Apollo*, lines 110
*seqq*. Despite references in Ovid and Propertius, nothing of
value from Philetas survives except his reputation as an elegist
and that one of his pupils was probably Theocritus. But with
Callimachus it is different: much has survived, and with it the
personality of a poet who is original, scholarly, and mordant
in the expression of his opinions. He flourished in the mid-
third century B.C., and early in life moved from his birthplace
in Cyrene to become a schoolmaster in Eleusis, a suburb of
Alexandria, during the reign of Ptolemy Philadelphus. He
quarrelled with other poets and scholars of his day, among
whom were Asclepiades and Posidippus. His enemies accused
him of inability to write a traditional epic. Callimachus regarded
the epic as out of date and concentrated on the epyllion, a
shorter poem, complete in itself, of 100–600 lines, taking as its
theme the life of a mythical hero or heroine. This was akin to
the hymns, which included any metrical address to a god and

contained an accumulation of names and epithets and a recital of his deeds. This type of poetry Callimachus preferred, and he quarrelled with his former pupil, Apollonius Rhodius, when he wrote his *Argonautica*. One of his epigrams expresses his feelings directly:

Ἐχθαίρω τὸ ποίημα τὸ κυκλικόν, οὐδὲ κελεύθῳ
χαίρω τίς πολλοὺς ὧδε καὶ ὧδε φέρει,
μισῶ καὶ περίφοιτον ἐρώμενον, οὐδ' ἀπὸ κρήνης
πίνω· σικχαίνω πάντα τὰ δημόσια.

*I loathe the cyclic poem, and find no pleasure in the road, which takes many this way and that, and I hate, too, the gallivanting lover and do not drink from the public well: I dislike all vulgar things.*       O.B.G.V. 519

It reminds one of Horace, *Odes* III. i. i:

'Odi profanum vulgus et arceo.'

*I loathe the uninitiate mob and keep them off.*

11 Of his hymns and epyllia, it is the *Bath of Pallas* written in elegiacs which concerns the development of elegy. The scholiast says that it was the custom of the Argive women, on a certain day, to carry the image of Athena and the shield of Diomedes to the River Inachos and wash them. This image is the Palladium, taken from Troy by Diomedes and Odysseus, and brought by the former to Argos. In the poem, Callimachus summons the Argive women to assemble, before inviting the presence of the goddess. Pallas is described in amazonian terms; praised to the detriment of Aphrodite and Hera, she is pictured as returning in her chariot from battle with the giants, her arms are stout, she has no need of mirrors, and while Aphrodite dallies with one, Pallas has been racing long distances and afterwards with a touch of olive oil blushes like the colour of a rose or seed of pomegranate. She is addressed as sacker of cities, golden-helmeted, and loving the clatter of horses and shields. Some goddess! No one is to approach the River Inachos today – the fountains, certainly – but not the river. No one must look on her as she bathes. To gaze on deity is to

go blind. Then Callimachus launches into the story of the blinding of Teiresias. Athena's bosom companion was a nymph Chariclo, the mother of Teiresias, and one day they undressed and bathed together:

μεσαμβρινὰ δ᾽ εἶχ᾽ ὄρος ἀσυχία.
ἀμφότεραι λώοντο, μεσαμβριναὶ δ᾽ ἔσαν ὧραι,
πολλὰ δ᾽ ἀσυχία τῆνο κατεῖχεν ὄρος.
Τειρεσίας δ᾽ ἔτι μῶνος ἁμᾶ κυσὶν ἄρτι γένεια
περκάζων ἱερὸν χῶρον ἀνεστρέφετο·
διψάσας δ᾽ ἀφατόν τι ποτὶ ῥόον ἤλυθε κράνας,
σχέτλιος· οὐκ ἐθέλων δ᾽ εἶδε τὰ μὴ θεμιτά.

*The noontide quiet held the mountain. Both were bathing, and it was the noontide hour and a great quiet covered that mountain. And Teiresias on his own, whose beard was just beginning to darken his face, was still ranging with his hounds the holy place. And unspeakably thirsty, he came to the flowing spring, wretched man. And unwillingly he saw what it is forbidden to see.*  O.B.G.V. 810

There was nothing Athena could do; he had to go blind despite the protests of his mother. Athena tells her how he was lucky not to suffer the fate of Actaeon, who was torn to pieces by his own dogs, because he had seen Artemis bathing. In return, she will give him as recompense the inward sight of the seer. After Athena has spoken, the poet again invokes the goddess. The story is beautifully told and the scene is set simply. Though the subject is very different, the passage above has the atmosphere of Ovid's encounter with Corinna in *Amores*, I, v:

Aestus erat, mediamque dies exegerat horam.

*It was hot and the noontide hour just past.*

Both Ovid and Propertius owe something to Callimachus, who in a literary age breathes fresh life into the myths of the ancient world. In another work, called the *Aitia*, he treats in a series of elegiac episodes all kinds of aetiological legends, connected with the history, religion, and customs of the Greeks. He imagines himself carried by the Muses from Libya to Helicon, where as he questions them they instruct him in all manner of legends. Propertius, in IV. 3. i, once again acknowledges his debt:

Visus eram molli recubans Heliconis in umbra

*I seemed to be reclining in the gentle shade of Helicon.*

There is no sign in Callimachus of love elegy as found in the Augustan poets, but it is clear from many themes present in their work that again the Roman poets were much in his debt.

12 It was, however, with the epigram that the Hellenistic poets were most at home, and while keeping within the traditions of the short poem, they extended its range. Callimachus was as perfect at this poetry as anyone, and along with Asclepiades and Meleager created the background from which the Roman elegists were to range more freely. Many will recognize from the translation the epigram by Callimachus on Heraclitus:

Εἶπέ τις Ἡράκλειτε τεὸν μόρον, ἐς δέ με δάκρυ
ἤγαγεν, ἐμνήσθην δ' ὁσσάκις ἀμφότεροι
ἥλιον ἐν λέσχῃ κατεδύσαμεν· ἀλλὰ σὺ μέν που
ξεῖν' Ἁλικαρνησεῦ τετράπαλαι σποδιή·
αἱ δὲ τεαὶ ζώουσιν ἀηδόνες, ᾗσιν ὁ πάντων
ἁρπακτὴς Ἀίδης οὐκ ἐπὶ χεῖρα βαλεῖ.     O.B.G.V. 513

*They told me, Heraclitus, they told me you were dead;*
*They brought me bitter news to hear and bitter tears to shed.*
*I wept, as I remembered, how often you and I*
*Had tired the sun with talking and sent him down the sky.*
*And now that thou art lying, My dear old Carian guest,*
*A handful of grey ashes, long, long ago at rest*
*Still are thy pleasant voices, thy nightingales, awake,*
*For Death, he taketh all away, but them he cannot take.*

William Cory.

The translation is fine, but nothing compared with the original. 'tired the sun with talking and sent him down the sky' fails to capture the simplicity of 'put the sun to bed'. The lament of the Greek has to be captured by extended paraphrase of unrestrained emotion in the English. Yet the translation expresses well the brevity of man's mortal life and the immortality which

77

surrounds the thoughts of a genius. But the English fails to capture ἁρπακτής and the sudden efforts of Death who tries in vain to catch the nightingales. Unlike the epigrams of an earlier age (Simonides, etc.), this is a literary epigram, not written for any special moment or occasion, but simply to express in as technically perfect a way as possible a poetic idea.

13 Asclepiades, whose pen-name was Sicelides, was a contemporary of Callimachus and a brilliant writer of epigrams. Moreover, these mostly concerned the themes of love, and perhaps he was the first poet consciously to associate elegiac writing almost entirely with love. His epigram on the fate of Danae, mother of Perseus, who was imprisoned by her father, Acrisius, in a bronze chamber, and despite this visited by Zeus as a shower of gold, foreshadows the allusive treatment of myth by Propertius and Ovid.

Νῖφε, χαλαζοβόλει, ποίει σκότος, αἶθε, κεραύνου,
   πάντα τὰ πορφύροντ᾽ ἐν χθονὶ σεῖε νέφη.
ἢν γάρ με κτείνῃς, τότε παύσομαι· ἢν δὲ μ᾽ ἀφῇς ζῆν,
   καὶ διαδὺς τούτων χείρονα, κωμάσομαι·
ἕλκει γὰρ μ᾽ ὁ κρατῶν καὶ σοῦ θεός, ᾧ ποτε πεισθείς,
   Ζεῦ, διὰ χαλκείων χρυσὸς ἔδυς θαλάμων.

*Snow, send hail, shed darkness, lighten, thunder, over the earth shake all your darkening clouds. If you kill me, then I will cease. But if you let me live, even going through worse than this, I shall revel. I am in the clutches of the god who won power over you, by whose persuasive power you, O Zeus, once went as gold through the chamber of bronze.*   O.B.G.V. 524

There is the humour and wit present here which later lightens the melancholy of much Latin love elegy. Under the passion of love, the great sky god, Zeus, stoops to subtleties of metamorphosis which seem to ridicule his more usual expressions of authority. In yet another the poet in anguish of passion begs Cupid to set him free:

Οὐκ εἴμ᾽ οὐδ᾽ ἐτέων δύο κεἴκοσι, καὶ κοπιῶ ζῶν.
   Ὦρωτες, τί κακὸν τοῦτο; τί με φλέγετε;
ἢν γὰρ ἐγώ τι πάθω, τί ποιήσετε; δῆλον, Ἔρωτες,
   ὡς τὸ πάρος παίξεσθ᾽ ἄφρονες ἀστραγάλοις.

78

*I am not yet twenty-two and I'm worn out with life. O Loves, what evil thing is this? Why do you burn me up? For if anything happens to me, what will you do? Clearly, loves, just as before you'll play your aimless game of dice.*

O.B.G.V. 529

Notice the genuine conversational tone of most love elegy, the same frankness, at once serious and absurd, the same longing for an end of passion and a craving for more, the same humour, for if all you, Cupid, are going to do is play at dice, you might just as well be giving me the works! The portrayal of Cupid as a naughty playful boy enters elegy perhaps for the first time. He becomes a constant symbol of the whimsical inconstancy of erotic passion.

14 The Hellenistic world developed the epigram, and nowhere more than here changed and enlarged a literary form. Its subjects were artificial, often about men long dead, as in Callimachus' epigram on Heraclitus, or on works of art or sentimental trifles. At the same time they infused these trifles with the intensity of feeling found in early elegy, and appear masterful and confident in the neatness with which they show off their varied skill. Meleager, a poet and philosopher of the Cynic School, who lived in Tyre and Cos, is best fitted to conclude these reflections on Greek Elegy, although the epigram continued as a live art form into Byzantine times. Perhaps he is over-florid, and owes more to lyric and poets like Anacreon than to the writers of elegy. But he is interesting because he lives at the beginning of the first century B.C. but a little while before Catullus, who first gave effective form to Latin Elegy. His mosquito plays a similar role to Lesbia's pet sparrow:

Πταίης μοι, κώνωψ, ταχὺς ἄγγελος, οὔασι δ' ἄκροις
    Ζηνοφίλας ψαύσας προσψιθύριζε τάδε·
" Ἄγρυπνος μίμνει σε· σὺ δ', ὦ λήθαργε φιλούντων,
    εὕδεις." εἶα, πέτευ· ναί, φιλόμουσε, πέτευ·
ἥσυχα δὲ φθέγξαι, μὴ καὶ σύγκοιτον ἐγείρας
    κινήσῃς ἐπ' ἐμοὶ ζηλοτύπους ὀδύνας.
ἢν δ' ἀγάγῃς τὴν παῖδα, δορᾷ στέψω σε λέοντος,
    κώνωψ, καὶ δώσω χειρὶ φέρειν ῥόπαλον.

*Fly away, mosquito, be my swift messenger, and touching the tips of her ears, whisper this to Zenophile: 'I lie awake for memory of you. But you, forgetful of your lovers, lazily sleep.' Here you, off you fly! Yes, as the muses love you, wing away! But say it softly, in case you wake her man and stir the pangs of envy against me. But if you bring the girl to me, I'll wrap you in a lion's skin, mosquito, and give you a club to brandish in your hand.*

*O.B.G.V.* 582

15 At the start it is somewhat affected, but very neat with the whirr of his wings caught by προσψιθύριζε in line 2 and his whine on approach in line 4 and ending up with a full-blooded erotic image. There is the trio situation, played up later in all its variations in Tibullus, Propertius, and Ovid, the fine sense of drama, and a colloquial style, which shows the influence of new comedy here, just as the plays of Plautus and Terence, derived from it, perhaps influence in their turn the plots and turn-about situations of the long Latin love elegy. It is important, however, not to overstress this, as the Latin love elegy, however playful and fanciful on occasions, could not contemplate the happy ending of comedy, as it depends for tension on an essentially tragic situation. 'They lived happily ever after' is as remote from elegy as marriage from the adventures of a knight-errant hero in a television serial.

16 Gaius Valerius Catullus (c. 84–54 B.C.) is the first Roman poet whose elegies have survived. It is true that many of his shorter love poems written in elegiac metre are epigrams, but as has been shown in considering Greek elegy, it is impossible to examine one kind apart from the other, as their history and influence on each other are so intertwined. Moreover, Latin elegy developed out of the epigram, and no one did more to hasten the development than Catullus. He was associated with a band of poets, referred to by Cicero as 'poetae novi' (known also as 'νεώτεροι' or 'the moderns') or derogatively as 'Cantores Euphorionis'. These, under the leadership of Publius Valerius Cato (b. c. 100 B.C.), called the Latin Siren, deliberately revolted against the poetic tradition of Ennius and turned for their inspiration to the Alexandrian tradition, especially as represented by Callimachus and lesser men, such as Euphorion of

Chalcis. Of this group two at least were friends of Catullus, Calvus, and Cinna. This tradition had already made its impact on earlier Latin poets, among them Lutatius Catulus, Consul in 102 B.C., who wrote love epigrams clearly under this influence. Though these earlier poets did not slavishly imitate, the real revolution in technique, style, and spirit did not emerge until Catullus. It is impossible to determine what factors caused this revolution, but since they were living in an age of revolution with the party of Caesar challenging accepted methods of government, it would be surprising if literary movements were not similarly affected. Yet if they inherited from Alexandria a more subjective treatment of poetry, the allusions, the imaginative and open-ended use of myth, the dramatic devices and bold experiment with rhythm, they instilled passion into their poems. Catullus did not just observe life analytically, he lived it in his poetry.

17 He wrote three long elegies which have survived, one of which is a direct translation from Callimachus (No. 66), but for the purposes of this chapter, number 68 is the most illuminating. As it stands, it is a long and complete poem, beginning with a letter to a friend. The middle section is an elaborately wrought elegy, dwelling on his first encounter with someone, who must be Lesbia (generally held to be Clodia, the wife of Quintus Caecilius Metellus Celer, Consul 60 B.C. and made notorious by Cicero's magnificent defence of his friend Caelius, who unlike Catullus, appears to have escaped moderately unharmed from his affair with her). It ends with an epilogue, expressing his thanks and presenting the preceding elegy as his gift. There are difficulties in regarding all these as parts of the same poem. One is the unlikelihood of Manius and Allius, to whom the letter and elegy are addressed respectively, being the same person. Secondly, in the opening letter Manius is obviously suffering from unrequited love and beyond the help of the Muses, while in the farewell at the end of the poem he makes no allusion to this except for a polite wish that Allius and his wife or mistress ('tu simul et tua vita') may be pros-

perous. Another oddity is the repetition in each part of the poem of lines written in grief on his brother's death, although granted it is one poem, the repetition is effective. More than that, if it is all one poem Catullus goes on to do exactly what he says in the introductory letter he cannot do. There is no easy solution, but if one regards the first forty lines as a different poem the rest certainly has a natural unity.

18 He will make Allius famous for his help, and in an original twist, summons the Muses to convey his story to posterity:

> vos porro dicite multis
> milibus et facite haec carta loquatur anus.

> *You in turn, tell it to many thousands and make this paper speak when it is old.*

Catullus could hardly have imagined the slender chance on which the survival of his poems depended, yet throughout so much of his poetry there is the confident hope of immortality for it, this time implied by:

> notescatque magis mortuus atque magis,
> nec tenuem texens sublimis aranea telam
> in deserto Alli nomine opus faciat.

> *When dead, let his fame spread more and more and may no spider weaving its suspended web build its work over Allius' abandoned name*

To continue his story, he burns like a volcano or geyser, with passion bestowed by treacherous (*duplex*) Venus. One simile then elaborately points his grief, another Allius' help, which was as welcome as the gentler breeze which comes as a response to prayer in a storm, and offered a spacious privacy (*clansum lato*) to indulge his love. The scene is set for the entry of his goddess:

> Quo mea se molli candida diva pede
> intulit et trito fulgentem in limine plantam
> innixa arguta constituit solea.

*This house my shining goddess entered with gentle step and placed her gleaming sole upon the well-worn threshold, resting on her tapping sandals.*

She is compared, rather strangely, to Laodamia, and this comparison leads to the digression or story so common in all Alexandrian hymns and epyllia (cf. *The Birth of Pallas*). The death of Protesilaus is connected in Catullus' version with a failure to sacrifice at his marriage and evokes a prayer from the poet:

> nil mihi tam valde placeat, Ramnusia Virgo,
> quod temere invitis suscipiatur eris.

*Maiden goddess of Ramnus (Nemesis), may nothing ever tempt me so strongly, that I would rashly grasp it against the will of my masters.*

This reads with splendid irony beside Carmen 76, when not even heaven can help him.

> Quin tu animo offirmas atque istinc teque reducis
> et dis invitis desinis esse miser?

*Why don't you take a grip of yourself, withdraw from your present state and leave off being unhappy against the will of the gods?*

19 The story of Protesilaus leads to Troy, an eternal symbol for many things, among them separated lovers, and Troy in turn evokes his own particular grief again over the loss of his brother. All his joys, he says, have perished with his brother, and this again reads curiously in an elegy, celebrating among other things his meeting with Lesbia, though perhaps from the start the note of tragedy sounded. Laodamia's grief at the death of her husband is described in a passage which abounds in a 'parade of mythological detail' (Fordyce: *Catullus*) typical of Alexandrian taste. Catullus continues:

> Sed tuus altus amor barathro fuit altior illo
> qui tamen indomitam ferre iugum docuit.

*But your love was deeper than that whirlpool, a love which trained you to bear the yoke of marriage, untamed before.*

Perhaps this gives a clue to Catullus' comparison of Lesbia's illicit love (*furtum*) for him, to Laodamia's married love for Protesilaus. Tragedy is part of the essence of love elegy, and both love affairs were doomed. Love, experienced under sentence of death, is only made tolerable by the wilful phantasies of the mind. There will come the day when Catullus will tame Lesbia! In later lines the poet sustains this thought with reference to a late-born heir and images of kissing doves, symbols of conjugal affection. Then back to the real moment of Lesbia's entrance, after all these thoughts had suggested themselves to Catullus as he beheld her standing in the doorway. No longer phantasy, this is the world of furta (thefts), even if Catullus boldly uses the word of Lesbia's infidelities to himself, when he had no more claims on her than anyone else. He calls her 'verecunda era'. It is a commonplace in love elegy that the liaison is one-sided. Catullus is a slave. Nothing suggests this more powerfully than *molesti*. He must not be a nuisance to her.

> Nec tamen illa mihi dextra deducta paterna
>     fragrantem Assyrio venit odore domum,
> sed furtiva dedit mira munuscula nocte,
>     ipsius ex ipso dempta viri gremio.

> *Nor yet did she come to me, handed over by her father's hand, to my home smelling of Assyrian incense, but secretly she gave her little gifts in a marvellous night, taken from her husband's very embrace.*

In these two couplets he neatly compares his hopeful phantasies with the reality of his secret affair. Though somewhat rugged, the poem has a splendid eloquence, and the mythological or rather legendary treatment provides the universal background for his own particular experiences, whether love for Lesbia or grief for his brother, and makes them as wide as the world. This poem then, with all its complexities of construction and variety of themes, ranging over all the stylistic devices, including a cyclic inversion of the arrangement of his material, achieves an intensity of personal feeling unknown in Alexandria, and together with Carmen 76, an elegy depicting his despairing efforts to overcome his unrequited passion for Lesbia, reaches heights unsurpassed by later writers of elegy.

20 Albius Tibullus (*c.* 48–19 B.C.), if lacking the more passionate qualities of Catullus, developed the elegy to a greater perfection, whatever claims are made for Cornelius Gallus, of whose four books of elegies only one pentameter survives. Quintilian describes him as 'tersus atque elegans', and Ovid describes his poetry with warmth:

> donec erunt ignes arcusque Cupidinis arma,
> discentur numeri, culte Tibulle, tui.

> *As long as fires and bow are the weapons of Cupid, men will follow your rhythms, stylish Tibullus.*

Both 'doctus', as applied to Catullus, and 'cultus' suggest an enormous care and concern for their poetry. It was all the result of much 'labor', and it is through the skill which he acquired that Tibullus' work possesses the ease, fluency, and restraint, the formal qualities which are as satisfying in poetry as they are in a Haydn symphony. 'Ars est celare artem.' Not only did Ovid praise him, but Horace makes him the subject of an *Epistle* (Horace, *Epist.* 1. 4) and an *Ode* (1. 33), displaying a touching friendship and underlining how small was the circle in which these poets moved and the influence they had on each other. His patron was Marcus Valerius Messalla Corvinus (64 B.C.–A.D. 8), who first distinguished himself at Philippi in support of Brutus and Cassius, then served under Antony, and though later he joined Octavian, never forsook altogether his republican ideals. Tibullus had soldiered under him in his youth, and this explains the prominence of the abhorrence of war in his elegies and the pastoral ideal he vainly pursues to acquire peace of mind. He was the most un-Roman of them all.

21 Basically his themes are love and the blessings of country life. In the first book five poems concern his passion for Delia (Nos. 1, 2, 3, 5, 6), three with his admiration for Marathus, a 'puer delicatus' (Nos. 4, 8, 9), Elegy 7 was written to celebrate

Messalla's birthday, and the last one (No. 10) contrasts the blessings of peace with the futility of war. As has been shown in a comprehensive treatment of Elegy by Georg Luck, the debt of Tibullus to Callimachus and Alexandria is equally as great as that of Catullus, but less apparent through a more subtle approach. The birthday poem for Messalla is as complex as Carmen 68 of Catullus, though without the same unity, and defies easy analysis because it makes use of so many categories – a birthday poem, a triumphal ode, an autobiographical sketch of the poet's own campaigns leading into a hymn to Osiris, invited to share in Messalla's birthday festivities, ending with mention of his family and a brief prayer to the Natalis. It was the fusions of these different kinds of poem, all common in Hellenistic literature, which marked Rome's peculiar contribution to the development of elegy. Why the hymn to Osiris? Perhaps Tibullus visited Egypt as a comrade-in-arms of Messalla and both fell under the spell of the country. There could scarcely be a more fitting tribute to their friendship than to reproduce and develop echoes in his poem of the Egyptian genius of Callimachus (who also wrote for a birthday [Iambus XII], and about the Nile [*Fr.* 384. 27]). Osiris' presence is invited in company with Messalla's genius (representing the individuality of the birthday king). Though this is a Roman idea, the genius is described in the Hellenistic manner:

> illius et nitido stillent unguenta capillo
> et capite et collo mollia serta gerat.

> *Let perfumes drip from his glistening hair and let him wear soft garlands round his head and neck.*

Likewise in the three Marathus poems, the theme of homosexual love, the dialogue structure, and the coming to life of Priapus' statue are all Hellenistic. The cult of Priapus, as a god of fertility, spread from the Hellespont to Greece and was popular in the great Hellenistic cities, such as Alexandria. At the end of Elegy 4 he pictures himself as a consultant psychiatrist to young lovers suffering from unrequited love (ll. 78–80):

Cunctis ianua nostra patet.
tempus erit, cum me veneris praecepta ferentem
    deducat iuvenum sedula turba senem.

*Our door is open to all. There will come a time, when a busy crowd of
young men will escort me home, while I expound the lore of love.*

Georg Luck compares them with lines from Book I of the *Aitia*
(*Fr.* 41)

γηράσκει δὲ γέρων κεῖνος ἐλαφρότερον
κοῦροι τὸν φιλέουσιν, ἑὸν δὲ μὲν οἷα γονῆα
χειρὸς ἐπ' οἰκείην ἄχρις ἄγουσι θύρην.

*That old man wears his years more lightly, whom young men love and as if
he were their father, lead him by the hand to his own door.*

Again, as in Catullus, here is the strong element of fantasy,
springing from unrequited love, which is shattered in the
following lines (ll. 81–4):

eheu quam Marathus lento me torquet amore!
    deficiunt artes, deficiuntque doli.
parce, puer, quaeso, ne turpis fabula fiam
    cum mea ridebunt vana magisteria.

*Alas, how love for Marathus slowly tortures me! Vain are my skills,
vain my tricks. Spare me, boy, I beg you, from becoming a* News of the
World *story, when men will laugh at my empty warnings.*

Reason gives way to the irrational, the lover is helpless. Echoes
once again of Callimachus (*Fr.* 195. 30).

ἆ, μή με ποιήσῃς γέλω.

*Ah! do not make a fool of me.*

22 His genius comes to fruition in the Delia poems, where
themes of war, death, golden age, Elysium, country life, religion, and erotic love are exquisitely woven into one embracing
unity. Book I. 3 opens with Tibullus, ill almost to the point
of death, left behind in Corcyra by Messalla, who is on his way
to the East. The sound of lament was never more beautifully
expressed in the opening of a poem:

Ibitis Aegaeas sine me, Messalla, per undas,
  O utinam memores ipse cohorsque mei.

*You will cross the Aegean waves without me, Messalla; may you and
your company remember me.*

The long diphthongs of Aegaeas are a gorgeous wail. His
situation is desperate. He is ill in a foreign country, and the
hands of death are approaching, expressed by pathetic repetition:

  abstineas avidas Mors modo nigra manus.
  abstineas, Mors atra, precor:

*Just keep your greedy hands away, black death.*
*I pray you, keep them away, dark death.*

He pictures his funeral, without friends, without his mother,
without his sister to perform the last rites, without Delia.
Delia had consulted all the gods, Cupid himself. All promised
a safe return, but Delia was not reassured. She was also a de-
votee of Isis, whose cult had spread all over the Mediterranean
during the Hellenistic period. We are left guessing whether
Delia's devotion to Isis was a sign of her regard for the poet
or an excuse to avoid his passionate advances ('puro secubuisse
toro'). Tibullus now combines his prayer to Isis that Delia is
praying on his behalf with a Roman's wish to see his home
again and to put the monthly offerings before his household
god. The nostalgia created by this turns the poet's thoughts
from Isis to the golden age when Saturn reigned; the union of
Alexandria and Rome is complete. The world of Saturn is
shown with its freedom from violence and all need for effort
(in this case travel abroad), so different from Virgil's picture of
the countryside, which is more realistic with its emphasis on
*labor*.

  nunc Iove sub domino caedes et vulnera semper,
    nunc mare, nunc leti mille repente viae.
  Parce, pater, tumidum non me periuria terrent,
    non dicta in sanctos impia verba deos.

*Now under Jupiter's tyranny, there are always the wounds of bloodshed, the sea and a thousand sudden ways to die. Forgive me, father. Though I'm a coward, I'm not bothered by perjury or blasphemies against the holy gods.*

Saturn was a king (Saturno . . . rege), Jupiter is a tyrant and the poet's experience of life likewise one of tyranny. The whole of this passage is shot through with a gentle humour and irony at his situation. Being a devout man, he can speak frankly to the gods, for his blasphemous feelings are the results of his faithfulness. Anyway, if he has got to die his tomb must have an inscription:

hic iacet immiti consumptus morte Tibullus,
  Messallam terra dum sequiturque mari.

*Here lies the victim of harsh death, Tibullus, Messalla's companion on land and sea.*

In a neat compliment, patron's and poet's names are juxtaposed. It was his friendship that brought him on his travels and to his death.

23 But what now? The Golden Age gives way to the picture of Elysium, whither the poet's guide will be Venus herself. But Elysium is after judgement, and what happens to the faithless (*impia turba*)? Here Tibullus imagines them suffering the commonplace fates of Hades, where Ixion, Tityos, Tantalus, and Danaus' brood all have a couplet each (cf. Horace's *Ode to Lyde*). Whom has the poet got in mind for this fate? We might have known:

illic sit quicumque meos violavit amores,
  optavit lentas et mihi militias.

*Let him be there, whoever has pillaged my love, and prayed for me a tedious, long campaign.*

This is the delightful humour of a man who has the sympathy to know what his prayer would be in another man's shoes. Despite all protestations, 'all is fair in love and war'.

'At tu casta precor maneas . . .'

*But you, I beg, remain chaste.*

Only a writer of love elegy would use 'casta' here, but the warning is clear to Delia, otherwise she might be joining the other fellow. This is an elaborate passage with the contrast between heaven (Saturn) and hell (Jupiter) on earth balanced by the description of Paradise and Hell in life after death, the pivot being the death of Tibullus. To avoid the pains of Hell, poor Delia is doomed by the poet's fancy to a closely chaperoned existence, sewing samplers or the equivalent in the long evenings until overcome by slumber. Then the poet will come like a god sent by Heaven in the night. How typical, again, of the hyperbole of elegy and yet true because only a miracle would solve the poet's problems. Finally, no one is allowed to see romanticism in the Roman's approach to love, yet in the last four lines of the poem it breathes in every word:

tunc mihi, qualis eris longos turbata capillos
    obvia nudato, Delia, curre pede.
hoc precor, hunc illum nobis Aurora nitentem
    Luciferum roseis candida portet equis.

*Then, Delia, just as you will be with your long hair in disarray, run barefoot to me. This is my prayer, may the brightness of dawn with her rose-flushed steeds carry to me the shining morning star.*

The imagery speaks for itself, and the poem, which began with a death-bed scene, closes with the imagined and vainly anticipated rites of love. Tibullus's contribution to the development of elegy was to refine it. Gone are the long elaborate, often clumsy, subordinated sentences of Catullus. With few exceptions, the couplet is the length of a sentence, often epigrammatic in its force, the allusions to myth are restrained, the lines more dactylic in metre and hence smoother, the pattern of words (nouns and adjectives), foreshadowed by Catullus, are perfected in Tibullus.

24 Contemporary with Tibullus and a rival comes Sextus Propertius, born at Assisi. Little can be gathered of his history,

except that in common with Tibullus, his family lost property in the distribution of land among the veterans of Antony and Octavian. His patron was Maecenas, he was disliked by Horace and friendly with Ovid (*Tr.* IV. 10. 45). It was his experience of love for Cynthia, a woman whose real name was Hostia, which brought to flower the poet in him. Of all the women, celebrated in elegy, Cynthia possesses the most attractive and genuine personality. She is not a beautiful monster like Lesbia, nor remains undefined like Delia, nor overshadowed by literary artifice like Ovid's Corinna. The reason for this is perhaps that none of the other poets apart from Catullus have written of their women with quite such intensity of feeling and given them so concrete an existence as the object of their passion. In Book I. 3 she reproaches Propertius for coming to her too late after a drinking bout. Her pique on this occasion provides a lively and unexpected contrast to the drunken approach of the poet towards his slumbering beauty as she lies caught in the beams of moonlight streaming through the open casement. Again, both the elegies on Cynthia in Book IV, one where she returns from the dead as a ghost, and the other when she breaks up a dice party, effectively dramatize her personality. Querulous, imperious, wilful, disarming in bed ('toto solvimus arma toro') she has in some degree the 'infinite variety' of Shakespeare's Cleopatra.

25 Nevertheless, it is impossible to build up any history of their love affair from the poems, to know what is genuine experience and where fiction begins. Book I, which is almost entirely devoted to Cynthia and was called by Martial *Monobiblos Properti*, is not arranged biographically but to provide as much variety as possible. The introductory poem, addressed to Tullus, begins with Cynthia's name. The first couplet contains epigrammatically Propertius' falling in love; the second and later couplets his unwillingness to fall:

> Cynthia prima suis miserum me cepit ocellis
> contactum nullis ante cupidinibus
> tum mihi constantis deiecit lumina fastus
> et caput impositis pressit Amor pedibus.

*Unscathed was I by Cupid's dart till Cynthia's eyes enslaved my heart;*
*Then staring down my brave conceit, love trampled me beneath his feet.*
Translation from *Elegies of Propertius* by
Seymour G. Tremenheere

Many details of these lines echo an epigram of Meleager (*A.P.* XII. 101), and once again Propertius proclaims the debt of his new art form, the love elegy, to the Hellenistic writers. This poem at the beginning is balanced by the last poem to Cynthia in Book I, Elegy XIX, a work of feeling, where like Tibullus he turns his thoughts to death and the separation it would bring, and like Catullus he employs the legend of Protesilaus to heighten his own profession of faithfulness. Protesilaus was the grandson of Phylacus; on his death his ghost was allowed to visit Laodamia, his widow, who killed herself after his departure to be with him in Hades. The other elegies of the book are also arranged in pairs, though not always side by side, and in this way give the book variety and unity. Many of the themes of the poems have already occurred before or in other poets. The violent distaste for girls who dress themselves up and plaster their faces with make-up, expressed in II and XV, is also treated in a different setting by Tibullus in I. 8. 9. In Elegy XVI, Propertius addresses the door which bars him from Cynthia's embrace and compels him to spend the night on the pavement. This was a commonplace in literature, *cf.* Callimachus *A.P.* v. 23 and Tibullus I. 1. 56 and also Horace's *Odes.* So also the theme of the witch with echoes of Theocritus, the contrast between lover and man of action and many others. It is not suggested that Propertius copied Tibullus, but it is easy to imagine them in the fashionable literary circles of the capital rivalling each other in their treatment of similar themes. Unlike Tibullus, his poetry is far more allusive and rich in the use of mythological detail. Occasionally these allusions are merely rhetorical (cf. lines 15–24 in Elegy II), but more often they are intensely evocative as in XIX. 7–18, a poem already mentioned:

illic Phylacides iucundae coniugis heros
non potuit caecis immemor esse locis

sed cupidus falsis attingere gaudia palmis
　　Thessalus antiquam venerat umbra domum.

*There the hero, Phylacides (Protesilaus), in the regions of night could not*
*forget his loving wife: but longing to clasp his joy in phantom arms, had*
*come to haunt his old Thessalian home*

This finely expresses the faithfulness demanded of true 'amor'
and to the three poets who were the priests of 'amor', all anti-
social or unconventional behaviour was justified, if the demands
of love were satisfied by constancy between the lovers. Hence
the continuous attack on riches which so easily tempted a
courtesan to prove faithless. Furthermore, the moral anarchy
suggested by these poets' attitude to 'amor', while in part it is
a literary device to enlarge the scope of their work, afforded
opportunity for postures of nonconformity to the established
order and it should not go unnoticed that all the elegists considered here were Italians rather than Romans; Catullus from
Verona, Tibullus from the neighbourhood of Praeneste, Ovid
from Paelignia, Propertius himself from Umbria. Propertius'
elegies on Augustus and Rome are his least successful and his
hatred of war runs too deep to be a fashionable pose cf. II. 7.

26 The love theme is not inexhaustible. This was Propertius'
experience and though the last three books contain many fine
poems to Cynthia, particularly in Book II, where he possesses
her in joyful triumph or fears her lost at sea in a dream, and in
the final poems to her in Book IV he tries to extend the range
of elegy. In Book II there are two elegies addressed to Maecenas,
his patron, two also in praise of Augustus, and four which concern his art as a poet. These are not only full of references to
the Hellenistic writers Callimachus and Philetas but to recent
poets like Catullus, Gallus and Calvus, and Virgil from his own
circle. He is the first poet to discuss his art at length. In Book
III. 1 he claims to be the Roman Callimachus, and the poem
ends with a ringing claim to the immortality of a genius. All
man's achievements, the Pyramids, the temple of Jupiter at
Elis, Mausolus' tomb –

aut illis flamma aut imber subducet honores
    annorum aut ictu, pondera victa, ruent.
at non ingenio quaesitum nomen ab aevo
    excidet: ingenio stat sine morte decus.

*Either fire or storm will remove from them their fame or battered by the years they'll tumble, chunks of broken stone. But the title sought by genius will never fade through age: genius wins immortal fame.*

27 His range is further extended by two laments, and detailed poems on Cynthia give way to poems which generalize about the foibles of women. Later in Book IV he follows the path of Callimachus and his *Aitia* and investigates the origin of Roman cults. He ends the book with a noble lament on Cornelia, the wife of one Paullus, in which he praises her devotion and tenderness as a wife and mother. This is all the finer because the praise of Cornelia is implied by the nobility of the sentiments which in a dramatic touch she herself speaks to her family from beyond the tomb. Its dominant position at the end of the book suggests that Propertius has bidden farewell to the stormy and fugitive moments of adolescent passion to admire a married love which has proved deeper, happier, and more lasting.

28 The celebration of a triumph by a conquering general brought people flocking into the streets of Rome. The procession, so spectacular and gaudy, and having the additional lure of watching the behaviour of captive princes soon to perish in the culmination of the ceremonies, at the same time gave opportunity for the expression of Roman pride in the mastery of their race and seemed a certain pledge of the immortal nature of their power. Few conceits of Ovid can have had more immediate impact than his portrayal of Cupid, drawn in triumphal chariot, and receiving popular acclaim and, in the procession, the poet himself as captive, together with all social restraints personified (ll. 31–4 from Elegy II):

Mens Bona ducetur manibus post terga retortis
    et pudor et castris quidquid Amoris obest.
omnia te metuent, ad te sua bracchia tendens
    vulgus 'io' magna voce 'triumphe' canet.

*Good sense will be led in manacles, shame and all things opposed to the armies of love. All will fear you, the mob will wave their arms towards you, 'hail day of triumph' will be their clamorous song.*

This impudent image, at once Hellenistic and Rococo, sets the tone for nearly all Ovid's elegies, as contained in the three books called *Amores*. Puritan ages have consistently banished Ovid, partly at least for the same reason he was banished to Tomi by Augustus. Yet the attraction of Ovid's elegies is this escape into the world of erotic fancy where all the necessary restraints of society are pictured as removed or rather as there to be removed; for what excitement is there when love ceases to be illicit?

> quidlibet eveniat, nocet indulgentia nobis:
>   quod sequitur, fugio; quod fugit, ipse sequor.
>
> *Whatever happens, indulgence spoils us: what follows me, I run from; what runs from me, I follow.*                                  II. 19. 35–6

Thus he rebukes a man because he is indifferent to his wife's amours. He has made the game too easy and spoilt its delight. So we escape with Ovid to a world where the barriers must be there but we enjoy the vicarious pleasure of breaking through them. It can just as well be argued the effect of his poem is cathartic and beneficial and the acceptance of the moral life more palatable. To Ovid, the elegies and their themes provide the theatre for the exercise of intellect, wit, and fancy. It is no good looking for 'sincerity' in these poems. The sincerity, if it can be called this, exists in the liveliness and sheer joy of his creative power. In Catullus, Tibullus, and Propertius the key-note is minor with forays into the major, in Ovid it is the reverse. Corinna is a literary abstraction and less compelling, but Ovid is a mannerist, and it is his technique and art as a poet he exposes, not his soul.

29 The couplet above reveals much about the techniques of Latin poetry – the conflict between natural stress of a word

and the rhythmic beat, in the hexameter and first half of the pentameter, the parallelism, whereby the pentameter expands or varies the statement in the hexameter (cf. Hebrew poetry), the chiasmic arrangement of the pentameter, the epigrammatic style – taken out of its context it will stand on its own – *indulgentia* with its lazy spondaic rhythm admirably contrasting with the restless dactyls which suggest the endless 'tip and run' of the furtive love affair. Many of these skills of composition were employed in the heroic couplet of the Augustan age of English literature, though the heroic couplet is more monumental and fails to capture the lyricism expressed in the pentameter of the elegiac couplet. Following Propertius, Ovid expanded the treatment of elegy. He used it for didactic purposes in the *Ars Amatoria*, for the dramatic rhetoric of the *Heroides* (letters from deserted or separated heroines to their men), and inevitably for poems in exile where *flebilis elegia*, the note of lament, offered the most suitable form. I have called him a mannerist, albeit a brilliant one, because he had the misfortune of some geniuses to arrive late on the scene when what could be said had been said and only fresh opportunities for treatment existed. This is perhaps why most critics have not called him great. Yet of all writers none, apart from Virgil and Horace, has been more pervasive in his influence on European and particularly Elizabethan literature, beginning with the courtly love of the medieval period and the songs of the troubadors, then Chaucer (' "Ovydes Art" was one of the books owned by the fifth husband of the Wife of Bath' – L. P. Wilkinson, *Ovid Recalled*), then the Renaissance writers, Petrarch and Boccaccio, both richly influenced by Ovid, later the pictorial arts where his mythological images provided inspiration and then to Spenser, Jonson, Marlowe, and Shakespeare. The last heralded his 'Venus and Adonis' with:

vilia miretur vulgus: mihi flavus Apollo
    pocula Castalia plena ministret aqua.

*Let the crowd admire worthless things: for me may golden-haired Apollo supply cups brimming from Castalian springs.*          *Amores* I. 15

96

30 Parallels from other poets are almost endless. A. G. Lee, in an essay on Ovid (*Critical Essays in Roman Literature, Elegy* – ed. J. P. Sullivan), quotes three poems of original English verse in which Ovidian tones prevail, *The Bait* by Donne, Dryden's *Song of the Zambra Dance* (this remarkably echoes *Amores* I. 5 – *Corinnae Concubitus*) and *Down Wanton Down* by Robert Graves (cf. *Amores* III. 7). Perhaps it is the poems of John Donne (1572–1619) which make the most interesting comparison, interesting because they are at once so alike and so different. Donne, in *The Sunne Rising*, deliberately borrows from *Amores* I. 13 to provide a setting for the all-sufficient love of two lovers, which is completely un-Ovidian:

> Must to thy motions lovers' seasons run?
>   Sawcy pedantique wretch, goe chide
>   Late school boyes, and sowre prentices.

> tu pueros somno fraudas tradisque magistris,
>   ut subeant tenerae verbera saeva manus.

> *You cheat boys of their sleep and hand them over to their masters to endure upon their tender hands the cruel whip.*   *Amores* I. 13. 17–18

In another poem, *The Flea*, a wonderful display of wit, in which two lovers are united in the flea which has bitten them both, there is a similar idea to that in *Amores* II. 15, where Ovid sends his girl the gift of a ring, though the treatment is very different and Ovid unashamedly more erotic.

A comparison between the last lines of Donne's fifteenth elegy, *The Expostulation*, and *Amores* III. 2, must end what is inevitably a selective study which can only hint at the continuing tradition of elegy in English literature. Donne is at the theatre with his mistress, who is proving hard to keep, once got:

>           and at maskes and playes
>   Commend the selfe same actors, the same ways;
> Aske how you did, and often with intent
>   Of being officious, be impertinent;
> All which were such soft pastimes, as in these
>   Love was as subtilly catch'd, as a disease;

Ovid is at the races with Corinna. For me this is his most attractive elegy, humorous, witty, descriptive, and colourful:

> Non ego nobilium sedeo studiosus equorum;
>> cui tamen ipsa faves, vincat ut ille, precor.
> ut loquerer tecum, veni, tecumque sederem,
>> ne tibi non notus, quem facis, esset amor.
> tu cursus spectas, ego te: spectamus uterque
>> quod iuvat atque oculos pascat uterque suos.

> *I do not sit here to see the noble horses: yet I pray your favourite wins. I came to speak with you and sit with you, to let you know the love you arouse in me. You watch the races, I you: let us both watch what delights the eyes of both to feed on.*　　　　　　　　　　*Amores* III. 2. 1–6

The unity of this poem is confirmed by its ending where, seeing Corinna's favourite horse come home first, Ovid hopes that his girl's delight will gain him more easily the triumph he anticipates.

> 'Sunt dominae rata uota meae, mea uota supersunt;
>> ille tenet palmam, palma petenda mea est.'
> risit et argutis quiddam promisit ocellis:
>> 'hoc satis hic; alio cetera redde loco.'

> *'My mistress' prayers are answered, mine remain; he holds the palm, my palm must yet be won.' She laughed and gave some promise in her sparkling eyes: 'this is enough here; give me the rest in another place.'*
>> *Amores* III. 2. 81–4

# Bibliography

CAMPS, W. A. *Propertius, Elegies*, Cambridge, 1961.

LEE, A. G. *Tenerorum Lusor Amorum*
　Essay from *Critical Essays on Roman Literature, Elegy*, edited by J. P. Sullivan, London, 1962.

WILKINSON, L. P. *Ovid Recalled*, Cambridge, 1955.
　*Golden Latin Artistry*, Cambridge, 1963.

CAMPBELL, D. A. (Ed.) *A Selection of Greek Lyric, Elegiac and Iambic Poetry*, London, 1967.

HIGHET, GILBERT, *Poets in a Landscape*, London, 1957.

LUCK, GEORG, *The Latin Love Elegy*, London, 1959.

LEISHMAN, J. B. *The Monarch of Wit*, London, 1967.

FORDYCE, C. J. *Catullus*, Oxford, 1961.

PLATNAUER, M. *Latin Elegiac Verse*, A study of the Metrical Usages of Tibullus, Propertius and Ovid, Cambridge, 1951.

SELLAR, W. Y. *Horace and the Elegiac Poets*, 2nd ed., Oxford, 1899.

POSTGATE, J. P. *Tibullus* – Loeb Classical Library, London, 1912.

WILSON, W. M. *Tibullus: Select Elegies*, London, 1967.

BARBER, E. A. *Edition of Propertius*, Oxford, 1953.

POSTGATE, J. P. *Select Elegies of Propertius*, 2nd edn., London, 1885.

SHACKLETON BAILEY, D. R. *Propertiana*, Cambridge, 1955.

FRÄNKEL, H. *Ovid: A Poet Between Two Worlds*, California, 1945.

KENNEY, E. J. *P. Ovidi Nasonis Amores etc.*, Oxford, 1961.

KENNEDY, E. C. *The Heroides of Ovid*, (Selections), London, 1964.

# IV

# Pastoral Poetry
### *Robert Coleman*

1 The Pastoral is one of the latest genres to appear in classical Greek literature. There are no serious grounds for doubting that it was invented in the early third century B.C. by the Syracusan poet Theocritus.[1] The ancient commentators record no earlier writers of Pastoral, and their accounts of its origin, in the worship of Artemis and such like, are most implausible.

2 Theocritus established many of the characteristics of the genre – the use of the hexameter verse[2] and the Dorian dialect;[3] the familiar forms, like the conversations of herdsmen[4] as they watch their flocks or rest in the heat of the day, and their singing recitals and competitions; the melancholy themes of unhappy love and the absence or death of friends.

3 Of the Greek Pastoral after Theocritus we have a few poems and fragments by Moschus and Bion and the anonymous

1. Of the Thirty *eidullia* ('little scenes') traditionally attributed to him a number are not by him and only a minority are in fact Pastorals. Apart from *Idylls* 1 and 3–11, formed into a Bucolic collection in the first century B.C., a few others, e.g. *Id.* 13, 20, 27, exhibit pastoral themes or colouring.

2. Already long established in narrative and didactic poetry and later used by the Latin satirists. [Theocritus] 8. 33–60 is a competition in elegiac couplets.

3. Often praised by critics, e.g. Dryden in his dedication to *Virgil's Pastorals*. However, attempts to reproduce it, whether in translations from Greek or in original compositions, produce a bizarre pastiche of rusticity, archaism, and 'poetic diction', such as Ben Jonson and Pope ridiculed in Spenser's *Shepheardes Calender*.

4. The dialogue form owes something to Dorian Mime, but the only attested parallels are in the non-pastoral Idylls, 2 and 15, for which cf. a fragment of Sophron (Page, *Greek Literary Papyri*, 1. 328) and Herodas's fourth Mime.

*Lament for Bion*, all of uncertain date within the period 250–100 B.C. The ten *Eclogues*[5] that make up Virgil's *Bucolics* were his first major work and are the earliest known examples of the genre in Latin. Although they are rich in echoes of the Greek Pastoral, there was no Latin equivalent to the use of literary dialects, and Virgil rarely introduces rustic colour into his diction.[6] His imperial successors in the Pastoral are represented by Calpurnius Siculus and the anonymous author of the *Einsiedeln Eclogues* from the time of Nero and by Nemesianus from the late fourth century. The immense influence in later literature of what was thus a minor classical genre is due chiefly to the fact that its exponents included two of the greatest poets of Greco-Latin Antiquity, Theocritus and Virgil.

4 The Pastoral represents a protest by urban man against certain distasteful aspects of his environment; it may be an excessive sophistication of intellectual activity, a preoccupation with industry and commerce or the hatreds and jealousies of political and military intrigue. Believing that the development of civilization had corrupted human life, man longed to escape, now and again in the imagination, to an idealized world of simple shepherds, happy in the innocence and freedom of pastoral life and love.

5 Some of the ingredients of the Pastoral ideal were, of course, already well established in earlier Greek literature: the 'ideal landscape', for instance. This was usually treated not as a set piece for its own sake[7] but in organic relation to the surrounding context, to evoke a specific mood. In Homer the dwelling-places of gods and nymphs and of the noble dead are depicted as scenes of great beauty, peace, and plenty,[8] and they

5. *eclogae* ('excerpts') need not imply that the *Bucolics* are a selection from a larger body of work.

6. One example in *Ecl.* 3. 1 was the subject of a parody, cited in Donatus's *Life of Virgil*, 43. The 'plain style' which Servius saw in the *Bucolics* (in contrast to *Georgics* and *Aeneid*) certainly does not imply any colloquial or rustic flavour in the language.

7. At least not until late Antiquity, e.g. Tiberianus's *Amnis ibat inter arua*, Asmenius's *Adeste Musae, maximi proles Iouis*.

8. Olympus in *Od.* VI. 43–6, the home of the nymphs in *Il.* xx. 8–9, Elysium in *Od.* IV. 566–8.

offer a wistful contrast to the incessant conflicts and harsh conditions of life that dominate the foreground of the two epics. Rural scenes are prominent on the shield of Achilles, and at this point in the epic they put the disruptive violence of war back in its true perspective alongside the peace of normal human life that is nostalgically evoked.[9]

6 In the *Odyssey* the ideal landscape is a recurrent feature in the series of temptations that the hero must undergo before his homecoming is accomplished. Thus the description of Calypso's island embodies many of the details found in the later pastoral landscape:

> Around her cave was a forest in bloom, alder and poplar and sweet-smelling cypress. And long-winged birds nested there, owls, falcons and chattering sea-crows. . . . And round the hollow cave stretched a luxuriant vine with rich clusters of grapes, and there were four springs, one behind the other, all close together, with their streams of clear water flowing away in different directions. And all around were soft meadows abounding in parsley and violets. Even an immortal god coming to this spot would marvel at the sight and be glad in his heart    v. 63–74

Yet close by all this Odysseus sits 'weeping on the shore as he had done earlier . . . and as he wept he gazed wistfully over the unharvested deep'. Paradise is alien to him, and in his longing for home is symbolized the spirit of the true citizen of the Greek city-state, restless and ill at ease amidst the tranquil beauties of Nature.

7 This spirit is found explicitly much later, in the opening pages of Plato's *Phaedrus*.[10] After describing the ideal landscape beside the river Ilissus Socrates says:

> Forgive me, my friend; for I am a lover of learning. So you see, it is not the fields and trees that are in the habit of teaching me, but men in the town.

9. *Il.* XVIII. 483–608, especially 509–40, contrasted with 542–72 and 587–606.
10. Plato, *Phaedrus*, 230 B-D.

The delights of the countryside tempt man to retreat from his real world, the world of the city-state, and their allurements must be resisted.

8 Euripides' Hippolytus does seek to escape from the city, where his bastard status and the moral temptations to which he is exposed make life intolerable. He takes up the pursuits of a country gentleman with his horses and his hounds; but the ideal of rural existence that he expounds in his famous 'Meadow of Innocence' speech[11] in honour of Artemis is too narrow and repressive, and in fact becomes the instrument of his own tragic destruction.

9 By contrast the cult of Dionysus is a total and whole-hearted flight from civilization, which rejects neither Aphrodite nor the demonic savagery of Nature in its pursuit of ultimate peace and purity of heart.[12] Whoever tries to civilize the cult destroys its true character.[13] The ecstatic sense of communion with Nature that forms the climax of the rites has much in common with the Romantic 'call of the wilderness'. However, the Romantic experience of Nature is essentially a private one, to be sought in solitude, not in company; and it depends on the civilized sensibilities and philosophical doctrines which its exponents bring with them into the countryside.[14]

10 The Pastoral Concept is not, like either of these, a longing for wild Nature but for an ideal human community set in an ideal landscape. The values of Arcady depend, like those of the Bacchants, on their being shared with others. But the community of Arcadian herdsmen retains for the most part the civilized sensibilities of its creators. Their songs, like the

11. Euripides, *Hippolytus*, 73–87. Later in the drama the chorus long to escape from disaster to the ideal landscape of the Hesperides (742–51).

12. All brilliantly expressed in the odes of Euripides' *Bacchae*, especially 73–82, 135–50, 402–32, 862–81.

13. And even, like Teiresias in *Bacchae*, becomes ridiculous – an outcast from both sides. Note how his demythologizing (287–97) is twice rejected by the Bacchants (88–99, 519–25).

14. As the reviewer of *Lyrical Ballads* in the *Monthly Review*, 28 (1798), 210, says, with reference to *Tintern Abbey*: 'Is it not to education and the culture of the mind that we owe the raptures which the author so well describes . . .?'

Nature poetry of the Romantics, are the polished products of a refined literary culture, far removed from both the rough simplicity of folk poetry[15] and the realistic portrayal of the grimmer side of rustic life which distinguishes the poetry of the true countryman.[16]

11 The fiction of Arcady has its basis in traditional mythology.[17] The citizens of the classical city-state may have been too close to the real countryside to sustain an idealized view of it for very long, but they could still cherish the illusion of a Golden Age somewhere in the remote past or in some remote corner of the world. In the famous account of the sequence of metallic ages Hesiod had depicted a Golden Race of men who under the rule of Cronus

> lived as gods with hearts free from care, without labour or sorrow. The misery of old age never came to them, but retaining the vigour of their hands and feet they continued to take pleasure in dancing, without any afflictions. When they died, it was as if they had been overcome by sleep. All good things were theirs. The fertile fields brought forth their fruits in abundance and of their own accord. Their way of life was pleasant and peaceful, with good things in abundance. *Works and Days*, 112–19.

12 The pre-agricultural stage of human history is thus seen as a period of leisure and contentment; men's wants and desires were simple and easily satisfied, and as yet they knew nothing of the acquisitiveness which inspires commerce and sea travel or

15. Meliboeus in Calpurnius, 4. 147–51, remarks that the shepherds' songs have displayed an Ovidian polish not at all like the usual 'rustic verses fit for cloddish ears'. Even the uncouth goatherd of Theocritus 3 can manage a learned ditty for Amaryllis (40–51).

16. Such as Hesiod or Crabbe. *The Village* is, of course, an explicit protest against the illusion which 'consists in exposing the best side only of a shepherd's life and in concealing its miseries' (Pope, *A Discourse on Pastoral Poetry*, §5). In *As You Like It* Shakespeare develops with great subtlety the complex relations between the courtiers who are exiles in the Forest of Arden, the Arcadian natives like Corin, and the realistic countrymen like William and Audrey.

17. Pope, *Discourse*, §5: '. . . Pastoral is an image of what they call the Golden age. So that we are not to describe our shepherds as shepherds at this day really are, but as they may be conceiv'd then to have been; when the best of men follow'd the employment.'

of the jealousies and ambitions which compelled their successors to arm themselves and gather together in fortified cities. Their way of life was both amoral and anarchic; for men could live peacefully together without the constraints of legal codes or political organization. The myth of the Golden Age is thrown into sharp relief by the grim account that Hesiod gives of contemporary rural life. In the Pastoral, however, the Myth is brought closer to the present: the scenes and stories are usually set in the past, but it always seems a very recent past, and there is the suggestion of a world that is permanently there and unchanging. The harmony that linked the ideal landscape to the Golden Age perfection of human life[18] also carries over into the Pastoral, where it merges with another traditional idea, that of a sympathy between events in the natural world and the behaviour and fortunes of its human inhabitants.[19]

13 Opposed to the 'soft primitivism' of the Golden Age was the 'hard primitivism' which emphasized the rigours of early human society and the simple virtues which they inculcated. Both primitivisms agree in seeing the progress of civilization as a corruption of man's true nature, but the one concentrates on the loss of happiness, the other on the decline of moral standards. The latter in fact became a commonplace of Cynic and Stoic philosophy and of popular moralizing generally, with its veneration for 'the good old days'.[20] The soft primitivism of the Pastoral has affinities rather with Epicureanism,[21] particularly in its pursuit of inner peace and detachment from worldly designs and exertions.

14 Both types of primitivism have a geographical as well as chronological specification, arising from the tendency at all

18. Re-enacted in the Golden Age transformation of Nature that accompanies the Bacchants' attainment of serenity. See Euripides, *Bacchae* 677–713.

19. Typical examples are the pestilence in Sophocles' *Oedipus the King* and the storm which accompanies the fateful union of Aeneas and Dido in *Aeneid* IV. The idea formed one of the bases of divination and reappears in the Stoic doctrine of *sumpatheia*.

20. E.g. Seneca, *Epistle* 90; Juvenal, *Sat.* 13. 28–59; Maximius Tyrius, *Dissert.* 36.

21. Epicurus (341–270 B.C.) was an older contemporary of Theocritus. Before writing the *Bucolics* Virgil seems to have been a follower of the Epicurean Siro.

times to idealize the life of remote lands.[22] The Scythians, for instance, provided the stock example of hard primitivism for generations of poets and moralists.[23] The location of the Pastoral world was usually remote enough for the fiction to be insulated from contact with the real countryside. Sicily and Cos, where some of Theocritus's idylls are set, were no doubt familiar enough to him, but their impact on his public owes much to their distance from most of the great centres of Hellenistic civilization.

15 For the Latin poets the recent history of Sicily with its agrarian uprisings perhaps made it unsuitable for the Pastoral. At all events Virgil transferred the setting to Arcadia,[24] the homeland of Pan, divine patron of countrymen and their music, and an area of Greece proverbially isolated and old-fashioned, whose inhabitants were devoted to music.[25] But Virgil's Arcadia has no pretence to being more than a concept: the two Arcadians of the seventh Eclogue sing to each other beside the River Mincio. The ideal landscape henceforth was an inseparable blend of Greek and Italian features. Virgil's successors extend the Italian detail,[26] but the convention, dependent as it was on a constant tension between myth and reality, was too fragile to allow the actual countryside to obtrude too much.

16 Occasional touches of realism, of course, preserve the myth from sterility. Usually it is a brief detail like an animal straying from the flock or the description of Menalcas 'drenched from

22. E.g. in Homer the Abioi are 'hard' (*Il.* XIII. 3–6), the Syrians 'soft' (*Od.* XV. 403–11).

23. E.g. Strabo, VII. 301–3; Horace, *Odes* III. 24. 1–32; Virgil, *Georgics* III. 349–83.

24. In view of the subsequent importance of this change, it should be noted that Arcadia is the explicit setting only in *Ecl.* 10 and perhaps *Ecl.* 8 (l. 22). *Ecl.* 2 is set in Sicily (l. 21), 7 in Virgil's native country near Mantua (*Mincius* in l. 13), 1 and 9 more vaguely in Italy.

25. So Polybius, IV. 20, who sees their devotion to poetry (apparently not Pastoral poetry) as a palliative to the harsh conditions of life; cf. Lucretius, V. 1379–411, for the role of music in primitive society.

26. E.g. the finger game and the Italian deities Flora and Pomona (cf. Silvanus in Virgil 10. 24) in Calpurnius, 2. 25 ff.

steeping the winter's store of acorns[27] or the occasional reminders that there is work to be done when the singing is over.[28] It is rare to find a vein of realism running through a whole poem, as in Theocritus's fourth idyll, with its discussion of the cattle's ailments, the incident of the thorn in the foot, and the coarse vividness of its dialogue.[29]

17 The intimations of reality in the tenth Idyll of Theocritus came very close to exploding the whole convention. The love-sick Bucaeus is too distracted to pull his weight in the harvest – a reminder, incidentally, like the description of Menalcas above, that even Arcadian herdsmen had other tasks to perform. At his friend Milon's suggestion he sings to relieve his feelings. It is a most polished and sophisticated song, and he is reprimanded for it by Milon, who, having already pointed out to him that such high aspirations to love are not for a 'working man', proceeds to quote from 'the inspired poet Lityerses' a sample of what a true countrymen's song ought to be, a homely series of rustic maxims:[30]

> That's what men who toil in the sun ought to sing. As for that starved love of yours, Bucaeus, that's a tale fit only to tell to your mother when she wakes in bed of a morning. (ll. 56–8).

18 But such uneasy intrusions of realism, reminding us perilously of the gulf between the myth and the actuality of country life, are very rare. In general, the toilsome character of many of the herdsman's routine tasks is played down, there are no disagreements as to what aspirations might be appropriate to the inhabitants of Arcady, and no doubts that these aspirations ought to be embodied in song.

27. Virgil, 10. 20, underlining by contrast the incompleteness of Gallus's conversion to the humble Arcadian life.

28. E.g. Theocritus, 11. 73–4; Virgil, 3. 94–9; Calpurnius, 4. 168–9.

29. Censured by Pope, *Discourse* §9, cf. Johnson's view (*Adventurer*, No. 92) that the 'invective' of Virgil's third Eclogue 'degraded from the dignity of pastoral innocence'.

30. In Calpurnius 5 the aged Micon (a rare intruder in the Pastoral world, which seems to be peopled by adolescents) sings to his foster-son a song even more prosaic and edifying than that of Lityerses.

19 Music-making with voice and pipes, is the central activity of the whole pastoral way of life. It is natural therefore that Corydon, who has been left in charge of Aegon's flocks, should also be the keeper of his pipe,[31] and that the ideal landscape of Arcady should provide the setting for the beauties of Arcadian song.[32] The value of music both as a palliative to the laborious monotony of many of the routine tasks in the real countryside and as a recreation when the actual work is over or interrupted for the midday rest was a commonplace in Antiquity,[33] but for the pastoral poet the power of music to free man from the burdens of life becomes in its Arcadian associations the power to transform Nature itself, to re-create the Golden Age. The singing herdsmen thus acquire the mythological status of Orpheus, the prototype of all poets:

> . . . The Music of the shepherds Damon and Alphesiboeus, whose contest excited such wonder in the heifers that they forgot their pasture, and whose song stopped the lynxes dead in their tracks and made the rivers change direction and still their currents.[34]

20 Music-making is in fact closely bound up with the religion of the Arcadians. Occasionally there are realistic glimpses of ordinary rustic superstitions,[35] but the deities who are honoured most are those who preside over the countryside and its music, Pan, Apollo,[36] and the Nymphs,[37] who at times seem to be almost identified with the Muses.[38] The Muses themselves

31. Theocritus, 4. 2 and 29.

32. Theocritus, 1. 1–8 (cf. Virgil, 5. 45–7, 82–4), and 5. 31–4, 45–9. Cf. Nicaenetus's epigram cited by Athenaeus, 15. 673 b. Calpurnius, 6, 61–72, has an interesting realistic variation on the theme.

33. Cf. Homer, *Il.* XVIII. 567–72, and Polybius, IV. 20. Meliboeus's objection in Calpurnius, 4. 19–28, is presumably that the present music-making falls into none of the approved categories, a decidely unarcadian consideration!

34. Virgil, 8. 1–4, cf. 6. 27–30, Calpurnius, 2. 10–20.

35. E.g. Theocritus, 6. 39–40; Virgil, 3. 103.

36. For Pan: Theocritus, 1. 3, 123–4, *Epigram* 2; Virgil, 2. 33, 4. 58–9; cf. the epigram of Alcaeus of Messene, *Anthologia Planudea* 226; for Apollo: Theocritus, 5. 82; Virgil, 3. 104, 4. 10, 6. 82–3.

37. E.g. Theocritus, 1. 12, 141–5 (together with the Muses), 5. 80–2 (with Apollo), 53–8 (with Pan). They are often present in their normal role, e.g. in the harvest festival scene of the seventh idyll (ll. 137, 148, 154).

38. E.g. Theocritus, 7. 92–5; Virgil, 7. 21.

occupy a prominent place in Arcadian worship, and their patronage extends beyond the inspiration of pastoral music to the protection of the lives and fortunes of the pastoral musicians in general:

> Cicada is dear to cicada, ant to ant and hawk to hawk;[39] but to me it is the Muse and song. May my house always be filled with Music! Indeed sleep is not more sweet, nor the sudden coming of Spring nor flowers to the bees. That's how much I love the Muses. For those whom the Muses rejoice to look upon are never harmed by the potions of Circe.[40]                        *Id.* 9. 31–6

21 Artemis is a notable absentee from the devotions of the Arcadians. Hunting had played no part in Golden Age life, and is rarely mentioned as one of the activities of the herdsmen in the Pastoral, even though they are familiar with it. Hence, when Polyphemus boasts of his captures,[41] it is a sign that his love for Galatea has inspired him to venture into the wilderness outside Arcady. Moreover, the chastity that Artemis enjoins on her followers has no place in the life of the Arcadians, who like the Bacchants are devotees of her rival Aphrodite.

22 The association of the ideal landscape with the perfection of love was again traditional,[42] but it obviously finds its fullest expression in the context of the Pastoral. The promiscuousness of Arcadian love[43] is a symptom of the amorality of a human society freed from the restraints of civilized convention; but it has its roots, perhaps, in the traditional mythology which represented the annual regeneration of Nature in terms of the

39. For the rustic analogy cf. Theocritus, 10. 30–1, 12. 3–9; Virgil, 2. 63–5, 5. 32–4, 76–8.

40. For the protection of the Muses see the tale of Comatas in *Id.* 7. 78–88 and cf. Horace, *Odes* III. 4. 1–36.

41. Theocritus, *Id.* 11. 40–1.

42. Cf. the wistfulness of Tibullus, *Elegies*, 1. 5. 21–36. The ideal landscape of Plato's *Phaedrus* forms the setting for Socrates' famous discourse on love.

43. In Theocritus 5 Lacon sings of his love affairs with Cratidas and Eumedes; Comatas of Clearista, Alcippa and a sexual frolic with Lacon himself. In Virgil 3 Damoetas sings of Galatea, Phyllis and Amaryllis, Menalcas of Phyllis and Amyntas. In Virgil 2 Amaryllis and Menalcas have preceded Alexis in Corydon's affections.

sexual acts of gods and goddesses[44] and filled the rustic scene with tales of their amorous exploits with shepherds and nymphs.

23 Spring, the fairest season of the year,[45] when Nature comes to life again and men have a glimpse of the Golden Age once more, is the time for love[46] and song. Indeed, the very presence of the loved one ensures the continuance of the spring transformation, as absence brings desolation to the scene:

> Everywhere it is spring and there are pastures, everywhere the udders pour forth milk and the newborn calves are fed, every-where that fair Naïs comes; but if she departs, then the herdsman and his herd will wither away.[47]    *Id.* 8. 45–8

For, as we have observed, the Pastoral inherited from the Golden Age myth the idea of a sympathetic bond between the Natural world and its human inhabitants. Love in the ideal landscape forms one of the chief themes of Arcadian song.[48] When Bion attempts to instruct Eros in the art of country music he finds himself learning the music of love instead; and the Muses are most propitious to his pastoral songs when they express his love for Lycidas.[49]

24 Yet even in Arcady love has its bitterness. In the eighth idyll Menalcas sings of the surpassing joy of rustic love and music, but Daphnis's reply strikes a more sombre note (ll. 57–60):

> To the trees a storm brings fearful harm, to waters drought, to birds a trap and to wild beasts the hunter's net; but to man it is the desire for a tender maid. Ah, I am not the only one to have

44. In *Il.* XIV. 346–51, the physical union of Zeus and Hera is accompanied by a Golden Age transformation of Nature.

45. Bion, *frag.* 2 (Gow), Virgil, 3. 55–7; Calpurnius, 5. 16–22; cf. Meleager's epigram, *Anthologia Palatina* XI. 85.

46. For the perfection of love in the Golden Age, Theocritus, 12. 16; cf. Tibullus, II. 3. 71–4. For Venus as patroness of Nature's fertility and human passion in the spring season see the late Latin *Peruigilium Veneris* and Ausonius's *de rosis nascentibus.*

47. Cf. Virgil, 7. 53–60. Nemesianus, 2. 44–52, brings out the 'fallacy' of this sympathetic association; cf. ibid., 27–36.

48. Cf. Meleager's epigram, *A.P.* v. 139.

49. Bion, *Frs.* 9 and 10.

felt this longing, Father Zeus; you too have known love for a mortal woman.

The ambivalence of love was a traditional theme of erotic poetry[50] and was depicted in the charming fable of *Eros and the Bees*[51] which forms the subject of the nineteenth idyll. Indeed, it is not too fanciful to see in the image of the bee a link between the poetry which is the Muses' honey and the bitter-sweet of love which forms its theme.[52]

25 Now and again the Arcadian singers protest against the cruelty of Love, as if it were an unnatural monster intruding into their world. So the goatherd of the third idyll complains (ll. 15–16):

Now I have come to know Eros: and a harsh god he is. Surely he was suckled by a lioness and reared by his mother in the wild woods.

But in general they accept it with fatalistic resignation, and this contributes to the vein of melancholy that runs through the whole Pastoral tradition.

26 Theocritus handles the theme of unhappy love in a variety of ways. The serenade which the goatherd sings outside Amaryllis's cave in the third idyll is an amusing variation on the 'excluded lover' theme which is well attested outside the Pastoral.[53] The subject of the twentieth idyll is the anger of a cattleherd at his rejection by the haughty town girl Eunica; after preening himself absurdly his feelings became violent and he calls down a curse on her head. In the tenth, as we have seen, Theocritus brings out the lover's alienation from his normal life and the power of love to inspire uncharacteristic

50. The epithet *glukupikros* ('sweet-bitter') is already found in Sappho.
51. Cf. the Hellenistic *Anacreontica* 33.
52. The bee as a symbol of the poet is as old as Pindar, e.g. *Pythian Odes*, 6. 54, cf. Theocritus, 7. 81–2; *Lament for Bion*, 33–5. In Virgil, 3. 108–10, Palaemon seems to be saying that the finest poetry comes from the sad experience of love.
53. For the *paraclausithuron* ('poem beside the closed door') see [Theocritus] *Id.* 23; Bion, *Fr.* 11; cf. Callimachus, *A.P.* v. 23; Asclepiades, *A.P.* v. 145, 164; Tibullus, 1. 2. 7–14; Horace, *Odes*, 1. 25, III. 10.

flights of poetry. Both themes recur in the famous eleventh idyll, where Polyphemus's serenade to Galatea is offered as an illustration of the power of music to soothe the lover's pain.[54] In the *Odyssey* the Cyclops had been a terrifying monster inhabiting an ideal landscape; now the power of love has assimilated him to his environment. He is still grotesque, as he is in the sixth idyll, though not more so than the goatherd of the third idyll; but his serenade is a fine blend of the comic and the pathetic, which makes him the prototype of all the 'passionate shepherds' of the later pastoral tradition.[55]

27 The other great melancholy theme of the Pastoral is that of death, which since the seventeenth century has been linked with the phrase *et in Arcadia ego*. Although Arcady is peopled by youthful herdsmen and shepherdesses, there is a brooding sense of doom[56] which seems almost symbolic of the tenuous nature of the Arcadian myth itself.

28 The cycles of death and rebirth in Nature have often been contrasted by poets with the finality of human death,[57] but the contrast has a special poignancy in the ideal landscape of the Pastoral:

> Alas, when the mallows die away in the gardens and the green parsley and the exuberant dill with its curly leaves, they live and grow again for another year; but we men, tall and strong as we are, and wise too, once we are dead, lie unhearing in the hollow earth in a long sleep that is without end or awakening
>
> *Lament for Bion*, 99–104

29 The association of unhappy love with untimely death, found in the folk literature of all nations, was a recurrent feature of

54. For this doctrine of the 'medicine of the Muses' (*Id.* 11. 1–6, 80–1) see Bion, *Fr.* 3; cf. Callimachus, *A.P.* XII. 150.

55. Beginning with Corydon in Virgil's second Eclogue. The reversion to Homeric type in Ovid's *Metamorphoses* XIII, though not in the genre, made Polyphemus a kind of pastoral anti-hero over against the gentle shepherd Acis, and so opened the way to such diverse developments as the Polifemo of Gongora's great allegorical Pastoral, Caliban in Shakespeare's *Tempest*, and the depiction of the Serpent in the Garden in Milton's *Paradise Lost*.

56. E.g. Theocritus, 1. 62–3, 4. 38–40.

57. E.g. Horace, *Odes*, 1. IV and 4. 7.

Greek mythology. Particularly relevant here are the tales of pastoral characters, nymphs and shepherds, to whom the love of a god or goddess had brought disaster and subsequent metamorphosis:[58] Adonis, Daphne, Hyacinthus, Syrinx . . . This introduces yet another mythological element into the sympathetic relation between the Natural world and its human inhabitants; for the whole Arcadian landscape is full of permanent living monuments to the pathos of love and death. The author of the *Lament for Bion*, describing the way in which all the creatures of Nature joined in the dirge for his beloved friend and fellow poet, explicitly recalls the sorrowful circumstances of their own metamorphoses (ll. 37–40, 44–45):[59]

> The lament of the Siren beside the banks of the sea was never so mournful, nor was the song of the nightingale among the rocks nor the dirge of the swallow in the long hills nor the wailing of Ceyx for the sufferings of Halcyone . . . as when they all mourned for the destruction of Bion. Begin, Sicilian Muses, begin your song of woe!

30 It is to the same mythological background of suffering lovers that Daphnis[60] the handsome cattleherd and master poet of the first idyll belongs. The poem begins with an evocation of the ideal landscape. Then follows an elaborate description of the scenes carved on the cup which is to be Thyrsis's reward for singing 'the sufferings of Daphnis': first the pathos of love itself is represented by the two handsome suitors vainly wooing a hooded woman, then a realistic picture of a fisherman, the proverbial brother of the herdsman,[61] but in the Pastoral the representative of a life of hardship and toil,[62] and finally a rustic fable, the little boy, the foxes, and the grapes.

58. Moschus in fact wrote a narrative poem on Europa and the Bull, with a digression on Io, which is rich in pastoral and marine imagery.

59. In Bion's own *Lament for Adonis* Aphrodite's farewell (40–61) is enclosed by a description of the metamorphosis of the dead shepherd (25–8, 65–7).

60. His tale was first treated, apparently, by the sixth-century lyric poet Stesichorus. In Theocritus 5 he appears as the typical master singer (80–1) and suffering herdsman (20).

61. Cf. the dedication to Pan in Archias, *A.P.* x. 10.

62. Cf. lines 40–3, [Theocritus] *Id.* 21. 1–18, 39–42, 66–7; Moschus, *Fr.* 1.

31 The major part of the idyll is occupied by Thyrsis's song. The precise cause of Daphnis's plight is left obscure. The angry scorn of his opening words to Aphrodite (ll. 100–3):

> Cruel Cyprian, vengeful Cyprian, hated by all who are mortal, do you really consider that all my suns have now set? No, even in Hades Daphnis will bring grievous sorrow to Eros.

and the taunting references that he makes to Adonis and Diomede are reminiscent of Hippolytus's proud defiance. Although there is no tradition elsewhere in the Pastoral that he was so unarcadian as to be celibate,[63] he must clearly have offended the goddess by eventually renouncing love. He calls on Nature not only to mourn him but also to demonstrate that the times are out of joint by a transformation which is a kind of pessimistic parody of the Golden Age (ll. 132–6):

> Now bear violets, ye brambles, and violets too, ye thistles, and let fair narcissus blooms cover the juniper and all things go awry; let pines bring forth pears – for Daphnis now is dying – let the stag tear the hunting dogs to pieces and the owls cry from the mountains to the nightingales! Cease, Muses, cease the pastoral song!

Aphrodite finally relents, but she is as powerless to save her enemy, 'friend of the Muses and the Nymphs', from death as she had been to revive her beloved Adonis:[64]

> I will treasure this last kiss as I treasure Adonis himself, since you are fleeing from me, hapless Adonis, fleeing far away to Acheron and its loathsome savage monarch; while I live on in misery and am a goddess and cannot come in search of you. Take my husband, Persephone, for you are much stronger than I and all that is fair is swept away to you ...          Bion, *Lament for Adonis*, 49–55

As in the old mythology, so too in the new mythology of the Pastoral not even the gods can alter the fate of mortals.

63. In *Id.* 7. 73–7 his love for Xenea is linked to his destruction, in [Theocritus] *Id.* 8. 93 he marries Nais, in [Theocritus] *Id.* 27 he woos Acrotime.
64. *cf.* Bion, *Fr.* 1 for Phoebus's inability to save Hyacinthus.

32 The presence in Arcady of the universal human pathos o love and death[65] enabled the convention to be adapted allegorically to the expression of the real sorrows and concerns of poets and their friends. The image of the shepherd in the ideal landscape as an ideal poet could be reversed to represent the living poet of the real world, in search of the leisure and relief from material cares that provide the ideal conditions for the practice of his art, as an Arcadian shepherd.

33 Already in the seventh idyll, although much is now obscure, it is plain that Theocritus is portraying something more than the familiar singing herdsmen of Arcady. Simichidas, the narrator, speaks throughout in the first person[66] and among the unusually large caste are a number of unpastoral names,[67] so it is a fair inference that the poem alludes in some way to Theocritus's own interests and activities.

34 Much of the detail of the idyll is pure Pastoral; the closing description of the setting for the Harvest Festival is one of the richest examples we have of the ideal landscape motif. The countrymen who converse animatedly as they make their journey to the Festival seem at first no different from the herdsmen of the other idylls. Yet when the laughing goatherd Lycidas suddenly declares (ll. 45-8):

> I hate the builder who strives to raise a house as high as the peak of Mount Oromedon and all the Muses' cocks that crow in vain rivalry with the minstrel of Chios,

we catch an echo of the literary polemic of Theocritus's fellow poet Callimachus.[68] Moreover, the songs which Lycidas and Simichidas sing in their competition,[69] though full of pastoral colour, have more in common with the erotic themes of other

65. Well illustrated in Marvell's *Damon the Mower* among English pastoral poems.
66. As does the anonymous narrator of *Id.* 8.
67. Eucritus (1), Phrasidamus and Antigenes (3-4) occur nowhere else in the idylls, and Philitas, Sicelidas, and Aratus are all names of contemporary poets.
68. Cf. *Aetia*, 1. 1 (Trypanis, Loeb edition, pp. 4-8).
69. Lines 52-89, 96-127.

genres. Lycidas's hopes for the safe arrival of his beloved Ageanax to Mytilene recall the *propemptikon* ('*bon voyage* poem') of Elegy and Lyric.[70] Simichidas's message of goodwill to Aratus in his love for the boy Aristis is again typical of the erotic genres and concludes with a reference to the 'excluded lover' theme and an hysterical appeal to the Erotes. Finally, the beginning and end of the idyll exhibit features that are typically Hellenistic but alien to the Pastoral.[71]

35 The whole poem thus seems to be an oblique declaration of Theocritus's support for Callimachus in the current literary controversy. If so, then we have here the first instance of the allegorical use of the genre that was to prove so important in its subsequent history.

36 In the *Lament of Bion* the themes of the first and seventh idylls are brought together in a poem celebrating the achievements of an actual poet, 'the fair minstrel', 'the Dorian Orpheus',[72] and mourning his untimely death. For the first time the values of the peaceful world extolled by the pastoral poet explicitly claim equality with the epic world of violence and conflict portrayed by Homer (ll. 76–85):

> Both poets were dear to springs, the one drank from the fountain of Pegasus, the other from Arethusa. The one sang of Tyndareus' fair daughter and the mighty son of Thetis and Menelaus son of Atreus. The other's music was not of war and tears but of Pan; as a herdsman he sang with a clear voice, and as a poet he pastured his herds; he fashioned pipes and delighted in milking the heifer; he taught the boys to kiss, he cherished love in his breast and roused the desire of Aphrodite.
>
>     Begin, Sicilian Muses, begin the song of woe!

37 The first and seventh idylls of Theocritus and the *Lament for Bion* were the major sources of inspiration for Virgil's most

70. Cf. Meleager, *A.P.* XII. 52; Horace, *Odes* I. 3, III, 27; Propertius, *Elegies*, I. 8; Ovid, *Amores*, II. 11.

71. The myth of the origin of the spring Burina (6–9), the comparisons to Heracles and Cheiron and to the Homeric (not Theocritean) Polyphemus (149–52).

72. Lines 8, 18. The poem was the model for Milton's *Lycidas*.

creative work in the Pastoral. Many of the original features of the genre do, of course, recur in the *Bucolics*, and the seventh Eclogue, for instance, the singing match between Corydon and Thyrsis, is as pure a Pastoral as could be found anywhere.[73] Yet even in this context Virgil was constantly exploring new aspects and new dimensions.

38 In the eighth *Eclogue* Damon's song is inspired by the first idyll and Alphesiboeus' is a pastoral adaptation of the sorceress of the second idyll. Out of the Theocritean material Virgil has created something quite new, a kind of didactic pastoral. The two songs balance each other symmetrically, thus enacting the contrast between the *suffering* of the passive victim of love, the inefficacy of the 'medicine of the Muses' to which he wistfully resorts and the desperation of his longing for the pessimistic transformation of Nature and the *success* of the lover who boldly reacts to the loss of her lover and turns to the positive aid of the *carmina* of witchcraft in her determination to transform the world to her own will.[74]

39 In the last poem of the collection Virgil again uses the image of the dying Daphnis to depict his friend Gallus in despair at the loss of his mistress Lycoris. In an elaborate song, which like the *Lament for Bion* seems to contain allusions to Gallus's own poetry, the dying poet declares his longing to have been an 'Arcadian', hunting and riding and composing pastoral verses. But like Bion he finds all his Pastorals turn to love and to his frustrated passion for Lycoris. Love may inspire fine poetry, but once again poetry is incapable of curing the lover's sorrows (l. 69):

Love conquers all things, and so let us yield to love.

40 In the earlier fifth *Eclogue* Mopsus's lament for the dead Daphnis takes up again the themes of the *Lament for Bion* and the first idyll, this time stripped of all its erotic content.

73. Along with *Ecl.* 3 it provides the model for Pope's *Spring* pastoral, *Damon*.
74. Pope in his *Autumn: Hylas and Aegon*, modelled on *Ecl.* 8, reverts to the purely Arcadian melancholy of love and death.

Menalcas, who is revealed at the end as Virgil himself, responds with a precisely symmetrical hymn of thanksgiving for the deification of Daphnis. Although the *Eclogue* is, unlike the seventh idyll, a completely homogeneous and self-contained Pastoral[75] and Daphnis is throughout the great Pastoral singer and benefactor of his fellow Arcadians, the allusion to the death and deification of Julius Caesar is unmistakable. The Arcadian herdsman has now become the image of the statesman, shepherd and benefactor of his people.

41 The mood of optimism that followed the appearance of the 'Julian comet' in 44 B.C. had been disappointed in the event, but there were expectations of peace when Pollio, the architect of the pact of Brindisi between Octavian and Antony, was elected consul for 40 B.C. Virgil greeted the latter event with a poem prophesying the return of the Golden Age:

> Now the last age of the Sibyl's prophecy has come. The great cycle of the ages is born anew. Now the Virgin is returning and the reign of Saturn. Now a new generation is being sent down to us from high heaven. *Ecl.* 4. 4–7

'A somewhat loftier theme' (l. 1) to be sure, but the treatment of it is still thoroughly pastoral. For the myth of the Golden Age, which Virgil is perhaps the first poet to envisage as capable of returning in the future,[76] is, as we have seen, profoundly linked to the whole pastoral conception; and the child, from whatever source he came to Virgil,[77] is perennially the symbol of carefree innocence and therefore very much at home in the pastoral setting.

75. E.g. The Golden Age manifestation of Nature's rejoicing (62–4), balancing the earlier signs of mourning (25–8). A similar homogeneity is preserved in Pope's *Winter, Daphne*; '*to the Memory of Mrs Tempest.*'

76. There is no hint of this, for instance, in the *Phaenomena* of Theocritus's contemporary Aratus, with whose account of the Golden Age (ll. 96–136) the *Eclogue* has some affinities.

77. Possibly from current oracular material, which was infiltrated by Judaeo-Hellenistic apocalyptic of the kind that was interpreted in the Gospels as prophetic of the coming of Christ. The rich pastoral imagery of the Bible, from the Garden of Eden to the Good Shepherd, provided a new axis of associations for the Arcadian concept; cf. Pope's *Messiah*, '*in imitation of Virgil's Pollio*'.

42 Yet in the very centre of this message of hope Virgil inserts a dark warning (ll. 31–6):

> A few traces of the old sin will still linger on, however, to bid men assault the sea-nymph Thetis with their rafts, surround their cities with walls and plough furrows in the earth. There will be a second Tiphys then and a second Argo to carry its chosen complement of heroes. Then there will be another period of warfare and mighty Achilles will be sent once more to Troy.

Between the prophecy and its fulfilment lies a return to the heroic wars that sealed the end of the first Golden Age.

43 The Pastoral had always been pacifist in character. The troubles that disturbed the tranquil contentment of Arcady were those common to the human condition, unhappy love and untimely death. But the peace of Arcady might be threatened from outside, by the forces of ambition and avarice that had first corrupted the Golden Age itself. The threat of political strife and warfare was one that the real countryside had known only too well in the recent past, and in two of his *Eclogues* Virgil meditates on the effects of the civil wars on the countrymen of Italy.

44 The first is a dialogue between two farmers, one of whom has had his land confiscated by the triumvirate and is forced to emigrate; the other, threatened with the same fate, has made the long journey to Rome to win a reprieve. The poem moves continually between the traditional pastoral imagery and the realistic portrayal of the historical setting;[78] and Meliboeus follows his realistic description of the poverty of his friend's lands (ll. 47–8) with a wistful Arcadian picture (ll. 51–8):

> Happy old man, here amidst the familiar streams and sacred springs you will be able to seek out the cool shade. Over here the hedge which marks the boundary with your neighbour will often provide a feast of willow blossoms for the Hyblaean bees,

78. E.g. the contrast between Meliboeus's plight and Tityrus's contentment (1–5) and the ingenious development of the Sympathy-of-Nature figure out of the signs of neglect on the farm during Tityrus's absence in Rome (36–9).

just as it has always done, and its gentle rustling will lull you to sleep; while over here will be the leaf-gatherer singing to the breezes from beneath the steep rock. And all the husky wood-pigeons so dear to your heart and the turtle doves high up in the elm will keep up their song unbroken.

The paradise from which Odysseus felt himself an alien is now poignantly portrayed by one who is forced to leave it.

45 At first Tityrus shows a smug callousness towards his friend's plight, but the tensions of the dialogue are resolved in a final act of hospitality, which reasserts the values of friendship that belong to the Arcadian world (ll. 79–83):

You could, however, rest the night here with me on the green leaves. I've sweet apples and soft chestnuts and plenty of cheese. And already the smoke is rising from the rooftops of the farm houses in the distance, and the shadows cast by the high hills are lengthening.

46 In the ninth *Eclogue* Virgil's concern is for the sadness of those who are left behind. Moeris and Lycidas, on their way to town, lament the departure of their friend, the poet-farmer Menalcas. They wistfully recall to each other snatches of his poems, the character of which leaves little doubt that Menalcas is once again Virgil himself. But Moeris, who was closer to Menalcas, finds himself unable to carry on in spite of his friend's insistence (ll. 51–5):

Time carries off everything, even a man's mind. I remember how often as a boy I used to lay the sun to rest with song after a long day. Now so many of the songs I knew are forgotten, and Moeris's voice has gone too. The wolves have seen Moeris first. However, Menalcas himself will recall the ones you're after well enough.

In his sorrow he has lost even the Arcadian solace of song.

47 The treatment of contemporary social troubles and the strains that alien forces place on countrymen's lives and

friendships is something quite new in the Pastoral. Arcady is now identified with the ideals not of an urban literary coterie but of the real countryside, in a way that looks forward to the blend of soft and hard primitivism in the *Georgics*.[79] The peace of Italian Arcady is threatened, and unlike the Bacchants the humble countrymen cannot call on any demonic powers to ward off aggression:

> . . . our songs, Lycidas, have as much power among the hostile weapons of war[80] as they say the prophetic doves of Chaonia have when the eagle comes         (*Ecl.* 9. 11–13)

The protest against the disruption of Arcady is Virgil's protest against the way in which war had undermined all that was worthwhile in civilization. In treating contemporary social and political events in the Pastoral Virgil was boldly confronting the ideals for which the pastoral concept had traditionally stood, peace, leisure, simple contentment, friendship, and love, with the harshness of the world as it actually was.

48 Thus transformed into a vehicle for the treatment of profound issues in contemporary life, the Pastoral became a model of the universality of poetry itself, and of the poet's power to create myths which impose meaning and value on the brute experience of life. The sixth *Eclogue* begins as a pure Pastoral, with the nymph and the two shepherd boys catching the drunken Silenus asleep. But the song that he sings to them is decidedly unpastoral. It begins with a philosophical cosmogony and passes through a succession of myths, telling of tragic loves and fantastic metamorphoses, to the initiation of Gallus as successor to the divinely ordained poet Hesiod. By linking the recital of 'things true' and 'things like the truth'[81] through Gallus to the work of the contemporary 'new poets' Virgil has produced his own version of the seventh idyll, his own literary manifesto.

79. E.g. especially II. 455–74.
80. Cf. the 'impious soldier' in *Ecl.* 1. 70–2.
81. Hesiod, *Theogony*, 27–8.

49 With Virgil the classical Pastoral reaches its definitive form.[82] Yet in it lay the seeds of its own corruption. For the convention was too fragile to stand too much reality, and Virgil's bold juxtaposition of reality and myth was too delicate and precarious to last. Already for his Latin successors the genre has become either a pretty divertissement[83] or the irrelevant framework for the presentation of what concerned them most. Thus in Calpurnius' first *Eclogue* the true subject, the praise of Nero (42–88), is hardly given even a pastoral guise;[84] and in the seventh the poet's real theme is the urban spectacles that Nero provides (23–72) for all those who unlike Lycotas do not prefer to stay at home in the country. This allegorizing attitude to the genre, elaborated in the commentaries on the Eclogues themselves,[85] was responsible for the Medieval and Renaissance conception of the genre as primarily allegorical, and for its use in political and ecclesiastical polemic.

50 If we are nowadays in a position to appreciate the classical genre more fully it is because we are able to see something of the forces that shaped it and the various ways in which it was developed by poets who really believed in the Arcadian ideal and found the Pastoral a medium for some of their finest creative work.

82. From the Renaissance onwards it was Virgil rather than Theocritus who was the model for pastoral poets and critics. In the mid-eighteenth century Joseph Warton, in his *Essay on Pope*, preferred Theocritus for his 'romantic Rusticity and Wildness', but the precursors of the Romantic movement who praised the 'naturalness' of Theocritus were already finding the Pastoral itself 'cold, unnatural and artificial'.

83. E.g. Calpurnius, *Ecl.* 2, 3, and 6; Nemesianus, *Ecl.* 2, 3, 4; which, however, do occasionally contribute, as we have seen, fresh and appropriate details to the genre.

84. As it is at least, though absurdly, in *Ecl.* 4. 82–146.

85. Theocritus, significantly, escaped this fate, but the tendency for the Greek pastoral conception itself to degenerate into an empty conceit is illustrated by Longus's *Daphnis and Chloe*, where, for all its tender delicacy, the rustic lovers turn out to be like Florizel and Perdita in *Winter's Tale*, aliens in disguise.

# Bibliography

Texts, translations, and commentaries:

CONINGTON, J., and NETTLESHIP, H. *P. Vergili Maronis Opera*, vol. I: *Bucolics and Georgics*, London, 1881.

DUFF, J. W. and A. M. *Minor Latin Poets*, including *Calpurnius Siculus, Einsiedeln Eclogues, Nemesianus*, Loeb, London, 1934.

EDMONDS, J. M. *The Greek Bucolic Poets*, Loeb, London, 1919.

FAIRCLOUGH, H. R. *Virgil*, Vol. I: *Eclogues*, etc., Loeb, London, 1916.

GOW, A. S. F. *Bucolici Graeci*, Oxford, 1952.

GOW, A. S. F. *Theocritus*, Vol. I: Introduction, text, translation; Vol. II: Commentary, etc., Cambridge, 1952.

Scholarship and criticism:

CURTIUS, E. R. 'The Ideal Landscape', *European Literature in the Latin Middle Ages*, English translation, London, 1952, Ch. 10.

EMPSON, W. *Some Versions of Pastoral*, London, 1935.

KERMODE, F., *English pastoral poetry from the Beginnings to Marvell*, London, 1952.

LOVEJOY, A. O., and BOAS, G. *Primitivism and Related Ideas in Antiquity*, Baltimore, 1935.

PANOFSKY, E. '*Et in Arcadia Ego*: Poussin & the Elegiac Tradition', *Meaning in the Visual Arts*, New York, 1955. Ch. 7.

PARRY, A. M. 'Landscape in Greek Literature', *Y.C.S.*, 15, 1957, pp. 3–29.

POGGIOLI, R. 'The Oaten Flute', *Harvard Library Bulletin*, 11, 1957, pp. 147–184.

SNELL, B. 'Arcadia, The Discovery of a Spiritual Landscape', *The Discovery of the Mind*, English translation, Oxford, 1953, Ch. 13.

# V

# Didactic Poetry
### *Alister Cox*

1 The improbable art of harnessing poetry to severely technical instruction[1] originated almost accidentally in Greece, blossomed near-miraculously in Rome, and was never afterwards to be convincingly revived. Since many would now claim that the art-form is defunct because it is in principle impossible (resting upon a fusion of incompatible elements),[2] an investigation of its evident success in the ancient world has an obvious interest.[3]

## Hesiod and the Didactic Tradition

2 Hesiod is the fount and figurehead of didactic poetry as Homer is of epic, and the two names stand together at the dawn of Greek literature.[4] But whereas the *Iliad* and the

---

1. Such a definition distinguishes the ancient genre of didactic poetry from the more general class of *admonitory* poetry – a common ingredient in ancient didactic (see para. 4 below), but not its defining characteristic.

2. A point well discussed in Sikes (24), Ch. 1, who quotes with disapproval Coleridge's view that 'whatever in Lucretius is poetry is not philosophical, whatever is philosophical is not poetry'. See para. 15 below.

3. For brief surveys of the genre see Huxley (38c), Intr. ch. II; Sellar (42), pp. 182–4; Page (38a), pp. xviii–xxii; and the articles in *O.C.D.* Wilkinson (44), ch. III, surveys the literary influence of earlier didactic upon the *Georgics*. My sincere thanks are due to Mr Wilkinson not only for advance information about his book but also for valuable comments on my typescript.

4. West (2), pp. 40–6, dates Hesiod to the late eighth century B.C.

*Odyssey* established the definitive outline of epic poetry, the *Works and Days* of Hesiod was a stimulus rather to divergent experiment. It had too little clarity of form and too great an infusion of its author's personality[5] to encourage wholesale imitation, and it is only in certain *incidental* features of this idiosyncratic work that we see the earliest marks of what was to be the didactic tradition.

3 First there is its close association with epic. In the centuries before written literature, when inherited knowledge was commonly transmitted in recited hexameters, we may postulate two related traditions – narrative saga (issuing into Homeric epic) and non-narrative folk-lore (enjoying particular vogue in Boeotia and selectively incorporated by Hesiod). The theory of an influence between these pre-Homeric and pre-Hesiodic traditions[6] perhaps best explains the markedly Homeric tone of Hesiod's writing – its epic metre, dialect, and even phraseology, and its narrative interludes in authentic (if somewhat rugged) epic style.[7] The same close links with epic were to be maintained by later didactic poets, Greek and Roman, who adhered (with the significant exception of Ovid[8]) to the hexameter form, aspired to epic phraseology, and learned to incorporate narrative and descriptive passages sometimes in conscious imitation of epic authors.[9] A further link with epic is Hesiod's opening invocation to the Muses, but when this merges almost imperceptibly into a supplementary appeal to Zeus, the all-powerful dispenser of Justice,[10] we see the origins of a distinctively 'didactic' fashion – the summoning of deities

---

5. A remarkable amalgam of dour realism and prophetic earnestness, the former relating to his place in the Boeotian peasant community and the latter to his role as poet: see Sinclair (1), Chs. II and III respectively.

6. Lattimore (3), pp. 1–4.

7. West (2), Intr. chs. V–VIII. Cf. *O.B.G.V.* Nos. 57–8 (*Pandora*, and the *Five Ages of Man*).

8. See para. 26 below.

9. E.g. Empedocles was Ὁμηρικός (see para. 9 below), Lucretius consciously in the Homeric and Ennian tradition (Maguinness (26d), pp. 82 ff.), Virgil experimenting with epic form (Otis (41), p. 194).

10. 2–10: note the transition from third person (8) to second (9).

of a specific *relevance* to the ensuing theme.[11] For Justice *is* the burden of the work.[12]

4 The missionary urgency with which Hesiod proclaims this gospel was to be another determining influence upon the genre. 'Listen to justice, and put away all notions of violence. Here is the law, as Zeus established it for human beings; as for fish, and wild animals, and the flying birds, they feed on each other, since there is no idea of justice among them; but to men he gave justice, and she in the end is proved the best thing they have. If a man sees what is right and is willing to argue it, Zeus of the wide brows grants him prosperity.'[13] The motive of self-interest is even more evident in the interlocking theme of Hard Work.

λιμὸς γάρ τοι πάμπαν ἀεργῷ σύμφορος ἀνδρί . . . .
ἐξ ἔργων δ' ἄνδρες πολύμηλοί τ' ἀφνειοί τε·
καὶ ἐργαζόμενοι πολὺ φίλτεροι ἀθανάτοισιν.
ἔργον δ' οὐδὲν ὄνειδος, ἀεργίη δέ τ' ὄνειδος.

*Famine is the unworking man's most constant companion. It is from work that men grow rich and own flocks and herds; by work, too, they become much better friends of the immortals. Work is no disgrace; the disgrace is in not working.*[14]

Though the earthiness of these sentiments is characteristic of the peasants who probably first coined them and of Hesiod who selected them, we may see in the underlying moral earnestness the origins of a *mood* which pervaded the later masterpieces of didactic poetry and was perhaps an essential element in their success as works of art: for poetry seems most easily to combine with a didactic purpose when teaching rises to *preaching*.[15]

11. Zeus the sky-god in Aratus (para. 10 n. 61), Venus in Lucretius and Ovid (paras. 14 and 26), rustic deities in Virgil (para. 23 with n. 184). Cf. para. 27 (Mercury in Manilius).

12. For the formative importance of this departure from the 'Homeric' system of morality, see Jaeger (5).

13. 275–81 (cf. *O.B.G.V.* No. 61). The translation is Lattimore's but without his line-divisions.

14. 302; 308–9; 311. For other such maxims in Hesiod see *O.B.G.V.* Nos. 62-6.

15. See on Empedocles, Lucretius, and Virgil below (paras. 9, 12–13, 20), and n. 70 for a relation between poetry and rhetoric. For an opposite view see Sinker (20c), p. xviii.

Hesiod furthermore originated a method which greatly increased the admonitory impact of such works – the 'open letter' form. At the receiving end is his misguided brother Perses: with a mixture of indignation and goodwill ('I mean you well, Perses, you great idiot, and I will tell you . . .'[16]) the poet rebukes him first for his injustice in seizing *his* part of the inheritance, and second for the idleness which induced him to go for such quick money.[17] And although the double sermon is intended for a wider public, especially for the 'bribe-devouring barons', with their assumption that might is right,[18] and for the harassed Boeotian peasantry, for whom the virtue of work is a necessity, nevertheless Perses is always there in the forefront. By accident or design a powerful weapon was thus put into the hands of didactic poets: for by a natural identification the reader feels *upon himself* the tirade intended by Hesiod for the delinquent Perses, the cajolery directed by Lucretius at the reluctant Memmius,[19] or the gentle, deferential persuasiveness of Virgil's offering to Maecenas.[20]

5 Another Hesiodic influence upon the genre is the loose-knit *structure* of the *Works and Days*.[21] With the frailest of connecting links it incorporates catalogues of proverbs,[22] 'epic' episodes,[23] autobiographical digressions,[24] as well as a series of practical tips on farming[25] and gloomy warnings about navigation.[26] It is not surprising that editors find neat analysis of the work a puzzling exercise and are inclined to suspect interpolation.

16. 286.

17. 27–41; 314–16, 396–404.

18. 38–9; 202–12 (the animal brutality illustrated in this parable of the hawk and the nightingale should be seen in the light of 277 ff., quoted above: injustice, that is, is *sub-human*); 248 ff. See *O.B.G.V.* No. 61 (i) and (ii).

19. See n. 122 below.

20. See n. 155 below. Empedocles similarly directs his poem *On Nature* to an individual, Pausanias (Guthrie (12), p. 137). Compare also para. 25 (the *epistolary* poetry of Horace) and contrast para. 27 (Manilius).

21. See Sinclair (1), Ch. 1, and the running analysis in Lattimore (3).

22. See n. 14 above and add 765 ff. (an appendix of lucky and unlucky days).

23. See n. 7 above.

24. 633–40; 651–9. Lattimore (3), p. 4.

25. 383–617 (cf. *O.B.G.V.* No. 67).

26. 618–94.

The truth may simply be that Hesiod did not have the strict standards of relevance to a set theme which logic requires – and in this he was to prove curiously influential upon the later didactic genre. Even of the more sophisticated Hellenistic and Roman poets, at least one (Horace) opted for Hesiodic informality,[27] and they all learned the tactical advantages of interspersed 'digressions' – for whatever purpose they might be used.[28]

6 Despite these influences of expression, tone, and structure, the *Works and Days* is far removed from the didactic poetry of later centuries and lies quite as firmly in the ancestry of other Greek genres such as personal poetry,[29] religious drama,[30] and moral and political reflection.[31] Typical of this breadth of influence is the subsequent history of Hesiod's Golden Age theory (in which rustic bliss is linked with justice, and both with a scarcely recoverable past);[32] it is reflected not only in Aratus,[33] Lucretius and Virgil,[34] but in such diverse writers as Plato[35] and Tibullus.[36] Furthermore, the 'versified instruction' which was to be the determining feature of the didactic genre occurs only in a sub-section of the *Works and Days* and is in the form of *practical* advice,[37] which few poets before Virgil chose to imitate.

7 In these respects an earlier influence was exercised by Hesiod's other main work, the *Theogony*,[38] a reverent and yet systematic

27. See para. 25 below with note 191, and cf. n. 186 for Virgil.

28. In Ovid, ornamental (para. 26); in Aratus and Manilius, ancillary to the theme (para. 10 n. 59 and para. 27); in Lucretius and Virgil, of central thematic importance (paras. 12 and 20).

29. See Rose *H.G.L.*, p. 57.

30. Along with the *Theogony* of course. See Solmsen (4), whose pp. 103–6 act as a neat summary of Hesiodic literary influence.

31. See Sinclair (1), pp. xxx–xxxvi.

32. 117–19, 225–39. See Solmsen (4), p. 87.

33. See para. 10.

34. See para. 20 below with nn. 152–3; Ryberg (53); Wilkinson (54).

35. See Solmsen (7), pp. 181 ff.

36. See Grimal (7). For Ovid's rejection of the concept see para. 26 below.

37. See n. 25 above.

38. Scholarly interest has recently shifted to this: see especially West (2).

classification of the gods in terms of genealogy and function. Hesiod claims to speak with prophetic authority as the inspired mouthpiece of the Muses, who once taught him the poetic art 'as he was shepherding his lambs on holy Helikon', experts (we are told) in matters of fiction *and fact*: 'you shepherds of the wilderness,' they say, 'poor fools, nothing but bellies, we know how to say many false things that seem like true sayings, but we know also how to speak the truth when we wish to'.[39] This claim to authoritative exposition, which was taken seriously by the Greek world at large, was echoed by a line of poets who wished in their turn to utter in poetry the 'truth' about the nature and government of the universe.

## Cosmological Didactic

8 The next important didactic poets after Hesiod are thus the 'cosmological' poets of the sixth and fifth centuries B.C. Though they adopted in part the *form* of the *Theogony* (notably its metre) and were preoccupied with some of the same questions, they nevertheless diverged further and further from the religious orthodoxy which it came to represent. Indeed, a sufficient reason for studying the fragmentary relics of their writings is the sample they give of a movement from the theological through the philosophical towards the scientific. The pioneering Xenophanes advocates a reformed theology. He scornfully rejects the multiplicity of Hesiod's gods with their all-too-human weaknesses, exposing the anthropomorphic fallacy with ruthless logic and satire (if horses had artistic talent they would draw gods like horses, he observes).[40] He urges belief in 'one god, greatest among gods and men, in no way similar to mortals either in body or in thought', one who 'always remains in the same place, moving not at all'.[41] This conception of a single static god, the constructive contribution

39. 22–8 (*O.B.G.V.* No. 70). Rose, *H.G.L.*, pp. 61–2, sees this as a deliberate departure from the epic tradition.
40. Kirk–Raven (8), No. 172.
41. Kirk–Raven (8) Nos. 173–4.

to theology of Xenophanes, was one of the influences behind the truly bizarre philosophizing[42] of Parmenides, reputed to be his pupil: for in *his* view it is the universe itself which is static, in the form of a single, ageless, and unchanging sphere,[43] and no evidence from the 'fallible' senses is allowed to disrupt this picture of reality. By contrast, Empedocles, influenced though he was by Parmenidean assumptions, deserves an important place in the history of science.[44] His theory that the universe is an intermixture of four elements (earth, water, air, and fire) was to mould Greco-Roman and indeed Medieval ideas of physics, cosmology, and psychology,[45] and equally noteworthy was his explanation of the constant fusion and dissolution of these elements in terms of the opposed cosmic principles of 'Love' and 'Strife':

καὶ ταῦτ' ἀλλάσσοντα διαμπερὲς οὐδαμὰ λήγει,
ἄλλοτε μὲν Φιλότητι συνερχόμεν' εἰς ἓν ἅπαντα,
ἄλλοτε δ' αὖ δίχ' ἕκαστα φορεύμενα Νείκεος ἔχθει.

*And these things never pause in their continuous movement, at one time fusing together through Love, at another each travelling its separate course through the divisiveness of Strife.*[46]

But 'Love' means more to Empedocles than an impersonal principle or process. He writes of it in terms of reverence and awe:

42. The forthright attack by Symonds (11), pp. 187–90, written in 1893, will be seen as prophetic by those who accept the thesis of A. J. Ayer's *Language, Truth and Logic* (1936), Ch. I.

43. E.g. Kirk–Raven (8), Nos. 350–1. See Guthrie (12), pp. 26 ff.

44. See Sambursky (10), pp. 16–19, and cf. Kirk–Raven (8), Nos. 419, 453. In *attitude* he is transitional between seer and scientist, alternating between 'pride in possession of certain truth' and 'consciousness of the fallibility and inadequacy of the human faculties' (Guthrie (12), p. 248).

45. See E. M. W. Tillyard, *The Elizabethan World Picture*, Ch. 5, Penguin Books, 1963. It was Aristotle's acceptance of the theory which ensured this lasting influence (Guthrie (12), p. 143).

46. Kirk–Raven (8), No. 423; see Guthrie (12), pp. 147–59. Love as a cosmological force can be traced back to Hesiod, *Theog.* 120–2 (see Solmsen (4), p. 26), but the attempt to find a Hesiodic pairing of Love and Strife (Sale (6), pp. 687–9) is unconvincing.

τὴν σὺ νόῳ δέρκευ μηδ' ὄμμασιν ἧσο τεθηπώς·
ἥτις καὶ θνητοῖσι νομίζεται ἔμφυτος ἄρθροις,
τῇ τε φίλα φρονέουσι καὶ ἄρθμια ἔργα τελοῦσι,
Γηθοσύνην καλέοντες ἐπώνυμον ἠδ' Ἀφροδίτην.

*Gaze at her in your mind, and do not sit bemused. For she is recognized as dwelling in the human frame; by her men think thoughts of love and do deeds of harmony, calling her 'Joy' and 'Aphrodite'.*[47]

In scientific detail as well as in this breadth of vision there are close links between the περὶ φυσέως of Empedocles and the *De Rerum Natura* of Lucretius – the pre-eminent examples of Greek and Roman didactic poetry.[48]

9 All these cosmological speculations were couched in the rhythms of the hexameter – a curiosity which cannot be explained solely in terms of 'tradition', since others such as Heraclitus were already writing on similar themes in prose. The reasons which suggest themselves for such conservative adherence to poetic form are important in the subsequent history of the genre. In the first place these philosophers were no doubt reluctant to put off the poet's mantle of *authority*: as mouthpiece of god they could claim immunity from criticism and enunciate their doctrines from a safe height. Parmenides, for instance, prefaces his theories with a claim to divinely inspired insight into the 'unshaken heart of well-rounded truth' and thus gains in prophetic impact what he lacks in poetic.[49] A similar attitude is evident in Empedocles, who went so far as to claim for himself divine status: 'Friends, I appear before you all an immortal god, mortal no longer. . . . No sooner do I enter their proud prosperous cities than men and women pay me reverence . . .'[50] Not surprisingly his propounded theories have an oracular quality, springing (as Lucretius aptly put it) *ex adyto tamquam cordis*, 'from the inner

47. Kirk–Raven (8), No. 424; cf. No. 466.
48. See para. 14 below.
49. Kirk–Raven (8), No. 342, with appended comments; Guthrie (12), pp. 6 ff.
50. Kirk–Raven (8), No. 478 (*O.B.G.V.* No. 347). See Symonds (11), Ch. VII, Guthrie (12), p. 246 with p. 123 ('something of the magician about him and a corresponding touch of arrogance and showmanship').

sanctum of the heart',[51] and as such they are entirely suited to the hexameter form long used at Delphi. But the poetry of Empedocles embodies two further attitudes: a deep *emotional* commitment – a passionate, evangelistic, concern with that message of sin and salvation which overlays his physical theories;[52] and an aspiration to *literary* achievement – a desire to harness the best resources of the Homeric tradition even to the technicalities of his theme.[53] This first infusion of fine poetry into expository writing probably caused its author none of the qualms later felt by Lucretius,[54] but it puzzled the critics. Aristotle described Empedocles as 'Homeric' ('Ομηρικός), noting his use of metaphor and 'the other admirable instruments of poetry',[55] and yet observed in a different context that 'there is nothing in common between Homer and Empedocles except their metre, so that it is right to call the former a poet (ποιητής) and the other a natural philosopher (φυσιολόγος)'.[56] The view that there was a tension between these two roles was typical of the fourth century, when prose had swept in as the medium for systematic instruction. Empedocles stood at the end of an era. Didactic poetry was soon dormant and apparently dead.

## Hellenistic Didactic

10 Revival came in the third century, when Hellenistic scholars – impelled by their characteristic enthusiasm for archaic poetry and for systematized knowledge – experimented with 'imitations' of Hesiod, unaware perhaps of the widening gulf caused by their own innovations in the tradition. The new fashion

51. *D.R.N.* 1. 737.

52. Cf. Kirk–Raven (8), Nos. 466 ff.; Symonds (11), pp. 204–5; Guthrie (12), pp. 244 ff.

53. E.g. to the description of the four elements: see Kirk–Raven (8), Nos. 417, 424 (line 18), 432, 441, and (closely related and pleasingly Homeric) 425. See Symonds (11), p. 203, for Homeric phraseology, sometimes tangential to the scientific purpose.

54. See para. 15 below.

55. *Fr* 70. For examples of metaphor see Guthrie (12), p. 136.

56. Poetics 1. See Symonds (11), p. 202.

was for (1) almost unrelieved catalogues of fact, and (2) mere versification of the prose treatises of others.[57] From an array of such poems[58] the only one to acquire any lasting fame was the *Phaenomena* of Aratus, a hexameter version of works on the constellations by Eudoxus and on weather-signs by Theophrastus. In his aspiration to authentic ancestry Aratus borrows Hesiod's phraseology, stresses the importance of his theme to farmer and sailor,[59] and devotes almost the only long digression to a Hesiodic treatment of Justice and the Golden Age.[60] But even if the work is informed by a noble Stoic faith[61] and is not without literary grace,[62] it lacks that combination of primitive moral urgency and sophisticated poetic artistry which characterized the best Greek and Roman didactic poems. The immense prestige which it enjoyed for many centuries is a reflection, not of its merits, but of an educational system which preferred its science in literary guise.[63] The poem does, however, have historical importance: for it was the young Cicero's Latin paraphrase of it (the first of three such versions)[64] which launched didactic poetry into the Roman world.[65]

57. It was left to Romans to impose artistry upon these unpromising developments – upon (1) by more sophisticated use of 'digressions' (see para. 5 n. 28), and upon (2) by more inventive treatment of prose originals (see paras. 11–13 below and Bailey (19), p. 28, for Lucretius; para. 25 for Horace).

58. See Rose, *H.G.L.*, 329–30. Nicander deserves special mention only because two of his works survive and a third's title was borrowed by Virgil (Γεώργικα, 'Points of Agriculture').

59. The former especially in 6–9; the latter in numerous tiny digressions about the hazards of the sea (149 ff., 287 ff., 408 ff.). For these themes in Hesiod see para. 5, nn. 25–6.

60. 100–36 (= *O.B.G.V.* No. 506).

61. See Webster (14), pp. 34–8: the grudging gods of Hesiod (*Works and Days* 42) give way to the benevolent Zeus of *Phaen.* 768–72 and 1–18 (= *O.B.G.V.* No. 505, the Invocation). Cf. N.T. Acts, xvii. 28. Aratus' comfortable teleology (e.g. 10–13) influenced Virgil (see n. 167 below).

62. Webster (14), pp. 33–4; Jermyn (56), p. 29.

63. See H. I. Marrou, *A History of Education in Antiquity* (trs. Lamb), pp. 184–5, Sheed and Ward, 1956.

64. Rose, *H.G.L.*, p. 327. A similar enterprise (in the 50s B.C.) was the Latin version of Empedocles by Sallust – probably not the historian (Syme, *Sallust*, p. 10, C.U.P., 1964).

65. There are isolated examples of earlier Roman experiments in the genre, e.g. Ennius on the *Art of Dining* (Rose, *H.L.L.*, p. 38).

## Lucretius

11 Within a few decades the *De Rerum Natura* of Lucretius (*c.* 94–*c.* 55 B.C.) was to outshine all Greek achievement in the genre and to achieve a harmonious interplay of poetry and instruction never surpassed. The system of the Greek philosopher Epicurus which he set out to expound[66] might well seem an unpromising theme for such poetic treatment, since its admonitory message is outweighed by a bulk of supporting technical argument. But Lucretius triumphantly met the challenge, (*a*) by a judicious interweaving of the technical and the non-technical,[67] and (*b*) by a skilful infusion of poetry into both.[68]

12 THE EPICUREAN GOSPEL – ROLE OF THE PROLOGUES. Lucretius, following Epicurus,[69] offered a prescription for happiness. Happiness, they both proclaimed, lies not in wealth or power or unstinted pleasure (where it will at best be unstable or marred by frustration) but in a passive state of equilibrium, achieved by the mind's victory over the causes of unhappiness: bodily pain, for instance, can be made tolerable by reasoned detachment, and those mental fears and forebodings which religion instils can be dispelled by a knowledge of the laws of physics, which leave no place for divine intervention in life or human survival after death. These latter points require a substructure of scientific argument to which Lucretius devotes his main exposition, but he is none the less careful to highlight the central doctrines in a series of emotionally charged excursuses, strategically placed either in mid-argument or as prologues to the six books. What in Hesiod or Aratus were haphazard *digressions* are thus in Lucretius calculated *intrusions*, in which

66. See note 57 (2) above. A contemporary vogue for Epicureanism is attested by Cicero, who is horrified at the proselytizing efforts of a certain Amafinius (*Tusc.* IV. 5–7), on whom see Boyancé (22), p. 8. According to Crawley (33), Lucretius aimed specifically to convert the Roman *aristocracy*.

67. See paras. 12–14 below.

68. See paras. 15–16 below.

69. See Bailey (19), pp. 60–6; Sikes (24), pp. 91–7; Warner (9), pp. 154–8 (translation of the *Principal Doctrines*).

high-flown rhetoric[70] and pungent satire,[71] as well as all the resources of poetry,[72] are effectively used in the service of an intensely serious purpose. The prologues represent an ingenious fusion of ends and means, designed (like any rhetorical *exordium*) to secure the reader's sympathetic attention to what follows, and yet enshrining the very essence of the Epicurean gospel – salvation through Reason from the cares and fears which beset mankind,[73] and from the specific human follies which are their causes or effects: superstition (I. 62–101), power-lust (II. 7–53), crime (III. 41–86), vice (V. 43–8), spiritual malaise (VI. 9–23). They can thus be seen as related sermons on a common theme, and their likeness to Christian pulpit oratory is increased by the element of reverential praise for the Founder himself.[74] In the three great hymns which open alternate books, Epicurus is hailed successively as heroic '*man* of Greece' (I. 66), benevolent '*father*' to his devoted followers (III. 9), and veritable '*god*' for the salvation he has offered (V. 8) – a planned triad of praise in which we may see confirma-

70. E.g. in the prologue to Book V – *conduplicatio* (*deus . . . deus*, 8), *anaphora* (*tantis . . . tantis . . . tam . . . tam*, 11–12), and thirteen rhetorical questions. Book III has been likened *in toto* to a classically composed speech (see Sikes (24), p. 136), and it is interesting though perhaps fruitless to isolate the relevant structural elements. C. S. Lewis discusses rhetoric in relation to poetry in *A Preface to Paradise Lost* (Oxford Paperbacks, 1960), p. 53: 'the differentia of Rhetoric is that it wishes to produce in our minds some practical resolve . . . and it does this by calling the passions to the aid of reason' – a neat summary of the role of Lucretian *poetry*? (see para. 15 below).

71. E.g. III. 1060–7, IV. 1121 ff., V. 1120–35, with lighter touches in V. 228–34 (animals manage without rattles and baby-talk), 1009–10 (progress from accidental to deliberate poisoning): see Sikes (24), pp. 30–2, Dudley (26f), Boyancé (22), pp. 311–14.

72. See paras. 15–16 below.

73. For condemnation of *curae* and *timores* in the name of *ratio* (in all its senses) see especially: I. 102–11, 130; II. 40–53; III. 14–17, 37 ff.; V. 9–10, 45–6; VI. 24–34. The motif is reinforced by imagery of calm out of storm and light out of darkness (II. 1–4, 14–16; III. 1–2; V. 10–12), darkness being specifically associated with *terror animi* in the three-line refrain which recurs in four prologues (I. 146–8; II. 59–61; III. 91–3; VI. 39–41). That 'casting out fear' is the main burden of the prologues can therefore be in no doubt.

74. The uncritical discipleship implied particularly in III. 9–13 conforms with Epicurus' own wishes, but is not typical of the Roman temperament. See Boyancé (22), p. 34 ('c'est parce qu'il est si fidèle qu'on peut vraiment dire de Lucrèce, comme on le dirait d'un chrétien, qu'il a la foi').

tion of the three-part structure of the whole work.[75] We need not therefore be surprised that the prologues of Books II, IV, and VI open differently.[76]

13 THE SCIENTIFIC ARGUMENT. The missionary purpose which is most evident in these excursuses has a controlling influence also on the scientific argumentation which fills the rest of the work. For just as Epicurus adopted atomism from Democritus[77] primarily as a prop to his ethical system, so Lucretius arranged his exposition of it as a three-stage attack upon that *fear* which was in his view the arch-enemy of happiness. (1) Foundation principle: the sole cause of events is the movement of atoms in accordance with fixed natural law (Books I and II). Corollaries: (2) the soul is physically composed and mortal (Book III), visions of the dead being explicable in terms of *simulacra* without reference to immortality (Book IV); (3) cosmic and human evolution (Book V) and such intimidating phenomena as lightning (Book VI) have natural – not supernatural – causes. The last two pairs of books thus successively combat the fear of death and the fear of divine displeasure in life.[78] Although Lucretius himself stressed this three-fold

75. See para. 13 with n. 79. One might expect each Epicurus-hymn to be relevant to the theme of the following *pair* of books, and I. 75–7 may be seen as a summary of Books I and II (cf. v. 56–8), III. 25–7 as allusion to the theme of Books III and IV. But is there any such reference in prologue V?

76. The best evidence that Lucretius was not planning an Epicurus-hymn for *every* book is the finished state of prologue II, in which Epicurus must share credit with other unnamed *sapientes* (8). Prologue VI does contain a fourth eulogy, but it differs from the others: (*a*) in its close links with the end of the preceding book, with an unbroken chain from the *summum cacumen* of v. 1457 through *Athenae* (VI. 2) to Epicurus (VI. 4 ff.), and (*b*) in its less effusive, more expository, tone (the fullest account of Epicurean psychology). Prologue IV (see n. 99 below) may well be a stop-gap (Bailey (19), pp. 756–8), but recent criticism stresses the common *motifs* which link it with the other prologues. For illuminating analysis of all six prologues see Boyancé (22), pp. 46–53; Wormell (26c), pp. 38–49; Minadeo (30), pp. 451–7: the latter sees the motifs as *creation*-themes, by contrast with *destruction*-themes at the close of each book.

77. On atomism see Guthrie (12), Chap. VIII; Bailey (17); Sambur, (10), Ch. V; Lowenstein (26a).

78. On the remote gods of Epicureanism see Bailey (19), pp. 66 ff.; Sikes (24), Ch. VI; Festugière (16), Ch. IV. Lucretius dutifully adheres to the positive tenets (III. 18–24; v. 148–9), but is more at home with angry denunciations of traditional beliefs (I. 62–101; v. 1194–203).

structure and its evangelical purpose,[79] he was (perhaps un-wittingly) impelled by an additional *scientific* interest in his theme.[80] He dwells at length on points of dubious 'relevance' (such as the whole range of sense-perception in Book IV) and exhibits the recognizable marks of a scientific spirit: a close and critical observation of the natural world; an unflagging insist-ence on the universality of natural causes; an over-mastering (and in the event over-optimistic) faith in reasoned argument; and a concern (matched by a capacity) for clear and systematic exposition.[81] The *De Rerum Natura* thus paradoxically com-bines the passionate intensity of a proselytizing tract with qualities which place it firmly among the ancestors of modern science.

14 AN EMPEDOCLEAN MOTIF. If Lucretius gave a scientific twist to the Epicurean heritage, we may trace this to the influence upon him of his Greek predecessor in the genre, Empedocles, whom he certainly greatly admired:

carmina quin etiam divini pectoris eius
vociferantur et exponunt praeclara reperta,
ut vix humana videatur stirpe creatus.

*Indeed, the songs that took shape in his divine breast proclaim in ringing tones such glorious discoveries that he scarcely seems born of mortal stock.*[82]

This eulogy, praising as it does the *thought* rather than the *poetry* of Empedocles, raises an interesting and little-discussed

79. Most incontrovertibly in v. 55 ff., where 56–8 refers to Books I and II, 59–63 to Books III and IV, and 64–90 to Books V and VI. See also I. 127–35, summarizing the last two pairs of books in inverse order (compare IV. 33–45 for the stress on 'visions of the dead' as the *main* feature of Book IV) and VI. 48–91 (where the anti-religious purpose is underlined). The discussion of these 'programme' passages in Bailey (19) is hampered by his assumption that the 'main purpose' of the work was to 'set forth the physical theories of Epicurus' (p. 22). See rather Boyancé (22), pp. 71, 77.

80. Is it Epicurean orthodoxy which leads him to mask the element of pure scientific curiosity in his work? His attitude to poetry may be compared (para. 15).

81. See Sellar (23), pp. 331–9.

82. I. 731–3. Translation here and below by Latham (21a). There was current interest in Empedocles (see n. 64).

problem: what *are* the Empedoclean *praeclara reperta* which earn such approval? Not, it would seem, the four-element theory: for, despite its obvious links with atomism,[83] its *defects* are what Lucretius emphasizes in the immediately following lines. We may, however, plausibly trace back to Empedocles that theme of a cosmic balance between Creation and Destruction which finds a central place in Lucretian thinking.[84] The plain processes of Epicurean physics – indestructible atoms constantly realigning themselves to form new compounds – are elevated to a philosophic and poetic level, and conceived as an endless battle between destructive and creative forces:

nec superare queunt motus itaque exitiales
perpetuo neque in aeternum sepelire salutem,
nec porro rerum genitales auctificique
motus perpetuo possunt servare creata.
sic aequo geritur certamine principiorum
ex infinito contractum tempore bellum.
nunc hic nunc illic superant vitalia rerum
et superantur item. miscetur funere vagor
quem pueri tollunt visentes luminis oras;
nec nox ulla diem neque noctem aurora secutast
quae non audierit mixtos vagitibus aegris
ploratus mortis comites et funeris atri.

*The destructive motions can never permanently get the upper hand and entomb vitality for evermore. Neither can the generative and augmentative motions permanently safeguard what they have created. So the war of the elements that has waged throughout eternity continues on equal terms. Now here, now there, the forces of life are victorious and in turn vanquished. With the voice of mourning mingles the cry that infants raise when their eyes open on the sunlit world. Never has day given place to night or night to dawn that has not heard, blended with these infant wailings, the lamentation that attends on death and sombre obsequies.*[85]

83. In an adapted form it finds a prominent place in Lucretian physics (cf. v. 235–305, 380 ff., 432 ff.) – more prominent than in the atomism of Democritus (Guthrie (12), pp. 413–14). The influence of Empedocles *is* surely here at work.

84. Sellar (23), pp. 300–1, 352, saw this clearly enough, but not its detailed outworkings.

85. II. 569–80. See n. 95 below.

There are countless allusions in the *De Rerum Natura* to this cyclical process of Birth and Death,[86] some stressing the ambivalence and essential relatedness of the two concepts,[87] and others the state of war between them. In the latter category we may now with some confidence place the work's opening invocation to Venus and closing account of the Plague at Athens, individually a source of long bafflement to critics[88] but perhaps yielding at last to joint interpretation. Why does an author who denies the possibility of divine intervention begin his poem with a forty-line address to Venus?[89] The convention of invocation[90] was, of course, congenial to him as a poet, but his readiness to employ it *must* be interpreted in the light of his materialistic philosophy and of his declared views about the legitimate use of gods' names.[91] In short, his Venus, for all the vividness of her poetic presentation, is a symbol – a personification of those generative processes with which the natural world pulsates, the *motus genitales auctificique*. Parallel allusion to the *motus exitiales* ('destructive processes') may be seen not only in the glamorous mythology which follows[92] but in the stark precision of the closing account of the Plague: for *morbus* (elsewhere described as *leti fabricator*, 'artificer of death'[93]) is the very reverse of that creativity which Venus symbolizes.[94] The work thus starts with the rush of animals to

86. For this and what follows see Minadeo (30); Liebeschuetz (31).

87. E.g. *natura creatrix* can dissolve a compound (I. 628) and *mors* create a new one (II. 1002–4). See further Minadeo (30), p. 451.

88. See Bailey (19), pp. 589–90 (the invocation), p. 1724 (the plague-sequence, with three unconvincing explanations).

89. Recent scholarship offers many incompatible answers to this question. The view of Boyancé (22), pp. 64 ff., that *Venus = Voluptas* (the Epicurean ideal) is attractive, and many will prefer it to the explanation offered in the text.

90. But even this required relevance to the ensuing theme (see n. 11 above) – an important clue.

91. II. 655–60: Neptune = sea, Ceres = corn, etc.

92. Liebeschuetz (31), note 30, assumes that Mars in I. 31 ff. symbolizes *mors*, and Wormell (26c), p. 39, suggests that the form *Mavors* (l. 32) is intended to encourage the identification.

93. III. 472. See the whole context and also v. 380 ff. (the same view applied on the cosmic level).

94. Bailey (19), p. 1724, and Sikes (24), p. 90, toyed with this interpretation, which Boyance (22), p. 79, later described as 'arbitraire et sans valeur philosophique'. But neither objection remains valid against the eloquent statement of

give birth and ends with the rush of desperate men to bury
their dead – poignant and poetic reminders of the great warring
processes of Creation and Disintegration which govern animate and inanimate nature alike.[95] It seems certain that
Lucretius drew inspiration for this majestic vision from the
Empedoclean conceptions of Love (or Aphrodite) and Strife,[96]
and that in this particular way his presentation of the *aurea dicta*
of Epicurus was influenced by his admiration for the *praeclara
reperta* of Empedocles.[97]

15 THE ROLE OF POETRY. A more obvious debt to Empedocles
was the whole idea of a scientific *poem* – certainly foreign to the
spirit of Epicurus, whose advice about poetry was 'to sail past
it with stopped ears, as from the Sirens' song'.[98] Lucretius was
careful to claim renown as a poet in terms which his master
might approve –

> quod obscura de re tam lucida pango
> carmina, musaeo contingens cuncta lepore,
>
> *because I shed on dark corners the bright beam of my poetry, touching
> everything with the charm of the Muses.*[99]

There is a double emphasis here upon his didactic purpose:[100]
the 'banishment of darkness' is a didactic rather than a poetic
aim, pre-eminently achieved in prose by Epicurus himself, as

---

the case by Minadeo (30), who demonstrates that 'disintegration' forms the
closing theme for four of the other five books. See also nn. 76 above and 128
below.

95. Animate and inanimate are not different in kind in Lucretian physics:
II. 569–80 (quoted above) well exemplifies the poet's instinct to illustrate the
*universal* law in terms of *human* life and death.

96. See para. 8 above.

97. Note that *De Rerum Natura* = περὶ φύσεως, the title of works by Empedocles *and* by Epicurus. For early Epicurean interest in Empedocles see Bailey
(19), p. 29, n. 1.

98. See Sikes (24), p. 25; Boyancé (22), pp. 58 and 315.

99. IV. 8–9. This is the only prologue which Lucretius devotes to his own
rather than to Epicurus' achievements, but I. 136–45 may be compared. See n. 76
above.

100. See Boyancé (22), pp. 62–5 and p. 35 for the precept of Epicurus ('always
behave as though Epicurus were watching you') which may be significant in
this context.

we are told elsewhere;[101] and as for the poetic grace of language
to which *musaeus lepor* refers, it is (we are at once assured) only
a means towards an overriding therapeutic end. Just as doctors
use honey to make unpleasant medicine palatable for children,

> sic ego nunc, quoniam haec ratio plerumque videtur
> tristior esse quibus non est tractata, retroque
> vulgus abhorret ab hac, volui tibi suaviloquenti
> carmine Pierio rationem exponere nostram
> et quasi musaeo dulci contingere melle,
> si tibi forte animum tali ratione tenere
> versibus in nostris possem, dum percipis omnem
> naturam rerum.

*In the same way our doctrine often seems unpalatable to those who have not
sampled it, and the multitude shrink from it. That is why I have tried to
administer it to you in the pleasing strains of poetry, coated with the sweet
honey of the Muses. My object has been to engage your mind with my verses
while you gain insight into the nature of the universe.*[102]

This proclamation of an ancillary role for poetry is not only
abhorrent to modern taste but arguably a distortion of Lucretius' own true priorities: modern critics prefer to think of the
philosophy and the poetry as inextricably intertwined.[103] What
is certain is that the poetic highlights – passages of unmistakably exalted feeling and expression – are not normally digressions *from* the didactic theme but embodiments *of* it. Thus:
(1) In the *prologues and excursuses*, finely wrought poetry is used
to give emotional force to the central message of Epicureanism.[104] (2) In the famous '*illustrations*', which mark Lucretius
out as a pastoral and descriptive poet of the highest order,[105]
the content is integral to the scientific argument – more so
than is sometimes assumed. For Lucretius aims not (as in a
simile[106]) to stimulate the imagination by comparing diverse

---

101. III. 1; V. 11–12. See para. 12 above.
102. IV. 18–25. Cf. VI. 82–3: *multa tamen restant et sunt ornanda politis/versibus.*
103. Boyancé (22), p. 308; Wormell (26c), p. 46; Maguinness (26d), pp. 69–70.
104. See para. 12 above.
105. See Sellar (23), pp. 398–403.
106. A misleading term used by Maguinness (26d), pp. 86 ff., and Townend
(26e), pp. 100 ff.

fields but to impart conviction by appealing to the precisely analogous: the pleasingly poetic description of grazing sheep, for instance, stresses above all their movement whether slow (*reptant*) or fast (*ludunt . . . coruscant*), contrasts that with their seeming immobility at a distance, and thus actually *explains* the invisibility of atomic movement;[107] the whirling dust-particles, described in unforgettable metaphor, provide a precise analogy with such atomic movement ('from this you may infer what it is like for atoms to be incessantly tossed about in the mighty void'[108]), as well as an actual instance of its effect.[109] In such arguments from analogy Lucretian thought and Lucretian poetry triumph simultaneously.[110] (3) Even in his rare but memorable *excursions into mythology*[111] Lucretius does not depart far from his didactic aim – either pointing a moral[112] or appending a rationalistic explanation.[113] From all this it is clear that Lucretius, while aspiring to high poetry, yet keeps it within his framework of moral purpose. Here lies the secret of the work's unity and power.

16 Among the more easily identifiable ingredients of Lucretian poetry are: sensitive and varied use of *hexameter rhythms*;[114] the exploitation of *verbal sound effects* (alliteration and assonance);[115] *metaphor*, especially to endow inanimate nature with

107. II. 317–22.

108. II. 121–2.

109. II. 125–41. See Boyancé (22), pp. 112 and 136; Cox (20e) App., p. 80.

110. Boyancé (22), p. 6. But we may guess that he first wrote them in an abbreviated and precisely 'relevant' form, and then filled out the description: the cryptic *errant saepe canes itaque et vestigia quaerunt* (IV. 705) may represent the first stage.

111. See especially West (32), pp. 50–3, 97–114.

112. I. 84–101 (Iphigeneia).

113. II. 600–60 (Magna Mater); v. 396–404 (Phaethon). There is a double irony in the description of the sun as *aeternam lampada mundi* (402): the myth itself cast doubt on the epithet, and Lucretian science flatly rejected it.

114. Bailey (19), pp. 109 ff.; Sikes (24), pp. 52–6; Maguinness (26d), p. 71, warns against unthinking application of Virgilian canons.

115. Bailey (19), pp. 146 ff. Linked with this are the *archaizing* features of Lucretian language, usefully listed in Maguinness (26d), p. 85, and Duff (20a V), pp. xiii–xix, and mentioned even as a symptom of poetic genius in Wormell (36), p. 384, quoting Palmer, *The Latin Language* (Faber & Faber, 1954), pp. 106 ff.

feelings and purposes;[116] and a complex tapestry of *images*.[117] Although such poetic artistry (*musaeus lepor*) particularly characterizes the passages mentioned in the preceding paragraph, there is some justice in Lucretius' claim that it permeates every part (*cuncta*) of the work.[118] Even the most technical discussions are lifted above the prosaic, as for instance the account of the atomic constitution of extra-hard objects: formed of interlocked atoms (*haec magis hamatis inter sese esse necesse est*, an accumulation of *s*'s which symbolizes the jarring friction), diamonds can 'stand in the front line and unfailingly defy the blows', as also the bronze plates 'which scream as they hold out against the bolts' (metaphors which aptly describe the capacity to survive intense pressures).[119] By contrast, there is much ugliness of rhythm, and plainness or redundancy of expression, where these best serve the didactic purposes of accuracy or clarity.[120] Thus poetry and 'prose' go hand in hand.

17 THE POET'S PERSONALITY. It will be clear by now that the *De Rerum Natura* is no mere transcription of Greek views into Latin, but a highly original creation: Lucretius has not only made a novel *organic unity* out of diverse elements but also suffused the prosaic with *poetry*. A third distinctive ingredient is the evidence of his vibrant *personality* in every part of the work. Although autobiographical allusions are few,[121] the man-to-man tone, which characterizes the address to Memmius throughout,[122] leads the reader to feel that he 'knows' its author, and an analysis of such subjective impressions is a

116. Maguinness (26d), pp. 89–91; Townend (26e), pp. 96–7.

117. Analysed for the prologues by Minadeo (30), and for the whole work by West (32) and Boyancé (22), pp. 291–7: the all-pervading symbols of *light* and *darkness* are natural enough in a missionary context.

118. IV. 9 (quoted in para. 15 above).

119. II. 444–50. See further Bailey (19), pp. 168–70 (the 'arid' not so arid).

120. Maguinness (26d), pp. 72–7.

121. For an interesting pair see I. 142 (working all night) and IV. 969–70 (dreaming about it): cf. also IV. 572–9 (hunting-party reassembling to return home?).

122. See para. 4 above and Boyancé (22), p. 32 (Epicurean preference for epistolary form), pp. 26–32 (Memmius); Farrington (26b), pp. 27–33.

fascinating and tantalizing exercise. Is he an independent thinker – or a slavish disciple?[123] a perfectionist in the ordering of his thoughts – or content with 'discontinuity'?[124] an exponent of authentic Epicurean composure – or victim of a mental imbalance verging on insanity?[125] a dedicated believer in his own materialistic dogma – or a secret doubter of it?[126] devoted to the pure and unsullied – or preoccupied with morbidity and unpleasantness?[127] optimistic and cheerful – or pessimistic and gloomy?[128] sociable and good-humoured – or lonely and ascetic?[129] The second, less favourable, alternative has been most stressed over the centuries, under the influence of Christian apologetic and of the one piece of external evidence about Lucretius' life – St Jerome's story of love-potion, madness, and suicide.[130] But in the twentieth century, when the theme of the

123. Paras. 12–14 above offer evidence of the former, and Farrington (26b), p. 20, can even claim that Lucretius was as original as Epicurus: for a different emphasis see Boyancé (22), p. 34, quoted in n. 74 above.

124. Minadeo (30), p. 444 with n. 1, lists champions of the latter view, which he effectively (at any rate in part) refutes. The view of Rose (H.L.L., p. 128) that the 'chief formal defect of the work' is 'a certain tendency to ramble' is now scarcely tenable.

125. The arguments for the latter are listed in Bailey (19), p. 10 – and demolished by Wormell (28).

126. The 'anti-Lucrèce chez Lucrèce' theory is supported by Sinker (20c), pp. xviii ff. but refuted by Kinsey (29).

127. Contrast the ideal of rustic purity (II. 29–33) with the seeming morbidity of III. 403–15, 634–63; V. 1310–40; VI. 1138 ff. But is the attitude sadistic – or clinical? An affinity with Thucydides (and therefore with the Hippocratic tradition) can be detected.

128. The argument in para. 14 above (symbols of creation and destruction *in that order*) might suggest the latter, and Green (27) argues that the stress on our world's decay and imminent collapse (II. 1164–74; V. 91–109) is not in Lucretius' sources but of his own making. But he concludes: 'his attitude seems rather to be one of fascination than of dread. As a detached spectator of the world's tragedy he found a beauty in death as well as in life.' So also Wormell (26c), p. 61; Minadeo (30), p. 458; and Kinsey (29). *Humour* in Lucretius is marked, but tends to be satirical (see n. 71 above) or polemical (II. 973–9) or grim (V. 104–9, 984–7).

129. For a balanced discussion see Sellar (23), pp. 291–4. It is often assumed that Lucretius was not temperamentally suited to that warmth of *friendship* which Epicurus advocated (on which see Festugière (16), Ch. III; Farrington (15), Ch. II). Note 121 above offers slender evidence both ways. He was certainly sensitive to affection within the family (III. 894–6; V. 1011–27), but his attitudes to contemporary society would alienate many.

130. See Bailey (19), pp. 8–12.

*De Rerum Natura* begins to command wide assent and universal respect, St Jerome's sensationalism is treated with suspicion,[131] and the character of Lucretius is more often vindicated and admired.[132] On any view the force of his personal impact upon the reader has never been in doubt.[133]

## Virgil: Georgics

18 Among the earliest readers to have felt this impact was the young and sensitive Virgil, in his late teens when the *De Rerum Natura* was published (soon after 55 B.C.): its formative and complex influence upon him is most clearly seen in his own didactic poem, the *Georgics*.[134] Not only is there a constant reminiscence of Lucretian phraseology,[135] an adaptation of the pattern of Lucretian argument,[136] and a deep reaction to Lucretian thought and attitudes,[137] but the overall structural similarities of the two works are too marked to be accidental. From Lucretius Virgil learned to harmonize three didactic levels – (1) technical exposition, providing the overt framework, (2) impassioned appeal to the emotions, characterizing the 'digressions', and (3) a subtler philosophical orientation, embodied in structural motif. These three levels represent the Hellenistic, the Hesiodic, and the distinctively Roman contri-

131. E.g. in Boyancé (22), pp. 17–20; Wormell (26c), pp. 36–7, (36), p. 380. See also Wilkinson in C.R. LXIII, No. 2, p. 47.

132. For sympathetic surveys see Boyancé (22), pp. 299–308; Wormell (26c), pp. 62–4.

133. For initial Roman reaction see Crawley (33), who argues that Cicero threw his influence against so 'dangerous' a work. For continuing controversy over the centuries see Boyancé (22), Ch. XI; Hadzsits (34); Gordon (35), Introduction. Sykes Davies (37) records and discusses Macaulay's pungent remarks.

134. For biographical and dating evidence see Perret (43), Ch. I and pp. 49–55.

135. Estimated at one in every twelve lines: see Bailey (47), and for some examples Duff (20a V), pp. xix–xxii, and n. 159 below.

136. See Perret (43), p. 72: Lucretian listing of arguments becomes Virgilian listing of imperatives, and in each writer a *summary* of the point precedes its *amplification* (cf. esp. *Georgics* II. 259–419).

137. See Sellar (42), Ch. VI; Liebeschuetz (31), pp. 33 ff; and cf. n. 153 below (sympathy) and para. 22 (aversion).

butions to the didactic tradition,[138] and their fusion within the two poems marks the full maturity of the art-form.

19 TECHNICAL INSTRUCTION. The *Georgics* purports to be a technical handbook. Witness its title,[139] its author's professed motive,[140] and its subdivision (in the manner of a textbook) into four sections – crops (Book I), trees and the vine (Book II), livestock (Book III), and bees (Book IV).[141] Furthermore, as a countryman himself, Virgil ensured that his practical advice was authentic, and only rarely can it be faulted.[142] But despite this expository façade, the *Georgics* is *not* a farmer's manual, and cannot have been conceived as such. On the author's own admission it is selective (*non ego cuncta meis amplecti versibus opto*[143]) and its content sometimes betrays a literary rather than a practical concern (influenced by Hesiod,[144] Aratus,[145] and others). A farmer who wanted full and contemporary advice would have gone rather to the recent prose work of Varro.[146] The lay-out of the *Georgics* is in fact an ingenious exploitation of the traditional form for a non-traditional purpose, so that Seneca expressed at least half the truth when he

138. See paras. 10, 4, and 14 respectively.

139. See n. 58 above.

140. I. 41, pity for 'ignorant' countrymen. See Perret (43), p. 84, for the class for whom Virgil really wrote – wealthy and cultured landowners.

141. See Huxley (38c), pp. 10–14, for a useful analysis, and Saint-Denis (38b), pp. xx–xxi, for the antecedents of this subdivision: he well argues that it comes not from a *technical* tradition but from 'un éloge enthousiaste et lyrique de la vie champêtre' (Cato, via Cicero).

142. See White (57), Jermyn (55) and (56), and other works listed in Williams (40), p. 15 n. 1, p. 16 n. 2.

143. II. 42. For agriculturally important omissions see Williams (40), p. 15 n. 1, Liebeschuetz (51), p. 64 n. 5, Saint-Denis (38b), pp. xv ff.

144. Sellar (42), pp. 193–5; Otis (41), p. 155; Duckworth (50), pp. 226–7. Despite the claim to Hesiodic ancestry in II. 176, only Book I owes much to Hesiod, its structure representing the 'Works' and (from 204) the 'Days', but with a new astronomical slant in the latter. Specific Hesiodic allusions are always noted in Huxley's edition (38c).

145. Particularly the weather-signs in I. 351–463: the versions of Aratus, Cicero, and Virgil are compared in Jermyn (56). See Sellar (42), pp. 195 ff., for other Alexandrian sources.

146. Virgil no doubt 'used' material from Varro (see Saint-Denis (38b), p. xxix), but his technical sources can rarely be located with precision, and it is best to think of an 'agronomic tradition', the literature of which is largely lost to us: see Perret (43), pp. 56–9.

said of Virgil's intentions *nec agricolas docere voluit, sed legentes delectare* ('his wish was not to offer instruction to farmers but pleasure to his readers').[147] Seneca's mistake was to assume that these are all-embracing alternatives: there are other didactic levels where the essence of the poem may lie.

20 MORAL PURPOSE. If Virgil's role as a teacher in the *Georgics* was something of a literary pretence, his role as preacher was not: influenced by the mighty poetic sermon of Lucretius, he set out – by gentler means and with a humbler message – to inspire new attitudes in his fellow Romans. His theme is the glory of country life, implied in many a loving detail of his exposition,[148] but most clearly expressed in the 'digressions', particularly those of Book II.[149] The country life symbolized for Virgil all the values he stood for: peace as against war, purity as against vice, rustic Italy as against urban Rome, and the great heritage of the past as against contemporary decadence.

> O fortunatos nimium, sua si bona norint,
> agricolas; quibus ipsa, procul discordibus armis,
> fundit humo facilem victum iustissima tellus.

> *Oh, too lucky for words, if only he knew his luck,*
> *Is the countryman who far from the clash of armaments*
> *Lives, and rewarding earth is lavish of all he needs.*[150]

And after a satirical attack on the pomp and sham of the city, there follows a catalogue of the merits of rural life. There is every reason to believe in the sincerity of such Virgilian sentiments, corresponding as they do to the background and temperament of the shy Mantuan who rarely went to Rome and would then cower in doorways to avoid being pointed out.[151]

147. Ep. Mor. 86. 15. For the role of aesthetic *delectatio* see para. 24 below.

148. In particular, the attribution of human emotions to animals and plants (in Lucretian spirit, n. 116), conveying an impression of throbbing vitality: see Williams (40), pp. 16–17; Liebeschuetz (51), p. 64.

149. In praise of Italy (136–76), of spring (315–45), of country life (458–540). Williams (40), p. 16.

150. II. 458–60, trs. by Day Lewis (39). See Williams (40), p. 20.

151. Suet. Vit. Verg. 11. Sellar (42), p. 125.

Yet these deep-felt convictions had both a literary and a political setting, conforming not only with a traditional didactic theme, as old as Hesiod[152] and recently revitalized by Lucretius,[153] but also with the wishes of Octavian, who (through Maecenas) was Virgil's patron. We need not doubt that as early as 36–35 B.C. the young triumvir was foreseeing the need for that pursuit of national peace and purity, and that refurbishing of antique tradition, which later became his overt policies,[154] and even if the allusion to Maecenas' *haud mollia iussa*[155] is an ironical exaggeration, we may assume that there was some political encouragement for the work.

21 MOOD AND MOTIF. Until the mid-twentieth century the theme of the *Georgics* was interpreted on these two levels only – as a fusion of exposition ('the farmer's manual') and exhortation ('hymn to the country life'). This did justice to Book II, made some sense of Book I, but left important features of Books III and IV unexplained. Recent investigation into patterns of motif[156] has not only shown the structural unity of the work but also suggested a philosophical profundity in it, previously unsuspected, and indeed masked by Virgil's modest

152. See para. 6 above. For allusions in this passage to the Golden Age theory of Hesiod and Aratus, see Wilkinson (54), p. 83.

153. Lucretius, though no naïve adherent of the Golden Age view, associates the Epicurean ideal with rural peace (II. 29–33) as against the prevailing urban scramble for wealth, power, and pleasure (II. 9 ff., III. 1060 ff., v. 1120 ff.): Virgil's *secura quies* (II. 467) has Epicurean overtones, and his anti-urban satire is Lucretian in spirit.

154. Williams (40), pp. 17–18. Wilkinson (49), pp. 20–21, is perhaps too sceptical, though rightly critical of Page's talk of the 'Emperor's' wishes.

155. III. 41. Maecenas is also addressed in I. 2, II. 41, IV. 2 – the kind of pattern which modern criticism considers deliberate, e.g. Perret (43), p. 70. On Maecenas see Sellar (42), p. 215, Saint-Denis (38b), p. vii, and on the tradition of personal address, para. 4 above.

156. The views of Otis (41), summarized in Williams (40), pp. 20–1, and of Duckworth (50) are substantially the same: their structural and thematic analysis is supported by Perret (43), pp. 59–71, and Mountford (52), pp. 30–4, whose deductions, however, are in terms of artistry rather than meaning and purpose. Wilkinson's similar verdict in (44) will carry weight: he has told me that he accepts the 'conception of symphonic structure (responsion of themes and moods)', but doubts the further deductions drawn from it about Virgilian philosophy.

disclaimer.[157] Beneath the surface we may detect his considered response both to the views of Lucretius and to the anarchy of his own times.

22 It was always the thought as much as the poetry of Lucretius which made its impact on Virgil.[158] Tutored as he was by Siro the Epicurean, he learned to see to the heart of the *De Rerum Natura*, as his tribute to its author shows:

> Felix qui potuit rerum cognoscere causas
> atque metus omnes et inexorabile fatum
> subiecit pedibus strepitumque Acherontis avari.

> *Happy the man who could grasp the causes of things, and who trampled beneath his feet all fears and the intransigence of fate and the clamour of hungry Acheron.*[159]

There is clear recognition here of Lucretius' two dominant themes: (1) the denial of divine intervention by an insistence on natural causes, and (2) the denial of immortality by an insistence on the universality of decay.[160] Yet it was precisely these twin doctrines from which Virgil after mature reflection rebelled, and which he explicitly or implicitly rejected in the very material of his *Georgics*. (1) By contrast, he asserts providential guidance of human affairs, detecting it even in the farmer's toilsome struggle with the land –

> Pater ipse colendi
> haud facilem esse viam voluit; primusque per artem
> movit agros, curis acuens mortalia corda.

> *The Father of agriculture himself willed that the way should not be easy, and first ordained the working of the fields through human ingenuity, using worry to sharpen human wits.*[161]

157. II 483–6.
158. See note 137 above.
159. II. 490–2. *Subiecit pedibus* is a near-direct quotation from Lucretius (I. 78, *quare religio pedibus subiecta vicissim*), but by the change to *fatum* Virgil characteristically gives it a twist in the direction of his own thinking.
160. See para. 13 above.
161. I. 121–3.

This is the Hesiodic gospel of Hard Work,[162] given divine sanction in the spirit of Aratus,[163] and urged in precise contradiction of the Lucretian view.[164] Similarly, in the earnest appeals to the gods,[165] explicit advocacy of religious worship and ritual,[166] and passing assumption that weather-signs are a mark of the Father's benevolence,[167] we see a clear enough rejection of Lucretian theology. (2) More deeply concealed and more tentative is Virgil's answer to Lucretius' preoccupation with death and decay. For it lies not in any one passage but in an interrelation of passages, forming a motif which corresponds with the Lucretian scheme and is equally easy to miss.[168] The four books of the *Georgics* are arranged in contrasting pairs.[169] The theme of the first is the *effort* of farming, the struggle with recalcitrant nature, the *labor* which remains *improbus* despite its divine blessing;[170] the political epilogue, linked to what precedes by related images,[171] ends the book on a note of discord – *saevit toto Mars impius orbe* ('the wicked War-god runs amok through all the world').[172] Book II, in marked contrast, offers a happy optimistic vision, with emphasis in every detail on nature's *co-operation* with man, digressions which speak of harmony and happiness,[173] and a closing reference to political

162. See para. 4 above.

163. See n. 61 above. Wilkinson (54), pp. 77–8, sees a wider Stoic influence as well.

164. See especially *De R.N.* v. 206–17. Note that even the 'worries' (*curae*) from which Epicureanism proclaimed release (see n. 73 above) find a place in Virgil's scheme (123). For illuminating commentaries on this crucial passage see: Williams (40), pp. 19–20;* Otis (41), pp. 155–9; Wilkinson (49), pp. 23–5, and (54); Mountford (52), p. 32; Perret (43), pp. 79–82;* Ryberg (53), pp. 119–23;* those asterisked stress the implied rejection of Lucretian thought.

165. E.g. I. 5–23, 498–9; cf. II. 493–4. See Williams (40), p. 19; Sellar (42), pp. 217–227.

166. I. 338.

167. I. 231. See Otis (41), pp. 159–60, and n. 61 above for the influence of Aratus.

168. For a warning that these interpretations are controversial in the case of both poets see nn. 94 and 156 above.

169. Clearly summarized in Otis (41), pp. 151–4. See also Perret (43), p. 70.

170. Otis (41), pp. 157–8.

171. Boat out of control (202–3): chariot out of control (513–14). Otis (41), p. 161.

172. 511.

173. See n. 149 above.

peace which counterbalances the end of Book I.[174] Books I
and II must thus be interpreted together: Virgil combines a
realistic picture of discord (Book I) with an answering vision
of harmony (Book II), a pointed reversal of the Lucretian
order.[175] The parallel contrast between the second pair of
books is again most clearly seen in their conclusions. The culminating motif of Book III is Death, instanced in the horror
of a cattle plague,[176] which unmistakably echoes the grim
climax of the *De Rerum Natura*: the gloom of this Death-motif
is then dispersed by the Resurrection theme which closes the
final book.[177] It is typical of Virgil that he thus answered
Lucretius with a theme rather than a theory, though he was to
attempt the latter in the sixth book of the *Aeneid*.[178]

23 This overall pattern (I War, II Peace, III Death, IV
Resurrection) has also been seen as a socio-political comment
on the troubled times in which Virgil wrote, with emphasis
in this case upon the *conditional* nature of the promises in
Books II and IV. The peace and harmony idealized in Book II
is dependent on a right attitude of mind;[179] and, whereas the
death-theme in Book III is associated with the idea of blind
selfish passion (symbolized in animal mating), the Rebirth in
Book IV is reserved for the sexless, selfless, bees.[180] Virgil
seems to underline the allegorical implications of these animal
sequences:[181] was he delicately recommending a revitalized
Roman society, purged of the selfish ambition which had induced Civil Wars, and bound together by a common purpose

174. Otis (41), pp. 163–9.
175. See notes 76 (ad fin.), 94 and 128 above.
176. III. 470–566. See Liebeschuetz (51) for a study of the tone of Book III.
177. IV. 281–558. For this interpretation of the excursion into mythology see
Otis (41), pp. 190 ff. and Duckworth (50), p. 232 (who emphasizes its significance
as an answer to Lucretius). Few scholars now accept (without severe modifica-
tion) the assertion of Servius that Book IV originally ended with an encomium of
Virgil's friend, Gallus: see Williams (40), pp. 21–2; Perret (43), pp. 49–52; Rose,
*H.L.L.*, p. 246, and (for continuing dispute) Otis (41), Appendix 7.
178. 724–51. See Williams (40), p. 35; Rose, *H.L.L.*, p. 253.
179. See Otis (41), pp. 168–9.
180. Otis (41), pp. 174–6, 185–6.
181. Otis (41), p. 153 and *passim*, Sellar (42), p. 233.

and a common loyalty to a respected leader?[182] His personal attitude to Octavian emerges clearly. In the extended epilogue to Book I, which reflects the uncertainties of the Triumviral period, the nation's gods are implored to allow *hunc saltem iuvenem* ('at least *this* young man')[183] to restore peace out of anarchy. The diffident tone of this blossoms into adulation when Actium has set the seal upon Octavian's power and the hoped-for peace seems assured: for the prologues to Books I and III are certainly late additions to the work. In the one Octavian is ranked by a touch of sophistry among the gods of the countryside;[184] in the other his world-wide fame and Trojan descent are celebrated, and Virgil promises to record his 'blazing battles' in a later work.[185] Mercifully this formula for abject flattery was soon dropped in favour of the subtler scheme of the *Aeneid*. But we need not doubt that Virgil, who lacked the inbred republican sympathies of an aristocrat, saw in the strong personal control of Octavian (soon to be Augustus) the only hope of peace in a distracted world.

24 POETRY IN THE GEORGICS. Such are the didactic purposes of this highly sophisticated work: a surface level of technical instruction, a deeper vein of exhortation to the rural 'virtues', and (buried at a depth where only profound study can unearth it) a philosophical view which rejects the Lucretian and anticipates the Augustan. Yet Virgil's purpose in adopting these themes was not merely – and perhaps not even primarily – didactic: he chose them as material for *poetry*, and (being less tied to a missionary aim than Lucretius) allowed poetic considerations to affect his shaping of them, avoiding over-formal organization of the material,[186] taking an obvious de-

182. Otis (41), pp. 185–6, 190; Perret (43), p. 86; Saint-Denis (38b), p. xxxv; cf. Liebeschuetz (51), p. 75.

183. I. 500. The passage is well discussed in Williams (40), pp. 18–19.

184. Though not yet a god, he *will be* one (24–5), and *may* then have dominion over crops and weather (26–8). See n. 11 above.

185. III. 46. The poem closes with further allusion to the triumph of Octavian (IV. 560–2).

186. The articulation is not clear until an Otis makes it so: (41), pp. 148–51.

light in the mere *description* of nature,[187] and achieving a remarkably consistent finesse of literary style.[188] Whereas the all-night preoccupation of Lucretius was to find words which would *'illuminate'*,[189] Virgil spoke of imitating the she-bear and 'licking his poetry into *shape'*.[190] The difference of image pinpoints the characteristic genius of each poet.

## Other Augustan Didactic

25 The *Georgics* set a fashion for didactic poetry, which other leading Augustan poets followed in their characteristic and utterly diverse ways. The *Epistles* of Horace, the longest of which is known as the *Ars Poetica*, contain the author's considered reflections on the conduct of life and the role of poetry, and have the merit not of startling originality but of shrewd, witty, and congenial presentation. It is an uncanny fact that so sophisticated a collection, exhibiting the *urbanitas* of a fully mature society, should show marked similarities with didactic at its most primitive – the *Works and Days* of Hesiod.[191] Both are epistolary in form and 'philosophical' in content, and two further points suggest that Horace was *deliberately* experimenting in a 'reversion to the primitive'. First, in reaction to the high-flying poetry of Lucretius and Virgil, he defiantly conceives the hexameter as a 'prosaic' medium, ironically claiming that his poetic days are past.[192] The resultant lowering of the emotional tone conforms with a difference in his aim:

187. Hence Wilkinson's view, propounded in (49), pp. 26–8, and to be maintained in (44), that the *Georgics* is the first *descriptive poem* (a new genre). See also Liebeschuetz (51), p. 68. Such an emphasis is at variance with that of Otis (41), and the reader must take his choice – or attempt a synthesis, as Williams (40), p. 22. See also n. 156 above.

188. See Wilkinson (48), Perret (43), pp. 71–7; and for hexameter rhythms Huxley (38c), pp. 19–28.

189. I. 144–5 (*clara . . . praepandere lumina*).

190. Suet. Vit. Verg. 22 (*carmen . . . lambendo effingere*).

191. See Sinclair (1), pp. xiv–xvi. Mr L. P. Wilkinson has suggested to me that these 'Hesiodic' features in Horace are better explained in terms of the *sermo* tradition (cf. Cicero, *De Oratore*, III).

192. Ep. I i 10 (*nunc itaque et versus et cetera ludicra pono*).

he has no wish to convert,[193] but merely to stimulate reflection. Second, he contrives to obscure the drift of his reasoning by omitting all the familiar didactic sign-posts and by inter-weaving thematic points, illustrations, and digressions into a pattern which only the discriminating reader can discern. In the *Ars Poetica* any clarity of outline which the Hellenistic prose original of Neoptolemus may have had is consistently blurred.[194] This studied return to the prosaic and rambling discourse of the earliest didactic is perhaps a sign that the tradition had run its course.

26 Another such sign is the advent of parody. Already in his *Medicamina Faciei*, an uncompleted handbook on cosmetics, Ovid had challenged the Golden Age myth dear to didactic poets, by advocating *cultus* in place of old-fashioned *simplicitas* and wittily using the analogy with Virgil's *arvorum cultus* as justification.[195] Now in the *Ars Amatoria*, with a mock-seriousness of purpose which is evident even from his choice of metre,[196] he offered a 'monumental didactic, based on the triumphant paradox of teaching an art that all men know'.[197] The fun lay in the use – or misuse – of stock features of the tradition. Hesiod's claim to inspiration as well as the standard preliminary invocations to relevant deities are quietly mocked:

> Nec mihi sunt visae Clio Cliusque sorores
> > Servanti pecudes vallibus, Ascra, tuis:
> Usus opus movet hoc: vati parete perito;
> > Vera canam: coeptis, mater Amoris, ades!

> *Nor did Clio and her sisters [i.e. the Muses] ever appear to me as I guarded my flock in Ascra's valleys. It is experience which prompts this work – pay heed to a poet who knows. I shall utter the truth. Mother of Love, assist the undertaking!*[198]

193. See n. 15 above.
194. See n. 57 above, and Brink (58) for a full treatment.
195. *Med. Fac.* 1–26. Cf. *Ars. Am.* III. 101 ff. (= No. 5 in *Aestimanda* by Balme and Warman, Oxford, 1965, usefully juxtaposed with *Georg.* II. 458–74). See Higham (59), pp. 113–14.
196. The elegiacs of love-poetry in place of the expository hexameter.
197. Higham (59), p. 114.
198. I. 27–30. See para. 3 n. 11 and para. 7 above. For Ascra, Hesiod's home village, see *Works and Days*, 640.

The exposition consists of grouped 'proofs' or analogies leading to consecutive conclusions[199] (a truncated version of the
Lucretian method[200]), punctuated by episodes which in Ovid
really *are* digressions. Most are narrative sequences from his
favourite field of mythology,[201] but one is political and perhaps
indirectly satirical: its adulatory praise of the young Gaius
Caesar is of so thin a relevance, so cynically and amusingly contrived, that it makes unspoken comment on Virgil's political
episodes.[202]

27 Relatively dull is the other surviving didactic poem of the
Augustan period, an exposition of astrology in five books by
Manilius. The bulk of the work is formidably mathematical,
but the tedium is partly offset in traditional manner by *digressions* of some literary merit[203] and by *prologues*.[204] The latter
are didactic manifestoes of great interest to the study of the
genre. The poet is conscious of his distinctive place in the
tradition: he rejects the allurements of epic (III) as well as the
hackneyed themes of earlier didactic (II), and after diagnosing
human ills in expressly Lucretian terms (IV. 1 ff.) proudly offers
his Stoic panacea (*fata regunt orbem, certa stant omnia lege*, IV. 14).
But while rejecting the themes of his predecessors, he also let
slip some of the secrets of their success: in place of the solemn
invocation of a presiding deity, we find Mercury taking second
place to Caesar;[205] in place of the intimate or thrusting appeal
to a Perses or a Memmius or a Maecenas, we find a vaguely

199. See Wilkinson (60), p. 123.

200. E.g. the list in 1. 473–6 is lifted straight from Lucretius 1. 311 ff. See
Kenney (61) for the Lucretian (and Virgilian) didactic *formulae* employed by
Ovid.

201. See Wilkinson (60), pp. 123–7. They have been aptly termed 'serious
relief'.

202. I. 177–216. Note the pseudo-relevance given to it by 217–18, and the
daring humour of the imperative to the would-be lover (221) following on the
vocative in which Gaius himself is addressed (213). The 'skilful transitions' at
start and finish of Virgil's digressions, noted in Mountford (52), pp. 32–3, are
thus parodied by Ovid.

203. See *O.B.L.V.* Nos. 196–7, 199–200, 203–4.

204. The first four are *O.B.L.V.* Nos. 195, 198, 201, 202.

205. Cf. 1. 7 ff. and 32 ff.

worded invitation – and then not to a 'honeyed draught' but to unalleviated instruction:

> Huc ades, o quicumque meis advertere coeptis
> aurem oculosque potes, veras et percipe voces.
> impendas animum; nec dulcia carmina quaeras.
> ornari res ipsa negat contenta doceri.
>
> *Come hither, whoever can offer ears and eyes to my theme, and listen to the voice of truth. You must concentrate and not expect charming poetry. My theme spurns poetic treatment and asks only for plain exposition.*[206]

This brusque banishment of poetic artistry from the area of technical exposition reflects common practice among the hack didactic poets of the Augustan and later periods: their surviving works (on subjects such as hunting and fishing)[207] give us information but little literary uplift. Even poetic *digressions* become rarer, and Columella's feeling of 'guilt' after a competent attempt at one (in the versified tenth book of his *De Re Rustica*) is symptomatic.[208] The heritage of Hellenistic pedantry was to triumph in the end.

## Later Revivals

28 Those who wish to trace the influence of Roman didactic poetry upon its later European exponents must travel not a highway but a by-way of literature. They will glance at the sixteenth-century Italian vogue for Latin poems of rustic instruction (after Virgil)[209] or scientific exposition (after Lucretius),[210] and hurry on to the resurgence of the genre in eighteenth-century England.[211] Here they will find, on the one

206. III. 36–9 (= *O.B.L.V.* No. 201 *ad fin.*). Contrast Lucretius' attitude to *ornatio* (n. 102 above).

207. For names and some details see Huxley (38c), pp. 15–17.

208. *De R. R.* x. 215–29. See Dudley (62), p. 41.

209. See Wilkinson (64).

210. See Gordon (35), Appendix II.

211. See Dudley (62), Huxley (38c), pp. 18–19; and (more fully) Spencer (26g), pp. 137 ff, Wilkinson (64); Røstvig (63) deals with one aspect in minute detail. The coyness of eighteenth-century English didactic, with its conscious imitation of classical authors, contrasts with the rugged simplicity of Elizabethan works

hand, vigorous didactic works (such as *Cyder*, by John Philips which scarcely qualify as poetic literature, and on the other hand, the unbroken surge of 'poetic' emotion which characterizes James Thomson's *Seasons*.[212] Each claims Virgilian ancestry and with some justification, but neither breathes the whole spirit of the *Georgics*. For the true fusion of poetry with technical exposition is a Roman achievement, which baffled posterity by its inimitability.

## Bibliography

### Hesiod

1. T. A. SINCLAIR, *Hesiod, Works and Days*, London, 1932; reprinted 1966 by Georg Olms Verlagsbuchhandlung.
(Text, commentary, and a full Introduction which remains the best survey of the work in English)

2. M. L. WEST, *Hesiod, Theogony*, Oxford, 1966.
(Text, detailed commentary, and lucid Introduction)

3. RICHMOND LATTIMORE, *Hesiod*, Michigan, 1959. (A translation which combines the robust vigour of Hesiod with a racy modernity, with brief Introduction)

4. FRIEDRICH SOLMSEN, *Hesiod and Aeschylus*, Cornell, 1949.

5. WERNER JAEGER, *Paideia* (tr. Highet) Bk. 1, Ch. 4, Oxford, 1939.

6. WILLIAM SALE, 'The Dual Vision of the Theogony', Arion, 1965.

7. *Hésiode et Son Influence*, Fondation Hardt, Geneva, 1960.
Essays included survey influence on Plato (Solmsen), Virgil (La Penna, in Italian), Tibullus (Grimal, in French)

### Cosmological Poets

8. G. S. KIRK and J. E. RAVEN, *The Presocratic Philosophers*, Cambridge, 1962.
(Extracts, with translations and running commentary)

---

such as Tusser's *Five Hundred Points of Good Husbandry* (1573). This is an interesting parallel with (not a derivative from) the primitive Hesiodic tradition: see A. L. Rowse, *The England of Elizabeth*, pp. 99 ff. (Macmillan, 1951).

212. A twentieth-century work, *The Land*, by Victoria Sackville-West, may be compared.

9. REX WARNER, *The Greek Philosophers*, Mentor, 1958.
(Translated extracts with brief commentary)

10. S. SAMBURSKY, *The Physical World of the Greeks* (tr. Dagut), London, 1956.

11. J. A. SYMONDS, *Studies of the Greek Poets Vol. $I^3$*, Chaps. VI–VII, A. & C. Black, 1893.

12. W. K. C. GUTHRIE, *A History of Greek Philosophy*, Vol. II, Cambridge, 1965.

## Aratus

13. G. R. MAIR, *The Phaenomena*, London, 1921.

(Text with translation in Loeb series – second half of a Callimachus volume)

14. T. B. L. WEBSTER, *Hellenistic Poetry and Art*, London, 1964.

## Lucretius

A. *Epicureanism* (see also 9, 19, 22)

15. BENJAMIN FARRINGTON, *The Faith of Epicurus*, London, 1967.

16. A. J. FESTUGIERE, *Epicurus and His Gods* (tr. Chilton), Oxford, 1955.

17. CYRIL BAILEY, *The Greek Atomists and Epicurus*, Oxford, 1928; Reissued 1964 by Russell & Russell.

18. KATHLEEN FREEMAN, 'Epicurus – a Social Experiment', G. & R., 1937/8.

B. *Editions of* De Rerum Natura

19. CYRIL BAILEY. In three volumes. Oxford, 1947.
(Outmoded in some matters of interpretation, but still the indispensable guide)

20. (*a*) DUFF, Cambridge (Books I, III, V separately). (*b*) LEE, Macmillan (Books I–III). (*c*) SINKER, Cambridge (rearranged extracts surveying Epicureanism). (*d*) BENFIELD and REEVES, Oxford (extracts, with relevant modern thought). (*e*) COX, Bell (easy, science-based, extracts).

C. *Translations of* De Rerum Natura

21. (*a*) LATHAM, Penguin (prose). (*b*) TREVELYAN, Cambridge (verse).

D. *General Surveys* (see also Intr. to 19)

22. PIERRE BOYANCE, *Lucrèce et L'Epicurisme*, Presses Universitaires de France, 1963.
(There is no comparable twentieth-century book in English)

23. W. Y. SELLAR, *The Roman Poets of the Republic³*, Oxford, 1889; Reprinted 1965 by Biblo & Tannen, New York.
(Still the fullest English treatment)

24. E. E. SIKES, *Lucretius, Poet and Philosopher*, Cambridge, 1936.
(A compact but suggestive survey)

25. J. WIGHT DUFF, *Literary History of Rome, from the Origins to the Close of the Golden Age*, London, new edn. 1953.

26. D. R. DUDLEY (Ed.), *Lucretius*, London, 1965.
(An invaluable volume, containing essays by (*a*) O. E. LOWENSTEIN, (*b*) B. FARRINGTON, (*c*) D. E. W. WORMELL, (*d*) W. S. MAGUINNESS, (*e*) GAVIN TOWNEND, (*f*) D. R. DUDLEY, (*g*) T. J. B. SPENCER)

E. *Topics*

(*a*) *The Poet's Character* (see also 26c)

27. W. M. GREEN, 'The dying world of Lucretius', *A.J.Ph.*, 1942.

28. D. E. W. WORMELL, 'Lucretius: the Personality of the Poet', *G. & R.*, 1960.

29. T. E. KINSEY, 'The Melancholy of Lucretius', Arion, 1964.

(*b*) *The Poem's Form and Purpose* (see also 26b)

30. RICHARD MINADEO, 'The Formal Design of the De Rerum Natura', Arion, 1965.

31. W. LIEBESCHUETZ, 'The Cycle of Growth and Decay in Lucretius and Virgil', P.V.S., 1967/8.

(*c*) *Language and Poetic Artistry* (see also 26d and 26e)

32. DAVID A. WEST, *The Imagery and Poetry of Lucretius*, Edinburgh, 1969.
(An enthusiastic and sensitive approach to Lucretian poetry)

(*d*) *Changing Attitudes to Lucretius* (see also 26g)

33. L. W. A. CRAWLEY, *The Failure of Lucretius*, Auckland, 1963.
(Assesses the immediate reaction of the Roman world to the challenge of Lucretius: a pamphlet well worth getting)

34. G. P. HADZITS, *Lucretius and his Influence*, London, 1935.

35. COSMO GORDON, *A Bibliography of Lucretius*, London, 1962.
(The General Introduction surveys attitudes to Lucretius in relation to published editions)

36. C. BAILEY and D. E. W. WORMELL, *Fifty Years (and Twelve) of Classical Scholarship*, ch. X, Oxford, 1968.
37. SYKES DAVIES, *Macaulay's Marginalia* (= appendix to 21b).

## Virgil: Georgics

### A. *Editions*

38. (*a*) T. E. PAGE, *Bucolics and Georgics*, London, 1898. (*b*) E. DE SAINT-DENIS, *Géorgiques*, Paris, 1966. (*c*) H. H. HUXLEY, *Georgics I and IV*, Methuen, 1963.
   (The commentaries in (*b*) and (*c*) provide a much-needed supplement and corrective to the notes in (*a*))

### B. *Translation*

39. C. DAY LEWIS, London, 1940.
   (A classic of poetic translation: Day Lewis reads extracts on an Argo record, RG 27)

### C. *General Surveys* (see also Intr. to 38b)

40. R. D. WILLIAMS, *Virgil* (Greece and Rome, New Surveys in the Classics, No. 1), Oxford, 1967.
   (Provides useful preliminary bearings on the subject and its bibliography)
41. BROOKS OTIS, *Virgil: A Study in Civilised Poetry*, Oxford, 1963.
   (Offers detailed commentary within a controversial general interpretation)
42. W. Y. SELLAR, *The Roman Poets of the Augustan Age: Virgil*[3], Oxford, 1897. Reprinted 1965 by Biblo and Tannen, New York.
   (A full and still valuable treatment)
43. J. PERRET, *Virgile*, Hatier, Paris, 1965.
   (A compact and useful paperback)
44. L. P. WILKINSON, *The Georgics of Virgil*, Cambridge, due 1969.
   (Will be invaluable as the only comprehensive treatment in English)
45. F. KLINGNER, *Virgils Georgica*, Artemis, Zurich, 1963.
46. K. BÜCHNER, *P. Vergilius Maro*, Stuttgart, 1956.
   (Nos. 45 and 46 are in German)

### D. *Topics*

   (*a*) *Language and Poetic Artistry*

47. CYRIL BAILEY, 'Virgil and Lucretius', P.C.A., 1931.
48. L. P. WILKINSON, 'Expressiveness in Georgics', I, 43–392 (pp. 74–83 of *Golden Latin Artistry*), Cambridge, 1963.

(*b*) *Structure and Purpose*

49. L. P. WILKINSON, 'The intention of Virgil's Georgics', *G. & R.*, 1950.

50. G. E. DUCKWORTH, 'Virgil's Georgics and the Laudes Galli', *A.J.Ph.*, 1959.

51. W. LIEBESCHUETZ, 'Beast and man in the Third Book of Virgil's Georgics', *G. & R.*, 1965.

52. JAMES MOUNTFORD, 'The architecture of the Georgics', *P.V.S.*, 1966/7.

(*c*) *The Golden Age and the Role of* Labor

53. I. S. RYBERG, 'Virgil's Golden Age', *T.A.P.A.*, 1958.

54. L. P. WILKINSON, 'Virgil's Theodicy', *C.Q.*, 1963.

(*d*) *Technical Aspects*

55. L. A. S. JERMYN, 'Virgil's agricultural lore', *G. & R.*, 1949.

56. L. A. S. JERMYN, 'Weather-signs in Virgil', *G. & R.*, 1951.

57. K. D. WHITE, 'Virgil's knowledge of arable farming', *P.V.S.*, 1967/8.

## Other Augustan Didactic

58. C. O. BRINK, *Horace on Poetry*, Cambridge, 1963.

59. T. F. HIGHAM, 'Ovid: some aspects of his character and aims', *C.R.*, 1934.

60. L. P. WILKINSON, *Ovid Recalled*, pp. 120–43, Cambridge, 1955.

61. E. J. KENNEY, 'Nequitiae Poeta', *Ovidiana*, ed. Herescu *Les Belles Lettres*, Paris, 1958.
    (Reminiscences of Lucretius and Virgil in the *Ars Amatoria*)

## Later Didactic (see also 26g)

62. D. R. DUDLEY, 'Some Literary Descendants of the Georgics', *P.V.S.*, 1964/5.

63. M. RØSTVIG, *The Happy Man*, 2 vols., Blackwell, 1958.
    (Studies the influence of Roman idealization of country life and of related Virgilian attitudes upon English poetry of the seventeenth and eighteenth centuries)

64. L. P. WILKINSON, 'The Georgics in After Times', Ch. X of (44) above.

# VI

# Epic Poetry
## *David Gaunt*

*In order to deal with this immense subject in the space available, it has been necessary to assume that the reader has to hand the following texts, with translations if required:*
Homer, Iliad *and* Odyssey
*Apollonius Rhodius,* Argonautica
*Valerius Flaccus,* Argonautica
*Virgil,* Aeneid
*Lucan,* Bellum Civile (=Pharsalia)

*The Bibliography gives a complete list, under authors in alphabetical order, of most works referred to in the text, together with some others. In the text and footnotes all works of criticism are referred to simply by the author's name and year of publication: reference to the appropriate section of the Bibliography will immediately give the full title, etc. The text is primarily intended for continuous reading by students: the footnotes give documentation and further reading.*

## Introduction: I. The Nature of Epic

1 Epic is the oldest literary 'genre' in European history. With Homer it springs into being fully formed, mature in its techniques, and presenting to the reader or listener a complete world of its own, three-dimensional and alive, as different from the twentieth century as J. R. R. Tolkien's world of Mordor and Minas Tirith,[1] yet wholly credible and convincing. From

this fountain-head, resembling a spring of clear water which springs suddenly and in full flood from limestone slopes, a great river of poetry runs through western literature.[2] It would be impossible in one chapter to give full factual information even about classical epic; our purpose here is rather to create a frame of mind in which epic can be approached and to suggest certain tools which may be employed in order to obtain a right understanding of the poetry. This will be done largely by reference to the text of the poems, and in this connection it is necessary to say that, useful as translations may be to give an 'aerial view' of a poem too long for the student to manage in the original, no translation can ever be more than a makeshift; the colour, shape, and very being of the poem under consideration are all lost when the forms of another language are obtruded. Epic is, by reason of its length, particularly liable to be studied in translation; yet, as Bruno Snell says,[3] 'We can become acquainted with the ideas of foreign peoples only when we receive them in the language in which they are expressed.' Not only are 'intellectual systems' untranslateable but poetry is by its nature fragile, and the message which is being broadcast can be received only by an apparatus directly in contact with the transmitter. The point may be briefly illustrated: probably even so much proof will be unnecessary for anyone who has enough command of the language to hear even a faint and distant signal from that lost world.

2 Homer is describing (*Od.* XIII. 79 f.) the return of Odysseus from the magical island of Phaeacia to his own Ithaca – a return from fairyland to reality. Odysseus falls asleep on deck:

καὶ τῷ ἥδυμος ὕπνος ἐπὶ βλεφάροισιν ἔπιπτε,
νήγρετος ἥδιστος, θανάτῳ ἄγχιστα ἐοικώς.

1. In *The Lord of the Rings*, Allen and Unwin, 1954.
2. Cf. C. M. Ing in Cassell's *Encyclopaedia of Literature*: 'The only ages and temperaments to which epic is entirely alien are the blasé and the commercial.'
3. B. Snell, 1961, p. 10.

Meanwhile the ship runs on:

ἡ δ’, ὥς τ’ ἐν πεδίῳ τετράορες ἄρσενες ἵπποι
πάντες ἅμ’ ὁρμηθέντες ὑπὸ πληγῇσιν ἱμάσθλης
ὑψόσ’ ἀειρόμενοι ῥίμφα πρήσσουσι κέλευθον,
ὣς ἄρα τῆς πρύμνη μὲν ἀείρετο, κῦμα δ’ ὄπισθε.
πορφύρεον μέγα θῦε πολυφλοίσβοιο θαλάσσης.

Something of the quality of this brilliantly evocative formulaic diction is caught by T. E. Lawrence, who, more than any other translator, seems aware of the poetry of Homer: 'The stern of the ship towered and shuddered and sank again towards the huge dark waves of the clamorous sea ever rushing in behind.' The colour of the original is here, but not the brocaded stiffness of the fabric; and above all, the movement of the verse is lost, with all that this implies for the 'spell-binding' which is an essential of all poetry, and especially of the greatest. Yet it is rare to find a version which comes as near even as this to the quality of the original.

## II. The Two Types of Epic

3 The *Iliad*, the *Odyssey*, the *Aeneid*, and *Paradise Lost* are all epic poems, but there is an important distinction to be made: and although all such categories are in some degree arbitrary, we may agree to call the first two 'primary' and the others 'secondary'.[4] By 'primary' epic is meant that type of poetry which stems directly from heroic deeds and is composed in the first instance in order that such deeds may not be forgotten.[5] This type of composition is noticed at *Iliad* ix. 186 ff., where the Achaean embassy finds Achilles playing on his lyre and singing the κλέα ἀνδρῶν, the 'glorious deeds of men'. The purpose of such singing is practical (it keeps the 'record' alive and gives pleasure to those participating). It makes use of 'formulaic' techniques (cf. §1 below) and describes a real world, however much glamour may be imparted in the process; this is particu-

4. Cf. C. S. Lewis, 1942, cc. III–VII.
5. Cf. *Beowulf*, 867 ff. and 2105 ff. (See J. de Vries, 1959, pp. 166 ff.)

larly noticeable in the *Chanson de Roland*, where deeds evidently superhuman are attributed to the heroes (e.g. the sound of human horns does not in real life penetrate 'thirty leagues'),[6] yet all readers correctly feel that the poem is basically a description of something which actually happened.

4 'Secondary' epic is a quite different type of poetry. It may deal with an existing legend, but that legend becomes something in the poet's head which he feels at liberty to alter as he wishes. Thus Apollonius Rhodius, in his *Argonautica*, follows a legendary outline, much as Greek tragedy does, but he invents incidents and alters characterization as he chooses. For example, the character of Medea in Book III is drawn with deep psychological insight, and her 'moment of doubt' at III, 645 ff. is as convincing as the hesitations of Mary Hardy at the end of Charles Morgan's *Sparkenbroke*.[7] It seems likely also that in the same poem the wanderings of the Argonauts along the Danube, the Po, and the Rhone are invented by the poet as a consequence of his own geographical interests.

5 In this kind of poem, composed at leisure, fully revised, and available for reading and re-reading (whether silently or aloud), the entertainment is more sophisticated, and the 'story', which was of vital importance in 'primary' epic, is reduced to the level of being only one among many components. Much is imagined and imaginary, so that (and this is especially true of Virgil and Milton) a new world is created. The combination of the poet's 'seeing eye' and his personal style together create something which is not based on reality but has a life of its own to be transmitted to the mind of the reader. Thus in *Paradise Lost*, IV. 131 ff., where we find Satan approaching the Garden of Eden, the site of Paradise with its cedar trees is described, and then:

> Yet higher than their tops
> The verdurous wall of Paradise up sprung:

6. Penguin tr., p. 119.
7. *Sparkenbroke*, Bk. VI, Ch. 4.

Which to our general Sire gave prospect large
Into his nether Empire neighbouring round.
And higher than that wall a circling row
Of goodliest trees load'n with fairest fruit,
Blossoms and fruits at once of golden hue
Appear'd, with gay enamelled colours mixed.[8]

This is a newly created world of the imagination which we have no right to expect from Homer, although we do find traces of it in the *Odyssey*, as, for example, at VII. 84 ff., where the riches and peculiarities of Phaeacia are imagined and described in a way which is hardly less vivid than Milton's description of Paradise.

6 A further characteristic of 'secondary' epic is that it may concern itself with a theme which is more abstract than the type available to 'primary' epic. It is true that the *Iliad* describes the abstract 'wrath of Achilles', and not merely the siege of Troy; but the wrath is clearly depicted in the events, which themselves form a strong narrative base. In the *Aeneid*, and still more in *Paradise Lost*, it is the theme (the greatness of Rome, the Fall of Man) which dominates, and incidents are introduced (e.g. Anchises' 'preview' of Roman history at the end of *Aeneid* VI) which are necessary if the poet's intention is to be executed, but are far from being demanded by the development of the story.

7 Where this happens, it may well be that the poet is not able also to sustain the characterization with quite the same intensity. Many readers have felt dissatisfied with Aeneas, not merely through an English dislike of priggishness ('*Sum pius Aeneas . . .*') but because he does not convince them of his reality. This is perhaps because, in the interests of his theme, Virgil has made Aeneas a repository of a very wide range of virtues – so wide that he ceases to be a human entity, or more particularly an epic character in a heroic world, and becomes instead a mere collection of *mores Romani*. Milton triumphantly

8. Detailed analysis in C. S. Lewis, 1942, pp. 49–51.

overcomes this difficulty in the case of Satan, but the impossibility of characterizing God the Father has been too much even for his genius.

8 The broad distinction between 'primary' and 'secondary' epic is thus made clear, as is the fact that neither kind is 'better' than the other. We should perhaps add that the epics of Apollonius Rhodius, Valerius Flaccus, and (still more) William Morris are, for all their charm and readability, a sub-species of their own, which may be entitled 'faded primary'. They use the mechanism and even some of the language of 'primary' epic: they do not take a 'theme', as Milton and Virgil do, but seek rather to re-create a past world of heroism seen through the eyes of a poet who is essentially an antiquarian enjoying a picture of something which he has never in fact experienced for himself. In these poets we find that psychological subtleties, which are in fact anachronisms, are the main new contribution. This happens in Virgil also, but it does not offend in the case of Aeneas, who, as we shall see (§3), moves in an 'inflated' world of the poet's imagining; it is less persuasive in the versions of the *Argonautica*, which do purport to be a restatement of the familiar Homeric setting.

## §1. Homer

9 The *Iliad* and the *Odyssey* appear to have come down to us substantially as they were known to the Athenians of the sixth century B.C. The Greeks themselves attributed both poems to a single author, although some of them, observing great differences in tone between the two poems, offered the hypothesis that Homer wrote the *Iliad* in his prime and the *Odyssey* in old age.[9] D. L. Page[10] offers strong evidence from the vocabulary of the two poems to show that in fact they are more likely to have come from different sources. However that may

9. Cf. '*Longinus*', IX 13: ἄθεν ἐν τῇ 'Οδυσσείᾳ παρεικάσαι τις ἂν καταδυομένῳ τὸν "Ομηρον ἡλίῳ – 'And therefore in the Odyssey one would liken Homer to the sun when it is setting.'

10. 1955, Ch. VI. (G. S. Kirk, 1962, takes a similar view.)

be, both poems are certainly the products of a poetic tradition very different from anything which has been common in Europe since the introduction of writing. They are both 'oral' or 'bardic' poems designed to interest an audience which looked to the bard for entertainment, much as our civilization looks to the television set. The bard carries in his head many stories about the heroic past, and the audience may ask for any which they happen to fancy: or the bard may tell whatever tale he pleases (cf. *Od.* VIII. 72 ff.). Such stories, whatever their period, are traditional, and although they spring in most cases from a kernel of fact (such as the campaign of Charlemagne in Spain in A.D. 777 and the death of his son Roland in the Pass of Roncesvalles), they are not 'historical' in the sense of attempting to give an accurate narrative of what happened so long ago. The bard describes not what happened but, as Aristotle says,[11] the kind of thing that is likely to happen: he is concerned with men, their deeds and their passions, and although he would claim, if questioned, to be telling the truth, it is a truth which has been altered, varied, and refined through the years so as to conform more completely than the reality may have done with the bard's idea of what is convincing.

10 When the bard is called upon for some such story as that of the Wooden Horse he does not, as it were, play back a tape-recording. He draws on two sources: his knowledge of the story as transmitted by his predecessors, and his knowledge of certain poetic formulae which centuries of bardic singing have proved useful and convenient – useful because they cover a wide range of heroic or natural activity, and convenient because they fit appropriately into the hexameter line. The formulae may extend to a whole paragraph[12] (e.g., *Il.* III. 330 ff., where Paris arms himself, and ten out of the eleven lines are 'from stock'); or a passage may be a skilful pastiche of smaller sections of formulaic diction.[13] The bard also has at his disposal

11. *Poetics*, 1451a, 37, οἷα ἂν γένοιτο.
12. Cf. J. B. Hainsworth, 1966.
13. Cf. Milman Parry, 1930, and W. Whallon, 1961.

different epithets for each of his major heroes which will fit the name in question so as to fill in as much of the line as may be required. Thus Odysseus may be δῖος 'Οδυσσεύς or πολυτλὰς δῖος 'Οδυσσεύς. Telemachus, if his name occurs after the caesura, will be Τηλέμαχος θεοειδής; alternatively, occupying a syllable more, he may be 'Οδυσσῆος φίλος υἱός. (There is great economy in the use of these formulae, and it is rare to find a pair of adjective–noun phrases which are in all respects interchangeable.) A very great part of the Homeric epic is composed of formulaic diction of this type, and it is clear that the bard, in such circumstances, shows his powers more by selection from a stock of themes than by the creation of new ones, and more by the extent of his knowledge of existing formulae than by adding to the repertoire. This is not to say that he will never invent a new phrase or line: he may well do so, and will no doubt use it in his own singing; whether such a phrase will thereafter go into the common stock will depend upon his successors' estimate of its popularity and effectiveness.[14]

11 It cannot be too much emphasized that the process described above is essentially *not* the reproduction of a memorized text, but the re-creation, in memorized formulae, of a story known to the singer and remade by him for a particular occasion. He will vary his story according to the time available and according to his assessment of the interests and capacity of his audience. What actually happens on such occasions has been well described by A. B. Lord,[15] who gives a vivid picture of modern Jugoslav singers of heroic poetry. It is clear, however, from the quality of the Jugoslav lays so far published, which are much inferior to the *Iliad* and *Odyssey*, that we must not necessarily think of early Greek bards as working in exactly the same way as their modern Jugoslav counterparts: both in metrical complexity and in imaginative quality, Homer is on a quite different level.[16]

14. Milman Parry, 1930, p. 146, goes even further.
15. A. B. Lord, 1960, Ch. II. Cf. also C. M. Bowra, 1952.
16. Cf. Adam Parry, 1966: and for a different view, J. de Vries, 1959, Ch. I.

12 It may perhaps be objected that under the conditions described above there can never be any one creative poet to whom an epic may be ascribed: any given poem must be the product of a long period of transmission[17] during which a bard learns from his elders and transmits to his juniors, making only very small contributions of his own. It is certainly true that the formulaic style, with its stiff 'embroidered' quality, must go right back into the Mycenaean period, and it seems likely that bards were singing in this way for centuries before the sack of Troy. This can be seen from the fact that some of the objects described by Homer can be shown to have a Bronze Age provenance: e.g. the curious 'boar's tusk helmet' (cf. *Il*. X, 261–5) certainly had Mycenaean and Minoan ancestry,[18] as also did the big shields ἤυτε πύργος such as the one described in *Il*. VIII, 267 ff. The Homeric poems are an amalgam whose origins go back a very long way, and research shows that, with care, we may find in Homer interesting sidelights on the Mycenaean period.[19]

13 So far, then, we have not found much scope for individuality in the poet or singer. But one must remember that, as in photography, choice of viewpoint and selection of the relevant are important, and that at every performance the bard is constantly choosing[20] to suit the occasion. Furthermore, by general consent the *Iliad* and the *Odyssey* are not, like much of the Icelandic sagas, shapeless or annalistic narratives: they are (with certain qualifications) artistic unities, so that the *Iliad* tells of the wrath of Achilles rather than the sack of Troy, and the *Odyssey* tells of the return of Odysseus rather than his wanderings. In each case the plot is very carefully controlled, and in the *Odyssey* we have an elaborate 'stranded' narrative of the type used by J. B. Priestley in his *Good Companions*: the stories of different participants are separately told and then carefully

17. Similarly with the *Chanson de Roland*: cf. J. de Vries, 1959, p. 32.
18. Cf. Wace and Stubbings, 1963, p. 516.
19. Further information: D. L. Page, 1959, Ch. VI.
20. Cf. A. B. Lord, 1960, p. 13: 'An oral poem is not composed *for* but *in* performance.'

brought together for the finale. This is combined with the 'flash-back' technique, whereby we plunge at once into the middle of the story: earlier details are filled in later by Odysseus in Phaeacia, where he tells his story before King Alcinous (*Od.* IX. 19 ff). Finally the characterization throughout each of the poems remains remarkably consistent. It is true that in some degree they are type-characters,[21] which makes consistency easier, and this was probably inevitable under 'bardic' conditions; but most readers will feel that they would recognize Odysseus or Eumaeus almost, though perhaps not quite, as readily as they would Emma or Mr Micawber, and this in itself is an achievement which suggests a single creative and controlling mind. How are we to reconcile these facts with what was previously said about the formulae?

14 Thanks to Milman Parry and A. B. Lord, we have a good knowledge of how, over a period of several centuries, the *Odyssey* and *Iliad* were probably performed; what we do not know is when and by whom they were first written down. Bards have no need of writing, and in fact the evidence from Jugoslavia suggests that the arrival of writing leads to the decline and eventual extinction of oral techniques. The poems themselves do not specifically refer to writing, although the σήματα λυγρά ('baneful signs') of *Iliad* VI. 168, which were intended to bring about the death of Bellerophon, are presumably a memory of the Linear 'B' script. It is not surprising that this specialized syllabary, known apparently only to a closed guild of writers and used simply for the bureaucratic record-systems of the great Mycenaean palaces, should have lapsed completely with the break-up of the Mycenaean empire at the end of the twelfth century B.C. We know approximately when the Greek world again became literate, this time using its own version of the Phoenician alphabet. There is strong evidence for written codes of laws in the Greek states by the mid-seventh century B.C.;[22] and it would seem that, as writing became

21. Yet cf. *Il.* IX. 308 ff., where Achilles' rejection of the first embassy goes far beyond the normal anger of the quick-tempered hero.

22. Cf. also Wace and Stubbings, 1963, Ch. XXIII, with bibliography.

common, so the craft of the ἀοιδός, or bard, declined, until, perhaps at Athens under Pisistratus, it became necessary, if the poems were to be preserved, to institute a quite different type of performance, that given by rhapsodes. In this the lyre of the bard disappeared and the performer was equipped only with a ῥάβδος or staff; and the poems were recited as wholes, one rhapsode beginning ἐξ ὑπολήψεως ('in sequence') where another left off. This was a memorized performance, presumably based on a standard text, and it is this standard text which the supposed 'Pisistratean' recension may have supplied.

15 If this account is correct the Homeric poems were being recited, in much the form transmitted to us, at the Panathenaic festivals some time before 527 B.C. The question which remains unsolved is where, in the development of the poems, we should look for 'Homer' himself; or, to be more precise, for the great figure or figures who finally cast the *Iliad* and the *Odyssey* into the evidently artistic and considered form in which we know them. It is clear that we should expect to find 'Homer' late in the development of the poems. First, it seems more likely, under the conditions of oral poetry which have been described, that the moulder of shortish lays suitable for an evening's entertainment into a single long poem should arise late rather than early in the history of the poems. Secondly, there was no need for a long poem until the emergence of the Panathenaic festival,[23] and under 'oral' conditions poems which are not needed are not likely to be produced. Yet, for reasons given in the previous paragraph, it does not seem that a great oral poet can long survive the advent of the written word. Logical considerations would seem to give the eighth century B.C.[24] as the most likely date for 'Homer's' lifetime; but one must emphasize that 'logical considerations', although they are all we have to go on, may well be erroneous.

16 When all this has been said, we may feel that we have a

23. Cf., however, H. T. Wade-Gery, 1952.
24. For a different view, cf. J. de Vries, 1959, p. 19: A Lesky, 1966, pp. 37 ff. See also G. S. Kirk, 1966.

better understanding of the Homeric poems, but that the reason for their greatness still eludes us. The best reason is perhaps that they fulfil C. S. Lewis's requirement:[25] 'The imagined world of the poem must have a consistency and vitality which lay hold of the mind. . . . It should remain with us as a stubborn memory like some real place where we have once lived – a real place with its characteristic smells, sounds and colours: its unmistakeable and irreplaceable "tang".' The world of Homer is presented to us in exactly this way, whether it be the field of battle, with its closely observed scenes of fighting and sudden death, or the subtler colours of Ithaca or the land of the Cyclopes. It would be difficult, for example, to find a more evocative passage in all European literature than *Odyssey* IX. 116–151, where Odysseus describes an islet on which his ships are eventually beached. The scene, with its sharply etched picture of an island harbour, complete with fresh-water spring and cypress trees surrounding a deep-water anchorage, is a model of vivid compression, and the moment of approach through darkness and mist, as the breakers are heard but not seen, has complete authenticity.

17 Effects such as this are obtained in a rather curious way. One would expect that such vividness would need a vocabulary full of words and phrases of a compelling power. Yet there is nothing in Homer either of Keats's 'magic casements' or of the consciously fresh-minted words of a Dylan Thomas with his 'sun-honeyed cobbles of the humming streets' and his 'bird-ounced boughs'. Homer is using the rounded pebbles of formulae smoothed and polished by centuries of bardic technique; yet the effect on the imagination is no less profound, and perhaps more lasting, than the striking word-coinages of our own contemporaries. It is worth considering how this effect is obtained: (*a*) The mere repetition of phrases creates an illusion of genuineness and reality. Just as, in E. M. Forster's[26] phrase, a 'flat' character in a novel becomes more credible with each

25. In Charles Williams' *Arthurian Torso*, p. 190.
26. Cf. *Aspects of the Novel*, Ch. IV.

successive appearance, however brief, so Homer's world, with its steady recurrence of normal events, each with its standard designation, becomes firmly imprinted on the mind. (*b*) Against this firmly drawn back-cloth, characters are depicted whose actions are heroic but wholly credible, because they are based on instincts fundamental to all human beings in a crisis. Thus the famous scene at *Iliad* VI. 390 ff. (Hector and Andromache) is effective because the thoughts are those which must be common to any husband and wife in wartime, when the man is carrying heavy responsibility and is about to leave on a dangerous mission. (The effect of the helmet-plume on the baby Astyanax is equally 'human', though a little surprising in a poem of this date; we should have expected it in Apollonius, but perhaps not in Homer.) (*c*) The 'neutrality' of a formulaic diction allows the reader to feel for himself, much as anyone who reads aloud today must not put too much emotion into his words but must leave room for the hearer's active participation.[27] The effect of this technique is that one's imagination is always ready to supply what the poet leaves implicit, as, for example, at *Iliad* III. 156-8, where Helen's beauty is hinted at rather than described.

18 There are two other features of Homer's style which help to produce his characteristic 'flavour'. They are the catalogue and the simile. The best example of a catalogue is at *Iliad* II. 484 ff.,[28] where a muster-roll of the Achaean host is given. Such lists are tedious to the modern reader, but they appear in other early oral epics and were evidently valued in their day as a form of history. Facts are easier to remember when they are in metre, as learners of Kennedy's gender-rhymes have found. The simile, whether short (Patroclus crying, Achilles says, 'like a silly girl' – *Il.* XVI. 7-8) or long (e.g. *Il.* II. 141-7) is constantly in use. Sometimes the effect is that of a spotlight which briefly

27. Cf. Scholes and Kellogg, 1966, p. 166, where the story of David and Bath-Sheba is used to illustrate 'the fundamental understatedness of primitive narrative'. See also C. Day Lewis, *The Lyric Impulse*, Lecture 3.

28. Cf. D. L. Page, 1959, pp. 118 ff.; C. M. Bowra, 1930, Ch. IV. For Virgil, cf. A. M. Guillemin, 1951,[2] pp. 226 ff.

illuminates a point of interest; when, however, the poet moves away from the immediate point and the simile becomes 'long-tailed' (cf. Milton, *P.L.*, I. 287 ff.) it will often be found that the mood of the expanded simile fits closely the mood of the poem at that moment.[29] The image is often based on the world of nature, and much of Homer's finest poetry will be found in these sections.[30] The general effect on the reader is like that of a painting of the Netherlands School, in which, behind the main action in the foreground, we glimpse through a window a brilliant miniature scene showing men at work or a pastoral landscape. It is worth noticing that in many cases the figures are drawn from the painter's or poet's own world; other similes appear to be 'formulaic', and may go back to the Mycenaean period.[31]

## §2. The Story of the Golden Fleece

19 This famous tale appears to contain all the ingredients of a high-grade narrative. The young hero, unjustly excluded from the throne which is his by rights, is dispatched by his wicked uncle on a quest for an ancestral possession. Collecting a band of heroic followers, he sails in a magical ship, and after a succession of adventures reaches his destination; there, helped by a beautiful princess and sorceress to complete a series of ordeals imposed by her father, he finally obtains the object of his quest. Escaping with the princess, whom he later marries, the hero returns home by an even more hazardous route, dispossesses the wicked uncle, and takes his rightful place as king of his country. Such is the story of the Argonauts. Brilliantly treated by Pindar (518–438 B.C.) in one of his most striking lyric narratives (*Pythian* IV. 70–261), it was also the theme of Apollonius Rhodius (third century B.C.) in his neo-Homeric *Argonautica*, of Valerius Flaccus (first century A.D.) in a Latin *Argonautica* of Virgilian tone, and of William Morris (1834–96)

29. Cf. C. R. Beye, 1966, pp. 104 ff.
30. Examples for study: *Od.* v. 488–90; *Il.* VIII. 555 ff.
31. Cf. C. M. Bowra, 1930, Ch. VI.

in his *Life and Death of Jason*, which although intolerably prolix, has many moments of vivid colour. In spite of the attractive material, none of these poems, taken as a whole, can be regarded as better than second-rate; each has its merits, and the third book of Apollonius Rhodius shows great psychological intensity in its analysis of a heroine driven by forces beyond her control; but none of them succeeds in creating an epic whole.[32] The verdict is not in dispute, and it may be profitable to consider the reason for the successive failures.

20 The basic difficulty resides in the character of the hero. If this poem is ever to be a unity it must become such by reason of Jason's heroic qualities. The nature of the poem will place him, like Odysseus, in a series of tight corners, and he will have under his command a crew composed not of faceless Ithacans returning home after a ten-year siege but of all the elder heroes of Greek myth; the catalogues given by Apollonius (I. 18–227) and Valerius Flaccus (who shrewdly defers the list till I. 350, when his story is under way) are muster-rolls of great names. If Jason is to control such figures as Heracles, Peleus, and Meleager he must show himself to be a super-hero, resilient and resourceful. Yet in fact he is far from doing this: as a single example, his defeatism after the passing of the Symplegades (Ap. II. 619 ff.) may be cited; there are many similar occasions.[33] Even in Colchis he can do nothing without the help of Medea's magic charms, whether in his ordeal with the fire-breathing oxen or in the final theft of the dragon-guarded fleece. It is true that Homeric heroes also derive help from external sources, but both Odysseus and Achilles are 'mighty men of valour' whose strength and endurance are repeatedly proved; Jason, on the other hand, obtains the command only after Heracles has refused it (Ap. I. 331–62), and even his liaison with Medea has an unhappy look of expediency.

32. It is true that Valerius Flaccus' work is unfinished, but we have enough before us to show that he is not likely to have improved on Apollonius' version of the return voyage.

33. 'It is not the presence of human faults which destroys him as a hero; it is the lack of heroic virtues' (J. Carspecken, 1952, p. 102).

21 All this has led Gilbert Lawall[34] to speak of Apollonius' Jason as an 'anti-hero' who is gradually educated against his will by a series of different adventures; even when the multiform experience of the outward voyage is over, it is only for a brief moment, in his fight against the bulls, that he attains heroic dignity; thereafter he is compelled to rely on flight and treachery in order to put to sea. He is 'a man of resounding success whom no reader has ever found himself able to admire'[35] (p. 168). Mr Lawall adds: 'This Jason is the creation of a poet with a largely pessimistic vision of man and the world.' But an epic cannot be based on such a figure; even the *Aeneid*, as we shall see, is weakened by its concessions to such a viewpoint.

22 Neither Valerius Flaccus nor William Morris is successful in correcting this fault. It is true that Valerius Flaccus introduces a new theme at Colchis, where Jason is immediately induced to fight for King Aeetes, Medea's father, against the rebel Perses; Jason (among others) acquits himself well in this fighting, and thereby affords a plausible pretext for Medea's falling in love; but the fighting is so prolonged and the whole episode so loosely attached to the plot that it becomes excessively tedious. Moreover, the poet's attention is concentrated at least as much on the fighting in general as on Jason in particular, and one cannot help feeling that the author is pandering to the contemporary love of mere carnage. William Morris's Jason is no more effective, and his whole poem, once Argo sails for home, falls away into a series of discursive episodes in which Jason plays no dominant part.[36]

23 Combined with this weakness of the central figure there is the tendency of all Alexandrian poetry to concentrate on individual scenes. (This can be well seen in the *Mimes* of Herodas and in such poems as the *Adoniazusae* of Theocritus.[37])

34. G. Lawall, 1966.
35. Cf. the equally anti-heroic Jason of Euripides' *Medea*.
36. Morris, however, by giving us a long account of Jason's childhood and by holding him more frequently before our gaze, does give him a greater degree of importance.
37. Cf. also the 'Orpheus and Eurydice' episode in *Georgic* IV, 452 ff.

Apollonius tends to string beads onto a necklace – compare the abduction of Hylas (I. 1207–39) and Polydeuces' defeat of Amycus at boxing (II. 1–163); Valerius even adds a completely new episode in Hercules' rescue of Hesione (II. 451–578); but these 'beads', though admirably worked, are really self-contained units which positively break up the structure of the poem. We thus have the paradoxical conclusion that in Homer, where a looseness of structure due to oral techniques might have been pardoned, the design is firm and unified,[38] yet the Argonautic poets, writing at leisure for a literate public, all fail to control their material or to make their poems into unities. Nor is this surprising; for, in spite of its superficial attractiveness, the story of the *Golden Fleece* is not in fact well adapted to the demands of epic. Many episodes on the way to Colchis, which must by tradition be included, such as the abduction of Hylas, the defeat of Amycus, and the story of Phineus, do little or nothing for the central character. Similarly, after the Fleece has been won, Argo must sail back to Thessaly by a roundabout route of high geographical implausibility; this gives scope for such episodes as William Morris's 'winter in the North' (Book XII):

> For day passed day, and yet no change they saw
> In the white sparkling plain without a flaw,

or Apollonius' fantastic portage across North Africa (IV. 1380 ff.), combined with an unlikely reappearance of Heracles, who was so conveniently 'lost' in Book I. Yet all these episodes are really contrivances, for in fact Argo could have returned home via the Bosphorus, now that the Clashing Rocks have lost their power to move (cf. Ap. II. 604–5). Such episodes as are to be included on the return should be made to centre on Jason himself; yet actually in all three poems they are a mere excuse for pictorial geography[39] (cf. W. Morris's fine picture

38. Consider, for example, how the figure of Odysseus dominates the early books of the *Odyssey*, when the narrative is primarily concerned with Telemachus.

39. Apollonius, both here and elsewhere, is also frequently led aside into learned 'Baedekerisms': cf. II. 841 ff.

of the Garden of the Hesperides in Book XIV), together with unavailing attempts, in the case of Apollonius, to keep the Colchians in the story by introducing an expeditionary force, faint but pursuing, in (of all unlikely places) the kingdom of Phaeacia, where it takes all the diplomacy of the legendary King Alcinous to bring about a satisfactory settlement. Valerius' poem breaks off at the entry to the Danube, so that we are happily spared the huge acreage of tedium which his rhetorical talent might have devised for the homeward journey. Apollonius and William Morris both bring their hero safe home to Iolcus; Apollonius ends lamely:

ἀσπασίως ἀκτὰς Παγασηΐδας εἰσαπέβητε.

*Gladly you disembarked on the shore at Pagasae.*     IV. 1781

whereas W. Morris goes on[40] to give us the full tale of Medea's murder of Pelias (with Jason once again in the background, patiently waiting aboard *Argo* for the agreed signal), and even a sad postscript at Corinth, where the hero is finally killed by a timber falling from the now rotting hulk of the great ship. The difficulty experienced by both authors shows that there is no clearly marked point where the plot can be laid to rest. This is often a problem for the ancient epic poet. It is interesting that even the *Odyssey* as we now have it drifts off in Book XXIV into a sequence of trivialities like a river spilling itself into the desert; only the *Iliad* and the *Aeneid* conclude at all worthily.

24 The instinct of most readers has been to concentrate on the events in Colchis, which are in fact the core of the poem, and upon which all three writers, feeling no doubt that at this point they have matter for a genuine *epyllion*, lavish their talents. Jason's two ordeals, in facing first the fire-breathing bulls and then the dragon, are worthy of a hero, as is the prize of the Fleece itself; Medea is as proper a figure for epic as

---

40. It is worth pointing out that Morris chose as his title not *Argonautica* but *Life and Death of Jason*.

Circe or Nausicaa, of whom indeed she is a kind of blend; and her abduction forms a splendid finale to the successive episodes of heroism, witchcraft, and romance.

25 Yet even here there are difficulties. One concerns the 'celestial machinery' which epic writers (apart from Lucan and Tolkien) have found it hard to avoid. Apollonius handles this most adroitly. The first 166 lines of Book III give us the famous picture of Hera and Athene appealing to Aphrodite for help; Aphrodite can only act through her son, Eros, who is an *enfant terrible* and has to be 'persuaded' with a science-fiction toy from the toy-cupboard of Zeus himself (III. 132–41). This is all done with the lightest of touches, and we feel ourselves spectators at a film in which a group of Hellenistic statuary has come to life. Except for the execution of Aphrodite's project at III. 275 ff., we see no more of the gods until Argo is homeward bound; Apollonius has paid his respects in his own way to the Olympians, and he goes on to give us a fully motivated story on the human level.[41] (Medea, it is true, derives her powers from Hecate, but Hecate is chthonian rather than Olympian.) Medea falls in love; but she knows that love for Jason implies apostasy from her father and her home, and Apollonius brilliantly describes her divided mind (III. 616 ff.) and her thrice-repeated (and finally successful) attempt to batter her way through the closed doors of modesty, shame, and loyalty. The simile of sunlight glancing off moving water on to a house-wall (III. 752 ff.), which Virgil borrows (*Aen.* VIII. 22 ff.), is tellingly introduced. Later, she meets Jason at the shrine of Hecate (III. 948 ff.). The moment is crucial; for the balance of the poem will be disturbed if Jason does not fall in love also. (Notice that 'being in love' is not a state which concerns Homer's heroes; Apollonius' epic world is one which psychologically is close to our own.) He first addresses her much as Odysseus addresses Nausicaa (*Od.* VI. 149–85) in a carefully calculated diplomatist's speech, and we think that Apollonius has failed to see the importance of the moment.

41. But see P. Händel, 1963.

Medea, head over heels in love, is content even with this mere husk of romance; but she looks at Jason, and he looks at her,

*ἱμερόεν φαιδρῇσιν ὑπ᾽ ὀφρύσι μειδιόωντες*

*with lovers' smiles on radiant faces*                          III. 1024

and suddenly he is in love too, and Apollonius is triumphantly over his hurdle. Apollonius has also contrived to make us believe in Medea as a genuine sorceress (cf. III. 828–84), whereas in Valerius it is her character as a young woman in love which is emphasized; Valerius makes the act of Medea's falling in love more credible (cf. VI. 657–80), but in literary quality there can be no doubt of Apollonius' superiority. William Morris also shows to good advantage at this crucial point; his narrative is both (by his standards) concise and also evocative; there is a beautiful pre-Raphaelite touch where Medea is hurrying back to the city after her mysterious rites (Book VII):

> Nor heeded she that by the river side
> Still lay her golden shoes, a goodly prize
> To some rough fisher . . .

Morris also rises to the occasion when Medea puts the dragon to sleep (Book IX):

> . . . till at last
> All feebly by the wondering prince he passed
> And whining to Medea's feet he crept.

The handling of the theft of the fleece is more convincing in Morris than in Valerius, who grotesquely makes Jason use the enchanted serpent as a kind of beanstalk for reaching the upper branches of the tree in which the fleece is kept. Both Apollonius and Morris see the need for instant departure once the fleece has been seized; only Valerius impedes his narrative with a rhetorical appeal by Medea's mother (VIII. 140–70).

26 The reader who seriously and in detail compares the three narratives will not doubt that in this section at least Apollonius

is the best poet. He has taken old, almost threadbare, diction and idiom, and has altered them (e.g. by the omission of formulae) to suit the style of his day; his conception of the gods, though conventional in form, is also fresh in tone, so that the picture of Eros in III. 111–66 is quite unhomeric; and above all, his handling of the relationship between Jason and Medea, whereby Medea remains both princess and sorceress, yet Jason's stature is not diminished by her help, is most impressive. William Morris follows Apollonius quite closely and adds some charming touches (e.g. the 'Old London Bridge' atmosphere of Colchis' 'four bridges fair Set thick with goodly houses everywhere'). Valerius, if read continuously in the Latin, impresses with his sub-Virgilian style[42] (such lines as VII. 21–5, where Medea lies sleepless, are perfectly effective); yet his greatest contribution, the rebellion of Perses, is completely frigid, and introduces large numbers of persons who are mentioned only so that they may at once be bloodily dispatched. Only in Apollonius can the whole section be read with a continuous and unaffected pleasure.

## §3 Ennius, Virgil,* and Lucan

27 C. S. Lewis said of the *Aeneid*: 'With Virgil, European poetry grows up', and 'No man who has once read it with full perception remains an adolescent'.[43] Certainly the reader can have no doubt that the *Aeneid* is a new kind of poem; although Virgil makes his debts to Ennius, Apollonius, and Homer plain enough,[44] it is evident that Propertius was right when he said:

Nescioquid maius nascitur Iliade,

*Something bigger than the Iliad is being born.*          *Eleg.* II. xxxiv. 66

recognizing that Virgil was creating the 'artificial' epic in which the underlying theme (in this case the greatness of Rome) is

* N.B. References to Virgil are always to the *Aeneid* except where otherwise specified.

42. Cf. H. MacL. Currie, 1959.
43. C. S. Lewis, 1942, Ch. VI.
44. See esp. G. N. Knauer, 1964.

what mainly holds the poem together. This theme Virgil owes in part to Ennius, who, annalist though he was, wrote a poem whose fragments often have something of the atmosphere of the *Aeneid.*

28 Of Ennius himself we can only speak briefly. His *Annales*, in eighteen books,[45] are a versified history of Rome down to 171 B.C. He was the first to use the hexameter in Latin, abandoning the native saturnians. Apart from his metre, Ennius owes little to Greek models; his poem is essentially Roman, and in spite of its obvious roughness, contains some magnificent lines, many of which Virgil adapts in the *Aeneid* – e.g.

Quis potis ingentis oras evolvere belli?

*Who can unroll this great war from end to end?*

Loeb, *Fr.* 173; cf. *Aen.* IX. 528

and

Summo sonitu quatit ungula campum.

*With a huge clatter their hooves shake the ground.*

Loeb, *Fr.* 283; cf. *Aen.* VIII. 596

Usually Virgil improves on his original, whom he honours by using in this way, but sometimes he retains the exact words, as at IV. 404:

it nigrum campis agmen,

*The black column crosses the plain.*

where the spondaic rhythm shows the slowness of the motion. (Virgil is describing ants: Ennius, perhaps more appropriately, elephants!) These detailed borrowings are of interest, but more important is the tone in which Ennius describes the death of Romulus[46] or the character of Quintus Fabius Maximus,[47] from which perhaps Virgil draws his feeling for Aeneas as a *pater*

45. Fragments in *O.B.L.V.* and Loeb, *Remains of Old Latin*, I.
46. Loeb, *Fr.* 117–21.
47. Loeb, *Fr.* 360–2.

*patriae* summoned by Fate to a destiny which is sometimes almost more than he can bear.

29 Many critics have felt dissatisfied with the character of Aeneas. The epithet *pius* has been objected to, often by those who do not understand that it means 'dutiful' and is therefore entirely appropriate. His desertion of Dido[48] has regularly caused English readers, with Dryden, to 'doubt there was a fault somewhere'; yet in abandoning Dido Aeneas was returning to his duty

> (Italiam non sponte sequor,
>
> *I am heading for Italy, but not of my own free will.* IV. 361)

and it was Dido, not Aeneas, who considers the liaison as a marriage (cf. IV. 172). Virgil shows us Aeneas undergoing the wanderings of an Odysseus and fighting the battles of an Achilles not for the sake of a longed-for return to wife and family, nor for his personal glory, but because he recognizes this to be the will of heaven (cf. Helenus' prophecy at III. 375–6). It is not surprising if Aeneas' shoulders are bent beneath the load, and modern critics[49] are increasingly aware of this. Readers born after 1918, with their assumption that all empires are wicked, are ill fitted to approach the *Aeneid* sympathetically, and Kipling's *Kim*, with its persuasive emphasis on the virtues of the British Raj in India,[50] should be a compulsory preparation for all intending readers of Virgil. Such phrases as 'Augustan propaganda' are not helpful; the question to be asked is whether or not Virgil succeeds in making an unprejudiced reader sympathize with his theme. Aeneas, in fact, is a model of the traditional Roman virtues – manliness (*virtus*), loyalty (*fides*), a sense of duty (*pietas*), an urge to get on with the

48. For Virgil's debt to Apollonius' *Medea*, cf. R. M. Henry, 1930.

49. Cf. P. Grimal, 1959; F. A. Sullivan, 1959; A. Parry, 1963; S. Clausen, 1964; Brooks Otis, 1964, Ch. VI.

50. Cf. also E. V. Arnold, *Roman Stoicism* (1911), p. 397: 'The great work of Roman government was carried on in silence, just as that of India in the present day.'

job and not waste words (*simplicitas*), and a basic decency (*humanitas*). It may be that Virgil has failed to make his hero credible, perhaps because he does not, except in Book IV, allow him enough human weakness. To say this would be a genuine criticism, but merely to dislike Aeneas' virtues is to show ourselves lacking in imaginative sympathy for qualities formerly held in esteem and now out of fashion.

30 Virgil has not abandoned the narrative framework (which seems essential even to non-oral epic – as also to the novel – if interest is to be maintained), but, in order to stress the theme of Roman greatness, he uses a number of devices, some of which were also used by Homer, though in a different way. For example, in *Iliad* XVIII Achilles' mother, Thetis, procures for him a new set of armour, including a shield, all made by the smith-god Hephaestus. Lines 478–607 contain a long description of scenes from everyday life which are depicted on this shield. It is not necessary here to consider Homer's reasons for including these; at any rate they do not bear closely upon the theme of the Wrath. In *Aeneid* VIII. 626–731 Aeneas is presented by Venus with a similar shield, but in this case the scenes depicted are carefully chosen to give a 'preview' of Roman history.[51] Thus Virgil adapts Homer's device to his own purposes. Elsewhere he makes the narrative itself work for him, as when, at VI. 703 ff., Anchises shows Aeneas, now in the underworld, the unborn souls of Romans destined to be great. It would be surprising indeed if on all these occasions the attempt had been equally successful; Virgil was using a new literary technique, and we know that he never gave the poem its final revision. He himself said:

Tanta incohata res est ut paene vitio mentis tantum opus ingressus videar.

*Such a task has been begun that I think I must have been mad to undertake it.*

---

51. Cf. esp. VIII. 731: *attollens umero famamque et fata nepotum* – 'lifting on his shoulders the glory and the destiny of his descendants'.

31 It is also necessary to admit that the second half of the poem is, despite many fine things, such as the death of Mezentius in Book X, less successful than the first. The fighting in Italy is prolonged and sometimes fails to convince.[52] Virgil dutifully describes the scenes of carnage which are expected in heroic battles, but we feel that his heart is not in them; or at least this would be a natural reaction after *Georgic* II. 367–70, and other passages showing intense sympathy with all living things. The structure, too, gives trouble: for example, in Book VIII,[53] Aeneas' visit to Evander, though it gives the opportunity both for a tour of the future site of Rome and for a contrast between the decadent luxury of Carthage and the heroic simplicity of Pallanteum, takes him inconveniently far from the main centre of operations, and one wonders whether Hector would have allowed himself to be sidetracked in this way. Finally, the *humanitas*[54] which Virgil so stresses in Aeneas does not go well with the butchery which he must perform in these books, and even the death of Turnus in the closing lines of the poem is a concession to savagery;[55] Aeneas would have spared his opponent but for the sight of the belt which Turnus took from Evander's son, Pallas (x. 495–7), and which now provokes an uncontrollable bitterness. Here and elsewhere Virgil regrets the bloodshed, but cannot find any alternative way forward.

32 Something must also be said about the Olympian gods, who appear in the *Aeneid* as they do in Homer and in Apollonius.[56] In Homer we became familiar with a world of gods who are hardly more than super-humans. They live for ever and enjoy great powers, but their morals are worse than those of humans and they make no pretence of a 'spiritual' existence. They have favourites, they bicker, they enjoy food and drink and sex. Virgil takes over the Olympians from Homer, but they are one

52. Cf. V. Pöschl, 1962, pp. 100 ff.
53. Cf. Brooks Otis, 1964, pp. 334–40.
54. Cf. VI. 853: *parcere subiectis* (to spare the beaten enemy).
55. But cf. Brooks Otis, 1964, pp. 371 ff.
56. In Lucan the celestial machinery is no longer found, no doubt because of the poem's Stoic colour; its place is in part taken by prophetic utterance of various kinds. Cf. C. H. Moore, 1921; B. F. Dick, 1963.

of the less satisfactory features of his poem. His tone is more elevated than Homer's, and Aeneas has higher values than Achilles: he is *pius*, he acknowledges *officia* ('duties'), he is the destined founder of a world-empire. But as soon as this high tone is imparted on the human level, it is seen to be unsatisfactory that the Olympians should continue to wrangle about their favourites (cf. IV. 90 ff.) as if this were still Homer's world. No doubt that is why Virgil's scenes in Olympus are often tedious. There is also the fact that Virgil is less successful than Homer in imparting individuality to his gods; they are stiffer, grander, less 'real'. This may well be deliberate; Virgil here and elsewhere 'inflates' both the personalities and the scenery of his epic, but where the gods are concerned the only result is to make us feel that they are intruders. Perhaps this is partly the fault of his period, in which the ancient *numina*, so potent in early Roman religion,[57] were no longer believed in. Certainly when for once (II. 604 ff.) Virgil allows us to imagine his deities not as mere 'out-there' figureheads, but as forces effectively at work in human affairs, the gain in power and vividness is very great.

33 There is a further difficulty to be considered. Throughout the epic tradition there is an opposition, explicit or implicit, between the Olympians, especially Zeus or Jupiter, and the power which Homer calls μοῖρα or αἶσα and Virgil calls *Fatum*.[58] In Homer, although the problem of how far Zeus and μοῖρα agree is never settled, it is no more obtrusive than the problem of how far the remaining Olympians are controlled by the will of Zeus.[59] In the *Aeneid*, however, where Virgil insists from the beginning that Aeneas is a 'chosen vessel' (*fato profugus*, I. 2), the opposition of Juno must appear foolish and unprofitable. Jupiter himself, at x. 96 ff., appears uncertain of his own position in relation to destiny,[60] and temporarily

57. Cf. W. Warde Fowler, *Religious Experience of the Roman People*, 1911, Lecture VI.      58. Cf. H. L. Tracy, 1964.

59. Cf. *Il.* XIII. 10 ff., where Poseidon flagrantly disobeys Zeus' orders.

60. Cf. x. 112–13: *Rex Iuppiter omnibus idem./Fata viam invenient.* (Jupiter is impartial king over all. The Fates will find a way.) For a different view see A. M. Guillemin, 1951², Ch. XII.

abandons his control so that events may take their own course. The picture is not unhomeric, but in Virgil's poem it is inappropriate.[61]

34 We must also mention two qualities which contribute greatly to the total effect of Virgil's style. First there is his technique of 'enlargement', whereby everything in a scene is made to appear not only grander than it can have been in reality but actually 'larger than life'.[62] For example, it is not possible that at the time described Carthage can have contained, even in embryo, the vast theatrical apparatus which Virgil hints at in I. 427 ff.; and the imperial splendour of Dido's hunting-outfit at IV. 133 ff. is more reminiscent of Cleopatra on her state-barge than of the resources which Dido might in reality have commanded. These are only two examples of something which may be felt throughout the poem: e.g. at VII. 373 ff., in the simile where Amata in her frenzy is compared to a spinning-top driven by whips, we observe that the boys in the simile are playing *vacua atria circum* ('around the empty halls'), and at once we see a huge empty 'Palladian' room, as Virgil no doubt intended. (Cf. the description of King Latinus' city and palace at VII. 170 ff., and the 'celestial choir' effect at IX. 111–12.) He wishes us to feel that the setting of his poem is as grand and noble as the events which he describes, and 'enlargement' is one of the means which he employs.

35 Secondly, there is the poet's ability to evoke a mood. This is often most delicately done, and the attentive reader may well be surprised by the way in which the local colour echoes the emotional key of the poem at that moment. As an example, the beginning of Book VIII is worth studying. Aeneas, whose affairs are in no happy state, has been encouraged in a dream by the river-god Tiber to seek aid from King Evander; he duly sacrifices and sets sail upstream. There follow (VIII. 91–6) six lines of memorable description, as the ships are reflected in the

---

61. Notice how skilfully this difficulty is handled in Matthew Arnold's *Balder Dead*. Cf. also A. Guillemin, 1951[1], for an interesting note on Virgil's technique.

62. Cf. A. Parry, 1963.

river: the feeling is of a 'green thought in a green shade', and this mood is entirely appropriate to the tranquil interlude. The effect was certainly intended, and one can only admire the masterly technique by which it has been achieved.[63]

36 To approach Virgil in the right frame of mind may require some effort, but it is nothing by comparison with that needed for Lucan, whose unfinished poem on the Civil War, generally known as the *Pharsalia*, bristles with difficulties for the modern reader. It is annalistic, and one cannot help feeling that Petronius was right when he said (*Satyricon* 118)

non enim res gestae versibus comprehendendae sunt;

*History should not be made the subject of poetry.*

No doubt we should think Ennius' *Annales* tedious if we had the whole poem. The known facts of history prohibit much innovation in the plot, so that inevitably the author's only area of invention is stylistic. In the *Pharsalia* there is no hero; or at least so many candidates have been put forward[64] that it is hard to believe in the claims of any single one. The writing is extremely rhetorical,[65] not only in the speeches but also in the narrative, where Lucan is perpetually looking for verbal effects, many of which seem to us strained both in conception and in expression.[66] The same criticism applies to the similes; a particularly grotesque example occurs at IX. 808–10.[67] Again, the moralist is always looking over the narrator's shoulder, and this effect is fatal to the reader's imagining. A particularly flagrant intrusion occurs in II. 1–15. Furthermore, the sheer vulgarity and sensationalism of the narrative is difficult to accept, as when at VI. 667 ff. the witch Erichtho adds various barely mentionable

---

63. Passages of similar quality: I. 159–69; IX. 806–18 (contrast between violence and tranquillity).

64. Cf. W. E. Heitland, 1887, liii ff.; H. C. Nutting, 1932. (Caesar, Pompey, Cato, the Senate, and Libertas have all been suggested.)

65. Cf. Quintilian, *Inst. Or.*, x. i. 90: *magis oratoribus quam poetis imitandus* (more to be imitated by orators than poets).

66. Cf., e.g., I. 56–9; II. 211–20; VII. 1–6; VIII. 84–5.

67. Cf. also IX. 781–2.

ingredients to her cauldron. Finally, the essential incapacity of Lucan for his task can best be seen in his delineation of character. Here, if anywhere, he had scope for imaginative writing, and it is here that the greatest of his predecessors had been greatest. Thomas Greene says:[68] 'One senses in Achilles . . . measureless reserves of living power . . . equally when he is active and at rest.' Lucan, however, fails through exaggeration to create any such impression, even though in real life some at least of his characters were vivid enough personalities. His Caesar is a double-dyed villain out of melodrama; his Pompey, memorably described in I. 135,

> Stat magni nominis umbra
>
> *a shadow of his former greatness*

is weak and vacillating, and his Cato is so saintly as to be incredible; cf. IX. 886–7, where dying soldiers restrain their groans because of his presence. In Cato there is shown a high idealism which one could respect if Lucan had brought it to life; but his passion for rhetoric has made him too self-conscious a writer to be convincing, at least for us, in whose age rhetoric has become subtler, more visual, and less formal.

37 It would be perfectly fair to reply that Lucan's rhetoric is in the same position as Virgil's patriotism, and that it is the critic's duty to try as hard to sympathize with the former as with the latter. If it were only rhetoric which were in question this would be a just comment; but if one looks for the good points in Lucan the list is short indeed. The poem contains some neat epigrams,[69] and parts of the narrative can be read with enjoyment if one summons up the mood of the viewer of a horror-film. There are also moments when one cannot restrain applause for a talented stroke, as when Cato refuses to consult the oracles of Ammon:

> Ille deo plenus tacita quem mente gerebat
> effudit dignas adytis e pectore voces.

68. *The Norms of Epic*, in *Comparative Literature*, XIII. 3 (1961), 193 ff.
69. E.g. I. 280–1; II. 287; V. 290; and many others.

*Cato, full of the power of God, which he carried in the silence of his mind, brought forth words of oracular quality.*                    IX. 564–5

This ingeniously expresses the Stoic sage's superiority to any oracular verbiage. There is not much else; and perhaps we are wrong in approaching the *Pharsalia* as if it were a true epic. It should rather be thought of as a young enthusiast's exposition of Stoicism, dramatized in rhetorical verse.

# Bibliography

§§1–3 correspond to §§1–3 of the text. Special emphasis has been laid on books published recently, and the obvious histories of literature are excluded unless mentioned in the text. Books of general reference are in §4.

Code: * = available in paperback
      † = specially recommended for background-reading
      B = contains useful bibliography.

§1. Homer

BASSETT, S. E. *The Poetry of Homer*, Berkeley, 1938.

BEYE, C. R. *The Iliad, the Odyssey, and the Epic Tradition*, New York, 1966.   * † B

BOWRA, C. M. *Tradition and Design in the Iliad*, Oxford, 1930.   †

BOWRA, C. M. *Heroic Poetry*, London, 1952.   * † B

COMBELLACK, F. M. 'Contemporary Homeric scholarship', *Cl.W.*, XLIX, 1955.  B

FINLEY, M. I. *The World of Odysseus*, London, 1956.   * † B

HAINSWORTH, J. B. 'Structure and content in epic formulae', *C.Q.*, XIV, 155 ff., 1964.

HAINSWORTH, J. B. 'Joining battle in Homer', *G. & R.*, XIII, No. 2, 158 ff., 1966.

KIRK, G. S. *The Songs of Homer* (Paperback title: *Homer and the Epic*), Cambridge, 1962.   * † B

KIRK, G. S. (ed.), *Language and Background of Homer*, Cambridge, 1964.   *

KIRK, G. S. 'Formular language and oral quality', *Y.C.S.*, XX, 152 ff., 1966.

LORD, A. B. *Singer of Tales*, Harvard, 1960.   * †

NOTOPOULOS, J. A. 'Studies in early Greek oral poetry', *H.S.C.P.*, LXVIII, 1 ff., 1964.

PAGE, D. L. *The Homeric Odyssey*, Oxford, 1955. †

PAGE, D. L. *History and the Homeric Iliad*, California, 1959. * †

PARRY, ADAM, 'Have we Homer's Iliad?' *Y.C.S.*, XX, 175 ff., 1966.

PARRY, MILMAN, *L'Epithète traditionelle dans Homère*, Paris, 1928.

PARRY, MILMAN, 'Studies in epic technique of oral verse-making', I and II, *H.S.C.P.*, XLI, XLIII, 1930, 1932.

RUSSO, J. A. 'Structural formula in Homeric verse', *Y.C.S.*, XX, 217 ff., 1966.

WACE, A. J. B. and STUBBINGS, F. H. (Ed.), *Companion to Homer*, London, 1963. †

WADE-GERY, H. T. *The Poet of the Iliad*, Cambridge, 1952.

WEBSTER, T. B. L. *From Mycenae to Homer*, London, 1958. *

WEIL, S. *The Iliad or the Poem of Force*, Pendle Hill Pamphlet No. 91, Wallingford, Pennsylvania, 1956. *

WHALLON, W. 'The Homeric epithets', *Y.C.S.*, XVII, 97 ff., 1961.

WHITMAN, C. H. *Homer and the Heroic Tradition*, Cambridge, Mass., 1958. * †

WOODHOUSE, W. J. *The Composition of Homer's Odyssey*, Oxford, 1930. †

## §2. The Golden Fleece

CARSPECKEN, J. 'Apollonius Rhodius and the Homeric Epic', *Y.C.S.*, XIII, 33 ff. (esp. 99–140), 1952. † B

CURRIE, H. MACL. 'Virgil and Valerius Flaccus', *V.S.L.S.*, No. 48, 1959.

GARSON, R. W. 'Critical Observations on Valerius Flaccus' Argonautica:

I. *C.Q.*, XIV, 267 ff., 1964.

II. *C.Q.*, XV, 104 ff., 1965.

GILLIES, M. M. *The Argonautica of Apollonius Rhodius*, Bk. III (Intro.), Cambridge, 1928.

HÄNDEL, P. *Die Götter des Apollonios als Personen*, Miscellanea Augusto Rostagni. Torino. 1963.

LAWALL, G. 'Apollonius' Argonautica: Jason as Anti-hero', *Y.C.S.*, XIX, 119 ff., 1966. †

MACKAIL, J. W. *Lectures on Greek Poetry*, 239 ff., London, 1911.

MOONEY, G. W. *The Argonautica of Apollonius Rhodius*, (Intro.), Dublin, 1912; Reprint, Hakkert, Amsterdam, 1964.

RIEU, E. V. *The Voyage of Argo* (tr. with intro.), Harmondsworth. 1959. * †

## §3. Ennius, Virgil, and Lucan

CLAUSEN, W. 'An interpretation of the Aeneid', *H.S.C.P.*, LXVIII, 139 ff., 1964.

DICK, B. F. 'The Technique of Prophecy in Lucan', *T.A.P.A.*, XCIV, 37 ff., 1963.

DILKE, O. A. W. *M. Annaei Lucani de Bello Civili*, Lib. VII (intro.), Cambridge, 1965. †

GRAVES, R. *Lucan, Pharsalia* (tr. with intro.), Harmondsworth, 1956. * †

GRIMAL, P. 'Pius Aeneas', *V.S.L.*, 1959.

GUILLEMIN, A. M. 'L'Inspiration Virgilienne dans la Pharsale', *R.E.L.*, XXIX, 214 ff., 1951.[1]

GUILLEMIN, A. M. *Virgile*, Paris, 1951.[2]

HEFFNER, J. E. 'Bibliographical Handlist on Vergil's Aeneid', *Cl.W.*, LX, 377 ff., 1967. B

HEITLAND, W. E. *Intro. to C. E. Haskin's Ed. of Lucan*, London, 1887.

HENRY, R. M. 'Medea and Dido', *C.R.*, XLIV, 97 ff., 1930.

KNAUER, G. N. 'Virgil's Aeneid and Homer', *G.R.B.S.*, V, 61 ff., 1964.

KNIGHT, W. F. JACKSON, *Roman Vergil*, London, 1944. * †

MAGUINESS, W. S. *Some Reflections on the Aeneid*, V.S.L., 1951.

MARTI, B. M. 'The meaning of the *Pharsalia*', *A.J.Ph.*, LXVI, 352 ff., 1945. †

MARTI, B. M. *Tragic History and Lucan's Pharsalia*, Studies in Honour of B. L. Ullman, I, 165 ff., Rome, 1964.

MORFORD, M. P. O. *The Poet Lucan*, Oxford, 1967.

MOZLEY, J. H. 'Virgil and the Silver Latin Epic', *Proc. Virg. Soc.*, III, 12 ff., 1963–4. †

NUTTING, H. C. 'The Hero of the Pharsalia', *A.J.Ph.*, LIII, 41 ff., 1932.

OTIS, BROOKS, *Virgil – A Study in Civilized Poetry*, Oxford, 1964. † B

PARRY, A. 'The two voices of Virgil's Aeneid', *Arion*, II, 4, 66 ff., 1963.

PERRET, J. *Virgile*, Paris, 1965. * B

PÖSCHL, V. *Image and Symbol in the Aeneid*, Michigan, 1962.

PRESCOTT, H. W. *The Development of Virgil's Art*, New York, 1926; Reprint, 1963.

PUTNAM, M. C. J. *The Poetry of the Aeneid*, Harvard, 1965.

SANFORD, E. M. 'Lucan and his Roman Critics', *Cl.Ph.*, XXVI, 233 ff., 1931. B

SULLIVAN, F. A. 'Spiritual itinerary of Virgil's Aeneas', *A.J.Ph.*, LXXX, 150 ff., 1959.

TRACY, H. L. 'Fata Deum and the action of the Aeneid', *G. & R.*, XI (N.S.), 188 ff., 1964. †

WILLIAMS, R. D. *Virgil*, Oxford., 1967.

WRIGHT, T. E. *The Augustan Poets: see* PLATNAUER, M. (§4).

§4 Miscellaneous (many of these span §§1–3)

ANDERSON, W. D. 'Notes on the simile in Homer and his successors', *C.J.*, LIII, 81 ff., 1957.

BOWRA, C. M. *From Virgil to Milton*, London, 1945. * †

BUTLER, H. E. *Post-Augustan Poetry from Seneca to Juvenal*, Oxford, 1909.

CHAMBERS, R. W. *Beowulf – an Introduction*, Cambridge (3rd ed., 1959).

LESKY, A. *History of Greek Literature*, tr. Willis and de Heer, London, 1966. B

LEWIS, C. S. *A Preface to Paradise Lost*, Oxford, 1942. * †

MOORE, C. H. 'Prophecy in the ancient epic', *H.S.C.P.*, XXXII, 99 ff., 1921.

PLATNAUER, M. *Fifty Years (and Twelve) of Classical Scholarship*, Oxford, 1968. †

RIDLEY, M. R. *Studies in Three Literatures*, London, 1962. †

SCHOLES, R. E. and KELLOGG, R. L. *The Nature of Narrative*, New York and Oxford, 1966. †

SNELL, B. *Poetry and Society*, Indiana, 1961.

SUMMERS, W. C. *The Silver Age of Latin Literature*, London, 1920.

THOMPSON, P. *The Work of William Morris*, London, 1967.

TILLYARD, E. M. W. *The English Epic and its Background*, New York and Oxford (Galaxy Books, 1966), 1953. * †

VRIES, J. DE (tr. TRIMMER, B. J.), *Heroic Song and Heroic Legend*, Oxford, 1959. * †

# VII

# Comedy
*Rosemary Harriott*

1 Nearly forty comedies have come down to us from classical antiquity, the work of two Greek writers, Aristophanes and Menander, and two Roman, Plautus and Terence. The official history of comedy in Athens began in 486 B.C.: from its very earliest years little survives but the names of one or two dramatists and titles of plays, but about 450 a writer called Crates won his first victory at a festival. In the *Poetics*[1] Aristotle links his name with that of the Sicilian Epicharmus, who proably lived about the same time, and says that both wrote general themes and plots. Aristotle says also that Crates' plays were free from lampoons, that is, attacks on named, living individuals. Taking both remarks together, it seems likely that Crates' plays lacked the topicality and political concern that were a feature of much Old Comedy. One of them, at any rate, called the *Animals* after its chorus, depicted a Golden Age in which there was no need of servants, since house-work and cookery were done spontaneously, on the word of command.[2] A slightly older contemporary of Crates, by contrast, was noted for the force of his satire. This was Cratinus, who with Aristophanes and Eupolis was chosen to represent Old Comedy in the way that Aeschylus, Sophocles, and Euripides represent

1. 1449b7.
2. *Frs.* 14–17K; in this chapter the fragments of Greek Comedy are from T. Kock, *Comicorum Atticorum Fragmenta*. An English version of the fragments may be found in J. M. Edmonds, *The Fragments of Attic Comedy*. Aristophanes, Plautus, and Terence are quoted from the Oxford Classical Text.

Tragedy, but whereas we have material for comparing the tragic poets, Cratinus and Eupolis have to be judged from the surviving fragments, sometimes substantial, and from accounts of their plays. Cratinus was a popular writer, winning nine victories, which included the defeat of Aristophanes' *Clouds* in 423 with a play called the *Wine-flask*. One of his chief butts was the statesman Pericles, but he was also a critic of poets and thinkers: besides open attack his methods included parody and mythological burlesque. The Greeks had long seen the comic possibilities of some of their myths, particularly those dealing with Heracles or Odysseus, and writers of Old Comedy used the figures of myth to represent well-known men and women of their own day. In Cratinus' *Dionysalexandros* Dionysus may have represented Pericles; in his *Nemesis* Zeus almost certainly did.

2 Eupolis was another of Aristophanes' rivals, and is known to have been writing between 429 and 412; like Aristophanes, he attacked the demagogues Cleon and Hyperbolus, the sophists and Socrates, and like him, he set a play, the *Demes*, in Hades. Aristophanes himself was born in about 450 and probably lived until about 385. Eleven of his plays survive, of which nine are classified as Old Comedy, while the remaining two have some of the characteristics usually ascribed to Middle Comedy.[3] The next complete play that has come down to us, Menander's *Dyscolos*, written in 317–6, belongs to the category of New Comedy, which is the source of the bulk of plays of Plautus and Terence and through them influenced many European dramatists down to the present day. There is so great a difference between even the last plays of Aristophanes and those of Menander and his contemporaries that we should like to know in much greater detail how and why Comedy changed in the intervening period. Some of the changes, evolutionary rather than revolutionary, are likely to have resulted from the changed political situation of Athens, both internally and in

3. The surviving plays of Aristophanes, like those of Plautus and Terence, are listed at the end of this chapter.

her relationships with other states. The mythological play continues, but concern with public affairs gradually gives way to stories about fictional ordinary people. Professor Handley writes:

> Alongside changes in subjects and attitude, comedy of the fourth century in general shows changes of style and form. Its language tends to the plainness of simple prose or ordinary conversation, losing much of the stylistic variety and the lively scurrilities which characterize Old Comedy as we know it best, from the fifth-century plays of Aristophanes; lyrics become sparse; the chorus declines to a band of interlude performers taking no part in the dialogue; the formal patterns of *agon*, *parabasis*, and scenes alternating with lyric, in strings or in pairs and groups, have all given way by Menander's time to a structure whose essential parts are what we call 'acts': that is, sequences of scenes forming more or less coherent units of composition, and marked off from each other by choral interludes ... In costume, there is little room for decorative elaboration, as with Aristophanes' Wasp-chorus, or his Hoopoe and birds in the *Birds*; the grossness of Old Comedy modifies towards decency; the range of masks worn by the players develops to include standard types suitable for a comedy of manners.[4]

3 Although no complete Greek plays survive by the writers of Middle or New Comedy except Menander, the fragments of their very considerable output are sufficient to give us some idea of their interests and individuality, of the differences between, for example, Antiphanes and Alexis in the earlier period, Diphilus and Philemon later. The fragments can tell us which philosopher or politician was an object of ridicule, what quirks of behaviour, what jokes were found diverting; they can also tell us about frequently represented characters – parasites, disgruntled old men, cooks, hetaeras – and so about some features of the plot. There is space here for no more than three passages from Middle Comedy, the first one of many about food, the second about philosophy, and the last a character-sketch.

4. *Dyskolos*, 4.

(a)  ὅμως δὲ λογίσασθαι πρὸς ἐμαυτὸν βούλομαι
καθεζόμενος ἐνταῦθα τὴν ὀψωνίαν,
ὁμοῦ τε συντάξαι τί πρῶτον οἰστέον,
ἡδυντέον τε πῶς ἕκαστός ἐστί μοι.
οἴσω τάριχος πρῶτον ὡραῖον τοδί.
διωβόλου τοῦτ' ἐστι· πλυτέον εὖ μάλα·
εἶτ' εἰς λοπάδιον ὑποπάσας ἡδύσματα,
ἐνθεὶς τὸ τέμαχος, λευκὸν οἶνον ἐπιχέας,
ἐπεσκέδασα τοὔλαιον· εἶθ' ἕψων ποιῶ
μυελὸν ἀφεῖλόν τ' ἐπιγανώσας σιλφίῳ.

A cook is speaking:

> *And yet*
> *I mean to sit and see what I've to get,*
> *Plan out my first wants, and think how each dish*
> *Should be flavoured. First I'll take this nice salt-fish –*
> *That's twopence – wash it clean as a new pin,*
> *Throw seasoning in the saucepan, put it in,*
> *Pour in some white wine, sprinkle it with oil,*
> *And then, till it's as soft as marrow, boil,*
> *And serve garnished with silphium.*

Alexis 186K (*Ponera*); cf. Menander 462 = 397Kö.,
tr. J. M. Edmonds.

I begin the next quotation after the first speaker has asked his
companion what progress the philosophers Plato, Speusippus,
and Menedemus are making; the second speaker tells how the
Academy students are classifying plants and animals while
Plato stands by, 'very gentle, in no way lacking calm':

(b)  ἀλλ' οἶδα λέγειν περὶ τῶνδε σαφῶς·
Παναθηναίοις γὰρ ἰδὼν ἀγέλην
τινὰ μειρακίων
ἐν γυμνασίοις 'Ακαδημείας
ἤκουσα λόγων ἀφάτων, ἀτόπων·
περὶ γὰρ φύσεως ἀφοριζόμενοι
διεχώριζον ζώων τε βίον
δένδρων τε φύσιν λαχάνων τε γένη·
κᾆτ' ἐν τούτοις τὴν κολοκύντην
ἐξήταζον τίνος ἐστὶ γένους. . .
καὶ κύψαντες

χρόνον οὐκ ὀλίγον διεφρόντιζον·
κᾆτ' ἐξαίφνης ἔτι κυπτόντων
καὶ ζητούντων τῶν μειρακίων
λάχανόν τις ἔφη στρογγύλον εἶναι,
ποίαν δ' ἄλλος, δένδρον δ' ἕτερος.

*Yes, I can certainly answer your question. During the Panathenaea I saw*
*a flock of youngsters, students at the Academy, and heard their extra-*
*ordinary talk; they were establishing classifications in biology, distin-*
*guishing between animals and trees and the* genera *of vegetables. They*
*came to the pumpkin, and were trying to discover its* genus ... *stooping*
*down they spent ages pondering over it. Then while they were still bent*
*double investigating one of them suddenly said it was a rotund vegetable,*
*another that it was a grass, the third, a tree.*

Epicrates 11K; cf. Menander 481,482K = 416, 417Kö.

(*c*)  εἶτ' ἔστιν ἢ γένοιτ' ἂν ἡδίων τέχνη
ἢ πρόσοδος ἄλλη τοῦ κολακεύειν εὐφυῶς;
ὁ ζωγράφος πονεῖ τε καὶ πικραίνεται,
ὁ γεωργὸς ἐν ὅσοις ἐστὶ κινδύνοις πάλιν.
πρόσεστι πᾶσιν ἐπιμέλεια καὶ πόνος.
ἡμῖν δὲ μετὰ γέλωτος ὁ βίος καὶ τρυφῆς·
οὗ γὰρ τὸ μέγιστον ἔργον ἐστὶ παιδιά,
ἁδρὸν γελάσαι, σκῶψαί τιν', ἐκπιεῖν πολύν,
οὐχ ἡδύ; ἐμοὶ μὲν μετὰ τὸ πλουτεῖν δεύτερον.

A flatterer speaks:

*A sweeter craft or trade men hardly ply*
*Than a clever flatterer's, and I'll tell you why.*
*The painter labours, just to win vexation,*
*The husbandman takes risks past computation;*
*There's work and worry in every such vocation:*
*We, on the other hand, live soft, live gay;*
*To be where the severest task is play –*
*Laughter, jest, tippling isn't that sweet as honey?*
*To my mind only one thing beats it – money.*

Antiphanes 144K (*Lemnian Women*);
cf. Menander 402K = 333Kö.,
tr. J. M. Edmonds

To end this selection, one passage of Menander in which a
father gives a shopper's guide for prospective husbands; the

199

matter-of-fact tone and easy style are typical of Menander, the
view of women typical of Middle and New Comedy.

καὶ τοῦτον ἡμᾶς τὸν τρόπον γαμεῖν ἔδει
ἅπαντας, ὦ Ζεῦ σῶτερ, ὡς ὠνήμεθα·
οὐκ ἐξετάζειν μὲν τὰ μηθὲν χρήσιμα,
τίς ἦν ὁ πάππος ἧς γαμεῖ, τήθη δὲ τίς,
τὸν δὲ τρόπον αὐτῆς τῆς γαμουμένης, μεθ᾽ ἧς
βιώσεται μήτ᾽ ἐξετάσαι μήτ᾽ εἰσιδεῖν·
ἀλλ᾽ ἐπὶ τράπεζαν μὲν φέρειν τὴν προῖχ᾽, ἵνα
εἰ τἀργύριον καλόν ἐστι δοκιμαστὴς ἴδη,
ὃ πέντε μῆνας ἔνδον οὐ γενήσεται,
τῆς διὰ βίον δ᾽ ἔνδον καθεδουμένης ἀεὶ
μὴ δοκιμάσασθαι μηδέν, ἀλλ᾽ εἰκῇ λαβεῖν
ἀγνώμον᾽, ὀργίλην, χαλεπήν, ἐὰν τύχῃ,
λάλον. περιάξω τὴν ἐμαυτοῦ θυγατέρα
τὴν πόλιν ὅλην· οἱ βουλόμενοι ταύτην λαβεῖν
λαλεῖτε, προσκοπεῖσθε πηλίκον κακὸν
λήψεσθ᾽· ἀνάγκη γὰρ γυναῖκ᾽ εἶναι κακόν,
ἀλλ᾽ εὐτυχής ἐσθ᾽ ὁ μετριώτατον λαβών.

*The right way to go marrying, by Saviour Zeus,*
*Is the same way you go shopping. You shouldn't haggle over*
*Irrelevant details – who was the girl's grandfather,*
*Or grandmother – while giving never a thought or look*
*To the character of the bride herself, the woman you mean*
*To live with; and what's the use of hurrying off to the Bank*
*With her dowry-money, to get the Banker to test the coin –*
*Which won't stay in the house five months – if you don't apply*
*A single test to the woman who's going to settle down*
*In your house for the rest of your life, but take haphazard*
*An inconsiderate, quarrelsome, difficult wife, who even*
*May be a talker. I shall take my own daughter round*
*The whole city: 'You want to marry this girl,' I'll say,*
*'Just chat with her; find out beforehand the true measure*
*Of the pest that you're acquiring. A woman is a pest –*
*That can't be helped; the luckiest man's the one who gets*
*The least unbearable pest.*

Menander 532K = 581Kö., tr. P. Vellacott.

4 The reputation of Menander, who met with varied success
during his lifetime, stood high through antiquity, but until

the beginning of this century he was known to us only by quotation and report and as reflected in the pages of Plautus and Terence. The discovery, in 1905, of a papyrus containing substantial parts of *Epitrepontes* (*The Arbitration*), *Periceiromene* (*The Unkindest Cut*), and *Samia* has been followed by the publication of the *Dyscolus* in 1958, and, more recently, of good portions of the *Sicyonian* and the *Misoumenos*; the publication of further fragments from several plays can be expected. In addition, a fourth-century mosaic in Mytilene shows groups of characters from each of eleven plays, among them the *Samia*, *Epitrepontes*, and *Misoumenos*. Although Menander was taught by Theophrastus, the successor of Aristotle and author of the *Characters*, and although the plays reveal an awareness of philosophical and ethical questions, Menander's development as a dramatist is likely to have been influenced much more vitally by seeing revivals of fifth-century tragedies, particularly those of Euripides, than by studying treatises on drama.

5 Menander died in 292 B.C., about forty years before the birth of Plautus, but Greek New Comedy continued to be performed in Athens and elsewhere. There is no room to discuss here the phlyax plays popular in the Greek cities of South Italy in the fourth century nor the evidence for early Italian comedy: in the surviving Roman plays Greek influence is paramount. It is possible that Plautus died in 184 B.C., not many years before the birth of Terence: the six comedies which constitute the entire production of Terence belong to the years 166–160, whereas the writing of Plautus' plays (twenty-one are likely to be genuine) covered a much greater time-span.

6 The brief account of the history of comedy given so far has made no mention of the conditions of performance, and little of the plays which survive complete, or nearly so. Both in Athens and in Rome comedies were performed at festivals under the auspices of the State; in Athens there were two festivals in the early part of the year at which comic dramatists competed, the Lenaea and the City Dionysia, both in honour of the same god, Dionysus. The plays of Terence are known to have been

produced not only at the September *Ludi Romani* dedicated to Jupiter and the April *Ludi Megalenses*, the festival of the Magna Mater, but also at funeral games in honour of Aemilius Paulus. The historian of comedy can point to continuity in some of the conditions of performance and in festival associations as well as in the literary sphere, but the reader of the surviving plays is first and chiefly conscious of the differences between the work, say, of Aristophanes and Terence, to say nothing of the differences between ancient comedy and that of a later age. Two obstacles may hinder the modern reader's approach, one shared, to some extent, with all students of classical literature, the other affecting only the reading of drama: reading plays requires a special technique, the ability to see in the mind's eye what is happening on the stage, and this is particularly necessary in reading comedy (where one may have, for example, to picture the reactions of a mute eavesdropper hearing no good of himself) and still more in reading plays written in an age when stage-directions were very rarely incorporated in the text; the appreciation of comedy is likely to be increased by understanding more about its development as a literary genre as well as about the politics and social conventions of the age which produced it.

7 Our knowledge of the theatres in which the plays were originally produced is tantalizingly incomplete, although we know more about Greek conditions than Roman. The theatre of Dionysus in Athens lies at the foot of the Acropolis; its acoustics were good, but to the more distant spectators the masked and costumed figures moving in the circular orchestra below, or on the slightly raised stage behind the orchestra, must have looked tiny. At the back of the stage was the actors' building, whose front wall formed, as it were, the backdrop before which the action took place. By the time of Menander, whose first play was not produced until after the completion of the reconstruction credited to Lycurgus, the stage was by convention a street, with the two or three houses belonging to the chief characters fronting on to it; the setting of Aristophanes' plays

was more varied, but the variety was achieved as much by verbal description as by physical means; at both periods there was also access to the stage from either side. Scenery was minimal, by modern standards, although we know of no obstacle to the use of portable stage properties. The costume of Old Comedy, grotesque because of the padding and leather phallus worn by the actors, was eventually replaced by the dress of ordinary life, although masks were still worn, very likely by Roman actors as well as Athenian. The producer of Old Comedy (often the playwright himself) was responsible for the chorus of twenty-four singers (with their musician) whose dances, vigorous or graceful, contributed more than visual interest to the play, as well as for the actors (probably three for the chief speaking parts, with 'extras' as needed); he also had at his disposal two scenic devices manipulated by stage-hands: by the use of the *mechanē* an actor could be shown in flight and the *eccyclema* (perhaps a wheeled platform) could be rolled through the central doors to reveal a tableau. Aristophanes took advantage of these devices to display Trygaeus in the *Peace* ascending to heaven on his dung-beetle and Euripides in the *Archarnians* composing tragedies with his feet up, since he was too engrossed, or too lazy, to walk out of his front-door.[5]

8 One of the difficulties of approaching Old Comedy is that the critic's hallowed topics, Plot and Character, are as often as not inadequate. Old Comedy has a story rather than a plot, in the accepted sense of the word, and when one has told the story critical description has hardly begun. For example: an old man has a son addicted to horse-racing; racing debts have almost overwhelmed him. He decides to take lessons in oratory and out-talk his creditors; he's too stupid to learn and his son goes to school in his place, so successfully that he worsts his father in argument; the father then sets fire to the school. A summary of the plot of almost any comedy written since the fifth century B.C. would not only be longer and more complicated but would

5. *Peace*, 80 ff.; *Acharnians*, 395 ff.

contain far more of the essence of the play. Others of Aristophanes' plays could be summarized still more briefly: the present state of their city so disgusts two Athenians that they decide to found a new city among the birds of the air: one of them becomes its king. This résumé of the *Birds* illustrates better than that of the *Clouds* the improbability, even the impossibility, of the events supposed to take place: an element of fantasy is normal, at least at the beginning of the story.

9 An account of the story does no more than hint at the theme of the play: the *Clouds* is 'about' education, just as the *Acharnians*, the *Peace*, and the *Lysistrata* are 'about' war and peace. But the plays are far more than animated debates on public issues: the fortunes of the individual and those of the *polis* are interwoven, and the distinction between public life and private life is not drawn where we should draw it. The *Wasps*, for example, like many plays of New Comedy, shows the relationship between a father and his son. The father, Philocleon, is old, tough and frugal, mad on jury-service, an uncritical supporter of the demagogue Cleon. Bdelycleon, by contrast, sees his father's passion as what we might call a senile obsession, to be restrained physically. He keeps him prisoner in his own home. One of the house-slaves describes the situation near the beginning of the play: 'I'll tell you what the old man's trouble really is. He's what they call a trialophile or litigious maniac – the worst case I've ever come across. What he's addicted to is serving on juries, and he moans like anything if he can't get a front seat at every trial.'[6] As the play develops we see that father and son are separated not only by the gulf between generations but also by class distinctions, yet where the author of a modern comedy might tend to see these as separate issues, Aristophanes makes them cohere.

10 Very often the public dimension of the play is established by the chorus. In the *Wasps* Philocleon has as his allies his fellow-jurors, men of waspish disposition and costume endowed with a sting they are glad to use. (Animal choruses are

6. *Wasps* 87–90, tr. D. Barrett.

known to have existed early in the history of comedy, and vase-paintings illustrate men dressed as birds as well as groups in which men dressed as horses or dolphins have riders on their backs.) The chorus of comedy may be a more active participant in the story than the chorus of tragedy, and usually is, but its function is not only that of participating in, and reflecting on, the stage events. Its first entrance, the Parodos, follows the play's exposition; its exit, singing the Exodos, marks the end of the play; in the intervening scenes it is continuously on view and its songs punctuate the action; moreover, Old Comedy has unique structural features in which the chorus has an essential place: the *Agon*, or contest, which is normally placed towards the centre of the play and followed by the *Parabasis*, an address to the spectators on topics of dramatic and public interest. These features are thought to go back to the period before Comedy as we know it came into existence and to have been part of a Dionysiac ritual.

11 Now it is time to try to draw together the elements we have been discussing, the story, the theme, the characters, and the formal structure of an Aristophanic play, and to begin to direct our attention also towards the language and style in which the plays are written, and the spirit, whether serious or comic, which animates the play. The *Frogs*, produced in Athens in 405, opens with repartee between master and slave. We can see from his dress that the master is Dionysus, himself the *raison d'être* of comedy, but we see also that he is partly disguised as Heracles. Dionysus visits Heracles, to find the best route to Hades, since he is in dire need of the recently dead Euripides. After rejecting the more sudden and painful routes he decides to wait for Charon's ferry. On reaching the water's edge, Xanthias, the slave is dispatched on his donkey to make his way by land, but Dionysus embarks. His attempts at rowing are mocked by a chorus of Frogs, whose song blends charm, reverence, and rudeness in a manner characteristic of its author but hard to convey in English. As children of the marshes, they sing to honour Dionysus and their other deities:

ἐμὲ γὰρ ἔστερξαν εὔλυροί τε Μοῦσαι
καὶ κεροβάτας Πὰν ὁ καλαμόφθογγα παίζων·
προσεπιτέρπεται δ' ὁ φορμικτὰς Ἀπόλλων,
  ἔνεκα δόνακος, ὃν ὑπολύριον
  ἔνυδρον ἐν λίμναις τρέφω.
  βρεκεκεκὲξ κοὰξ κοάξ.

*We are beloved by the Muses with melodious lyre, by horn-footed Pan who plays the tuneful reeds. Lyre-playing Apollo delights in us because of the reed which we grow in our marshy pools to hold his lyre-strings.*

But lyric degenerates into slanging-match until Charon's boat reaches land (270). At the far side of the lake Xanthias rejoins Dionysus, and the scene of comic terror which follows when Xanthias pretends to see monsters acts as a foil for the entry of the chorus, whose members are initiates of the Mysteries. The next hundred lines, the Parodos, are mainly sung, whether the initiates are invoking Dionysus, criticizing typical or even individual Athenians, or honouring their queen, Demeter.

12 So far we have had the opening scenes and the parodos; now, if Aristophanes is to adopt his usual pattern, we expect a spoken scene or two before the *agon*; in fact, the scenes are succeeded by the parabasis. The scenes portray Dionysus–Heracles' reception in Hades: Aeacus takes him for the Heracles who attacked Cerberus.

Ah, so it's you, foul, shameless, desperate, good-for-nothing villain that you are. Ought to be ashamed of yourself, you ought! Coming down here, trying to throttle a poor little dog! . . . I'll have you flung over the cliff, down to the black-hearted Stygian rocks, and you'll be chased by the prowling hounds of Hell and the hundred-headed viper will tear your guts out and the Tartessian lamprey shall devour your lungs and the Tithrasian Gorgons can have your kidneys and – just wait there a moment while I go and fetch them (465–78).[7]

This fine spate of mythological abuse so terrifies Dionysus that he begs Xanthias to assume his disguise. As we can guess, when Xanthias–Heracles is invited to a party Dionysus insists on

7. This and succeeding passages from the *Frogs*, tr. D. Barrett.

changing clothes again, just in time to come in for another lot of abuse. So the scene continues, exploiting not only shifts of identity but reversal of roles when from time to time the slave gets the upper hand.

13 Soon the stage is free and the chorus begin the parabasis. Just as Old Comedy regularly has the formal ingredients *parodos*, *agon*, *parabasis*, *exodos*, so *agon* and *parabasis* themselves have their own internal structure, a pattern composed of speech and song in balancing pairs. The *parabasis* of the *Frogs* (674–737), which lacks the usual opening address (the 'Anapaests'), consists of a song first invoking the Muse and then insulting Cleophon, followed by a speech eloquently pleading for the restoration of citizens disfranchised in the revolt of 411. A second song resembles the first in rhythm and tone, and the second speech, also twenty-eight lines long, reinforces the message of the first, in even wider terms:

> I'll tell you what I think about the way
> This city treats her soundest men today:
> By a coincidence more sad than funny,
> It's very like the way we treat our money.
> The noble silver drachma, that of old
> We were so proud of, and the recent gold,
> Coins that rang true, clean-stamped, and worth their weight
> Throughout the world, have ceased to circulate.
> Instead the purses of Athenian shoppers
> Are full of shoddy, silver-plated coppers.
> Just so, when men are needed by the nation,
> The best have been withdrawn from circulation.

14 A short iambic scene between Xanthias and another slave prepares us for the *agon*. Aeschylus, the present holder of the tragic throne in Hades, has refused to make way for the newly arrived Euripides (Sophocles is too easy-going to be a claimant). A contest is to be held. As the two tragic poets enter, in mid-quarrel, the chorus compare them, in grandiose language, to animals. A short slanging-match between the two leads to the formal *agon*, a pattern of speech and song like that of the

parabasis. But the contest does not end with the *agon*: Euripides, who has already defended his plays against the charge of immorality and attacked Aeschylus' high-flown incomprehensibility, now turns his attention first to his prologues and next to his choral lyrics; but he himself does not come off unscathed. In a final literary test each poet's lines are weighed in a pair of scales: Aeschylus wins. The political theme which runs through this play and is most obvious in the parabasis comes to the fore again at the end of the play when Aeschylus and Euripides are asked to advise the city how to treat Alcibiades. Finally, to Euripides' chagrin, Dionysus chooses Aeschylus, and while they feast before the return to Athens, the chorus in a final comment proclaim that the theatre, like Athens itself, needs men of good sense:

> μακάριός γ' ἀνὴρ ἔχων
> σύνεσιν ἠκριβωμένην.
> πάρα δὲ πολλοῖσιν μαθεῖν.
> ὅδε γὰρ εὖ φρονεῖν δοκήσας
> πάλιν ἄπεισιν οἴκαδ' αὖ,
> ἐπ' ἀγαθῷ μὲν τοῖς πολίταις,
> ἐπ' ἀγαθῷ δὲ τοῖς ἑαυτοῦ
> συγγενέσι τε καὶ φίλοισι,
> διὰ τὸ συνετὸς εἶναι.

> *So altogether we're glad to find*
> *That a man with a shrewd and intelligent mind*
> *(A man with a sense of proportion)*
> *Is returning to Earth, as this comedy ends,*
> *To the joy of his colleagues, relations and friends –*
> *Is returning to Earth, in this decadent age,*
> *To save the City and save the stage*
> *From politics, lies, and distortion.* 1482–90.

15 Menander's only surviving complete play was written when he was a young man of twenty-five. Like many other plays of New Comedy, it tells the story of the love of a young couple triumphing over parental opposition. The scene represents a country district near Athens, and the three doors of the stage-building belong to the houses of the Dyscolus himself,

Cnemon, his stepson Gorgias, and to a shrine between the two houses from which Pan appears to speak the prologue: he describes Cnemon, a misanthropist whose wife Myrrhine cannot stand him and has returned to live with her son by a former marriage, Gorgias, leaving her daughter with Cnemon. Because Pan felt sorry for the girl, he made a rich young man from the city, called Sostratos, fall in love with her at first sight. Pan withdraws, and Sostratos appears, accompanied by a parasite. Already it is clear that we are in a different world from that of Old Comedy; we are obviously concerned with character and temperament as mainsprings of dramatic action, and with family fortunes, not those of the *polis*; from the structural point of view, we notice that there is an explanatory prologue (which Menander sometimes placed *after* the first scene) delivered by a god, the sort of procedure we associate with Euripides. The opening scenes establish Cnemon's character by report, until the man himself enters, with a grumbling monologue which is a stock device of New Comedy. Cnemon is a figure of fun – often sarcastic himself, he complains of the rudeness of others – but too self-aware and rational to be seen as a buffoon. The young man, Sostratos, though lacking in self-reliance, is less weak than many of his New Comedy counterparts, and his willingness to do a good day's work in the fields wins Gorgias' approval, as well as amusing Gorgias' servant, Daos.

16 However, the humour is not all derived from contrast of character and class. The play is spaciously enough composed to allow for scenes which do not really forward the action or amplify the character-drawing. In one such scene we have a dialogue between Sostratos' man, Getas, and a cook (one of a series of comic cooks whose history can be traced from the beginnings of comedy right down to *Alice in Wonderland*, and further):

> This ruddy sheep's enough to break your ruddy heart.
> Ah, go to hell! If I pick it up and carry it,
> It gets its teeth on the branch of a tree and chews the leaves

And tears the branch off. Same if I put it down on the ground,
It won't get moving. Talk about slaughter! – it's not the sheep,
It's me, the cook, gets slaughtered, dragging this battleship.

393–9, tr. P. Vellacott.

The climax of the play is reached when Sostratos and Gorgias
rescue Cnemon from the well into which he has slipped and
Cnemon softens for long enough to entrust the arrangement of
his daughter's marriage to Gorgias. Often a play of this type
ends when the wished-for marriage has been arranged, but on
this occasion Menander chose to continue. The last section
begins with a conversation between Sostratos (joined later by
Gorgias) and his wealthy, upper-class father, Callippides. This
short scene demonstrates Menander's power of quickly
sketching not only a character but a relationship, and his way
of setting a passage of urbane courtesy and tact in contrast
with the harshness of Cnemon, still fresh in our minds, and the
crude baiting which is to follow. (The vivid feeling of the
locality in which the play is set is achieved with similar economy,
as Professor Handley shows in his introduction.[8]) The final
scene might be called 'Getas' Revenge': he and the cook, both
rather drunk, bully Cnemon into joining the revelry; the
boisterous ending, in which violence and feasting are combined, looks back to Old Comedy. While it serves to ensure that
it is with Cnemon, not the young lovers, that the play begins
and ends, the shift of mood is too great to be entirely agreeable.

17 The *Dyscolos* has been described as a morality play and as a
comedy of character: whether or not we are meant to draw a
lesson from observing Cnemon's fate, we can see to what
extent the play depends on his personality-traits. They clearly
provide the motivating force of the dramatic action, just as
Philocleon's litigiousness does in the *Wasps*; moreover, the
dominant characteristic is comic through exaggeration: we
cannot help laughing at an elderly man so excessively litigious
that he tries to get out of the chimney when all other exits

8. *Dyskolos*, 22–5; cf. the way in which a sense of locality is established in
Plautus' *Rudens*.

have been stopped, or one so unfriendly that he even regrets speaking to his neighbour Pan. It is interesting to compare comedies of character (not to mention different productions of single comedies) to see how far the comic characteristic is exaggerated and exploited. Among ancient comedies the _Aulularia_ of Plautus comes nearest to making the detailed portrayal of character not only motivate the play and provide amusing scenes but take on real substance. Its chief character, Euclio, the prototype of Molière's _L'Avare_, has not had an easy life: his sudden discovery of a pot of gold makes it much worse, since he now suspects everyone, rich and poor alike, of planning to acquire his treasure. His anxiety and his obsession lead at one point to a comic scene at cross-purposes with Lyconides, who has seduced his daughter. Euclio believes that Lyconides has stolen the pot of gold, Lyconides that Euclio knows about the seduction:

EUCLIO: What induced you to touch my property without my leave?

LYCONIDES: Love – and drink.

EUCLIO: Impudent rascal! You have the face to come to me with that kind of story! If that is what you call an excuse, we might as well all go round in broad daylight robbing women of their jewels, and if we're caught say we did it for love, and drink. Damn love and drink, I say, if a drunken lover is to do as he pleases with impunity.

LYCONIDES: But I have come of my own free will to beg your pardon for my foolishness.

EUCLIO: I've no use for people who when they've done wrong come whining with apologies. You knew you were taking what you had no right to take; you should have kept your hands off.

LYCONIDES: But having touched, my only plea is that I may possess entirely.

EUCLIO: What!! Do you think you're going to keep something that is mine, with my leave or without it?

_Aulularia_, 740–56, tr. E. F. Watling.

18 The type of characteristic that forms the subject of a play, ambition, meanness, gluttony, is not only likely to be familiar to the audience from personal experience but from other

dramatic presentations. This seems not to be a disadvantage, since once the stock character has been recognized individual quirks can be portrayed with greater subtlety. The stock situation, however, may be felt to be unpleasantly restricting, even granted the social conventions described by Professor Beare:

> Young ladies did not appear in public; their parents married them off to men they had never seen. Consequently, if a young gentleman is to fall in love, it must be with some girl who is of inferior social class, and whom therefore he will not be allowed to marry; and a young lady cannot fall in love at all. A costly sacrifice is offered by society at the altar of female chastity. Young gentlemen dangle after always expensive and sometimes heartless courtesans; they purchase slave-girls with money which has to be extracted from the grasp of cantankerous parents by intriguing slaves; or else they fall in love with some modest girl in humble circumstances and form illicit, unstable unions which only the fairy wand of Comedy can turn into real marriages by revealing the glad secret that the girl is of better birth than she seemed to be. Young ladies are still more unfortunate: if before marriage they are to win a man's love without betraying their sex and social class they must be exposed as infants or kidnapped in childhood; if they reach their teens in their parents' homes and venture to attend a women's night-festival they are raped by unseen, unknown assailants; if subsequently they marry, suspicion and scandal soon darken their lives and alienate their husbands; the baby born as a result of outrage has to be exposed, and still the young mother finds herself deserted by her husband. It is satisfactory to be able to set on the other side the fact that an exposed baby's chances of rescue are one hundred per cent; that kidnapped children are invariably recognized and restored to good and loving parents; that the drunken youth who assaults a maiden at a midnight festival and the husband who later disowns her for unchastity always turn out to be the same individual; that realization of guilt leads to remorse, and remorse to reconciliation.[9]

19 The modern theatre-goer, whether he prefers the witty and light-hearted treatment of an amorous triangle or the tragicomic study of society and family relationships perfected by

9. *The Roman Stage*, 54–5.

Chekhov, is likely to find the world of New Comedy limited. Although a restricted circle of characters does not necessarily make for boredom in comedy, the success of television series entirely devoted to the quarrels of father and son, or husband and wife can be seen to depend on a detailed portrayal of mood and mannerism which New Comedy could not have achieved. Broad contrasts between characters abounded, with Terence liking in particular to contrast in the same play a pair of young men and a pair of old. Thus, in the *Adelphi*, he gives us stern Demea, entrusting the education of one of his sons to his brother Micio, who is permissive and proud of it. After both boys have been involved in a series of scrapes Demea experiences a change of heart, but not quite the obvious one: 'I could also do with a bit of love and appreciation from my own children. If that comes from being generous and agreeable I can take the lead all right. The money may give out, but that needn't worry me – I'm old enough for it to last *my* time.'[10] Of the surviving plays of New Comedy this is the one most concerned with a social issue – that of upbringing. This is not to deny that social attitudes can be discerned in other plays – in the comic detestation felt for the *leno*, or in cynical allusions to marriage – but often enough one feels that these are attitudes expected of the dramatist, not necessarily his personal beliefs: the debate in Menander's *Arbitration*, however, is concerned with individual morality and shows a greater degree of involvement. Aristophanes' *Clouds* had also treated questions of education in terms of conflict between father and son, but there the scope had been wide enough to include not only religious and cultural issues but their embodiment in the person of Socrates and the Cloud-chorus. Moreover, in this play, as in the *Wasps*, the son gains ascendancy over his father in a way which would be shocking in New Comedy but is typical of the topsy-turvy nature of Old. The self-contained bourgeois world of New Comedy is less rich and less disconcerting than that of Aristophanes, but its range of mood, humour, and feeling is by no means narrow.

10. 879–81, tr. B. Radice.

20 We have seen that in Plautus and Terence rounded character-studies are rare; nor does plot have quite the importance it was to assume later. This is perhaps surprising, since we are accustomed to praise comedy of intrigue chiefly for its neatness of plot, and no doubt Wilde, Molière, or even Shaw would be pleased to receive this sort of compliment. Under the heading 'neatness of plot' one includes such qualities as economy in the number of characters required, the absence of 'padding' or of loose ends at the play's conclusion, and perhaps, too, a sort of artificial elegance in the ordering of component scenes. Modern critics have faulted both Plautus and Terence for lacking one or more of these qualities and for downright inconsistencies and contradictions in individual plots. Of course, plot was important to the writer of New Comedy: at the very least it enabled him to compose a succession of entertaining scenes which would grip our attention until the *dénouement*. We may, however, be misled if we suppose that dramatists valued neatness of plot and consistency of tone as highly as their critics. Coleridge wrote, 'A proper farce is mainly distinguished from comedy by the license allowed, and even required in the fable in order to produce strange and laughable situations', and I am suggesting that we should not think worse of plays that we could label 'romantic comedy' or 'comedy of manners' were it not for the admixture of farce (nor should we despise plays that are entirely farce). An admixture of farce is to be found in some types of scene, written by Terence as well as Plautus, such as those played by a *servus currens* or a slave tantalizingly withholding news. These, like the scenes of violence found mainly in Plautus, seem to need a broader and more boisterous style of acting than we expect in non-farcical comedy. Consider the scene near the beginning of Terence's *Phormio* in which the young Antipho, who has dreaded his father's return, panics and refuses to face him.[11] The *Phormio* is light comedy, but the extreme of cowardice shown, gratuitously as far as the plot is concerned, by a character for whom we have felt some degree of sympathy, is disconcerting. Geta, Antipho's

11. *Phormio*, 202–18, tr. B. Radice.

slave, tries to allay his fears: 'Come, come, sir, as things are there's all the more reason for making an effort. Fortune favours the brave.' 'I can't pull myself together.' 'But this is the moment when you must, sir. If your father sees you looking nervous he'll guess you've done something wrong.' Geta and Antipho's friend Phaedria finally persuade him to practise some brave faces and some excuses to offer his father, but once Demipho is in sight Antipho runs away. This scene is farcical to the extent that the production of a 'strange and laughable situation' is more important than unity of tone or consistency of character.

21 Molière modelled his *Les Fourberies de Scapin* on the *Phormio*, but his opening scenes achieve a deeper sympathy for Octavio, Antipho's equivalent, since we hear his love-story from his own lips and see him with his young wife, and the scene of cowardice, too, differs enough from its predecessor to put another complexion on Octavio's flight.

22 It may be that we should be content to enjoy without cavil any scene which has its own comic impetus. How far Plautus, in particular, aimed at strong contrasts between successive scenes we cannot say, but if his approach was at all like that of the composer of opera it seems likely that the variation between speech and song, and between songs of different type, was intended to change the emotional temperature. Let us now look at a Plautine farce, the *Menaechmi*, noting some of the passages likely to have been sung. Professor Beare summarizes the play as follows:

Two twin brothers had become separated in infancy; Menaechmus I, kidnapped and carried off to Epidamnus, has had the good fortune to be made heir to a wealthy old gentleman, who has since died. Menaechmus II (Sosicles), having grown to manhood in his native Syracuse, has started on a search for his brother and is now newly arrived at Epidamnus with his slave Messenio. The exact resemblance of the two brothers leads to a 'comedy of errors' which threatens to have serious consequences; eventually the brothers meet, and all is explained. The theme of mistaken identity was frequently exploited in New Comedy, to judge by the number of plays entitled 'The Twins' or 'The Doubles'. The interest of the *Menaechmi* lies chiefly in its well-handled if improbable plot and its amusing scenes; the two brothers alienate our feelings by their selfishness, but some of the minor characters are well portrayed, especially the doctor who is called in by the father-in-law of Menaechmus I to treat the young man's supposed insanity.[12]

23 After a prologue (which may not be by Plautus) the action begins with a monologue by a parasite, Peniculus, who is going to scrounge a meal from Menaechmus I. This monologue, in praise of eating for moral improvement, is only the first of a series distributed through the play. Their content, while not being quite unconnected with the dramatic action, is usually reflective and sometimes takes the form of a set-piece or aria, like the father-in-law's lament for old age (753–72). Not only do they provide a welcome relief from the quick-fire dialogue of the confusion-scenes which constitute the rest of the play but they help to give the play shape: one might perhaps say that their function in some respects resembles that of the chorus of Old Comedy. To return to the first scene. As Peniculus arrives, Menaechmus I is coming out of his house, nagging his (unseen) wife (we have noted a similarly realistic scene-opening in the *Frogs*). We know already that this is a comedy in which food matters and wives don't, and this attitude is further illustrated in the scene with Menaechmus I's girl-friend, Erotium. Next Plautus introduces us to Menaechmus-Sosicles, newly arrived with his slave Messenio, and *his* scene with Erotium quickly establishes how like his twin he is, in character as in looks. The encounters which follow succeed in getting the most out of the identical-twin theme and reach a climax when Menaechmus-Sosicles feigns insanity. Beginning with grimaces and gestures, he soon declares himself possessed by Bacchus and Apollo, and, obeying their commands, rids himself of his twin's wife and her father. The combination of invocations to these gods in tragic style and low insults is

12. *The Roman Stage*, 59.

more effective because it follows a scene of marital squabbling:

SOSICLES: euhoe atque euhoe, Bromie, quo me in siluam uenatum
uocas?
audio, sed non abire possum ab his regionibus,
ita illa me ab laeva rabiosa femina adseruat canes,
poste autem illinc hircus alus, qui saepe aetate in sua
perdidit ciuem innocentem falso testimonio.
OLD MAN: vae capiti tuo! SO: ecce, Apollo mihi ex oraclo imperat
ut ego illic oculos exuram lampadibus ardentibus.
WIFE: perii! mi pater, minatur mihi oculos exurere.

SOSICLES (raving): *Euhoe! Euhoe! Bacchus ahoy! Wilt thou have me go
hunt in the woods away? I hear thee, I hear thee, but here I must stay.
I am watched by a witch, a wild female bitch, on my left, and behind her
a smelly old goat, a lying old dotard whose lies have brought many an
innocent creature to ruin . . .*
FATHER: *Ay, ruin on you!*
SOSICLES: *Now the word of Apollo commands me, commands me to burn
out her eyes with firebrands blazing . . .*
WIFE: *Ah!! Father, father, he is threatening to burn out my eyes!* (835–42)

The mad scene, whose opening lines I have quoted, leads to an
episode of a different comic type, with a history even longer
than that of feigned stage madness. The father brings on a
doctor to treat Menaechmus-Sosicles: he turns out to be an
'expert' (and a coward) and employs medical jargon whenever
he can. In early comedy the 'expert', conceited and impractical,
was usually doctor or philosopher: later writers have added
the cleric, the schoolmaster, and the television pundit. The
characters of this play do not endear themselves to us and do
not need to; the deceptions which are practised from time to
time are the work of the twins, and so the plot does not need
the intriguing slave or parasite to manipulate the affairs of a
helpless young master; in fact, the slave, Messenio, is almost
convincing in the lyric proclaiming his virtue (966–89).

24 Shakespeare's early *Comedy of Errors* is close enough to the
*Menaechmi* to make the differences instructive. In a play which
is half as long again as its Latin model Shakespeare added twin

servants and a banquet-scene from another Plautine play, *Amphitruo* (the only surviving example of a mythological play), and other features whose source was probably his own imagination. The possibilities of confusion are increased by the addition of twin servants, and a new dimension of feeling is achieved both by a narrative prologue which arouses pity and fear and by letting us see the wife (and her sister) involved in, and distressed by, the mysterious changes in her 'husband'; moreover, the confusion, which in Plautus is purely comic, in Shakespeare produces moods of doubt and fear in which a man can be certain of nothing, not even of his own identity.[13]

25 The presence of so much that is recognizably Plautine, though not all from one play, in the *Comedy of Errors* should make us cautious in discussing the problem of the debt owed by Roman authors of comedy to Greek. Some specifically Roman references in the plays show that translation could give way to adaptation in certain cases, but over the question of major alterations in plot or character there is unlikely to be agreement unless the Greek original of a Roman comedy comes to light. Discussion of this problem, and of the related, but narrower, problem of *contaminatio* in Terence has been much affected by the feeling that originality is to be required of all good poets: put crudely, the attitude is this: 'I admire Plautus/ Terence: he must be original, not just a translator.' The scanty evidence about *contaminatio* is contained in the prologues to Terence's plays, and it is insufficient to produce agreement among scholars as to the exact meaning of *contaminari*, let alone agreement as to whether, or how, Terence combined material from more than one Greek play in composing for his Roman audience. Further, an author whose aim in discussing features of his literary practice is to win favour from the audience and discredit his rivals will perhaps conceal part of the truth or employ impenetrable irony.[14]

26 A farce succeeds if it continually arouses laughter: its

13. See *The Comedy of Errors*, ed. R. A. Foakes.
14. See particularly *Andria* 16 and *Heaut.* 16.

audience need not exercise intellect or sympathy. The aim and nature of other types of comedy is harder to define: the requirements that a comedy should end happily and arouse laughter are better met by ancient than by modern examples, but leave much unsaid. Aristotle's remark that comedy aims to represent people who are worse than us is perhaps not wholly acceptable either, but it suggests a helpful approach: is our attitude to the characters of the play one of scorn, amusement, or sympathy?[15] It is not certain that a Roman audience would have seen the young man of this passage with our eyes: Lysiteles, in Plautus' *Trinummus*, is talking to his father: 'I have always been obedient to your commands, father. From my earliest boyhood until now, your word has been my law. For my conscience I count myself a free man, but where your orders are concerned I am content to make my inclination your slave.' A little later he gives more details: 'Haven't I resolutely taken care to avoid bad company, stay home at nights, keep my hands from picking and stealing, and do nothing to upset your digestion? I have been scrupulously careful to keep the roof of your discipline in good repair over my head.'[16] As one judges this young man one should remember the amiable young asses whom the resourceful Jeeves rescues from scrapes; they are given character, apart from their idiocy, only by speaking in the accent and idiom of a particular class and period; endowed with a physical presence by an actor, they become sufficiently endearing and a good deal more amusing.

27 Our attitude to the protagonist, and so to the play, is largely determined by the first hundred or two lines: a reading of the opening scenes of the plays quoted and discussed in this chapter will reveal some of the different ways in which a playwright shapes our response – his choice of dialogue or monologue, the proportion of exposition of fact to description of feeling, the extent to which the hero is present on the stage, the urgency of the situation. There is space here to illustrate

15. *Poetics* 1448a16, 1449a32.
16. 301–17.

only the last of these points: the intrigue-plays of New Comedy normally begin at the eleventh hour (at any moment Antipho's father will return and all will be lost); in Old Comedy the initial situation is grave but may not yet be desperate. The practice of modern comedy is often to show a problem from near its beginning, as in the *Cherry Orchard*, or in several of its aspects, as in the Aristophanic *Mad Woman of Chaillot* by Giraudoux. The nature and distribution of verbal humour in the prologue, as elsewhere in the play, largely contributes to its effect. Xanthias' question which opens the *Frogs* – 'What about one of the old gags, sir? I can always get a laugh with those' – must often have occurred to the comic dramatist. For Aristophanes the old joke might be the mention of some *bête-noire*, for Menander some lines of exaggerated grumbling by an overworked cook: jokes of this latter sort, whether they evoke sympathy or dislike, are relevant to the portrayal of character, but others are there to dissolve tension or focus attention on what is being said after an episode whose chief effect is visual.[17] The response which the author achieves, in these and other ways, may be laughter, sympathy, a feeling of suspense or of our own superiority to the deluded men on the stage. When we leave the theatre it may be with increased understanding of character, with satisfaction because chaos has been replaced by order, or exhilarated by the success of the comic idea.

## Appendix: The Surviving Plays of Aristophanes, Plautus, and Terence

A. ARISTOPHANES

| | |
|---|---|
| *Acharnians* | 425 |
| *Knights* | 424 |
| *Clouds* | 423 |
| *Wasps* | 422 |
| *Peace* | 421 |
| *Birds* | 414 |

17. Compare, e.g., *Frogs* 465–78, quoted above, 66, with the argument at *Rudens* 938–1044; notice the verbal humour of *Menaechmi* 621–5 and cf. *Trinummus* 583–90.

| | | |
|---|---|---|
| *Lysistrata* | 411 | |
| *Thesmophoriazusae* | 411 | |
| *Frogs* | 405 | |
| *Ecclesiazusae* | 391 | |
| *Plutus* | 388 | |

**B. PLAUTUS**                 ORIGIN

| | | |
|---|---|---|
| *Amphitruo* | | ? Middle Comedy |
| *Asinaria* | ? early | Demophilus |
| *Aulularia* | | Menander (*Apistos*) |
| *Bacchides* | ? late | Menander (*Dis Exapaton*) |
| *Captivi* | | |
| *Casina* | ? late | Diphilus |
| *Cistellaria* | Before 201 | Menander (*Synaristosae*) |
| *Cuculio* | ? middle | ? Menander |
| *Epidicus* | Before *Bacchides* | |
| *Menaechmi* | | |
| *Mercator* | ? early | Philemon |
| *Miles Gloriosus* | ? 205 | |
| *Mostellaria* | | Philemon |
| *Persa* | | |
| *Poenulus* | | ? Alexis |
| *Pseudolus* | 191 | ? Menander |
| *Rudens* | | Diphilus |
| *Stichus* | 200 | Menander (*First Adelphi*) |
| *Trinummus* | | Philemon (*Thesaurus*) |
| *Truculentus* | ? late | |
| *Vidularia* | | ? Diphilus |

**C. TERENCE**

| | | |
|---|---|---|
| *Andria* | 166 | Menander (*Andria* + *Perinthia*) |
| *Hecyra* | 165 | Apollodorus (*Hecyra*) |
| *Heautontimorou-menos* | 163 | Menander (*Heauton timoroumenos*) |
| *Eunuchus* | 161 | Menander (*Eunuchus* + *Colax*) |
| *Phormio* | 161 | Apollodorus (*Epidicazomenos*) |
| *Adelphi* | 160 | Menander (*Second Adelphi*) |

# Bibliography

BEARE, W. *The Roman Stage*, London, 1968 (third edition also in paperback)

BIEBER, M. *The History of the Greek and Roman Theatre*, Oxford, 1961.

DUCKWORTH, G. *The Nature of Roman Comedy*, Princeton, 1952.

DUDLEY, D. R. and DOREY, T. A. (Ed.), *Roman Drama*, London, 1965.

LEVER, K. *The Art of Greek Comedy*, London, 1956.

Articles in the *Oxford Classical Dictionary*: 'Comedy' (Greek), 'Drama' (Roman).

WEBSTER, T. B. L. *Greek Theatre Production*, London, 1956.

WEBSTER, T. B. L. *Studies in Later Greek Comedy*, Manchester, 1953.

## Aristophanes

*The Frogs and other plays*, tr. D. Barrett, Harmondsworth, 1964.

*The Congresswomen*, tr. D. Parker, Michigan, 1962.

EHRENBERG, V. *The People of Aristophanes*, Oxford, 1951.

## Menander

*Theophrastus, The Characters, and Menander, Plays and Fragments*, tr. P. Vellacott, Oxford, 1960.

HANDLEY, E. W. *The Dyskolos of Menander*, London, 1965.

WEBSTER, T. B. L. *Studies in Menander*, Manchester, 1960.

## Molière

*The Misanthrope and other plays*, tr. J. Wood, Harmondsworth, 1953.

*The Miser and other plays*, tr. J. Wood, Harmondsworth, 1953.

## Plautus

*The Rope and other plays*, tr. E. F. Watling, Harmondsworth, 1964.

*The Pot of Gold and other plays*, tr. E. F. Watling, Harmondsworth, 1965.

## Terence

*The Brothers and other plays*, tr. B. Radice, Harmondsworth, 1965.

*Phormio and other plays*, tr. B. Radice, Harmondsworth, 1966.

# VIII

# Satire

## John Higginbotham

1 What do we mean by Satire? We think today in terms of Private Eye, Peter Simple, or those late Saturday evening shows on television. It could perhaps be described as comic irreverence. But it was not always so: Doctor Johnson defined Satire as 'a poem in which wickedness or folly is censured'. No hint of humour here. It pricks the bubble of pomposity, strips away veneers; it is not just meant to entertain, but has a serious – often crusading – moral purpose.

2 Can we equate this with Roman Satura – a genre more difficult than any other to pin down because of its own essentially diverse nature? And if so, can we point to Greek forebears, or must we accept Quintilian's famous dictum[1] about it being the only truly Roman genre? The answers to these questions are controversial, and therefore I do not pretend that they are matters of fact. What I aim to do in this chapter is to indicate where the answer to these riddles may perhaps be found, by examining the work of the principal satirical writers.

3 First let us look at the origins of Satire. Though Quintilian regarded the genre as purely Roman, Horace, at the beginning of *Satire* I. 4, looks back on the writers of Greek Old Comedy – 'Eupolis atque Cratinus Aristophanesque poetae' – as the true forebears of his genre. I must not poach on the subject of Comedy except to say that there is a good deal in it which we

1. *Institutio Oratoria*, x. 1. 93.

today would regard as satirical: Socrates in his basket in the *Clouds* contemplating τὰ μετέωρα καὶ τὰ ὑπὸ γῆς (things above and things beneath the earth), Cleon, the archdemagogue in the *Knights*, Euripides, to Aristotle τραγικώτατος τῶν ποιήτων (the most tragic of the poets), was to Aristophanes the one who demeaned the status of Tragedy by bringing on his characters in rags (Vd. *Acharnians*) or making them women ruled by wild passions (Vd. *Frogs*). All are characters magnified to a size much larger than life. Was Aristophanes primarily concerned with amusing his audience, or had he a serious moral purpose? His burlesque of Euripides seems good-humoured enough, and we know of no good reason that he had for hating him. Socrates certainly did not regard his darts as friendly, and in the *Apology*[2] attributes the false ideas popularly held about him largely to the influence of the comedists. When we come to Cleon, we come to a theme – the abhorrence of warmongers – which was clearly close to Aristophanes' heart, and pervades more of his plays than any other.

4 Not all Greek Satire was personal. Literary parody is apparent in the Homeric tradition – witness the *Batrachomyomachia*. Often it was concerned with attacking classes of people rather than individuals. Semonides of Amorgos' famous comparison[3] of women to various types of animals in the seventh century is one of the earliest examples of satirical writing, and echoes of it are to be found in Juvenal's *Satire* VI. His metre is iambic, the normal metre of satirical attack in Greek. It originated, according to Aristotle, from the Homeric *Margites*, and was developed by Archilochus, probably on the grounds that the rhythms of everyday speech were most suited to invective. Hipponax later lengthened the first syllable of the last foot and the *skazon* was born, a metre later to be used by Catullus and Martial for predominantly invective purposes; but the idea of the iambic as a metre of attack still survives into Latin in Horace's *criminosis iambis*.[4]

2. Plato, *Apology*, 19c.
3. Semonides, *Fr.* 7 (Diehls), *O.B.G.V.* No. 122.
4. Horace, *Odes* I. 16. 2–3.

5 The Hellenistic diatribe was undoubtedly satirical in that it was amusing, but had an underlying moral seriousness of purpose: to put across ethical teaching in a popular way by sugaring the pill with a strong element of parody. The principle on which it was based – σπουδογέλοιον (comic but in earnest) – later appears in Horace's 'ridentem dicere verum'[5] (to speak the truth with a smile). The style was a conversational one, again reflected in Horace's designation of his work as 'sermo'. Its chief exponent was Menippus, a Cynic philosopher of the third century B.C., who first interspersed prose with verse and founded the distinctive genre known as Menippean Satire, as later found in Varro, the *Apocolocyntosis* of Seneca and the *Satyricon* of Petronius. Lucian, although he wrote almost entirely in prose, was undoubtedly influenced by Menippus in his burlesque of philosophers and religious figures and often uses Menippus himself as a mouthpiece. In Βίων Πρᾶσις (*Philosophies for Sale*) and *Icaromenippus* he pillories a wide variety of philosophies. In Ζεὺς Ἐλεγκόμενος (*Zeus cross-questioned*) there are some awkward questions for Zeus about his relationship with the Fates, a theme later elaborated in *Zeus Tragodos*, in which we find the mixture of prose and verse used by Menippus.

6 Dubbed by Eunapius σπούδαιος ἐς τὸ γελασθῆναι (earnest in his laughter), he is in the main stream of true satirical writing in that his purpose in exposing false philosophies and absurd superstitions was a serious one (even though his treatment of ideas is never more than superficial), but his treatment is invariably lively and has a richly comic element.

7 It will now be apparent that Greek satirical writing presents us with several problems. Greek is so rich in the satirical that one is led to question Quintilian's dictum. Attempts have been made, such as that of Rennie,[6] to interpret his remark as meaning 'In Satire we are supreme' rather than 'In Satire we stand alone' but they have rarely been happy ones. Certainly there

5. Horace, *Satires*, I. I. 24.
6. Rennie, *C.R.*, 1922.

is a great deal in Greek that is closer to modern ideas of Satire than there is in the *Sermones* of Horace. Perhaps the mistake lies in too close an equation between Satura and the Satirical. It will therefore be necessary before going on to consider Roman Satire to look at the origins and meaning of Satura, and to realize that, though it owed a good deal to Greek models, it is in Latin a much more consistent and homogeneous genre.

8 The origins of Roman Satire are the subject for a great work of scholarship – even assuming that the fragmentary nature of our knowledge of Lucilius would allow it – and to attempt to sum them up in a chapter such as this is no doubt incredibly rash. However, from the evidence that we have the following points seem to emerge:

1. That it was Etruscan in origin is supported by historical evidence,[7] and the philological evidence of the word *satira* (Etruscan for *speech*, cf. Horace's use of the word *sermo*).

2. The word satura in Latin means a medley or *farrago*, as used by Juvenal in Satire I.[8] Variety was one of the main features of Roman Satire as is seen in its rapid transitions, multiplicity of examples, and wide-ranging treatment of the follies and vices of man.

3. The essential element of σπουδογέλοιον found in Greek satirical writing is found in Latin from Ennius onwards.

4. Nevertheless, there are two distinct branches: first, the sermo with its loosely constructed hexameters and colloquial language, invented by Lucilius and followed as their model by Horace, Persius, and Juvenal; secondly, the 'Menippean' satire, with its intermixture of prose and verse, introduced into Latin by Varro and copied by Seneca and Petronius.

5. Not only was Satura itself a medley, but within the genre there is considerable variety, ranging from the gentle observation of human weakness in Horace to the biting attacks on all the worst vices in Juvenal.

7. Livy, VII. 2.
8. Juvenal, *Satires* I. 86.

9 It is impossible to study the *Satires* of Horace effectively without knowing something of his distinguished predecessor, Lucilius. Lucilius, however, is one of those fragmentary authors whose works are hardly ever found in a form palatable for study, and hence he is more often referred to than read. But we know a good deal about him from Horace himself (especially from *Satires* 1. 4, where the poet speaks of his antecedents). He is spoken of as the inventor of Satire; his style of composition was apparently rapid, careless, and long-winded; it was also ruthless in the way that it stripped away all that was false and superficial. His use of the dactylic hexameter was in the tradition of Timon the Cynic who wrote a mock-epic in three books, the *Silloi*, ridiculing all dogmatic philosophers.

10 Horace did not follow him naïvely. In fact he is critical of his turgidness and superfluity:

cum flueret lutulentus, erat quod tollere velles;[9]

*As he flowed muddily, there was much that you would wish to remove*

his longwindedness and inaccuracy:

garrulus atque piger scribendi ferre laborem,
scribendi recte:[10]

*he was verbose, and too idle to take trouble with his writing, with writing accurately, that is:*

11 Clearly he was a profound influence on Horace, but not always a positive one. Horace reacted against his *libertas* – or it may have been a reaction against the violent political lampooners of the day who quoted Lucilius as their model. At any rate, his *Satire* is more a gentle attack on the vices and follies of man than blistering forays against individuals. It is also much tighter in composition; *brevitas* was one of Horace's watchwords. One has only to look at his economy in the use of words in the dialogue with the Bore to see this.

9. Horace, *Satires* 1. 4. 11.
10. Horace, *Satires* 1. 4. 12-3.

12 The main clues to Horace's intentions as a satirist are to be found in the first, fourth, and tenth *Satires* of his first book. In his first *Satire*, based on one of Lucilius which we do not possess, Horace makes clear the serious purpose of his writing. In fact, the way in which all lighter elements are subordinated to a supreme moral purpose is didactic, and his metaphor about teachers bribing their pupils with cakes is reminiscent of Lucretius' defence of his poetic treatment of a scientific subject in his first book.[11]

13 The theme is twofold: 'Men are never satisfied with their own state, but are constantly envying one another; also, money is only a means to an end so that man may live free from care, for what more can a man want but sufficiency?' The Sabine Farm philosophy is already in evidence – later to find expression in the Odes:

> Cur valle permutem Sabina
> divitias operosiores?[12]

*Why should I exchange my Sabine valley for riches which bring more toil?*

One is impressed by the clarity of the writing; a theme is stated, it is discussed, often in dialogue form, and at the end it is summed up: 'don't be a miser, but don't go to the other extreme; preserve the happy mean:'

> est modus in rebus, sunt certi denique fines,
> quos ultra citraque nequit consistere rectum.

*There is a mean to be observed; above all, there are certain limits beyond and short of which morality is not to be found.*

14 The poem contains (as do all the first three) a strong element of diatribe. In this poem it is against avarice, in the second against lust, and in the third against uncharity. The fourth returns to the theme of Satire. What is it, and what is its purpose? The pedigree of the genre (later echoed in the First

11. Lucretius, I. 936 *et seqq.*
12. Horace, *Odes* III. I. 47–8.

Satire of Persius)[13] is traced from the Attic poets, Eupolis, Cratinus, and Aristophanes, to Lucilius. He goes on to describe the horror in which poets are held by the masses; but, he says, he is not a poet. This reflection by Horace on his own style is interesting and shows that in fact he was closer to the diatribe than to Old Comedy. Aristophanes would have been shocked by any suggestion that he was not a poet, but here is a man who is writing verse, it is true, but using the down-to-earth language of the people; his style is 'sermoni propiora'. Moreover, Horace is at pains to explain not only his style but his aims in writing Satire – not to create notoriety for himself by a public display of backbiting. He writes not for a public but for his friends, following his father's practice of pointing out the follies of others so that steps may be taken to avoid them. Unfortunately Horace shows a fault which is apparent in much of his work – moral smugness.

15 The Fifth Satire describes the famous 'Journey to Brundisium', made in the company of Virgil, Maecenas, and others. Its inspiration was Lucilius' description of a journey from Rome to Capua and Rhegium. Perhaps Horace's attack on Lucilius' style in the previous Satire prompted him to show what he could do with a similar theme. The description is interesting, but frustrating; interesting because it gives us in detail the hardships of a journey in the first century B.C.: gnats and frogs, irritating delays, the deceit of innkeepers and prostitutes, bad water, etc.; frustrating, because it tells us nothing of the great issues which Maecenas was going to Brundisium to decide. In a way it is an untypically Horatian *Satire* in that it does not proceed by argument but is almost entirely descriptive. The style is varied; the easy-going Horatian sermo is at times blown up to epic proportions.[14]

16 This contrast in styles is again apparent in *Satire* VI, where the colloquial style is broken up by passages like:

13. Persius, I. 123–5.
14. E.g. vv. 9–11, 40–4, 51–4.

'sed fulgente trahit constrictos gloria curru
non minus ignotos generosis. Quo tibi, Tilli,
sumere depositum clavum fierique tribuno?'

*But Glory in her gleaming chariot carries in bonds the obscure no less than
the noble. What good did it do you, Tillius, to take up the robe you had
laid aside and become tribune?*

The passage also sums up the *Satire*, on the irrelevance of
noble birth, a favourite theme of the satirical writer. It contrasts sharply, however, with Horace's views on birth as expressed in his Fourth *Epode*, where his vehement attack on the
*nouveau riche* is reminiscent of that of Anacreon on Artemon.[15]

17 *Satire* VII is probably a very early piece; it has no moral
tone, is very slight, and has only one point which depends on
a very weak pun at the end. In *Satire* VIII Horace observes
witchcraft with the same Epicurean derision that we have seen
him pour on the supernatural at the end of *Satire* V. Once again
there are shades of Lucilius, who is said to have attacked witchcraft, and anticipation of Lucian, who in *Vera Historia* and
similar works takes great delight in parodying the supernatural.
Horace also owes a good deal to the *Greek Anthology* here in its
personification of inanimate objects, and to Theocritus'
Second *Idyll* for description of acts of sympathetic magic.

18 *Satire* IX deals with Horace's encounter with a Bore. It is a
celebrated piece, largely because Horace for the first time
shows the really dramatic possibilities of the 'sermo'. The per-
sistence of the Bore, his impertinence, his social and literary
pretensions, the cruel *Schadenfreude* of Fuscus Aristius, and the
ultimate cry of salvation are all felt in the short staccato
phrases of the dialogue. One has only to read Ben Jonson's
imitation in *Poetaster* to see how, in spite of skilled literary
handling, the sheer exasperation of the original is lost in a
flurry of words: thus:

'cum adsectaretur, 'numquid vis?' occupo. at ille,
'noris nos,' inquit; 'docti sumus.' hic ego, 'pluris
    hoc,' inquam, 'mihi eris.'

15. Anacreon 54 (Diehls).

becomes:

HORACE: I am bold to take my leave, sir; you'll nought else, sir, would you?
CRISPINUS: Troth, no, but I could wish thou didst know us, Horace; we are a scholar I assure thee.
HORACE: A scholar, sir. I shall be covetous of your fair knowledge.
CRISPINUS: 'Grammercy, good Horace, etc., etc.'

Yet Horace uses the staccato element sparingly; some lines even have the sonorous quasi-epic[16] quality already noted elsewhere, and serve to give the reader breath from the exacting pace of the poem. The rapid ending,

> rapit in ius; clamor utrinque,
> undique concursus. sic me servavit Apollo.

gives a vivid impression not only of the speed with which it all happened but also the breathless relief of the poet. Once again Jonson's 'Thanks, Great Apollo, I will not slip thy favour offered me in my escape for my fortunes.' is well wide of the mark. Time and again it is true, in appreciation of Greek and Latin authors, that the failings, inevitable perhaps, of a well-known translation or adaptation serve to enhance qualities in the original, which might not have struck the reader quite so forcibly but for the contrast.

19 Perhaps the closest in spirit to Horace's Bore is Theophrastus', who the moment a man opens his mouth tells him that his remarks are idle, but he knows all about it, and if only he will listen he will find out.[17] It contains something of the same relentless, self-opinionated arrogance. Also worth noting is the subtle characterization which makes the Bore talk in tones quite different from those of Horace, a quality which is rarely, if ever, noted in the characters of Persius or Juvenal.

20 In *Satire* X he returns to the subject of Satire, and in particular his criticisms of Lucilius, in a poem clearly intended

16. Cf. Homer, *Iliad*, xx. 443.
17. Theophrastus VII.

to round off the first book. The merits and demerits of Lucilius are again stressed:

> at idem, quod *sale multo*
> urbem defricuit, charta laudatur eadem.

> *But I applauded Lucilius in that very same poem* [Sat. IV] *in that he scoured the city with much salt.*

Note the pun here: Lucilius lashed the city with great wit, but his wit had a purifying effect akin to scouring with salt.

21 As in *Satire* IV, the ancient comic poets are cited as an example of the effectiveness of holding vices up to ridicule. He follows this up with a *reductio ad adsurdum* of the idea of mixing Greek with Latin and a deflation of the bombastic Alpinus. He clearly sees himself as owing much to Lucilius (inventore minor), but refining his rather rugged language (incomposito pede), and he sums up his merits and demerits in lines 64—71. There is a link between this and the previous *Satire* in the claim of both Lucilius and the Bore to great facility in the writing of verses. This kind of boast clearly stuck in the gullet of a poet whose great gift was craftsmanship in the choice, placing, and economy of words.

22 In passing on to Book II one is immediately conscious of a change of technique. Whereas in Book I the poet was always on top, either describing events, arguing a case, or justifying his poetry, in Book II the poet allows himself to be challenged and does not always answer the challenge. The result is something much more subtle and ironic, in that his interlocutors are condemned by the patent absurdity of their conclusions, and therefore do not need to be directly refuted. Fraenkel[18] and others have referred to the '*Platonic*' technique of the *Satires*, but W. S. Anderson[19] in a recent essay has gone further and argued that Horace in Book I portrays a *Xenophontic* Socrates who directly instructs, whereas in Book II we

18. Fraenkel, *Vd.*, Bibliography 1.
19. Anderson, *Vd.*, Bibliography 4.

see the εἰρωνεία of the *Platonic* Socrates, who with such disarming modesty leads his potential opponents into such deep philosophical waters that they have to admit defeat. This element, however, is only significantly present in the parody of the Stoic Stertinus in *Satire* III, Catius' lesson in gastronomy in IV, and the conversation between Ulysses and Teiresias in V. In the latter the similarity to the treatment in Lucian's *Menippus* is so striking that the poem may owe something to Menippus himself.

23 *Satire* VI is a plain account of the advantages of Horace's Sabine farm, and leads on without the least irony to a defence of country, as opposed to town life. *Satire* VIII is a delightful burlesque on the theme of a man of little breeding who tries to be grand by offering a great dinner party for distinguished people. The results are disastrous. The story is told to Horace by Fundanus – but the humour is direct rather than ironical, and there is little Socratic subtlety in the rumbustuous touches of broad comedy. It is more akin to an Aristophanic portrayal of Cleon, or Horace's own attack on a parvenue in the Fourth *Epode*. The comic figure of a person of little breeding trying to put on airs, typified in English by characters from Mrs Malaprop to Eliza Doolittle, was later to find a richly satirical portrait in Petronius' Trimalchio.

24 The Socrates analogy is an interesting and attractive one; εἰρωνεία is clearly present in *Satire* III of this Book; but it should not be overplayed. There is little that is Socratic about *Satire* II, in which Ofellus simply asserts his belief and there is no dialogue. Sometimes, like Juvenal, he uses the imaginary interlocutor descended from the Platonic dialogue via the Stoic diatribe.

25 *Satire* II, III contains a good deal of dialogue and gentle irony – yet Anderson is begging the question when he says that Horace is surrounded by his books (including Plato *the philosopher*) as he prepares to write. Other commentators (including

Palmer) [20] have taken this to be Plato *the comic poet* (428–389), who would certainly seem to be less incongruous in this company than the philosopher. Eupolis (already mentioned by Horace as a distinguished predecessor) and Menander were comic poets, while Archilochos was the earliest iambic satirist: in fact, his lines on the simple life may well have been in Horace's mind here.[21] If indeed Horace had Plato in mind it was doubtless a dialogue such as the *Ion* in which the interlocutor finds himself the victim of a *reductio ad absurdum* rather than direct refutation. There is also a certain amount of guying of the philosophical type reminiscent of Aristophanes' treatment of Socrates in the *Clouds*[22] or Lucian's in *Philosophies for Sale*. The *Satire* is full of types drawn with all the incisiveness and clarity of a Theophrastus, the avaricious man, the mean man, the superstitious man, and the braggart. There are differences, however. Theophrastus' avaricious man[23] is mean to others so that he can be self-indulgent; when he distributes the portions at dinner he says that it is fair for the labourer to receive double and loads his own plate. Horace's avaricious man allows himself no such luxuries; he may have three hundred thousand casks of the finest Falernian or Chian wine, but is content to drink vinegar.

26 The opening lines of II, IV are, allowing for the correction of a ὕστερον πρότερον, reminiscent of the opening of Plato's *Phaedrus*:[24] Unde et quo Catius? (Whence and whither, Catius), cf. ὦ φίλε, Φαῖδρε, ποῖ καὶ πόθεν. This sets the Platonic tone, and it is perhaps in the first ten lines of the poem that the Socratic influence is most apparent, especially in:

> quod si interciderit tibi nunc aliquid, repetes mox,
> sive est naturae hoc sive artis, mirus utroque.

*If anything has just slipped your mind you will soon recall it; whether this capacity is natural or acquired, you are remarkable in both.*

20. Palmer, *Vd.*, Bibliography 3.
21. Archilochus, *O.B.G.V.* No. 106 (W.22, Diehls).
22. Aristophanes, *Clouds* 31–42.
23. Theophrastus, XXVII.
24. Plato, *Phaedrus* 227a.

27 The *Satire* may be compared with Juvenal IV in that it not only deals with a culinary theme but carries it to absurd lengths. Far from being a satire on Epicureanism (which taught that more pleasure is to be derived from self-control than from self-indulgence, and of which Horace was a declared adherent),[25] it is an attack on the extremes to which men resorted to tickle the palate. It contrasts sharply with the previous *Satire*, which pilloried the Stoic paradox that *all but the wise are fools*: here men of sense are depicted with a fine sense of the ironic as desiring the shoulder of a pregnant hare or devoting their talents to making pastry:

> Sunt quorum ingenium nova tantum crustula premit.
>
> *There are those whose genius produces nothing but new kinds of pastry.*

The placing of the damning 'tantum' between 'nova' and 'crustula' is masterly. The theme was later taken up by Lucian (*Nigrinus*, 33).

28 The whole tone of the *Satire* suggests a parody of didactic poetry: it may well have been inspired by the Ἡδυφαγητικά of Ennius, or the treatise in three books of C. Matius on the Cook, the Picklemaker, and the Fishmonger. In fact, as Roman pseudonyms were often a metrical equivalent of the original, *Matius* may well be *Catius*.

29 *Satire* II, V owes two debts to Greece. The first is to Homer, who in *Odyssey* XI deals with the meeting of Odysseus with Teiresias to learn of his return to Ithaca. The question is: 'How to restore his shattered fortunes when he gets there?' Horace's answer is to become a *captator*, and by battening on to some rich and childless man to secure a substantial legacy. (The *captator* was later to find vitriolic treatment in both Juvenal and Martial.)[26] By choosing a humorous treatment of a social theme Horace approaches here most nearly the modern conception of satire. The humour is literary too, with unmistakable touches of epic style:

25. Horace, *Epistles* I. 4. 16.
26. Juvenal, *Satires* v and xii. *Vd.* also Martial i. 8. 27.

> fortem hoc animum tolerare iubebo;
> et quandam maiora tuli.

*I shall order my brave soul to bear this; for I have previously endured worse.*

Shades of 'τέτλαθι δή, κραδίη'[27] and 'O passi graviora'.[28] The second is to Menippus. In Lucian's *Dialogue of the Dead* XXVIII we see Menippus descending to Hades to consult Teiresias. Menippus is inquiring into the truth or otherwise of mythology. Was Teiresias blind? Did he really change sex? When and why did he become a prophet? Teiresias sticks to the traditional line, and Menippus loses his temper.

30 II, VI is on a typically Horatian theme – the contrast between the life of contentment in the country and the troublesome bustle of the town. Juvenal took up the theme in his famous attack on Rome in *Satire* III, later to be imitated by Samuel Johnson in '*London*'; but the emphasis here is quite different: whereas Juvenal speaks of the physical hazards

> incendia, lapsus
> tectorum assiduos ac mille pericula saevae
> urbis,

*fires, the continual collapse of buildings, and a thousand dangers of the cruel city*

and contrasts them with the mainly physical delights of country life, Horace is primarily concerned with people, the jeerers, the importunate, and those who want bail. The delightful fable of the town mouse and country mouse with which the satire ends is in the great tradition of animal analogy stretching from Aesop to La Fontaine.

31 II, VII is, like II, III, on the Stoic paradox. The treatment, however, is different: instead of lively dialogue which clearly owes something to the Platonic style, here we have almost a monologue in which Horace uses his slave Davus as an *alter*

27. Homer, *Odyssey* xx. 18.
28. Virgil, *Aeneid* i. 199.

*ego* to indulge in an orgy of self-criticism. His playful portrait of himself as seen by a slave is most endearing:

> aut insanit homo aut versus facit.

> *The man is either mad or composing verses.*

His candour is unusual in a satirist. As Swift put it: 'Satire is a sort of glass wherein beholders do generally behold everybody's face but their own.' Slaves were allowed considerable freedom of expression at the *Saturnalia*, and Horace uses this to lessen the embarrassment of talking about his follies direct. The *Satire* had a strong influence on the fifth *Satire* of Persius, who, it may be noted, was not afraid to be more personal:

> tibi nunc hortante Camena
> excutienda damus praecordia, quantaque nostrae
> pars tua sit, Cornute, animae, tibi, dulcis amice,
> ostendisse iuvat.

> *It is for you that I now allow my heart to be revealed at the bidding of the Muse; it pleases me to show you, my dear friend, Cornutus, how much of my soul is yours.*

Again the vanity of human desires theme with which Book I began is struck:

> Romae rus optas; absentem rusticus urbem
> tollis ad astra levis.

> *When in Rome, you long for the country; when in the country, you praise the distant city to the skies, fickle man.*

One might compare the restless man as portrayed by Theophrastus.[29]

32 *Satura*, according to some, means a mixed dish or hotchpotch. It is fitting that the climax of Horace's achievement in this field should be a description of a dinner. Gastronomy seems to have been a fruitful field for the satirist. Lucilius wrote on

---

29. Theophrastus, XVII; cf. Lucretius III. 1057 *et seqq.*

the subject. So has Horace already (II, IV). One of Juvenal's finest efforts is *Satire* IV, in which a turbot is honoured with a great debate which affords an opportunity for parodying flattery of the emperor and the pomposity of his minions. Boileau also deals with the theme in his third *Satire*.

33 The food is most expensive, but badly cooked and served. The wine is of the best, but hardly lavishly dispensed. The host points out the merits of practically everything on his table. And when a tapestry falls from the wall, bringing with it clouds of black dust, and the host weeps, this terrible warning to all who try to give dinner parties which are above their station is complete. Like Evelyn Waugh, Horace is far too good a moralist to moralize, but the lesson is clear amid the laughter. Perhaps closest in spirit to Horace's Nasidienus is Petronius' Trimalchio in his richness, his vulgarity, his boastfulness, and his gastronomic preciosity.[30]

34 Much has been written about the fine balance of Book II: the balance of I (consultation of Trebatius) with V (consultation of Teiresias); II with VI (both in praise of country life); III with VII (each refers to a Stoic paradox); and IV with VIII (each of which ridicules gastronomic excess). It is all very neat, but Rudd[31] is right, I think, to be rather sceptical of it. The connection of I with V is tenuous; the plan as a whole may simply have been dictated by a natural desire not to have two poems on a similar subject following one another; and we have no certain knowledge of whether it was Horace who arranged the book in this way.

35 Multum et verae gloriae, quamvis uno libro, Persius meruit.

> *Persius too, although he only wrote one book, has deserved a truly great reputation.*

Thus Quintilian.[32] He is the first Roman Stoic verse satirist, and the serious moral purpose of his work had a great influence

---

30. *Vd.* especially *Satiricon* 69–70.
31. Rudd *Vd.*, Bibliography 2.
32. *Institutio Oratoria*, x. 1. 94.

on later writers. But he has never achieved the popularity of Horace or Juvenal, due partly to his alleged obscurity and partly to his sermonizing. Only his first poem is genuine satire – on bad poetry. There was much in contemporary epic which reflected the worst excesses of a rhetorical education. Such senseless bombast he parodies in the famous lines:

'torva Mimalloneis implerunt cornua bombis'
et 'raptum vitulo caput ablatura superbo
Bassaris.'

(*Lines like* 'They filled their savage horns with Mimallonian boomings' *and* 'Bassaris about to tear off and take away the head of the proud calf.')

One is reminded of some of the lines attributed to Aeschylus in the *Frogs*.[33] Poetic platitudes and standard endings like 'Berecyntius Attis' are pilloried. Persius has a fine turn of phrase in his invectives: phrases like 'sartago loquendi' and 'trossulus levis' to describe the nonsense and the reaction it produces are particularly striking. We see here the beginnings of that pungent literary invective later to find expression in Charles Churchill's 'a happy tuneful vacancy of sense', in Dryden's lines on Shadwell, and in Pope's lines on Nahum Tate:

And he who now to sense, now nonsense leaning,
Means not, but blunders round a meaning:
All these my modest Satire bade translate,
And own'd that nine such poets made a Tate.'

36 *Satire* II, on the vanity of human prayer, foreshadows Juvenal X, especially in the prayers of an old woman on behalf of a newly born child. Underlying this theme is another – hypocrisy: how different are men's public prayers from their private thoughts, and how by their very acts they negate all that they desire. Γνῶθι σεωτόν is thus the real theme. Persius' realism and Stoic austerity is apparent in his condemnation of overdone sacrifices which do little to placate the gods and only serve to empty the purse.

33. *Frogs* 833 *et seq.*

37 *Satire* III opens with a vivid picture of a hangover and continues with a vigorous invective on a reprobate. It is a good example of Persius' variation of style, from the personal, in which he describes his own (fictional) stratagems as a boy, to the allusive, the philosophical, and the philistine. The dialogue with the friend and the fatal carousal which ensues are written in a racy style (hinc tuba, candelae, etc.) which foreshadows Juvenal. The conclusion – only Stoic detachment provides the answer to the problems of life; it is a sermon, true, but with rather more liveliness and pungency than one generally expects in a sermon.

38 *Satire* IV opens with words reminiscent of a Socratic dialogue: 'Rem populi tractas?' with its gentle irony reminds us of Alcibiades' encounter with Socrates in the *Symposium*.[34] Persius is typically allusive, perhaps even unnecessarily elaborate: even allowing for the fact that *Socrates* would not fit into a hexameter, 'barbatum . . . magistrum . . ., sorbitio tollit quem dira cicutae.' seems unduly prolix, unless it is Persius laughing at his own style. As in *Satire* III, so here the high moral purpose is apparent:

> rectum discernis ubi inter
> curva subit vel cum fallit pede regula varo.

> *You can see the straight line when it comes among curves even when the ruler with its straddling foot would lead you astray.*

(One notes, incidentally, the ancient pedigree of our moral metaphors, straight and crooked.) Apparent, too, is the Stoic disdain for the ignorant masses which we have already noted in Persius:

> auriculas asini quis non habet?

> *Who has not the ears of an ass?*

The *Satire* includes an attack on pride of birth –

> 'Dinomaches ego sum', suffla, 'sum candidus.'

> *Puff out your cheeks and say, 'I am Dinomache's son, a handsome fellow.'*

34. *Symposium* 213c et seq.

– the pomposity of which is wonderfully expressed in the imperative. It looks ahead to Juvenal's treatment of the theme in his eighth *Satire*. The last two lines show Persius at his incisive best as he strips away flattery and hypocrisy and reveals his victim in his naked poverty.

39 *Satire* V is modelled on Horace's II, VII, and deals with the Stoic Paradox – that *only the wise man who has conquered his emotions is truly free*. Its treatment, however, is much more dialectical, and therefore, as poetry, rather arid. It contains a number of *communes loci*, such as the elusiveness of tomorrow[35] and the evil nature of any action not prompted by wisdom:

> digitum exere, peccas.
>
> *Extend a finger, and you sin.*

It also contains a lively element of dialogue with Avarice and Luxury which owes much to Stoic diatribe and New Comedy. In fact, Persius quotes a section of the *Eunuchus* of Menander, which he knew, if not in the original, from the Latin translation by Terence. Boileau imitated the Avarice passage in his eighth *Satire*, but like Jonson's imitation of Horace, it lacks the concision and vigour of the original. One has only to compare the fine staccato tones of:

> 'surge.' negas. instat: 'surge,' inquit. 'non queo.' 'surge.'

with:

> 'Debout' dit l'Avarice, 'il est temps de marcher.'
> 'He laissez-moi.' 'Debout.' 'Un moment.' 'Tu repliques?.'

40 *Satire* VI deals with money and how to spend it. As in Horace and Juvenal, when money is mentioned the *captator* is never far away. Here, however, it is a dialogue with a supposed heir that brings the Satire to life. It is also notable for the fact that being addressed to a lyric poet, Caesius Bassus, it is

35. Cf. Martial v. 58.

more stylistically self-conscious than the other Satires; in fact, in the opening lines we see some of the mock grandeur which is a recurring feature in both Horace and Juvenal. Once again we see the rather prolix and elaborate style in his enumeration of non-existent heirs, contrasted with the economical, pungent lines which bring the poem to its close.

41 Persius is a poet of extremes: at his best there is colour, vigour, and point; at his worst prolixity, pretentiousness and obscurity. He is important in the history of Satire, in that he was the first poet to harness the satirical Hexameter to Stoic preaching. He fulfilled for Satire the claim which Martial makes of his *epigrammata*:

> Nescit, crede mihi, quid sint epigrammata, Flacce,
> Qui tantum lusus illa iocosque vocat.[36]

> *Believe me, Flaccus, a man does not know what epigrams are, if he calls them mere playful jesting.*

42 Difficile est saturam non scribere.[37]

> *It is difficult not to write satire.*

Thus Juvenal explains the compulsion which lay behind his writing. His work is more social, more of its time than Horace. The relationship between client and patron, the flattery of the emperor – both of which Juvenal saw as debasing the coinage of human relationships – the horrors of living in Rome and the constant exposure to *recitationes*, greed, fanaticism, and perversion are all themes which arouse in Juvenal an indignation which goes against the grain:

> si natura negat, facit indignatio versum.

> *Though nature may deny it, indignation prompts my verse.*      I. 79

One might compare Victor Hugo's invocation 'Muse Indignation, viens.' To Juvenal Satire is all-embracing; it is a hotch-potch of life:

36. Martial, IV. 49.
37. Juvenal *Satires* I. 30.

quiquid agunt homines, votum, timor, ira, voluptas,
gaudia, discursus, nostri farrago libelli est.

*All that men do – their prayers, their fears, their anger, their delight,*
*their joys, their comings and their goings, all are the varied subject of my*
*work.* I. 85–6

43 His technique is quite different from Horace's. He adopts
the dramatic form only once – in *Satire* Nine, a virulent attack
on sexual perversion discreetly omitted from all school
editions. Three of the *Satires* simply narrate, two are descriptive, eleven are arguments in which a premiss is stated at the
outset and continued with a multiplicity of examples which
leaves the reader breathless. 'He drives the reader along with
him,' observed Dryden. 'When he gives over, 'tis a sign that
the subject is exhausted; and the Wit of Man is able it carry it
no further.'

44 *Satire* I is a good example of his method. It starts with a
protest that contains the quintessence of his approach to
Satire: What is wrong with modern poetry? The quantities of
wishy-washy epic, comedy, and tragedy are so great that even
the marble columns are smashed by the non-stop *recitationes*.
They are boring; they are worse: they have absolutely no
relevance to life. Not for Juvenal the romanticism of the past:
res vera agitur. He is concerned with reality, and in Rome that
means vices:

et quando uberior vitiorum copia?

*and when was Rome richer in its crop of vices?* I. 87

Not for him the gentle irony of Horace; Juvenal's tirades are
full of vitriol. His lack of inhibition, his irreverence, his
exaggerations (Boileau referred to 'sa mordante hyperbole'),
and his sense of the ridiculous are probably paralleled in the
ancient world only in the works of Aristophanes, Lucian, and
Petronius. And yet the purpose, like that of all true Satire, is
serious, that by subjecting social injustice to a *reductio ad*
*adsurdum* people may feel that it is something to be opposed.

The enemy here is money. Nobles and magistrates defer to a rich freedman. The rich tycoon consumes an enormous meal and throws out a dole to his dependants at the gate.[38] It leads to affectation: Crispinus, Domitian's *Princeps Equitum*, shows off a special lightweight ring made specially for summer wear and not quite so heavily laden with gems. Money has not yet been given a temple alongside Pax, Fides, Concordia, and the rest, and yet:

> inter nos sanctissima divitiorum
maiestas.

> *From us no other deity receives such reverence.*      I. 112–13

Wealth leads to gluttony and sudden death. The old man has not even time to make a will. His natural heirs get the money and his friends are furious:

> ducitur iratis plaudendum funus amicis.

> *The funeral procession proceeds amid the cheers of enraged friends.*

Note the ironical use of *amicis* here, and the use of *plaudendum* instead of the expected *plangendum*, a striking παρὰ προσδοκίαν. Finally, Juvenal explains that he is attacking men of the past, yet from the virulence of his attack it is clear that the vices are contemporary. No doubt he uses names drawn from the past owing to the danger of attacking the numerous villains of his own day; or perhaps like Tacitus,[39] of whom he is in his bitter invective in may ways the poetic counterpart, he felt that the worst was over, Domitian was dead, and Nerva heralded the dawn of a new age.

45 Juvenal's main theme is decadence. It is a theme which he not only describes but diagnoses. Its root cause is insincerity. *Satire* II describes the mock philosophers who preached the virtues of Stoic restraint but gave themselves up to the most abhorrent vices. The name of Seneca springs immediately to

38. Cf. Martial III. 14.
39. Cf. *Agricola* II.

mind; but he is not mentioned. The Satire is an attack mainly on the nobility, and in particular on a man who was not fit to bear the name of Gracchus. It also contains several deft blows at Domitian himself.

46 *Satire* III is one of Juvenal's finest. It is full of contrasts: honesty and flattery, riches and poverty, Romans and foreigners, town and country. He particularly attacks a Rome infested by Greeks ('non possum ferre, Quirites, Graecam urbem'); he cannot bear their flattery. There are echoes of Theophrastus here, whose flatterer καὶ σκώψαντι ψυχρῶς ἐπιγελάσαι τό τε ἱμάτιον ὦσαι εἰς τὸ στόμα ὡς δὴ οὐ δυνάμενος κατασχεῖν τὸν γέλωτα.[40]

*If a man makes a stale joke, the flatterer laughs and stuffs his cloak into his mouth as though unable to restrain himself.*

Juvenal takes this sympathetic treatment further:

> rides, maiore cachinno
> concutitur; flet, si lacrimas conspexit amici,
> nec dolet; . . . si dixeris 'aestuo', sudat.

*If you laugh, he shakes with redoubled cackles; if he sees his friend's tears, he weeps, but does not grieve; if you say, 'I'm hot,' he sweats.*

The Greeks, like many a persecuted people, were hated not because they were bad, but because they were good at most professions they took up and overshadowed their rivals. The cultural inferiority complex of the Romans is apparent in Virgil,[41] and the distrust of their professional skills goes back to the elder Cato, who is recorded as having said of their doctors;

> iurarunt inter se barbaros necare omnes medicina.[42]

*They have sworn to kill all foreigners with their treatments.*

40. Theophrastus, II.
41. Virgil, *Aeneid* VI. 847 *et seq.*
42. Pliny, *N.H.* XXIX. 14.

47 The *Satire* is also an attack on poverty. Never since Jugurtha had exclaimed that the city was up for sale[43] had Rome been so preoccupied with money: 'omnia Romae cum pretio' (Everything at Rome has its price). Even the recognition of a great man costs money, and the people pay taxes so that his slaves may have an extra allowance of food; but it was not just poverty that was the evil, but the indignities that went with it:

nil habet infelix paupertas durius in se
quam quod ridiculos homines facit.

*The hardest thing to bear about poverty is the fact that it makes men ridiculous.*
                                                        III. 152–3

Crantor[44] of Soli had made the same point:

οὐκ ἔστι πενίας οὐδὲν ἀθλιώτερον
ἐν τῷ βίῳ σύμπτωμα· καὶ γὰρ ἂν φύσει
σπουδαῖος ᾖς, πένης δέ, καταγέλως ἔσει.

*Nothing more wretched can happen in your life than poverty; you may be of an earnest nature, but if poor, you will be ridiculous.*

Of the Augustans, Horace[45] and Tibullus[46] had sung the praises of the simple country life, and they were later echoed by Palladas. Juvenal is more down to earth: poverty in the country may be tolerable, but in the city there are burglars and drunks on the roads, crockery and slops falling from the windows, falling masonry and fires. One can hear in 'tabulata tibi iam tertia fumant' (III. 199) the crackle as the parched wood of a city tenement goes up in flames.

48 The sordidness of city life expressed in this Satire inspired Samuel Johnson's *London* and Boileau's *Les Embarras de Paris*. In our own time Eliot's *The Waste Land* is not so far from Juvenal's Rome in spirit; for contrast, one might take Wordsworth's *Westminster Bridge*. In Johnson we see the inescapable connection between the big city and wickedness:

43. Sallust, *Bellum Jugurthinum*, 35. 10.
44. Crantor, Vd. Stobaeus, Florilegia, 96, 13. *Cf.* also Lucian, *Nigrinus*, 21.
45. Horace, *Satires* II. 6.
46. Tibullus, I. 1.

Resolved at length from vice and London far
To breathe in distant fields a purer air.

There is the same rhapsodizing of country life:

For who would leave unbribed Hibernia's land,
Or change the rocks of Scotland for the Strand?

All the hazards of city life are there too:

Here malice, rapine, accident conspire,
And now a rabble rages, now a fire.

The Juvenalian themes are there; what is different is the tone.
The fierce lunge of Juvenal's hexameters is softened into the
rather lightweight rhyming pentameters and often reduced to
poetic clichés:

Some pleasing bank where verdant osiers play,
Some peaceful vale with Nature's paintings gay.

Boileau's imitation is more compact and incisive, closer to the
spirit of the original:

Bientôt quatre bandits lui serrant les côtés.
La Bourse! . . . Il faut se rendre; ou bien non resistez
Afin que votre mort, de tragique memoire
Des massacres fameux aille grossir l'histoire.

49 *Satire* IV starts with a short section of thirty-six lines which
tells of the voluptuary Crispinus, who paid 6,000 sesterces
(about £60) for a large mullet. Red mullet are rare even in the
Adriatic, and it is unusual to find one weighing more than a
pound.

> potuit fortasse minoris
> piscator quam piscis emi.

*You could perhaps have bought the fisherman for less than the fish.*

IV. 25–6

247

Thus the extravagance is brought home with typically Juvenal-ian incisiveness.

50 At line 37 Juvenal does something which is very typical of him: he starts a new subject, which has only a tenuous connection with the first. A turbot has been caught, so large that the only safe course is to hand it over to the Emperor. A solemn council is called to discuss its fate, and a bitter attack on the evils of the imperial system here finds a vehicle: the shores were infested with *delatores* – cf. Aristophanes attack on the συκοφανταί in the *Acharnians*. The council is called; its description is preceded by nine lines of mock epic which add to the ridiculous grandeur of the scene. Gross flattery follows:

> ipse capi voluit.
>
> *The fish wanted to be caught.*

The terror of the councillors is really felt:

> ergo in consilium proceres, quos oderat ille
> in quorum facie miserae magnaeque sedebat
> pallor amicitiae.
>
> *And so the Councillors were summoned to a meeting. The emperor hated them, and on their faces there rested a pallor which reflected a great and dangerous friendship.*　　　　　　　　　　　　　　IV. 73–5

It is a feeling which Juvenal does not allow us to forget. It recurs at the end of the poem and underlies the superficially frivolous conversation about the fish in a way that would excite the envy of Ibsen or Chekhov. Throughout Domitian is seen through the eyes of his terrified minions, whose relationship with him is symbolized by the oxymoron *oderat . . . amicitiae*.

51 *Satire* V is ostensibly about a dinner, but is in fact a biting attack on the relationship between *patronus* and *cliens* in imperial times. Once again, it is poverty that makes men ridiculous. A *cliens* is invited to dinner, but is it worth it? While his host dines on lobster garnished with asparagus, the *cliens* is served

with a stinking eel from the Tiber. His host drinks the finest wine from jewelled cups, while that of the *cliens* is absolute poison served by a swarthy and malignant-looking Ganymede. Even the bread is inedible:

> solidae iam mucida frusta farinae,
> quae genuinum agitent, non admittentia morsum.

*Lumps of solid dough now mouldy, which exercise the jaws, but are proof to every tooth.*

Apparently the habit was widely practised: Martial exclaims in one of his epigrams:

> Cum vocer ad cenam non iam venalis ut ante,
> cur mihi non eadem quae tibi cena datur?[47]

*When I am summoned to dinner, and not paid for it as formerly, why am I not given the same dinner as you?*

The Greek professional man, whom we saw so derided in the third *Satire*, was often treated in this way, according to Lucian, by his Roman *patronus*. Duff aptly compares Macaulay's account of the fare offered to an English domestic chaplain in the eighteenth century in the third chapter of his *History of England*.[48]

52 The first five *Satires* make up Book I. Book II contains just *Satire* VI. It is easily Juvenal's most elaborate effort, running to 661 lines, almost double the length of the next longest and containing his strengths – incisive description, poetic use of sounds, rapid movement – and his weaknesses – loose construction and abrupt changes of theme.

53 The tyranny of women is proverbial. As early as Homer we see witches at work – Calypso, Circe, and the Sirens. Euripides, in the *Medea* and the *Bacchae*, showed to what lengths they could go when their passions were roused. Aristophanes took Euripides beyond his logical conclusion in the *Lysistrata* and

47. Martial, III. 60. *Cf.* Lucian's Laws for Banquets, *Saturnalia*, 17.
48. Duff, *Vd.*, Bibliography 6.

*Thesmophoriazusae.* One of the most interesting examples of this theme is the longest surviving iambic fragment of Semonides of Amorgos, who compared women to sows, vixens, bitches, donkeys, weasels, monkeys, and bees.[3] Only the last are any good; the rest are a curse. If this seems cynical, one might reflect that Semonides, in admitting a class of women who at least have the merit of being industrious, goes further than Juvenal. The animal comparison is to be found in Juvenal: a woman annoyed is like a tigress who has lost her cubs:

tum gravis illa viro, tunc orba tigride peior. VI. 270

She is jealous and suspects everyone in the household of being a rival for her husband's affections, even the slaveboys. Not that wives themselves are moral: the *Satire* opens with a long lament for lost Chastity, and the way in which women lust after actors, gladiators, and all the worst types.[49] Extravagant women, domineering women, affected women, disloyal women, all are there in a ruthlessly vivid chamber of horrors. Even the perfect wife is shown to be a liability, as the story of Niobe shows. Besides, who could endure the odious comparisons that perfection brings:

quis feret uxorem cui constant omnia? malo,
malo, Venusinam quam te, Cornelia, mater Cracchorum.

*Who could bear a wife who is all-perfect? I would prefer a Venusian girl to Cornelia, the mother of the Cracchi.* VI. 166–7

At line 231 an even more sinister element than the wife is introduced – the mother-in-law, the ancestor of so many characters in farce, music-hall, and pantomime. Athletic women, busybodies, bluestockings are interspersed with incidental reflections on how good life was in the time of Hannibal. The pace is tremendous, but it is all as loosely connected as a comedian's patter. The poem is rich in sound effects: listen to a woman's chatter in the lines:

49. Cf. Praxilla, *O.B.G.V.* No. 410.

> verborum tanta cadit vis,
> tot pariter pelves ac tintinnabula dicas
> pulsari.

*Such is the flurry of words which falls from her lips that you would say that as many pots and bells are being struck.*

of the particularly vivid lines in which he describes their cruelty:

> hic frangit ferulas, rubet ille flagello,
> hic scutica; sunt quae tortoribus annua praestent.[50]

*One has a rod broken on him, another bleeds from the whip, a third from the strap. Some women engage their torturers on an annual contract.*

VI. 479–80

54 Once again we see the rich attacked: the poor woman has to bear the pangs of childbirth; the rich have abortions. Juvenal expresses it in that vividly allusive way which is typical of him:

> sed iacet aurato vix ulla puerpera lecto.

*Rarely does any woman bear a child in a gilded bed.* VI. 594

Then, as though fearing that he has not made his point, he goes on to be more explicit. Suppositious children recall us to the original theme. Women are unchaste and ruthless. Characters from tragedy bring up the rear.

55 In *Satire* VII it is the rich again who are the villains. They pay a schoolmaster no more in a year than a jockey who rides a winner; they buy tame lions, but will not give a penny to a young writer. The intellectual is not valued – but then he never has been. This criticism of human values was old in Juvenal's day. Look at Socrates. It is still true today when a singer of popular ditties can earn more in a week than a university professor in a year. Society has changed remarkably little in its sense of values. Patronage may help to restore the balance, and for some of the greatest Roman poets, for

50. Cf. Horace, *Satires*, I. 3. 119.

example, Virgil and Horace, it did. Martial expressed his confidence in patronage in the line:

Sint Maecenates, non deerunt, Flacce, Marones.[51]

*As long as you have a Maecenas, Flaccus, you will not lack a Virgil.*

But generally the lack of help given to the young poet was deplorable; he became a butt. Once again it is poverty that makes men ridiculous.

56 *Satire* VIII contains advice to Ponticus, who is likely to become a provincial governor. In fact, the name suggests descent from an earlier governor of Pontus. Juvenal, instead of urging him to live up to family traditions, takes just the opposite line, and the whole poem is an attack on pride of birth. It is this inversion of the trite that gives Juvenal his freshness and originality of treatment, although the theme was not a new one: it is found in a fragment of Phocylides of Miletus (sixth century B.C.), who denounced the high birth of those whose words or characters do not commend themselves to anyone.[52]

'Stemmata quid faciunt?' The usual leap *in medias res* is followed by the usual multiplicity of examples, and we are reminded of the opening of Persius' fourth *Satire*, in which the youthful Alcibiades is induced by thoughts of his illustrious guardian, Pericles, to want to conduct affairs of state. In fact, the opening of that poem – 'Rem populi tractas?' – a pithy, provocative question, is strikingly similar and may well have prompted Juvenal's expostulation. Moreover Juvenal seems here to be influenced by Persius' Stoic teaching:

tota licet veteres exornent undique cerae
atria, nobilitas sola est atque unica virtus.

*Though waxen images of great age may adorn your whole mansion, the
one and only nobility is virtue.*                                   VIII. 19–20

51. Martial, XI. 3.
52. Phocylides, 3.

Examples of patricians who have fallen from grace and plebeans who have achieved distinction follow; but Juvenal, typically, strays from the main theme of his poem to discourse on the evils of provincial misgovernment. He returns to his theme, and his invective reaches its climax in a fine passage on the evils of Nero, whose worst crime apparently was not parricide, evidently the prerogative of an emperor, but unseemly singing on a foreign stage:

> gaudentis foedo peregrina ad pulpita cantu. VIII. 225

The contract between Catiline and Cicero drives the point home: Marius, the Decii, and others serve to labour it, and when we come to Achilles, Thersites, and the people of Rome as a whole we are no longer in a mood to argue.

57 *Satire* X, like *Satire* VI, is on a theme which goes back to Semonides of Amorgos. It had already been touched on by Horace in his first and Persius in his second *Satire*, and was later to inspire the famous efforts of Johnson and Boileau. It is an attack not only against the uselessness of praying for beauty, eloquence, power, etc., but against ambition and desire for high place. The highest pinnacle offers the greatest fall, and human fortune often rests on a knife edge: the themes are trite enough; what brings them to life is the vividness of the illustrations. Sejanus might so easily have been emperor; as it was, his life and reputation lay in ruins, strikingly symbolized by the vigorous description of his statue being toppled and that proud bronze head being reduced to household utensils:

> iam follibus atque caminis
> ardet adoratum populo caput et crepat ingens
> Sejanus, deindo ex facie toto orbe secunda
> fiunt urceoli pelves sartago matellae.

*And now that head adored by the people glows in the furnace as the bellows roar, and the great Sejanus crackles; and from that face, the second most distinguished in the whole world, are being forged pots, pans, pails, and plates.* x. 61–4

Here, as at line 355, we see Juvenal's great sense of the ridiculous; but it is more than that: the anti-climax of the great man's fall is matched by the anti-climax of the poetry. The taunts of the crowd add to the vividness of the scene; just as eagerly would they have acclaimed him emperor had he been successful. Juvenal has a profound contempt for them:

> atque duas tantum res anxius optat
> panem et circenses.

> *They are only concerned in their desire for two things – bread and circuses.*
>
> x. 80–1

58 How much safer is obscurity! Johnson, taking Wolsey as a latter day Sejanus, writes:

> Shall Wolsey's wealth with Wolsey's end be thine?
> Or liv'st thou now with safer pride content
> The wisest justice on the banks of Trent?

Again the examples multiply, but are just saved by an incisive pen. Cicero would have fared better as a bad poet than as a great orator. Again the mock-epic flavour beloved by the satirist, the Stoic theme, the *captator*, the sharp *sententia*.

59 Military glory, as exemplified in Hannibal, Alexander, and Xerxes, is seen to lead only to misery and disaster. As for long life, this is the greatest of delusions. Juvenal's old man foreshadows Shakespeare's 'sans eyes, sans teeth, sans taste, sans everything'. He draws his examples from Homer (Nestor), Virgil (Priam – no doubt from Book II of the *Aeneid*) and the tragedians, especially Euripides (*Hecuba*). He may well have been influenced by Persius' picture of a gouty old man when dealing with a similar theme,[53] or his portrayal of a superstitious old woman praying for beauty in a child.[54] The greatness of the poem lies in the fact that the vividness of the examples and the incisive way in which they are presented freshen a trite theme. As Highet has said, 'His special talent is

53. Persius, *Satires* v. 58 *et seq.*
54. Persius, *Satires* II. 31 *et seq.*

to take ordinary thoughts and express them with extra-ordinary vigour.'[55]

60 *Satire* X is a poem of pessimism. As though for light relief, Juvenal follows it and completes his fourth book with a skit on extravagant dining (XI) and a poem of rejoicing for his friend Catullus' escape from shipwreck which develops into reflections on the hated *captator* (XII).

61 *Satire* XI is in two parts: the first is based on the famous maxim γνῶθι σεαυτόν (Know thyself) engraved on the temple of Apollo at Delphi and is an attack on the folly of those who try to be lavish on slender means; the second describes an invitation to Persicus to come to a simple feast which will be marked by its frugality and friendliness. It is reminiscent of Catullus 13.

62 For the structure one might compare *Satire* IV, which also is in two parts with only a tenuous link, and consider how far this was Juvenal's intentional method of writing. For the subject the obvious comparison is *Satire* V. It is difficult to imagine two Satires on a similar theme, but with such a totally different atmosphere. We have had the repeated theme that poverty makes men ridiculous; we have also seen the heights of arrogance to which they are raised by riches. The ideal is frugality. Quite apart from this preaching of the *aurea mediocritas*, there is a good deal in the peaceful contentment of this genial meal that is reminiscent of Horace.

63 The theme of *Satire* XII is the conflict between the love of life and the love of money. Many men are so conquered by their desire for wealth that they are prepared to put their lives in jeopardy to obtain it. Epicurus had spoken of the folly of being led into great danger by excessive desire.[56] Here the relation of life to wealth is expressed in a typically Juvenalian antithesis:

55. Highet, *Vd.*, Bibliography 5.
56. Epicurus, *The Extant Remains*, Ed. Bailey *Frr.* 68–72.

> Non propter vitam faciunt patrimonia quidam
> sed vitio caeci propter patrimonia vivunt.

> *Some men are so blinded by avarice that they do not make money to live,*
> *but live to make money.* XII. 50–1

The contrast between true affection and bogus wealth-in-spired love is beautifully brought out in the fine description of thanksgiving followed by a biting account of the lengths that legacy-hunters will go to to gain their ends. Catullus has children, and so all suspicion of this hateful practice is removed; contrast with this Martial's pungent warning to Gaurus:

> Munera qui tibi dat locupleti, Gaure, senique
> si sapis et sentis, hoc tibi ait 'Morere'.[57]

> *Why should anyone bring you, a rich old man, Gaurus, gifts? If you are*
> *wise, you will realize he is telling you, 'Drop dead.'*

One might compare also that bizarre passage at the end of the Satiricon in which legacy-hunters are bidden by the will of Eumolpus to eat his corpse, encouraged by examples of those who have eaten human flesh without such a bait. It is one of the most tantalizing features in Latin literature that the outcome of this grisly bidding does not survive.[58]

64 *Satire* XIII is ostensibly a poem of consolation written for a friend who has been cheated of a sum of money; but, as often, Juvenal departs from his stated theme to inveigh against some contemporary vice. Here he takes the Hesiodic theme of man's moral decline from a golden age,[59] and concludes that so corrupt is his own that there is no metal base enough to describe it. The Satire is remarkable for some striking mock-epic writing which bears all the rhetorical influences of the Silver Age as he compares the honest man to the rarest of prodigies (60–70) and enumerates all the oaths by which the guilty man denies his charge (75–85).

57. Martial, VIII. 27.
58. Petronius, *Satyricon* 141. Lucian too has some amusing scenes on the *captatio* theme in *Dialogues of the Dead*, VI–IX.
59. Hesiod, *Works and Days* 286 *et seq.*

65 The theme of perjury naturally takes him on to speculations on the after-life. Why be afraid of one's guilt? There is nothing but Chance to rule the world. Even those who do not believe in an after-life are prepared to take a chance provided they can become rich. Once again Avarice lurks behind it all: gain is worth whatever affliction it may cost:

> et phthisis et vomicae putres et dimidium crus
> sunt tanti.

> *Phthisis, running ulcers, and the loss of half a leg are all a fair price.*
> XIII. 95–6

Biting, cynical, pessimistic, Juvenal is master of the incisive line:

> ploratur lacrimis amissa pecunia veris.

> *True are the tears that mourn the loss of wealth.*     XIII. 134

Juvenal echoes Alcaeus' statement 'Money is the man'.[60] His conclusion is trite: think how many men are worse off. But again it is elaborated with such rhetorical flourish and wealth of detail that we are almost won over. Less convincing is his attempt to persuade Calvinus that revenge is not to be desired, followed by the consoling thought that the guilty are always punished by their consciences.

66 *Satire* XIV suffers from two defects in composition: it consists, like XI and XII, of two separate parts (1–106 and 107–331) with only a tenuous link (107–8), and its is almost pure sermon unspiced with the incisive wit which normally commends Juvenal to the palate. It illustrates well the schizophrenia of Roman Satire, never quite certain whether its true origin lay, as Horace suggested, in the rumbustious Old Comedy, or in the more earnest Stoic διατριβή. Certainly the latter is uppermost in this poem, typified by *sententiae* like:

> maxima debetur puero reverentia

> *The greatest respect is owed to the young.*     XIV. 47

60. Alcaeus, *Fr.* 101, Diehls.

and:

> Numquam aliud Natura, aliud Sapientia dicit.
>
> *Never does Nature say one thing and Wisdom another*     XIV. 321

It may well be that after Persius, and in view of the evil times, Satire could never be the genial castigation *mediocribus vitiis* that it was for Horace; or is it that the long *sermo* is now beginning to lose its bite to the more pithy and pungent epigram which Martial made popular in Rome?

67 The idea that children inherit their parents' vices is one of those recurring (it comes in the *Arrius* poem of Catullus),[61] but dubious beliefs: they are just as likely to revolt against them. When Juvenal presses this idea to extremes in his section on Judaeism he is indulging in special pleading, has clearly worn out his subject, and passes on to avarice. Even here he has little new to say, and there are echoes of *Satire* X in the section on the futility of the search for wealth.

68 *Satire* XV is remarkable for its bizarre theme and a return to the 'authentic' Juvenal treatment. How amazing is the religion of the Egyptians who worship animals and even vegetables:

> O sanctas gentes quibus haec nascuntur in hortis numina!
>
> *What a sacred race to have such deities growing in its gardens!*
>
>                                          XV. 10–11

Such reverence for life makes it all the more odd that they should be capable of brutality to men; yet such was the case in the fight between Ombi and Tentyra. Juvenal stresses the element of the fantastic in it by comparing himself as a story-teller to Odysseus. Then an Iliadic vignette emerges to balance the Odyssean in a horrific description of the actual battle. A more macabre element follows: so great is their haste that they do not even cook the flesh of the fallen man before eating it, and in the guttural alliteration of 'contenta cadavere crudo' the

61. Catullus, 84.

258

crushing of bones is heard. Here a cynical joke heightens the horror:

> Hic gaudere libet quod non violaverit ignem,
> quem summa caeli raptum de parte Prometheus
> donavit terris.

> *One may here rejoice that there was no violation of the fire which Prome-*
> *theus stole from highest heaven to present to those on earth.*   xv. 84–6

69 His reflection on the horror of the action, perhaps even allowable in times of dire hunger, leads up to the Stoic theme again:

> melius nos Zenonis praecepta monent.

> *We are better instructed by the teachings of Zeno.*          xv. 106–7

But what strikes us more forcibly and speaks to us direct across the ages is the tender humanity of a man who lived in one of the most barbarous centuries before our own:

> mollissima corda
> humano generi dare se natura fatetur
> quae lacrimas dedit; haec nostri pars optima sensus.

> *Nature confessed that she gave the tenderest hearts to human beings, when*
> *she gave us tears; for this is the best part of our make-up.*   xv. 132–3

Some Victorian critics found this *Satire* so repugnant that they tried to repudiate Juvenal's authorship. We, with our know-ledge of Belsen and Buchenwald, are more qualified to ap-preciate its horrific authenticity. True it is that there is greater loyalty among snakes: serpentum maior concordia.

70 *Satire* XVI deals with the privileges of being a soldier. Unfortunately what would have been a most intriguing social document tails off after sixty lines; the rest must have been lost at an early stage, or censored perhaps, or never written. What we have shows us enough of the rewards of soldiering – superiority and priority in law, riches, and the right to bequeath

property even during one's father's lifetime – to be really sinister in foreshadowing the military anarchy which was to descend on the Roman Empire in the third century A.D.

71 The origins of *Satura* are shrouded in mist – and yet two things are clear: Quintilian is surely right, in that, while in Greek literature there is much that can be called 'satirical', it was only with Lucilius and Ennius, unfortunately known to us only in fragments, that Satire became a distinctive genre, its matter being the castigation of human folly and vice, and its form the loosely knit, conversational hexameter which accounts for the total satirical output of Horace, Persius, and Juvenal. Lucilius and Ennius did for Roman literature with the hexameter what Hall and Marston did for English with the iambic couplet, later to find its full flowering in Dryden, Pope, and Johnson. They established the genre.

72 Secondly, to say that the genre originated with the Roman satirists is not to deny that it owed much to Greek influences, especially Aristophanes, whose technique of parody and exaggeration in the literary, social, political, and philosophical spheres was cardinal; but it goes back much earlier than that – to the *Batrachomyomachia*, Semonides, Archilochus, and Hipponax.

73 Satire in short is a product of society: it was born with European literature and is still vigorous within it today. Roman *Satura* was its main vehicle for over three centuries. Dryden defined the aim of Satire as 'the emendment of vices by correction'. Whether it has even done so is debatable – although it can undoubtedly influence a climate of opinion. Perhaps it is better to regard it as a safety-valve used for letting off steam against social pests. This, after all, is what Dryden himself was doing in *Absalom* and *Mac Flecknoe*; he certainly had no real hope of reforming Shaftesbury or Shadwell. Thomas Warton made the point well:

Could Boileau to reform a nation hope?
A Sodom can't be mended by a Pope!

Satire cannot of itself reform. It is simply a compulsive expression of indignation; the satirist looks at society and finds it almost impossible to write anything else, and so says, with Juvenal: 'Difficile est saturam non scribere.'

# Bibliography

1. FRAENKEL, EDUARD, *Horace*, Oxford, 1957.
2. RUDD, NIALL, *The Satires of Horace*, Cambridge, 1966.
3. PALMER, ARTHUR, *Horace, Satires* (edition), London, 1883.
4. SULLIVAN, J. P. (Ed.), *Critical Essays on Roman Literature, Satire*, London, 1963, includes:
   ANDERSON, W. S. on Horace, NISBET, R. G. M. on Persius, SULLIVAN, J. P. on Petronius, and MASON, H. A. on Juvenal.
5. HIGHET, GILBERT, *Juvenal the Satirist*, Oxford, 1954.
6. DUFF, J. *Juvenal, Satires* (edition), Cambridge, 1898.
7. GREEN, PETER, *Essays in Antiquity*, Chapter 8 'Roman Satire and Roman Society', London, 1960.
8. SULLIVAN, J. P. (Ed.), *Arion*, Vol. V, No. 3 (On Petronius), University of Texas, 1966.
9. THEOPHRASTUS and MENANDER, *Plays and Fragments*, tr. P. Vellacott, Harmondsworth, 1960.
10. LUCIAN, *Satirical Sketches*, tr. P. Turner, Harmondsworth, 1961.
11. CAMPBELL, A. Y. *Horace – A New Interpretation*, London, 1924.
12. FISKE, G. C. *Lucilius & Horace*, Madison, University of Wisconsin Studies, 1920.
13. FRANCIS, A. L. and TATUM, H. F. *Martial's Epigrams: Translation & Imitation*, Cambridge, 1924.
14. HOUSMAN, A. E. *D. Iunii Iuvenalis Saturae*, Cambridge, 1924.
15. SULLIVAN, J. P. *The 'Satyricon' of Petronius – A Literary Study*, London, 1968.
16. TATE, J. *Persius* (translation), Oxford, 1930.
17. VILLENEUVE, F. *Essai sur Perse*, Paris, Les Belles Lettres, 1918.
18. WIGHT-DUFF, J. *Roman Satire*, Cambridge, 1937.

# IX

# Tragedy
## *David Raven*

## Introductory

1 The comparative study of Greek and Latin literary *genres* is in many respects rather unrewarding when one reaches the field of tragic drama. Various reasons can be found for this. The first lies in the meagreness of the remains of Latin tragedy: while we possess thirty-two virtually complete fifth-century (B.C.) tragedies of Aeschylus, Sophocles, and Euripides (to say nothing of the disputed *Rhesus* and of numerous fragments, some of them very considerable in length), nothing survives but fragments, and mainly short fragments at that, from the work of such eminent Roman Republican tragedians as Ennius, Pacuvius, and Accius. Secondly, these latter tragedians wrote and produced early in the history and development of Latin literature, before language had been schooled, and metre sophisticated, under Greek literary influence; and, for all the natural vigour and robustness of their fragments, they seem to compare poorly with the mellowed maturity of their Greek models.

2 To both these statements an exception can be produced in the nine later plays usually (and not unreasonably) ascribed to the younger Seneca. These are indeed works of sophistication, do indeed provide some field for comparison with the Greek, and did indeed exert a remarkable influence over later European literature; but it has been widely accepted that they were never

designed for live production, and, be that as it may, their intention and emphasis carry us far from the spirit of the Greek tragedians. All this we shall observe in due course.

3 But a third reason may be put forward. This lies in the very derivativeness of Roman tragedy. It is, of course, true that nearly all Latin Literature was derivative to a high degree, and it would be foolish to regard it as second-rate on that account. Virgil's debt is immense to Homer, Hesiod, Theocritus, and many others; yet his greatness lies in his transforming touch: *nullum quod tetigit non ornavit*. The religious-cum-nationalistic dedication of the *Aeneid* (quite apart from its other merits) gives the poem a new and revitalizing dimension, which owes nothing to the Greeks. But the Roman tragedians, while adopting the form and substance and mythology of Greek tragedy,[1] could hardly hope to recapture the pervading religious spirit of what, to the Greeks, had begun and continued as a religious festival – a festival where (as we shall see) the very treatment of the dramatic themes tended to be 'religious', and to express a considerable 'moral attitude' (if not necessarily a conventional one) on the part of the poet. But what to the Greeks was entertainment under the aegis of the Gods must have tended to become entertainment pure and simple to the Romans: it is difficult to believe that the conscientious adaptations of the Republican dramatists (let alone the flashy verbal cleverness of Seneca) were aimed at reproducing the Greek idea of 'the poet as teacher'. The extent of the difference will be more apparent if we begin by surveying the growth and the spirit of Greek tragedy.

1. The *fabula praetexta*, described in §47 below, must have given the Romans far more scope for originality in this respect. In the absence of surviving *praetextae* (for the late *Octavia* ascribed to Seneca can hardly be ranked as a characteristic example) we are unable to judge how much use the Romans made of this opportunity.

## The Development of Greek Tragedy

4 On the origins of Greek tragedy much has been written,[2] but sadly little can be concluded. Its particularly close connection with the god Dionysus is attested not only by the annual tragic competition in Athens at the Great Dionysia but by the tradition (as old as Aristotle's *Poetics*) linking tragedy with the enigmatic dithyramb; by the frequency of Dionysus cult-stories actually treated by the tragedians, and the proverb οὐδὲν πρὸς Διόνυσον ('nothing to do with Dionysus') which grew up, according to Plutarch, as a complaint against the inclusion of other mythological treatments; and by the strongly Dionysiac element of the satyr-play which, whether it be regarded as the mother or the sister of tragedy, co-existed with it at the dramatic festivals.

5 Choral singing in honour of a god was a practice known to Homer,[3] and our own heritage of Greek lyric includes a notable early example in the beautiful *Partheneion* of Alcman. Of the special branch of cult-singing which grew into the dithyramb of Dionysiac worship we know all too little. But the development of the dithyramb, and even the appearance of satyrs in it, was attributed to Arion of Corinth (*c.* 600 B.C.), and the retention of Doric dialect-forms in all the lyrics of Athenian tragedy further emphasizes the strong Peloponnesian influence on the growth of the choral element. No dithyrambs survive from the pre-tragic period; but (whichever form actually influenced the other) one surviving fifth-century dithyramb (Bacchylides, xvi) forms a lyric dialogue between chorus and soloist, and it is tempting to conclude that, in the previous century, the introduction of dialogue into the choral song, through the medium of chorus-leader or actor, had provided the break-through from which drama could develop. The Athenians, at least, regarded the shadowy Thespis as the father of tragedy, both for his introduction of the actor's

2. Cf. especially A. W. Pickard-Cambridge, *Dithyramb, Tragedy and Comedy* (revised by T. B. L. Webster); A. Lesky, *Greek Tragedy*, Ch. 2.

3. Cf. Bowra, *Greek Lyric Poetry*, p. 5, and references there.

speaking part and for his productions (the first known) at the Great Dionysia about 535 B.C.

6 The derivation of the word τραγῳδία (tragedy) from τράγος (goat) gives rise to further dispute. The idea of peasant singers, at rude primitive festivals, competing for a goat as prize had much ancient backing. On the other hand, Aristotle believed the associated satyr-play to be the ancient precursor of tragedy, and the derivation of the word from 'goat-singers' – i.e. the satyrs of the Dionysiac retinue – also has much to recommend it. But the genuineness of the goat element in the traditional satyr figure has recently, and with good reason, been called into dispute. The works cited in note 2 above give a full summary of the arguments involved, and of the fascinating evidence from surviving works of art.

## Fifth-century Tragedy, and its Developing Styles: Formal Aspects

7 From Thespis through other important, yet almost equally shadowy, figures, such as Phrynichus and Pratinas, we reach the heyday of Athenian tragedy in the fifth century B.C. There is unfortunately no space here to examine the evidence for production, for the emergence of the elevated stage from the *orchestra* where the chorus remained, for primitive devices such as the γέρανος (crane) and ἐκκύκλημα (by which house interiors were represented), and for details of dress and of the indispensable mask.[4]

8 By the period now under discussion, three selected poets annually 'obtained a chorus', and each produced a tetralogy, consisting of three tragedies and one satyr-play, at the Great Dionysia in March. (Tragedies also came to be produced at the Lenaea.) At first it was a common practice for each competitor's three tragedies to form a genuine connected 'trilogy' in story (only one of the surviving Aeschylean tragedies is not in that

4. On these and kindred topics, cf. especially A. W. Pickard-Cambridge, *The Dramatic Festivals of Athens* (revised by D. M. Lewis and J. P. A. Gould); T. B. L. Webster, *Greek Theatre Production*.

class), but Sophocles and Euripides almost entirely abandoned this practice, although a much vaguer connection of themes is sometimes to be found in their productions.

9 On these productions, even if there is much ground for uncertainty and dispute, there is a reasonable amount of evidence. Apart from the surviving works and fragments of the three 'great' tragedians, valuable evidence is supplied by the *hypotheseis* existing for many plays, by many quotations or critical remarks in the works of other ancient authors, and by other literary sources ranging from Aristotle's *Poetics* to the *Suda* lexicon of *c.* A.D. 1000. We are helped, too, by inscriptions – notably the *Parian Marble* – and other catalogues: even since 1950 a new papyrus discovery has revolutionized our dating of Aeschylus' *Supplices*.

10 From such sources it is possible to name a high proportion of the works of the great tragedians, and in some cases to arrange the titles in tetralogies and assign certain or approximate dates to them. Although we possess only 7 tragedies each from the output of Aeschylus (to whom the *Suda* ascribes 90 plays in all) and Sophocles (some 120 plays), and 17 (excluding *Rhesus*) from Euripides' 66 tragedies,[5] we know the titles of a large percentage of the lost plays. Where external evidence is lacking, it is still often possible to 'date' surviving tragedies by criteria of style and technique.[6] For the very form

5. We lack a surprising number of titles for Euripides' satyr-plays. We know that the tragedy *Alcestis*, at least, was produced in the place of a satyr-play, and this and various other types of explanation have been given for the lack (cf. T. B. L. Webster as cited in n. 6). The form of drama may well have been uncongenial to Euripides: certainly his *Cyclops*, the one satyric drama surviving in full, seems sadly uninspired when compared with the lively fragments of Aeschylus' *Dictyulci* and Sophocles' *Ichneutae*.

6. In the case of Euripides, metrical criteria are particularly valuable: his growing freedom in allowing 'long' elements in his iambic trimeters to resolve into double-short makes it possible to group his plays with a high degree of probability. T. B. L. Webster (*The Tragedies of Euripides*, Ch. 2) combines this with other evidence to produce a plausible chronological order for the poet's whole tragic output. For discussion of the fragments of the other tragedians, cf. Vol. 2 of the Aeschylus Loeb translation (Weir-Smyth, revised by H. Lloyd-Jones), and Pearson's three-volume *Fragments of Sophocles*.

and structure of tragedies, quite apart from their internal content, developed and changed remarkably during the fifth century; and we must now consider this development.

11 Aeschylus' dramatic career lasted from about 496 B.C. to his death in 456; the career of Sophocles from 468 to his death (at the age of ninety) in 406, although *Oedipus Coloneus* was not actually produced until 401; Euripides' first production was in 455, and his last plays (including *Bacchae*) appeared very shortly after his death in 406. We have already seen that Thespis, according to tradition, had introduced an actor to balance the chorus; tradition also had it that Aeschylus introduced a second actor and Sophocles a third. (Certainly three actors are needed for the distribution of the parts in Aeschylus' *Oresteia*, produced ten years after Sophocles' *debut*; but some later tragedies – e.g. Euripides' *Alcestis* and *Medea* – strictly *need* only two actors, although it is, of course, possible that the parts were even so distributed round the usual three.)

12 Yet the tragedians were remarkably slow to exploit the possibilities of having even two or three characters on stage simultaneously. Our first surviving play, Aeschylus' *Persae*, was produced in 472 – some sixty years after the traditional date for Thespis' first production, and when Aeschylus himself had been producing for about a quarter of a century. Yet, for all its second actor, the play is still essentially an alternation of choric song with a single actor's soliloquies or dialogues with the chorus; only in two short stretches do the speaking characters actually converse. Similarly, even in *Agamemnon* (written after the introduction of the third actor), there is no conversation between actor and actor until after line 800. Sophocles and Euripides developed the effective use of dialogue, from brisk *stichomythia* (or line-for-line exchange, e.g. Soph. *Oedipus Tyrannus* 1007–46) to the lengthy and sophistical statements of the almost formalized *agon* (e.g. Eur. *Troades* 913–1032); but again years seem to have elapsed between the introduction of the third actor and any sustained use of three-cornered conversation. (It is illuminating to compare, say,

Sophocles' *Antigone* – produced in 442 B.C. – with Euripides' *Orestes* – 408 B.C. – in this respect.)

13 All this is evidence of the archaistic formality and somewhat statuesque nature of the production, of which other instances can be found. The Messenger Speech, for example, was a popular and almost indispensable survival from the days when narrative had not been replaced by dialogue: given the convention by which violence could not be portrayed on stage, and thus had to be narrated at second-hand, even so it is clear that Sophocles, and especially Euripides, revelled in the opportunity to indulge in lengthy and sensational descriptions often involving language much more grandiose than that of normal dialogue (e.g. Eur. *Bacchae* 677 ff., 1043 ff.).

14 The decline of the chorus, and of lyric song, was an inevitable consequence of the development of actors' parts and dialogues. In the plays of Aeschylus the chorus still often dominates to a degree where the actor seems subsidiary. We can surmise that, when first introduced by Thespis, the single actor often served merely to set the scene between one choral exposition of the theme and another. This can still be seen in Aeschylus, at *Persae* 532–680 and *Supplices* 524–709: in each of these passages two choral odes of some 60–80 lines each are separated by a mere twenty lines or so of dialogue setting the tone for the second ode. The first chorus, or *parodos*, of *Agamemnon* lasts 220 lines, and that of *Supplices* 175 lines: such unusual length is largely to be explained by the fact that each play opened a connected trilogy, and the chorus was being used to establish the background. There is in fact far more use made of lengthy choral song in *Agamemnon* than in the succeeding plays (*Choephori*, *Eumenides*) of the Orestes trilogy, and very likely the same could be said of *Supplices* as against the lost *Aegyptii* and *Danaides* which it preceded.

15 After Aeschylus, however, actors supersede the chorus both in length of parts and in concentration of interest. The proportion of lyrics declines from more than one-half in much

of Aeschylus to one-third in Sophocles, and to one-quarter or less in late Euripides. And the chorus, although it may be deeply involved (e.g. in Euripides' *Bacchae*), never dominates the action. There is a steady growth in the *episodes* of dialogue which separate the *parodos* and the other choral odes (*stasima*): Sophocles' *Antigone* and *Oedipus Tyrannus*, and Euripides' *Medea*, are good examples of this alternation, and the odes in these plays show well how the chorus, in spite of its subsidiary role, could still moralize effectively and relevantly upon the action. In the last years of the century (from about 420) the *kommos* or lyric interchange between actors (an old-established form) and the actor's *monody* (something of an innovation) tended to supersede the chorus. Choral odes became not only rarer but more incidental, and (especially in Euripides) served as interludes with little real connection with the action, although their themes were seldom actually irrelevant to it. (Euripides' *Orestes* is a good illustration of all these tendencies; the decline of the choral song to a mere interlude has its analogy in Greek Middle Comedy, and is also fatally illustrated by the Senecan lyrics which we shall consider later.)

16 The metrical practice of tragedy also changed during the century. We learn from Aristotle's *Poetics* that the original metre of spoken dialogue was the trochaic tetrameter, but that this was succeeded by the more wieldy iambic trimeter, which (in spite of differences in terminology) is basically the same length minus three syllables, as can be seen:

Trochaic tetrameter: – ∪ – ∪ – ∪ – ∪ – ∪ – ∪ – ∪ –
Iambic trimeter:              ∪ – ∪ – ∪ – ∪ – ∪ – ∪ –

The tetrameter is still used for normal dialogue in *Persae*, but later passed into virtual abeyance (except in occasional scenes of great excitement, e.g. the end of *Agamemnon*) until it was revived by Euripides after about 420 as an occasional substitute for the trimeter. Its presence is often another significant guide for dating.

17 Of the lyric metres of the chorus nothing can be said here. Mention may be made, however, of *anapaests* – rather four-

square marching measures basically of the form ∪∪ – ∪∪ – ∪∪ – ∪∪ –, which stand midway between spoken dialogue and the matching lyric strophes and antistrophes of choral song. Predictably, anapaests were associated with movement on stage (though not confined to it). In early tragedy they often formed the first part of the *parodos* (as in *Persae*) – perhaps always at the opening of a trilogy (*Supplices*, *Agamemnon*, Aeschylus' lost *Myrmidones*): their use is rarer, and more varied, in later fifth-century tragedy, though they seldom fail to appear for the gnomic tail-piece of Sophoclean and Euripidean tragedies.

## Tragic Themes in the Fifth Century

18 The preceding paragraphs have dealt only with the formal aspects of tragedy, and it is now time to look at the actual themes which the dramatists adapted before we consider the use that they made of them. With very few exceptions, these themes were drawn from mythology – the mythology of Homer and Hesiod, of lost poems of the Epic Cycle, and of localized hero cults. And it is not in theme alone that ancient critics considered the seed of tragedy to have been planted in epic. Apart from obvious points, such as the occurrence of speeches in epic narrative (and the temptation to oral poets to recite them 'dramatically'), an important reason for this conception is that in epic one first *sees tragic circumstances actually confronting human beings*. (Cf. Lesky, *Greek Tragedy*, Ch. 1.)

19 Apart from mythology stood a few Greek historical dramatizations: of these our only survivor is Aeschylus' *Persae*, which depicts the arrival at the Persian Court of the news of Xerxes' defeat in the Salamis campaign, and his own inglorious return home. But this type of play (which has some analogy in the Roman *praetexta*, cf. §47) was a rare one. Perhaps it was felt that the full implications of tragedy needed to be studied at a greater emotional distance; apparently Phrynichus' *Capture of Miletus* brought its author to be fined because of its all too effective emotional involvement of its audience.

20 In the main, then, the tragedians looked to mythology for their plots. But they allowed themselves very considerable freedom in their treatment of their themes and their management of the details. So much can be clearly seen from a comparison of Aeschylus' *Choephori* with the *Electras* of Sophocles and Euripides, where we possess all three tragedians' versions of the same story; and the ancient accounts of Euripides' lost *Antigone* suggest that it differed very sharply from its Sophoclean counterpart. Indeed, comparison of treatments seems to have played some part in the selection of plays that have reached us. Nine plays of Euripides appear (without *scholia*) in only one reputable MS. tradition, and (as Wilamowitz first suggested) are probably to be ascribed to the chance survival of one volume of a complete edition of the poet's plays in roughly alphabetical order, since their titles all begin with letters between E and K. But the remainder of our surviving tragedies reach us through a richer assortment of manuscripts, often copiously annotated, and it is generally believed that these were plays selected for educational use by the late Alexandrians. The selection of many of them can easily be attributed to their intrinsic excellence; but it is arguable that Euripides' *Phoenissae*, for example, owes its survival less to its quality than to its usefulness for comparison with Aeschylus' *Septem* and Sophocles' Theban plays, all covering much the same territory.

21 At any rate, the mixture of selection and coincidence leads to a remarkable concentration of plays on certain themes. If we discount the non-mythological *Persae*, but include the satyric *Cyclops* and the probably spurious *Rhesus*, of the 32 surviving works ascribed to the great tragedians, 16 deal with what we may call the 'Trojan cycle' of mythology, 6 with the 'Oedipus Cycle', and 4 with the 'Heracles cycle'. And the strength of these concentrations does not seem to have been entirely typical of the full conspectus of the tragedians' output, judging from the titles of the lost plays.

22 For reference purposes, a brief summary follows dealing with the place in different mythological themes of our surviving

tragedies. It need hardly be said that this summary has no relevance to the date of actual productions, and can be of no help towards an understanding of the tragedians' actual motivation, characterization, and treatment of the various themes. (From here onwards the abbreviations A., S., and E. are used in references for the full names of Aeschylus, Sophocles, and Euripides.)

A. THE TROJAN CYCLE. E. *Iphigenia in Aulis* shows us the Greek expedition delayed at Aulis, the summons to Iphigenia under the pretext of betrothal to Achilles, and her eventual sacrifice. *Rhesus* is a dramatization of the night operation (*Iliad* X) in which Odysseus and Diomedes kill the newly arrived Trojan ally Rhesus: this is, interestingly, the only surviving play within the action of the *Iliad*, although lost tragedies (e.g. Aeschylus' *Myrmidon* trilogy) covered various parts of it. S. *Ajax* and *Philoctetes* cover episodes in the post-Iliadic part of the Trojan war: the former describes Ajax's madness, death, and disputed burial after losing the famous contest with Odysseus for the arms of the fallen Achilles, and the latter the expedition of Odysseus and Neoptolemus to recover Philoctetes and his bow which is necessary for the taking of Troy. E. *Hecuba* and *Troades* describe incidents immediately following the sack of Troy, including Hecuba's blinding of the treacherous Polymestor, the killing of Hector's son Astyanax, and the allotment of Hecuba, Andromache, and other Trojan women to the victors. E. *Andromache* describes that heroine's persecution (when she has accompanied her master Neoptolemus home) at the hands of Hermione, Neoptolemus' new wife; this oddly divided play then proceeds to Hermione's abduction by her former betrothed Orestes, who has killed Neoptolemus.

Plays on the νόστοι (return home of the heroes) survive in the satyric E. *Cyclops*, lightly touching on Odysseus' captivity and subsequent blinding of the monster, and E. *Helen*, which dramatizes the old heresy that the real Helen had been imprisoned in Egypt, and only her phantom proceeded to Troy: the shipwrecked Menelaus meets his real wife accidentally and abducts her. A. *Agamemnon* of course shows us the hero's safe return to be murdered by Clytemnestra and her lover Aegisthus.

The avenging of Agamemnon's murder by his son Orestes, and Orestes' haunting by Clytemnestra's furies, is dealt with by the remainder of the Aeschylean trilogy (*Choephori* and *Eumenides*,

finishing happily with the cleansing of Orestes at Athens), by
S. *Electra* (which omits the furies and makes Orestes' revenge the
final triumph), and by E. *Electra*, whose progress and close is
savage and gloomy. Orestes' subsequent experiences are described by Euripides in *Orestes* (depicting various melodramatic
plans and frustrations in a hostile Argos), *Andromache* (already
referred to), and *Iphigenia in Tauris*, where he is wrecked among the
Tauri and meets and abducts his sister Iphigenia (previously
rescued from sacrifice by Artemis). This last play is problematic-
ally similar to *Helen* (above) in theme, progress, and structure.

B. THE OEDIPUS CYCLE. S. *Oedipus Tyrannus* works out at length
Oedipus' discovery that he unwittingly killed his father Laius
and married his mother Jocasta, and his self-blinding at this
discovery; in his later *Oedipus Coloneus* Sophocles shows us the
exiled Oedipus eventually granted asylum at Athens, his cursing
of his sons and his final, serene death. Different interpretations
of the sons' struggle for power in Thebes, the expedition brought
against his city by the ousted Polynices, and the death of the
brothers at each other's hands are shown by A. *Septem* (the third
play of a trilogy, following a lost *Laius* and *Oedipus*) and E.
*Phoenissae*. S. *Antigone* shows Antigone's defiant burial of her
brother Polynices, regarded in Thebes as a traitor, her consequent
death, and the concomitant disasters affecting Creon, who had
ordered it; E. *Supplices* portrays the similar refusal of Thebes to
grant burial to the remainder of the seven invading chieftains, and
its eventual capitulation to the prayers of their suppliant mothers
championed by Theseus of Athens.

C. THE HERACLES CYCLE. In E. *Alcestis* Heracles opposes
Death and recovers Alcestis, who had been permitted to die for
her husband Admetus. In E. *Heracles* he returns from his labours
to save his family from the threats of the Theban usurper Lycus,
but is subsequently maddened through the enmity of Hera and
kills his own children. In S. *Trachiniae* his wife Deianira sends him
a robe anointed with a charm which she supposes will recover
her his love; but the charm is a poison, and Heracles dies shortly
after her suicide. In E. *Heraclidae* the deceased hero's family is
persecuted by his old enemy Eurystheus, but finds asylum and
protection at Athens.

D. MISCELLANEOUS PLAYS
A. *Prometheus Vinctus*, our one genuinely Olympian play, portrays
the punishments inflicted on the Titan Prometheus for his rebel-

lion from the newly established Zeus. It is uncertain whether this most problematical play stood first or second in its trilogy, and how Aeschylus resolved the severe conflict of divine forces.

A. *Supplices*, the first play of a trilogy, shows Danaus' fifty daughters fleeing to Argos to escape marriage with their cousins; the lost remainder of the trilogy covered their reluctant marriage and their murder of all their husbands save one.

In E. *Medea* Jason has contracted a new marriage in Corinth, and the spurned Medea, in a singularly thorough revenge, kills the new bride and her father, and finally her own children, before escaping to Athens.

In E. *Hippolytus* (the poet's second play on this theme) Theseus' son Hippolytus has scorned Aphrodite, who in revenge drives his step-mother Phaedra to love him; his rejection of Phaedra, her suicide leaving a false accusation of him, Theseus' curse on his son and its subsequent fulfilment leaves Theseus destitute though forgiven by the dying Hippolytos.

E. *Bacchae* again deals with a spurned deity – Dionysus, whose special connection with tragedy we have already seen (§4) and whose epiphany in Greece was a favourite dramatic subject long after tragedy had established its independence of the dithyramb (cf. §5). This play depicts the god's rejection by Pentheus of Thebes, and his pitiless revenge by causing Pentheus' murder at the hands of the frenzied Bacchic revellers (including his own mother).

E. *Ion* introduces a less familiar Athenian cult-story – the restoration of Ion, a foundling child of Apollo, to his mother Creusa after she has attempted to kill him in the belief that he is a bastard son of her husband, Xuthus of Athens.


## Religious Spirit of Greek Tragedy

23 The foregoing survey of course helps little towards understanding the different attitudes and characteristics of the tragedies, which are discussed in succeeding sections. Nor does it show how essentially religious was the spirit behind Greek tragedy, a spirit which was surely communicated to its audience. There *are*, of course, occasional plays (Euripides' *Helen*, for example) in which it is hard to find a 'message' of any great profundity, or to feel that the audience imbibed

much material for serious reflection. Far more typical, however, is the depth of feeling which for Aristotle was so essential
to tragedy. So much has been written on the *catharsis* ('purgation') which tragedy should effect in its audience, in Aristotle's
judgement, that a lengthy statement here would be super-
fluous;[7] suffice it that, for him, this 'purgation' should be
effected by feelings of pity and fear, in a blend best produced
by certain conditions – such as when his ideal tragic hero (who
should not be faultless, but also not vicious) is brought
low, not through vice but through a mistake.[8] For these
purposes Aristotle found Sophocles' *Oedipus Tyrannus* the perfect
play.

24 Moral issues, then, predominate – most clearly when the
Gods can be brought in. The resolution of a problem by a
timely *deus ex machina* in the final scene may often seem, in
Euripides, a tired device (e.g. in his *Electra* or *Orestes*), but his
precursors probably made more significant use of it. In the
most serious tragedies the Gods are seldom unmentioned for
long, and hymns and prayers to them are common. The full-
length choral hymn is not rare – e.g. *Oed. Tyr.* 151 ff., *Ant.*
1115 ff., both examples of a particularly formal εἴ ποτε . . . καὶ
νῦν . . . type, not unfamiliar to readers of the psalms: the God
has been favourable in the past, may he be so again. The hymn
element is seldom absent from the choral odes of *Bacchae*. In one
(370 ff.) a prayer to Holiness ('Οσία) merges into another common form, the escapist hymn (403 ff.) quoted in §43 below,
which may be compared with *Hipp.* 732 ff. or with the psalmist's 'O that I had wings like a dove'.

25 In combining ecstasy and prayer with the story of the advent
of Dionysus, the God of the dramatic festival, the *Bacchae*

---

7. Cf. especially Lesky, *Greek Tragedy*, Ch. 1 ('What is tragedy?'); also J.
Jones, *On Aristotle and Greek Tragedy*.

8. This is a watered-down paraphrase of parts of Aristotle's *Poetics* XI–XIV.
That 'mistake' and not 'moral frailty' is the meaning of *hamartia* here may now
be taken as certain. Cf. most recently E. R. Dodds, 'On misunderstanding the
Oedipus Rex', *G. & R.*, 1966.

theme was clearly ideal. Its ecstatic worship ranges from the identification of the priest with the God (115),

*Βρόμιος ὅστις ἄγῃ θιάσους*

*whoever leads our dance is Dionysus.*

to the myth of the God's birth (88 ff.) and the pounding rhythm of the cry to worship in 83 ff.,

*ἴτε βάκχαι, ἴτε βάκχαι,*
*Βρόμιον παῖδα θεὸν θεοῦ*
*Διόνυσον κατάγουσαι . . .*

*Come, come, Bacchants, leading Bromius Dionysus, God and Son of a God . . .*

The Dionysiac ritual was, of course, a favourite theme in tragedy, and the hymns of this play may be contrasted with a substantial fragment from Aeschylus' *Edonoi*

*σεμνὰ Κοτυτοῦς ὄργι' ἔχοντες . . .*
*ὁ μὲν ἐν χερσὶν βόμβυκας ἔχων,*
*τόρνου κάματον,*
*δακτυλόδικτον πίμπλησι μέλος,*
*μανίας ἐπαρωγὸν ὁμοκλάν.*

*Holding Cotyto's holy rites . . . one, with the pipe, worked on the lathe, in his hands, blows his fingered melody, the sound that brings on frenzy.*

This passage continues for a further six lines of equally powerful expression.

26 More formalized elements also bring the hymn to mind. There are passages in *Bacchae* (e.g. 877 ff.) where the hymn-like refrain, in its simplicity and rhythm, recalls Anacreon's hymn to Artemis (348 D.L. Page, and cf. Catullus xxxiv) and rhythmical 'refrains' in a few other tragic choruses (cf. the structure of Aeschylus' *Supp.* 630 ff., *Agam.* 367 ff., and *Heracles* 348 ff.). Not without its religious significance, too, is Euripides' strange practice of mentioning, late in nearly all

his surviving plays, future religious cults connected with the characters involved (e.g. *Hipp.* 1423).

27 Almost as noticeable is a strong nationalistic fervour. The glories of Athens are the subject of two of tragedy's most famous odes, which should be compared (Soph. *O.C.* 668 ff., Eur. *Med.* 824 ff.); apart from the beauty of the poetry, it must be realized that in each case Athens has offered *asylum*. And it is noticeable how often Athens (sometimes through the agency of one of her Kings, such as Theseus) is found as the champion of liberty or the saviour of the oppressed. (See the plots of *Eum.*, *Oed. Col.*, Eur. *Supp.* and *El.*, *Med.*, *Heraclidae*, and *Heracles.*)

## Individual Characteristics of the Tragedians:
## (1) Aeschylus

28 With the exception of *Persae*, all our surviving Aeschylean tragedies form part of the connected trilogy-form in which this poet specialized, but which other tragedians avoided. It can hardly be disputed that this form gave him a welcome opportunity to develop themes at great length. Thus, in *Oresteia* he has ample space in the early long choral odes (see §14) to give the background for Agamemnon's murder; *Agamemnon* is followed by *Choephori*, in which Clytemnestra (who had slain Agamemnon in requital for his own slaying of Iphigenia) receives *her* death at Orestes' hands. At the end of *Choephori* the chorus can pessimistically sing

ποῖ δῆτα κρανεῖ, ποῖ καταλήξει
μετακοιμισθὲν μένος "Ατης;

*Where will an end be found, where will the fury of Calamity sink into slumber?*

as Orestes is maddened in requital for his matricide; yet there is still space in *Eumenides* for the conflicting moralities to be reconciled, and the triology can end in triumph

Ζεὺς ὁ πανόπτας
οὕτω Μοῖρά τε συγκατέβα.
ὀλολύξατε νῦν ἐπὶ μολπαῖς.

*All seeing Zeus and Fate have come down together. Cry joyfully in echo to our song!*

Thus (as so often) it is the gravity of the issues, and not a 'tragic' conclusion in the English sense, which is necessary to tragic trilogy; and other works of Aeschylus finished with similar reconciliation. For example, although we do not know whether *Prometheus Vinctus* stood first or second in its trilogy, we may be sure that the reconciliation of Prometheus with Zeus formed the conclusion.

29 Indeed, for Aeschylus even more than for the other tragedians, tragedy is fashioned from moral issues. (Even the single *Persae* shows the familiar pattern of *hybris*, insolence, leading to *nemesis*, its avenger.) Zeus is constantly referred to in the *Oresteia* and *Supplices*, and his contrasting 'tyrannical' presentation in *Prometheus* would surely be explained if we possessed the whole trilogy. Even where the Gods themselves are not in evidence, there is a near-personification of such forces as *Hybris* and *Nemesis*, and of *Atè*, a force embracing the process of mental infatuation, mad act, and consequent ruin (see the last lines of *Choephori* quoted above). *Agam.* 763–82 is a classic example of such personification, opening

φιλεῖ δὲ τίκτειν ὕβρις μὲν παλαι—
ὰ νεάζουσαν ἐν κακοῖς βροτῶν
ὕβριν . . .

*But old insolence is wont to bring forth young insolence in wicked men.*

This personification is linked also with the theme of hereditary ill at *Septem* 720 ff., a lengthy statement which should be compared with its counterpart (again in a Theban play) in Sophocles, *Ant.* 582–625.

30 This deep-set and restless moral awareness, together with his elevated language and style (for which see §31), compensates

in Aeschylus for the static nature of much of the action. For him drama had simply not reached the sophistication of plot and characterization which we see in Sophocles' work. His characters are statuesque, even if on a grand scale: the stubbornness of Prometheus and the single-minded revenge mania of Clytemnestra are glorious creations, but their inflexibility removes them from our plane. Yet he shows a sure touch in drawing his less 'exalted' personalities, such as the watchman in *Agamemnon* and the Nurse in *Choephori*, and the latter's homely prattle about the most sordid aspects of baby-nurture (*Cho.* 749–60) gains rather than loses from the splendid elevation of its language.

31 And certainly the language and style of Aeschylus form an essential part of our appreciation of him. One can often best appreciate an author by seeing him parodied; and no student should fail to benefit, in this respect, from the contest between Aeschylus and Euripides in the second part of Aristophanes' *Frogs*, where a superb burlesque is made of both these tragedians' characteristics. In particular, one should notice what Aristophanes calls Aeschylus' ῥήμαθ' ἱππόκρημνα ('big-beetling phrases'); in his most grandiose descriptions these culminate in the famous three-word iambic lines such as (*Prom.* 799)

δρακοντόμαλλοι Γοργόνες βροτοστυγεῖς

*snake-haired man-hating Gorgons.*

Prometheus' prophecy of Io's wanderings (*Prom.* 700 ff. and 786 ff.), and Clytemnestra's description of the beacons and the fall of Troy (*Agam.* 281–347) are fine examples of his style. A notable feature is his tendency to load one noun with numerous agreeing adjectives or adjectival phrases, an extreme case being *Agam.* 154–5 (the weird end of a weird prophecy)

μίμνει γὰρ φοβερὰ παλίνορτος
οἰκόνομος δολία μνάμων μῆνις τεκνόποινος.

*For there abides wrath, terrible, recurrent, ranging the house, crafty, of long memory, child-avenging.*

32 Yet his style is not always so rugged. There is a softer
quality, for example, in his description of the Erinys (Revenge-
spirit) on its first, deceptively calm, entry into Troy, appearing
as

μαλθακὸν ὀμμάτων βέλος,
δηξίθυμον ἔρωτος ἄνθος.

*a soft arrow of the eyes, a flower of love that stings the heart.*

*Agam.* 742–3

And his flexibility is shown by his ability to relax into the contrasting frivolity of the satyr-play: the recently discovered fragments of his *Dictyulci*[9] are most pleasing in this respect, as
when the satyrs are seen hauling Danae away to her 'marriage':

. . . καὶ τήνδ' ἐσορῶ νύμφην ἤδη
πάνυ βουλομένην τῆς ἡμετέρας
φιλότητος ἄδην κορέσασθαι.

*And I see that the bride is already yearning to have a surfeit of our love.*

There is an almost Aristophanic simplicity in parts of these
fragments. The master of the elevated and grandiloquent
knew how to relax.

## (2) Sophocles

33 No genuinely early work survives of any of the three great
tragedians. In the case of Sophocles this lack[10] is particularly
deplorable, for it leaves us without evidence for the spectacular
advance in structure, plot, and characterization separating his
earliest surviving plays from Aeschylus' latest. As it is, this
poet has often suffered unjust criticism through comparison
with Aeschylus and Euripides – for lacking the deep moral
preoccupations of the one, and the pioneering unconven-

9. These can most readily be found, edited and translated by H. Lloyd-Jones,
in the Appendix to the 1957 edition of the Loeb Aeschylus, Vol. 2.

10. *Antigone* was presented in 442, when the poet had already been producing
for twenty-five years, and it is unlikely that *Ajax* was very much earlier.

tionality of the other. Yet the technical development which must have characterized his early plays must also have excused the former criticism and rebutted the latter.

34 On moral and religious subjects, his difference from Aeschylus lies not in apathy but in his acceptance of traditional principles *without discussion*. Aeschylus, in the spacious field of a trilogy, had leisure to consider Orestes' matricide as a moral issue. Sophocles in writing his *Electra*, a single play, was concentrating on problems of characterization and accepted, undiscussed, the traditional view of Orestes' rightness which Aeschylus had perhaps been the first to question and which even Aeschylus had eventually approved. Sophocles' play contrasts more remarkably with Euripides' *Electra*. Euripides had launched a harsh attack on some elements of Aeschylus' *Choephori* (revived shortly beforehand); and that Sophocles could answer[11] this attack with his own morally unconcerned version – accepting traditional views *but without underlining the fact* – must be taken as perfect evidence for the serenity first attributed to him by Aristophanes' famous judgement (*Frogs* 82):

ὁ δ᾽ εὔκολος μὲν ἐνθάδ᾽, εὔκολος δ᾽ ἐκεῖ

*but he was serene in life, and is serene after life.*

Only in a few phrases reminiscent of the *Oresteia* (including Clytemnestra's death cries, *El.* 1415–6, which echo those of Aeschylus' Agamemnon) do we find, perhaps, a hint that we can look back to Aeschylus for Orestes' moral justification.

35 Orestes' matricide is accepted as justifiable because it is 'blood for blood'. No such justification can be extended to Oedipus' (unconscious) murder of his father and marriage with his mother. In *Oedipus Tyrannus* Sophocles seems again content to accept the fact that such actions are *ritually* unclean and lead

11. That the Sophoclean *Electra* (certainly one of his later plays) followed the Euripidean cannot be proved, but becomes more highly probable now that the latter is securely dated to a period *before* 415. Cf. Zuntz, *The Political Plays of Euripides*, pp. 64 ff.

to extreme disaster in consequence. It is notable how carefully he avoids any *moral* condemnation of Oedipus, to whom only a pedant could attribute any moral blame for his 'mistake' (*hamartia*),[12] and who is indeed portrayed sympathetically and at length in the last scenes of this play, and in the late *Oedipus Coloneus*; yet how unwaveringly his uncleanness is accepted. *Inevitability* is perhaps the key word for understanding *Oedipus Tyrannus*, which since Aristotle's day has been regarded as 'the perfect tragedy'. By the standards of modern detective stories, the plot shows some culpable incongruities and some improbable coincidences of time, place, and character;[13] but its reputation is amply justified by its continual tragic ironies, and by the forcefulness of the *peripeteia* (reversal of fate), as well as by Oedipus' presentation as a figure ideal to produce the pity-and-fear reactions necessary for the Aristotelian *catharsis* (see §23 above).

36 Although *Oedipus Tyrannus*, in particular, derives so much of its greatness from its plot-construction, Sophocles' advance on Aeschylus is hardly less striking in characterization. The relatively early *Antigone* is essentially a play of conflict, the type of conflict which Goethe regarded as germane to tragedy: to obey the Gods' laws (by burying a brother's corpse) or to obey a King's edict (by denying it burial)? But even here it is the conflicting portrayal of Antigone and Creon which gives the play its bite. Again, the characterization of Ajax, and of Deianira (in *Trachiniae*), are central to their respective plays; and in his last surviving plays (*Electra*, *Philoctetes*, and *Oedipus Coloneus*) Sophocles shows an interest in drawing characters in isolation, which supersedes 'plot' to a degree which some find objectionable. (Thus in *Electra*, which has already been seen to ignore *moral* issues of matricide, the heroine is characterized in 1,300 lines of comparative inactivity before the crowded 120 lines which embrace the actual murders.)

12. Cf. E. R. Dodds in *G. and R.*, 1966.

13. See A. J. A. Waldock, *Sophocles the Dramatist*, pp. 163 ff. Yet the coincidences should not be considered as flaws, but as an intentional build-up of events to *prove* the inevitability.

37 Sophocles (according to Plutarch) claimed to have rid himself early in life of the inflated style of Aeschylus. Certainly his appeal lies less strikingly in his actual language, though this, too, may halt the reader by its sheer power – as in his graphic account of the battle before Thebes (*Ant.* 100 ff., which may be compared with another description at *Oed. Col.* 1044 ff.), or in his praises of Athens already referred to (§27) at *Oed. Col.* 668 ff., e.g.

> τὸν ἀργῆτα Κολωνόν, ἔνθ'
> ἁ λίγεια μινύρεται
> θαμίζουσα μάλιστ' ἀη-
> δὼν χλωραῖς ὑπὸ βάσσαις.

*gleaming Colonus, where the shrill nightingale comes full often to sing beneath the green glades.*

But on the whole the stature of his language depends vitally on his matching of ideas with expression – as in Antigone's self-explanation (*Ant.* 523),

> οὔτοι συνεχθεῖν, ἀλλὰ συμφιλεῖν ἔφυν

*my nature is to join not in hating but in loving*

where the poet coins two compound verbs – in Electra's address to the urn supposedly containing her brother's ashes (*El.* 1126 ff.) – in Oedipus' curse on his sons (*Oed. Col.* 1348 ff.) – or in Antigone's appeal to the unwritten laws of heaven (*Ant.* 450 ff., which should be compared with the choral utterance at *Oed. Tyr.* 863 ff.).

38 Among other Sophoclean characteristics one may note a strong sense of dramatic relevance. This shows itself excellently in his prologues, where the reader is (except in *Trachiniae*) introduced to the story through the natural medium of dialogue: this contrasts notably with the leisurely exposition of Aeschylus in prologue and parodos, and with the often artificial ῥῆσις (set speech) which we shall see to be typical of Euripides. Sophocles has also a strong feeling for contrast:

*Electra*, for example, alternates sharply between scenes of misery and of optimism, and in *Antigone* the chief character's isolation is emphasized by her confrontation with a chorus which is (unconventionally) of the opposite sex and (also unconventionally) opposed to her. What is more, five of the seven surviving plays show a special device of contrast where a disaster[14] is shortly preceded by a particularly cheerful or hopeful choral ode (cp. *Aj.* 693 ff., *Ant.* 1115 ff., *Trach.* 633 ff., *Oed. Tyr.* 1086 ff., *El.* 473 ff.).

## (3) Euripides

39 Among his contemporaries Euripides ranked relatively low: it is remarkable how seldom he won the first prize at the Dionysiac festival, even the production which included the powerful *Medea* being placed third. His reputation as a *poet* is established by the tradition that Athenian prisoners in Sicily won favours for reciting his verse; and it is hard not to conclude that his unpopularity lay mainly in the unconventionality of his views – his portrayal of degraded or embittered women, his alleged attacks on the Gods, his merciless picture (in *Troades*) of a ravaged city in reaction to the Athenians' outrageous treatment of Melos. As in the case of Aeschylus, his characteristics are beautifully illustrated by the parodies and burlesques of the *Frogs*; but Aristophanes' presentation of him elsewhere (in *Acharnians* and *Thesmophoriazusae*) is also significant for his status in Athens.

40 Indeed, so common is the realization of his unconventional qualities that a word of caution is needed. Euripides' Medea is a diabolical creation, as was (we gather) the Phaedra in his first (lost) *Hippolytus*; but he is capable enough of presenting 'conventional' heroines such as Alcestis and Andromache. Apollo is criticized in *Electra* and abused in *Ion*; yet the latter play contains also a lyrical glorification of his worship (82–183) which cannot be the writing of a soured atheist. And the

14. Or, in *Electra*, an untrue report of a disaster—a uniquely unconventional use of the messenger speech.

pitilessness of Dionysus in *Bacchae* is still compatible with the deep and joyous worship of the same God pervading the play (see §25 above). It seems rather that Euripides was ready enough to worship the natural forces represented by the traditional Gods – but also to realize that much in nature *is* cruel, illogical, and hard to justify *morally*, and to suggest as much forcibly to an otherwise uncritical audience.[15]

41 This is not to deny that much of Euripides' appeal comes from his unconventionality. *Medea* is remarkable not only for its 'heroine' but for a preoccupation with femininity (cf. 230–51, 410–30, 1081–115). *Electra* gains its power from its contrast with Aeschylus' *Oresteia* and Sophocles' (probably later) *Electra*: we are confronted with a savage heroine, a cowardly Orestes, redeeming features in Clytemnestra and Aegisthus, and a round condemnation, if not of Apollo, certainly of his oracle. Unqualified approval is given only to Electra's farmer husband; indeed, approval of the 'honest peasant' is characteristic of Euripides' later work (*El.* 380 ff., *Or.* 917 ff.) and should be compared with the choral praises of the simple and unsophisticated which occur throughout *Bacchae* (e.g. 395–432).

42 In some ways the poet's urge to experiment led him to lose, rather than gain, in realism. Sophocles' use of dialogue in his prologues is (as said in §38 above) far more natural than the Euripidean set ῥῆσις. This method of exposition can be effective, as in the opening prayer of Medea's nurse

εἴθ' ὤφελ' 'Αργοῦς μὴ διαπτάσθαι σκάφος . . .

*would that the Argo had never sped . . .*

which was translated by Ennius

utinam ne in nemore Pelio . . .

in his *Medea*, and echoed also by Catullus (LXIV. 171) and Virgil (*Aen.* IV. 657). But more often this ῥῆσις becomes a formal

15. Cf. E. R. Dodds' edition of *Bacchae*, xxxvii–xliv, for an excellent study of the poet's motivation.

narrative, which Aristophanes makes Aeschylus parody in his 'oil-flask' scene (*Frogs* 1198 ff.), e.g.

> Eur. Σιδώνιόν ποτ' ἄστυ Κάδμος ἐκλιπὼν
> Ἀγήνορος παῖς—Aes. ληκύθιον ἀπώλεσεν.

> *Cadmus, son of Agenar, leaving once Sidon's city . . . lost his oil-flask*

The point of the joke lies in the narrative style and the pause in syntax at a point in the line which enables Aeschylus to slip in the oil-flask. Similarly Euripides' *agon* scene (set argument between two characters) becomes stereotyped in its form – cf. *Medea* 465–575, *Troades* 914–1032, *Phoenissae* 469–525; and similar stylization can be observed in his recognition scenes and actors' monodies. His messenger speeches also lapse severely from 'probability': in *Ion* a messenger arrives in great haste, yet spends 107 lines explaining why he must hurry on!

43 Euripides' actual style is enormously varied, and often used as a vehicle for characterization. The tutor in *Medea*, for example, shows his pomposity in addressing a fellow-servant (49),

> παλαιὸν οἴκων κτῆμα δεσποίνης ἐμῆς

> *O ancient chattel of my mistress' house,*

and the style if not the exact meaning is echoed in Ennius' *Medea* (262W)

> antiqua erilis fida custos corporis.

Medea herself is given several truly 'catty' remarks, in the simplest language, presenting yet another side to her character (Eur. *Med.* 623–4, 1394, 1396). Still more important is a taste for the epigrammatic or the clever, as in Hippolytus' famous forswearing (*Hipp.* 612)

> ἡ γλῶσσ' ὀμώμοχ', ἡ δὲ φρὴν ἀνώμοτος.

> *my tongue has sworn, my mind has not.*

286

which we find echoed in Shakespeare (2 *Hen. VI*, v. i. 182–3);
or in a fragment of *Alcmaeon*

—μητέρα κατέκταν τὴν ἐμήν, βραχὺς λόγος.
—ἑκὼν ἑκοῦσαν, ἢ οὐχ ἑκοῦσαν οὐχ ἑκών;

*I killed my mother, to put it briefly. — Were you both willing or both un-*
*willing parties?*

Such verbal trickery explains his particular influence upon
Seneca's tragic style (see §49 below); and it is also notable how
strongly Virgil, in rhetorical passages in *Aeneid*. iv, draws on
soliloquies in *Medea* (cf. *Med.* 376–409 with *Aen.* iv, 504–52;
and see also §42 above). The quality of Euripides' choral odes
likewise varies, both in depth of sentiment and in originality
of thought. In particular, one can sometimes detect an almost
monotonous sameness of theme and rhythm, as may be seen
by comparing three passages referring to the Nereids (*Ion*
1080 ff., *Iph. Taur.* 427 ff., *Iph. Aul.* 1055 ff.). But this is not
always so. There is a continual warmth and appeal in many of
his nature-descriptions – as of the dawn in a *Phaethon* fragment,
of the night sky in *Iph. Aul.* 6 ff. (see §48 below), of sunrise
over the gleaming rocks of Delphi in *Ion* 82 ff. The escapist
hymn is a common element (see §24 above), but there is
nothing common or unoriginal in *Bacch.* 403 ff.

ἱκοίμαν παρὰ Κύπρον,
νᾶσον τᾶς Ἀφροδίτας,
ἵν' οἱ θελξίφρονες νέμον-
ται θνατοῖσιν Ἔρωτες.

*O that I might go to Cyprus, Aphrodite's isle, where dwell the Loves*
*which charm the hearts of men.*

## Development of Tragedy under the Roman Republic

44 Of Greek tragedy after the fifth century we possess practically nothing substantial, except (probably) the pseudo-
Euripidean *Rhesus*, and our knowledge is correspondingly

limited. Much new tragedy was, however, produced, and old tragedy revived, as the form of entertainment gained popularity outside Athens and theatres flourished elsewhere. It is likely enough that later tragedy lacked much of the intensely religious spirit of the fifth century, and (with the growth in importance of characterization) far more emphasis was placed on the virtuosity of individual actors. This is certainly borne out by our scanty evidence for Roman Republican tragedy.

45 Of the origins of Roman drama something is said elsewhere in this book. We are here concerned with the revival of interest in tragedy (as in comedy and epic) on the part of the authors who spread Greek literary influence, and effectively both created and limited Latin literary merit, under the later Republic. We possess very few fragments of the pioneer work in this field of Livius Andronicus, who in 240 B.C. first translated a Greek tragedy, and of Naevius, who in addition to this type of work created the essentially Roman *fabula praetexta* (cf. §47). More substantial fragments survive of the tragedies of Ennius, Pacuvius, and Accius, who successively developed the *genre* in the second and early first century. Many of these fragments, and much of our information, are gathered from Cicero,[16] who tells us, for example, of the Romans' taste for sheer spectacle gratified by the sight of hundreds of mules in the theatre (*ad Fam.* VII. 1. 2), and of the specializations of different actors in chosen parts (*de Off.* 1. 114). The latter characteristic was, as we have seen, probably derived from late Greek tragedy; the former, typically Roman, shows us yet another new circumstance with which tragedy had to reckon.

## Characteristics of Republican Tragedy

46 The relatively low reputation of Republican tragedy is due to other factors besides its fragmentary survival. First, we may consider those of language and metre. It must be remembered

16. Cicero himself (*Tusc. Disp.* ii. 10) made his own translation from Aeschylus' lost *Prometheus Unbound*.

that we are surveying an early stage of literary development; and although such lines as Pacuvius' (*fr.* 352 W[17])

Nerei repandirostrum incurvicervicum pecus

*Nereus' snout-upturned awry-necked herd.*

may have an Aeschylean ring for some (cf. §31), even ancient critics regarded them rather as uncouth. Metre also presented difficulties. Not only did Republican dramatists find the complexity of Greek *lyrics* unattainable, but even in dialogue metres and anapaests (cf. §§16–17) they were faced with the grave difficulty of applying Greek quantitative principles to a language which relied strongly on word-accent and was embarrassingly rich in long syllables. By the first century this difficulty was mastered; but at this earlier stage the poets were content, for example, to replace the scheme of the Greek iambic trimeter

$$\underset{-}{\cup} - \cup - \underset{-}{\cup} - \cup - \underset{-}{\cup} - \cup -$$

with the far heavier $\quad \underset{-}{\cup} - \underset{-}{\cup} - \underset{-}{\cup} - \underset{-}{\cup} - \underset{-}{\cup} - \cup -$

– though the frequent coincidence of word-accent with the essentially long elements emphasized the basic rhythm.

47 A still more important factor is the attitude of the poets concerned. We have already seen that the great Greek tragedians were all pioneers in the form and interpretation of one specialized field, influenced in their own ways by strong religious associations. Livius, Naevius, and Ennius were, on a much wider and less dedicated scale, experimenters with several literary forms, adapting Greek comedies as well as tragedies. Roman tragedy was, in fact, highly derivative, not only in its titles but in its plots and even, often enough, its words (cf. §48). It is true that nearly all Latin literature was derivative to a considerable degree; but in this case originality of approach would seem to have been unusually scarce. The attitude of the audience is also significant: the Romans' pleasure

17. These references are to Warmington's two-volume *Remains of Old Latin* in the Loeb Classical Library, which also contains the original Greek models where they survive.

in histrionic effect and gorgeous spectacle (§45) was probably as unfavourable to the cause of serious or original moral thinking in tragedy as was, later, the educated citizen's pre-occupation with rhetoric (cf. §49). A striking indication of the tragedians' unoriginality lies in the relative failure of the *fabula praetexta* (§45). Though not profound theologians, the Romans were nationalistic to a degree which Virgil could later almost sanctify; yet the nationalistic possibilities of the *praetexta* seem never to have been fully exploited, and few titles survive. Yet its possibilities are well demonstrated by this quotation from a prophecy in Accius' *Brutus* (36–8 W):

> Haec bene verruncent populo! nam quod ad dexteram
> cepit cursum ab laeva signum praepotens, pulcherrume
> auguratum est rem Romanam publicam summam fore.

> *May this turn out well for our people! For in that the most powerful star
> moved from left towards the right, thus was the Roman state's supremacy
> most favourably foretold.*

48 In actual language we can observe an unusual closeness of expression between the fragments and such original Greek models that survive. The fragments of Ennius' *Medea*, for example, are practically translations from Euripides (cf. 253–95 W, and see quotations in §§42–3 above); almost as close is his adaptation (157–61 W) of Athena's invocation of the Eumenides' blessings (Aesch. *Eum.* 903 ff.). The opening of his *Iphigenia*, on the other hand, is less dependent in detail on Euripides, although clearly derived, e.g.

(*a*) – τίς ποτ' ἄρ' ἀστὴρ ὅδε πορθμεύει;
    – Σείριος ἐγγὺς τῆς ἑπταπόρου
    Πλειάδος ἄσσων ἔτι μεσσήρης.

*What star passes there? – Sirius, faring still in mid-heaven near the
seven Pleiades.*                                          Eur. *Iph. Aul.* 6–8

(*b*) – Quid noctis videtur in altisono
    caeli clipeo? – temo superat
    stellis sublime agitans etiam atque
    etiam noctis iter.

*What of the night is seen in heaven's high-echoing shield? – The Wain*
*dominates the stars, driving ever onward through night's lofty path.*

Enn., 222–5 W

Accius' debt to Euripides can easily be seen in the fragments
of *Bacchae* (201–26 W); but this poet's language has a fine
vigour which repays study for its own sake. Alliteration is
striking in this passage from his *Philoctetes* (552–3 W):

> Cum ex viperino morsum venae viscerum
> veneno imbutae taetros cruciatus cient.

> *When my body's veins, poisoned by the viper's bite, arouse hideous torments.*

In this equally vigorous passage from his *Argonautae*, a shepherd describes the approaching Argo (385–8 W):

> Ita dum interruptum credas nimbum volvier,
> dum quod sublime ventis expulsum rapi
> saxum aut procellis, vel globosos turbines
> existere ictos undis concursantibus . . .

> *So you might think now that a riven cloud rolled on, now that a rock was*
> *thrown aloft by winds and tempest, or that a rounded mass of water rose,*
> *beaten by conflicting waves.*

And his celebrated *oderint dum metuant* (168 W, *let them hate,*
*so long as they fear*) has an epigrammatic quality which points
forward to Seneca.

## Later Roman Tragedy: Seneca

49 The period just discussed brings us virtually to the end of
what we can meaningfully call 'live' classical tragedy. Its comparative insignificance, under the Roman Empire, can be explained largely by features already familiar – the audience's
lack of enthusiasm for serious thought or presentation, and
the preoccupation of the intellectual *élite* with verbal cleverness.
The tragic *genre*, as handed down from the Greeks, was scarcely
likely to flourish in such surroundings, any more than the

celebrated histrionics of Nero were likely to evoke distinguished literary material. We have some evidence for the revival of older tragedies, together with a few names of later tragedians such as the Augustan Pollio and Varius, and the later Pomponius Secundus. It is probable enough that in Ovid's *Medea* we have lost a literary masterpiece; but Ovid himself denies that he wrote for the stage (*Tristia* V. vii. 25 ff.), and *Medea* may well have been, like his *Heroides*, a brilliant *tour de force* of rhetorical display, owing much to the popularity of *recitatio*.

50 Both in manner and in detail, Ovid's influence on the Senecan tragedies is considerable. Even if these tragedies were ever intended for the stage rather than for public recitation, their *staging* possibilities are of small interest: first and foremost they are displays of dazzling rhetorical skill, whose strength (even in their most tasteless and ill-proportioned passages) certainly favours their ascription to the philosopher Seneca. (On all grounds it is likely that *Octavia*, the *fabula praetexta* attributed to Seneca, is by a later hand in spite of its Senecan traits; but it is omitted from separate discussion here, owing to its colourlessness and lack of individuality in nearly all respects save that of its theme – Octavia's tragic death at Nero's orders.) Of the nine Senecan tragedies four (*Troades, Medea, Phaedra*, and *Hercules Furens*) are principally drawn from Euripides, one (*Agamemnon*) from Aeschylus and two (*Oedipus* and *Hercules Oetaeus*) from Sophocles; *Phoenissae* owes something to all three of the Greek tragedians, and *Thyestes* perhaps something to a lost play of Sophocles, though probably more to an earlier Roman tragedy by Varius. The particular influence of Euripides may well be due to that poet's tendency to rhetoric and epigram already observed (§43).

51 The Senecan tragedies are typical of their age in their virtues as in their faults: in the effectiveness of individual passages as in the disproportions of whole plays, in the brilliance of separate phrases as in their tastelessness or irrelevance to the action. They show a masterly control of metre and of language. In metre, Seneca (like Catullus and Horace before him) achieved

the lighter form of the iambic trimeter which the early dramatists had found unmanageable (cf. §46), and his technical
dexterity is excellent. This shows itself especially in *stichomythia* (12), the line-for-line dialogue inherited from Greek
tragedy and later taken on with such effect by Elizabethan
drama. The brisk sequence of thought, for instance, in
Euripides' *Medea* 324 ff. may be compared with this Senecan
passage (*Med.* 192 ff.):

MEDEA. Quod crimen aut quae culpa multatur fuga?
CREON. Quae causa pellat, innocens mulier rogat.
M.      Si iudicas, cognosce: si regnas, iube.
C.      Aequum atque iniquum regis imperium feras.
M.      Iniqua numquam regna perpetuo manent.

*What crime or fault is punished by my exile?—'What cause banishes?' is
for an* innocent *woman to ask. – If you act as judge, hear my case;
if as king, command. – You must obey a King's commands, just* and
*unjust. – Unjust rule never remains for ever.*

And the same effect may be studied in Shakespeare, e.g. *Rich.
III*, IV. iv. 344 ff.

52 In his longer speeches Seneca again shows his mastery of
language. The descriptions, in *Oedipus*, of ill-omened sacrifices
(352 ff.) and of the grove of Dirce (530 ff.) are brilliant
language – but, in their length, wholly disproportionate digressions. Theseus' lament for his wife and son (*Phaedra*
1201 ff.) has all the power of developed rhetoric – yet is
marred by a typical unrealism when the hero lapses into
comparison of himself with other mythological sufferers, e.g.
1233–4

vultur relicto transvolet Tityo ferus
meumque poenae semper accrescat iecur.

*Let the fierce vulture leave Tityus and fly here, and let my liver ever renew
itself for punishment.*

There are superbly epigrammatic lines such as *Phaedra* 249

pars sanitatis velle sanari fuit.

*To wish for healing has ever been the half of health*

but – to our taste – they are too often ruined by an amazingly perverse (though brilliant) imagination, as when, after Oedipus' self-blinding and Jocasta's suicide, Oedipus soliloquises (*Oed.* 1050–1):

> ingredere praeceps, lubricos ponens gradus,
> i profuge vade – siste, ne in matrem incidas.

> *step quickly, planting uncertain feet, go – fly – make haste – yet stop, lest you fall over your mother!*

Indeed, the number of deaths – and, still more, the fullness of their description – in the text powerfully supports the common view that these plays were never actually staged. Be that as it may, the preoccupation with the gruesome is alien to Greek, although one must admit that the lost part of Euripides' *Bacchae* may have contained a scene not unlike Theseus' ghastly reconstruction of Hippolytus' limbs (*Phaedra* 1256 ff.), e.g.

> . . . quae pars tui sit dubito; sed pars est tui.
> hic, hic repone, non suo, at vacuo loco.

> *I know not what part of you this may be; but it* is *a part. Lay it here – not in its own but in an empty place.*

From such macabre horrors descended elements in Elizabethan melodramas, such as *Titus Andronicus* and Shakespeare's admirable parody in *Midsummer Night's Dream*, V. i. 259 ff.

53 Two other Senecan features deserve special attention. One is the growth of stock minor characters, especially Nurses: these appeared not infrequently in Greek tragedy (e.g. Euripides' *Medea* and *Hippolytus*), but in Senecan tragedy the heroine's nurse is almost indispensable (cf. *Medea, Phaedra*), and is a clear literary ancestor of nurses in *Romeo and Juliet* and in Restoration comedy. The second feature is the decline of the chorus, which is Seneca practically ceases to participate: the choral odes show occasional beauty, as in the nature description at *Hercules Furens* 125 ff., which opens like a Euripidean dawn-hymn (cf. §43):

iam rara micant sidera prono
languida mundo . . .

*now few and faint shine the stars in the declining sky*

but more often we find a wearisome preoccupation with
mythology (see §52 above), or a ghastly platitudinarianism, as
at *Agam*. 57 ff., which in places is a mere colourless paraphrase
of Horace, e.g.

quicquid in altum Fortuna tulit,
ruitura levat . . .

*Whatever Fortune raises on high, she raises to bring low,*

etc; cf. Hor. *Odes* II. x. The appallingly uninventive monotony of Seneca's choral metres makes the effect worse. Indeed
(as in Greek New Comedy), the chorus serves merely as an
interlude between acts, and the five-act formalization which
results is another legacy of Seneca to Elizabethan drama.

## Later Influences of Classical Drama

54 The enormous impact of Seneca on Renaissance drama has
been observed in preceding sections; more may be read in
F. L. Lucas' *Seneca and Elizabethan Tragedy*. That so indifferent a
*dramatist*, and one so little related to Greek and earlier Roman
tragedians, had such impact may be partly explained by his
availability to a host of students who had some Latin but no
Greek; yet Latin translations from Greek tragedy *did* exist,
and it is clear that (especially in France) Renaissance tragedians
genuinely found Seneca's stylized framework and rhetorical
elaborations very congenial to their tastes.[18] In England,
apart from some direct translations, writers such as R. Edwards and Marston, and more considerable dramatists such
as Ben Jonson and Kyd, owe very much to Seneca in actual
verbal expression; Marlowe and Shakespeare, poets of far

18. I am much indebted to Dr R. M. Griffiths for valuable advice on this
point, and to Mr F. J. Barnett for much information on the growing and changing aspects of French tragedy.

greater originality and imagination, relied on him less, but throughout the Elizabethan period his influence is descried in the five-act structure, formal devices like *stichomythia* (cf. §51), macabre plots, and abstract rhetoric.

55 Senecan influence is still stronger in French and Spanish drama of the sixteenth–seventeenth centuries. In France, particularly, almost slavish imitations were created during the sixteenth century, with lyric chorus parts as well as the other devices mentioned above; there was also, however, some genuinely pioneering originality in thought and style, and Garnier's *Hippolyte* and *Antigone* are good examples of actual classical plots in drama of the period. Like their Senecan models, most French tragedies of the period are clever exercises with no real stage potentiality. It was left to the seventeenth-century dramatists to revitalize tragedy in this respect; the greatest of them, Corneille and Racine, coincided with a real and practical assimilation of the Classical principles sometimes ill digested in the previous century, and with a return of interest in Greek tragedies and works of dramatic theory such as Aristotle's *Poetics*. These eminently practical dramatists have little use for the chorus (though it was reintroduced in Racine's last two tragedies), or for abstract and (to them) out-dated ideas such as the Greek concept of fatality; however, a Christian (or more specifically Jansenist) counterpart of the latter can be seen in Racine (particularly his *Phèdre*). Rhetoric is still enjoyed for its own sake (although more concentrated in Corneille than in the simpler Racine), but is linked more realistically with action; plots become better constructed, and far more attention is paid to characterization and to the moral dilemmas facing individuals. Corneille's *Oedipe* shows all these features and a classical plot as well; Racine concentrates particularly on female characterization, and his *Phèdre*, *Iphigénie*, and *Andromaque* can all be studied beside their classical prototypes.

56 After Racine followed a period of comparative sterility, as the rediscovered Classical principles became almost fossilized: only in Voltaire's free thinking, linked with some

timid technical innovation, does this period show much distinction within the field of French tragedy. Meanwhile, tragedy in England had become sparse. Milton's *Samson Agonistes* shows classical influences in form, use of chorus, and (most strikingly) in the *motif* of tragic endurance, but as a stage work it is too stiff to be convincing; Addison's *Cato* was praised in its time, but had little impact on later drama. Dryden's *All for Love* is almost the only lasting English tragedy from the century following Shakespeare's death, and in spite of classical features in its structure and plot, its outlook and approach show a romanticism which carried it far from classical models.

57 The later eighteenth century presents us with some revitalization, and some reaction. The German literary revival of this period is finely represented by Goethe's *Iphigenie*, which combines a classical theme with the philosophist attitude characteristic of the nation. In France, meanwhile, the influence of *drame bourgeois* and of nineteenth-century Romantic writers (such as Victor Hugo) ousted the Classical approach as thoroughly as it was ousted in England, where Swinburne's *Atalanta in Calydon* and *Erechtheus* are merely skilful exercises in Greek form and ideas without dramatic significance. The development of the novel probably contributed very strongly, at least in England, to the decline of the tragic *genre*. Farther afield in Europe such eminent dramatists as Chekhov, Ibsen, and Strindberg also show little of the Classical influence.

58 But the twentieth century has seen a reversion to Greek forms. In England the work of T. S. Eliot is remarkable especially for its revival of the role of chorus as commenting bystanders (as in *Murder in the Cathedral*); in France Sartre and Anouilh have produced powerfully fresh adaptations of Classical themes. Sartre's *Les Mouches* gives a new and arresting presentation of the Electra–Orestes story; Anouilh's *Antigone* concentrates (like so much of his work) on *social* concerns, especially the notion of individual liberty as against obedience to the State (a notion to some extent foreshadowed in Ibsen) – where it certainly merits close comparison with its Sophoclean

prototype. Not that these dramatists are in general close to their original models; on the contrary, the reader is left with almost too violent a sense that they are hard at work to find new and paradoxical positions and angles on the old stories. Thus, in such new angles, the themes of tragedy continue to fascinate, and its influence to grow, as much as the prototypes can be trusted to preserve their stimulus and abiding appeal.

## Bibliography

Besides standard texts and editions of the plays and fragments (some of which have been mentioned already), the following books and recent articles may be specially recommended. (A. Lesky gives a very full bibliography at the end of his *Greek Tragedy*.)

KITTO, H. D. F. *Form and Meaning in Drama*, London, 1956.

KITTO, H. D. F. *Greek Tragedy: A Literary Study*, London, 1961.

LESKY, A. (tr. H. A. Frankfort), *Greek Tragedy*, London, 1965.

LUCAS, D. W. *The Greek Tragic Poets*, London, 1959.

PICKARD-CAMBRIDGE, A. W. (revised T. B. L. Webster), *Dithyramb, Tragedy and Comedy*, Oxford, 1962.

PICKARD-CAMBRIDGE, A. W. (revised D. M. Lewis and J. P. A. Gould), *The Dramatic Festivals of Athens*, Oxford, 1946.

WEBSTER, T. B. L. *Greek Theatre Production*, London, 1956.

BOWRA, C. M. *Sophoclean Tragedy*, Oxford, 1944.

DODDS, E. R. 'On Misunderstanding the Oedipus Rex', *G. & R.*, April, 1966.

JONES, J. *On Aristotle and Greek Tragedy*, London, 1962.

KNOX, B. M. W. *The Heroic Temper: Studies in Sophoclean Tragedy*, California, 1965.

LATTIMORE, R. *Story Patterns in Greek Tragedy*, London, 1964.

LLOYD-JONES, H. 'The Guilt of Agamemnon', *Classical Quarterly* 1962. 2.

MURRAY, G. *Aeschylus the Creator of Tragedy*, Oxford, 1940.

PODLECKI, A. J. *The Political Background of Aeschylean Tragedy*, Michigan, 1966.

PATHMANATHAN, R. SRI, 'Death in Greek Tragedy', *G. & R.*, April, 1965.

WALDOCK, A. J. A. *Sophocles the Dramatist*, Cambridge, 1951.

WEBSTER, T. B. L. *The Tragedies of Euripides*, London, 1967.

WINNINGTON-INGRAM, R. P. *Euripides and Dionysus, an interpretation of the Bacchae*, Cambridge, 1948.

ZUNTZ, G. *The Political Plays of Euripides*, Manchester, 1955.

WATLING, E. F. (Penguin Classics), Introduction and Appendix to *Seneca: Four Tragedies and Octavia*, Harmondsworth, 1966.

WIGHT-DUFF, J. *The History of Rome*, London, 3rd edition, 1960.

WIGHT-DUFF, J. *A Literary History of Rome in the Silver Age*, London, 1960.

ANDERSON, M. J. (Ed.), *Classical Drama and its Influence* (Essays presented to H. D. F. Kitto), London, 1965.

BUSH, J. N. D. *Classical Influences in Renaissance Literature*, Cambridge, Mass., 1952.

LUCAS, F. L. *Seneca and Elizabethan Tragedy*, Cambridge, 1922.

DRIVER, T. F. *The Sense of History in Greek and Shakespearean Drama*, Columbia, 1960.

HARVEY, P., and HESELTINE, J. E. *Oxford Companion to French Literature* (s.v. 'Tragedy', etc.), Oxford, 1959.

*Le Dictionnaire des Lettres Françaises*, XVIe–XVIIIe siecles, Paris, 1951.

LANSON, G. *Esquisse d'une Histoire de la Tragédie Française*, Paris, 1954.

LEBEGUE, R. *La Tragédie Française de la Renaissance*, Brussels, 1944.

POMMIER, J. *Aspects de Racine*, Paris, 1954.

# X

# History

## Christopher Turner

### I. Two Thousand Years

1 Every Roman schoolboy knew that Herodotus was the father of history;[1] and Cicero was rather shocked that the title should be given to a man who still followed the epic poets' habit of telling stories. After all, the first rule of writing history was to tell the truth,[2] a rule be it said, which need not be kept in a panegyric of Cicero's own consulship.[3] It seems quite clear, however, that the Greek professors of rhetoric who so described Herodotus wanted to draw attention not so much to his truthfulness as to his ability to write prose for entertainment.[4] His predecessors had either been epic poets or compilers of local traditions ($\sigma\upsilon\gamma\gamma\rho\alpha\phi\epsilon\hat{\iota}\varsigma$). Herodotus succeeded in fulfilling both functions in prose and in giving his work

1. Cic. *de Leg.* I. 1 §5: 'patrem historiae'.

2. Cic. *de Or.* II. 62: 'Nam quis nescit primam esse historiae legem, ne quid falsi dicere audeat? Deinde ne quid veri non audeat? Ne quae suspicio gratiae sit in scribendo? Ne quae simultatis?'

3. Cic. *ad Fam.* V. 12, especially §3 and §6. Cicero acknowledges that such a work will be more in the nature of a 'laudatio' ('quasi fabula') than part of a 'perpetua rerum gestarum historia', and promises Lucceius that he will supply him with 'commentarii' of all 'suae res gestae'.

4. Cic. *de Or.* II. 55: 'princeps genus hoc ornavit'.

Cic. Orator 39: 'primisque ab his (Herodotus and Thucydides), ut ait Theophrastus, historia commota est, ut auderet uberius quam superiores et ornatius dicere'.

Dion. *Hal. de Thuc.* 5. There are very good reasons for supposing that Cicero, Dionysius, and Quintilian all used the same school text-books on rhetoric. See, especially, Usener's edition of the *de Imitatione*, pp. 113 ff., and, inspired by it, Peterson's introduction to his edition of Quintilian, Book X (1891).

an artistic shape. Granted the definition of 'historian' implicit in these accounts, Herodotus has every right to his title. But the election has led to serious misunderstanding and absurd controversies in the last eighty years. To begin with, Herodotus was not the first writer of Greek prose; nor was he the first historian interested in the world outside his own city; nor were his sources confined to oral tradition and local chronicles. He admits himself that he used the works of a man who could with much more justification answer all these descriptions, Hecataeus of Miletus.

2 A few fragments still survive of Hecataeus' *Historiae*, written near 500 B.C. He began with a preface, explaining that he wrote because he wished to preserve the truth and complaining of the wide circulation given to absurd Greek legends.[5] Evidently his contemporaries saw no reason to dispute even the Theogony of Hesiod as a sound record of fact. But, says Hecataeus,[6] there are two mistakes in it about Aegyptus: it was his sons, not he, who went to Argos, and there could hardly have been even twenty of them, fifty being utterly absurd. But Herodotus treated his predecessor with great respect,[7] borrowed from his *Periodos Ges* extensively, and pulled his leg about his genealogical pretensions[9] and his geographical theories.[10] If context is any guide, Herodotus owed his chronological system to Hecataeus.[11] When describing his exploits in the Ionian Revolt (499–493) against Persia he shows sympathy with the level-headed advice he gave the Ionian leaders.[12]

3 Estimates of Herodotus himself[13] have varied from that

5. *Fr.* 1 (*a*) (F Gr H I) Preface to the 'Ιστορίαι.

6. *Fr.* 19, from the 'Ηρωλογία.             7. Book VI. 137.

8. N.E.L. Herodotus, pp. xi–xiv (W. G. G. Forrest).

9. Book II. 143.             10. Book II. 21, 23.

11. See How and Wells, Appendix XIV (Vol. I) and Introduction, §20, for the theory that these references to Hecataeus are an Alexandrian forgery. See also Gomme, *Commentary*, Vol. I, Introduction, p. 2; Bury *A.G.H.*, Ch. I, especially pp. 33–5; Jacoby, *Atthis*, pp. 198–204, 300 n. 28, and 354 n. 13; Pearson *Early Ionian Historians*, 1939.

12. Book V. 36, 125.

13. For all major historians see Bibliographical Section. Footnotes are for further reference.

of Ludovicus Vives,[14] that he was the father of lies, to Collingwood's[15] that he invented the 'science' of history, that he was
'side by side with Socrates' one of the 'great innovating
geniuses of the fifth century'; indeed, that he created history
and Thucydides killed it. Quot homines . . . is too obvious
a comment. Uncontroversially Herodotus is important because
he tried to record the truth,[16] he asked questions;[17] he was
interested in men as men and in their destiny.[18]

> He was a man whose width of human sympathy, and interest in
> human things places him nearer to Shakespeare than to Thucy-
> dides.[19]

He wanted to be readable, and learnt the art from the poets,[20]
above all 'Homer'. He wanted to explain the great upheaval
of the Persian wars that had overshadowed his childhood, and
so he wrote about war. As an exile from Halicarnassos and its
tyranny, who found asylum, freedom, and a congenial intellectual climate at Athens, he applauded democracy.[21] He
lived in the city of Aeschylus and knew that arrogance is at
least one recipe for disaster.[22] He was well aware of the intellectual movements in Ionia: anthropology,[23] geography,[24]
technology, mineralogy, literary criticism, medicine. He was
interested in the nature of historical evidence, little though he
knew how to use it. His greatest charm for the modern reader
lies in his enjoyment of life and in his avid curiosity about
men and about life. In this, above all, he was a worthy successor to Homer.

14. *Libri XII De Disciplinis* (ed. 1612), p. 87. 'Herodotus quem verius menda-
ciorum patrem dixeris quam quomodo illum vocant nonnulli, parentem historiae.'
15. *Idea of History* (1961 ed.), pp. 18–19, 28–9.
16. I. 1, 5.
17. II. 3, III. 43–4, 106.
18. I. 5, 30–2; II. 10–12; III. 38; V. 9; VII. 45–56.
19. Livingstone, *The Greek Genius*, p. 152.
20. II. 53, 116–17; IV. 32. The Greeks usually attributed all epic to Homer.
21. V. 66–73; III. 80–4.
22. I. 27, 34, 53–4, 73, 76–7, 86–91; VII. 56–58; VIII. 114. Cf. Aeschylus:
*Persae*, esp. 800–42.
23. I. 74.
24. III. 115; VII. 129; II. 19–34.

4 There is no room for doubting his influence on his successors. But should Thucydides be called a 'successor'? Herodotus was still adding afterthoughts to his work as late as 431,[25] so it is arguable that Thucydides started writing before he had read a word of his senior's masterpiece.[26] It is much harder to decide whether it is Herodotus or his lost contemporaries whom Thucydides is correcting in his preface,[27] in his excursus on the years 478–432[28] (where he actually mentions Hellanicus as at fault) or in his various digressions on subjects related or skimmed by Herodotus.[29] Nowhere does he mention him by name, and experts are sharply divided in their judgements of the issue.[30] Directly or indirectly, Herodotus convinced later writers that prose could be entertaining. He set the fashion for writing a historical preface stating his purpose in writing; he adapted the Homeric traditions of a limited theme, of dramatic debate,[31] of digression, of epic description of single combat; he incorporated geographical detail, he discussed political issues, he took no interest in social conditions,

25. VII. 137.
26. Thuc. I. 1.
27. Thuc. I. 20–2.
28. Thuc. I. 97.
29. The rights of Spartan kings: Hdt. VI. 57; Thuc. I. 20. The names of Spartan military divisions: Hdt. IX. 53; Thuc. I. 21. The truth about the murder of the tyrant Hipparchus: Hdt. V. 55–6; Thuc. VI. 53–60; I. 20, corrected in turn by Aristotle's *Ath. Pol.* 16 and 18.

The truth about Cylon: Hdt. V. 70–2; Thuc. I. 126.

The truth about Pausanias: Hdt. III. 3; V. 32; IX. 64, 78–82; Thuc. I. 95, 128–34.

The truth about Themistocles: Hdt. VIII. 57–8, 75–125; Plut. *Mal.* 5; Thuc. I. 135–8.

The Thracians: Hdt. IV. 46; V. 3; Thuc. II. 97 §6.

The Battle of Mycale and its sequel: Hdt. IX. 13, 103–6, 117, 121.

Earthquakes and eclipses: Hdt. VII. 129; I. 74; Thuc. II. 8, 28; IV. 52; VII. 50.

30. Gomme (*Commentary*, Vol. I, pp. 2–8, 148–9, 257) is extremely sceptical about Thucydides' interest in Herodotus. Others are more certain (or less critical), e.g. Collingwood, op. cit., p. 19; Glover *Herodotus*, esp. pp. 69–71. A. D. Momigliano, *Studies in Historiography*, Ch. 8, gives a very strong version of the view questioned by Gomme. Professor Syme, *Lecture on a Master Mind*, pp. 41–2, is discreetly and wisely impersonal about the identification of those whom Thucydides refuses to name.

31. See especially the great debate in VII. 4–19, in which Xerxes contemplates the invasion of Greece.

but confined his account to the rulers; he discussed causation, with the fundamental assumption that 'the story is the explanation' or, in more formal terms, that 'history is self-revelatory'. Herodotus was not content with a single version of an incident, and he did not suppress the one he rejected.

5 The controversies which have raged over Herodotus are nothing to the storms Thucydides has roused. Here was a man who rejected the past as beyond the reach of verification and who chose the present, in which he himself even played a minor part and was banished for it, as the only fit subject for a truthful history. Where Herodotus was casual and superficially informal, Thucydides was disciplined, formal, didactic, ruthlessly selective. Again he chose war as his subject, a war in which he fought and which he only just outlived. His interest was in men, in their politics and ideas, and in the way they reacted to the stress of conflict, more especially in strains felt by a democracy which ruled an empire. The surprising fact is that he never saw Athens in the period of greatest strain, 424-404, the period of his own exile; he had no personal knowledge of the Corcyrean civil war nor of the sufferings of the Athenian army in Sicily, and yet his accounts of those events are among the most celebrated of his descriptive literary achievements.[32] Critics, ancient and modern, have mostly fastened on those features of Thucydides as a historian which had so great an influence on later writers and thinkers – his preface, his speeches, his '*sententiae*' (pronouncements on 'life'), his famous narratives, his discussion of the causes of war, his principles of selection, his sources, his chronological system, the varying dates at which he wrote different parts of the work, the unfinished look of Books V and VIII, his own involvement in the events he describes, his choice of a contemporary subject, his biographical interest – and restraint – his desire for posterity and the whole problem of the work's design. All these matters have to be discussed, but when discussing them piecemeal it is easy to forget the greatness of the work as a whole. Thucydides

32. Corcyra, Book III. 69-85; Sicily, Books VI-VII.

drew together a variety of interests – medical, diagnostic, rhetorical and political, philosophical and psychological, dramatic, epic, historical (in the strict sense of discovery and reporting the truth of events), and focused them all on the fundamental issues of human conflict. He discussed the strengths and weaknesses of democracy,[33] but he also recovered in vivid detail the excitement of a night attack which failed and of an escape by 300 determined men which succeeded against all odds.[34] The very range of discussion on him illustrates his versatility.

6 Herodotus wrote to entertain his readers and to record the achievements of great men truthfully. In his search for truth he gave the word 'ἱστορία' a new meaning. Thucydides also searched for truth and also wrote to preserve it. In so doing both of them developed techniques of research unknown before them. But Thucydides wanted to preserve the truth because he believed he was benefiting the generations to come, and helping those with intelligence to be better statesmen. This is why some describe him as the founder of scientific history and others accuse him of murdering history. However, Xenophon[35] proves that both lessons could be unlearnt. Xenophon is unique as one who reported facts without embellishment and with little political understanding. We would call him, without disparagement, a war-correspondent. In Xenophon's favour it has been said that he had 'method in ascertaining facts', moral earnestness, and 'a nice sense for harmony', all legitimate forms of historiography. It should be added that Xenophon was a modest man. He began his *Greek*

33. On democracy: I. 68–85; II. 35–47, 60–5; III. 37–48; VI. 89–92.

34. Night attack: VII. 43–5. Escape: III. 20–4 (omitted from the N.E.L. abbreviated translation, no doubt because it is too brilliantly written to bear translation).

35. Apart from a useful summary in the *O.C.D.* there is one good modern discussion of Xenophon now in English, in Lesky's *History of Greek Literature*. Bury (*A.G.H.*) pays him scant attention, and Hammond (*History of Greece*, Oxford, 1959) gives him ten lines, p. 582. Momigliano (*Studies*) gives a helpful summary of the eighteenth-century critic (Creuzer)'s dissertation on him, pp. 78–80. There is also a ten-page chapter covering all his works in Murray's *Literature of Ancient Greece* (3rd ed., Chicago, Ch. XV, pp. 314–24).

*History* without parade or preface, ostensibly as a simple continuation of Thucydides Book VIII, though leaving a controversial gap between. His *Anabasis* is businesslike, vivid, and justly renowned as the first known traveller's tale. One day it is to be hoped that an English scholar will publish an objective assessment of Xenophon the historian.

7 Xenophon is the last fully extant Greek historian of Greece. Of the three, the influence of Thucydides has been incomparably the greatest and longest-lived. Unconsciously he established a pattern and a technique in handling 'historical' material. He spoke so authoritatively that he came to be regarded definitively as the ideal historian. Even before his death, prose-writing split into: (1) oratory (Lysias (459–380), Isocrates (436–338), and Demosthenes (384–322) being particularly influential) often of a highly elaborate form; (2) 'straight' history in the hands of Xenophon, Ephorus,[36] Theopompus,[37] and others of less note, sometimes flat, sometimes rhetorical, with little interest in chronological accuracy; (3) philosophy (Plato and Aristotle). But simultaneously literary criticism developed as an art, and it was hard for anyone to write any type of literature without self-consciousness about style. The critics were the practitioners of oratory, who recognized no division between categories of literature, merely between styles. Rhetorical schools replaced independent sophists in supplying literary training. In their hands (and Isocrates and the Peripatetics must bear much of the blame) Thucydides was, for two centuries, only remembered for his most artificial rhetorical conceits. These were often slavishly imitated.[38] Truth was no longer the purpose of writing history; the order of the day was to produce more elaborate and more

36. See Gomme (*Commentary*, I, pp. 44–6, 52–4, 59, 65–6, 70); Bury, *A.G.H.*, pp. 162–5, 198–9; and G. L. Barber, *The Historian Ephorus*, Cambridge, 1935, and next note.

37. Gomme, *Commentary*, I. 46–9, 65, 69–70; Bury, *A.G.H.* 167; Bloch, *Athenian Studies Presented to W. S. Ferguson, Harvard Studies, Supplement I* (1940), pp. 303–41. This includes a discussion of his contemporaries.

38. E.g. Thuc. III. 39 §4 imitated by Philistus of Syracuse in the next generation (F 67). On this whole period see Momigliano, pp. 215–7.

sophisticated prose than your rivals or predecessors, usually in the form of national panegyrics. If Polybius is to be believed,[39] Timaeus of Tauromenium (352–256) was the worst offender. He was offensive to others, inaccurate, of little critical sense but of wide learning.

8 When Polybius burst on the scene in the middle of the second century B.C. with a new subject for history (Rome) and a new concept of history, he decided to revive the Thucydidean model (in Greek), discussing and illustrating it in his own history at inordinate length. His success dealt a deathblow to the Hellenistic tradition of historical writing which had hitherto supplied the model for historians of Rome. His example was followed, in Latin, by Sallust. Further education in those days was in the hands of Greek rhetoricians, in spite of Cicero's efforts to translate their text-books into Latin. Sallust was reacting against the orators of his day, Cicero above all, but he was only able to find other inspirations because Thucydides, abridged, was a set text in the schools whose function was to manufacture orators and statesmen. In his enthusiasm for 'archaizing' he blended Thucydides with Cato, the second-century champion of Hellenophobia. But whereas Polybius had used Thucydides as a model for a universal history in the heyday of the Republic, Sallust used him as one for rhetorical monographs on periods of acute civil war while the Republic lay dying. He hoped to record for posterity the calamity which had overtaken the ancient Roman virtues since Sulla's tyranny.[40] Sulla had reinstated a class who had already, in the time of Jugurtha, shown their corruption and unfitness to rule. What better subject than that very Jugurthan War to demonstrate the inherent corruption of the traditional senatorial class?

9 In the next generation after Sallust, the Age of Augustus, Livy assiduously pillaged Polybius as a source for a major

---

39. Polybius on Timaeus: Walbank, 'Polemic in Polybius', *J.R.S.*, 52, pp. 1–12. Polybius, esp. Book XII. 25k–26a.

40. Sallust, *Catiline*, 5 §6–8; *Bellum Jugurthinum* 5 §1, 15 §3-5, 29 §2, 31 §12.

history of Rome from the earliest beginnings, thus perpetuating stylistically Thucydides at second hand. His other sources were keen political partisans of the age of Sulla, who were in their turn nurtured in the Hellenistic tradition. But he often resorted to Sallust as a stylistic model, sometimes to copy him, sometimes to improve.[41] His language he owed to Cicero more than anyone, a debt which he acknowledged with enthusiasm.[42] He hoped when he began his history to demonstrate the old Roman virtues and the essential part they had played in the growth of Rome; he also did his best to explain the true meaning of liberty (not easy in the 20s B.C.). At the same time he must make it clear that the Augustan glory had been Rome's destiny from the start.[43] Opportunities for political digression frequently cropped up as he wrote his monumental work, and he seized them eagerly. The Second Punic War provided him with two heroes on a Homeric scale. But when he reached the second century the size of his undertaking began to tell, and sheer exhaustion and haste reduced the magnificence of his artistry.

10 Contemporary with Livy, the Greek Dionysius of Halicarnassos taught rhetoric, wrote intelligent text-books but revived unblushingly the Hellenistic tradition, antipathetic to Thucydides. In spite of that, however, it was to Thucydides he turned as a model when writing his own history: a history of Rome in Greek to serve as a demonstration model to his pupils and successors.

11 A century later Tacitus, a trained orator and at heart a Republican, lamented the passing of the great days of eloquence[44] and did his utmost to recapture and re-establish the excellence of Cicero's Latin. But he finally despaired of a return to a thriving legal practice and took to history. First he tried a monograph. It is not difficult to recognize Sallust among its

41. E.g. Livy, II. 12 §8 with Sall. *B.J.* 20 §2; 12 §15 with *B.J.* 64 §5.

42. M. Seneca *Suas.* VI. 21–3; Quint. II. 5 §19.

43. See Preface and Book I. 48 §8–9; II. 1–2, 5, 10, etc.; XXX. 29–31, as illustrations of these points.

44. Tac. *Dialogus*, e.g. 17, 22, 32–5.

models,[45] both in style and pattern. The Thucydidean tradition thus moved down another generation. But Tacitus' debt to Cicero in the *Agricola* remained prominent,[46] and, for all his prejudices against him, he used Livy – possibly only at second-hand.[47] His sources on the Empire, A.D. 14–96, are lost; but it is clear that they contained many tedious commonplaces of style and comment, with forerunners stretching back to Thucydides. The late second-century historian, Arrian, one of the best in later antiquity, was Polybian in outlook but not in the main stream of Thucydides' influence.

12 About the time of Tacitus' death was born one of the most level-headed critics known to antiquity. Lucian was a critic of manners, morality, and culture, as well as of literature. He gave some forthright advice in Greek on how to write history. Thucydides, in his opinion, was the ideal model and example.[48] Just after the year A.D. 200 Dio Cassius[49] followed his advice most conscientiously. In his monumental history of Rome he wrote speeches of intolerable length full of quotations and echoes from the great original. His narrative represents the extremes to which rhetorical elaboration could twist the Greek

45. For Tacitus and Sallust see Ogilvie, *De Vita Agricolae*, pp. 23–7; Syme, *Sallust*, pp. 292–7, 324; *Tacitus*, pp. 144 f. and Ch. XIII in general.

46. For Cicero in the *Agricola*, cf. Ogilvie, p. 22, e.g. Cic. *pro Plancio*, 66; *Orator*, 35; *de Or* III., 8; *Brutus*, 4 f.; *Agricola*, 1 §1 (with Ogilvie's note) §4, 45 §1 and §3, 46 §1.

47. For Tacitus and Livy see Ogilvie, loc. cit., pp. 25–9; Syme, *Tacitus*, pp. 137–42, 148, 359, 685–6, 733–4. The debt is various: (*a*) evocation of Livy's comments on historically parallel situations, e.g. Livy Book XXVIII. 27–9, used extensively as in *Hist.* IV. 58, 73; I. 37; *Ann.* I. 54, 42; (*b*) echoes of similar occurrences, e.g. *Ann.* II. 53 §2 and Livy, XLV. 27 §5 (*c*) echoes of Livian epigrams, as in *Ann.* II. 88 §2 and Livy III. 53 §2; (*d*) cases where Tacitus' meaning is made plainer by reference to Livy, e.g. *Ann.* II. 61 §2 explained by Livy XXXVI. 17 §15 and XLII. 52 §14.

48. See *Way to Write History*, 41–2, etc.

49. For Dio in general see Fergus Millar, *A Study of Cassius Dio*, Oxford, 1964. For his debt to Thucydides, pp. 7, 40–7, 52, 72, 76, 78 f. – these mainly on style. For Thucydidean traits in his work and attitude – civil concord, p. 78; purpose, pp. 28–9 (LXXII. 23); comments on early writers, p. 35; design, p. 40; biography, pp. 60–72; human beings, pp. 76–7. His interest seems largely to have been to create atmosphere at the expense of detail and to concentrate on selected dramatic incidents. His style is an amalgam of much more than just Thucydides, and he even took pains to translate Cicero's mannerisms into Greek (esp. p. 52).

language. It is far from certain what sources Dio used for much of his extant history; one name (Sallust) at least can be mentioned with confidence, and it is most unlikely he did not use Livy. Of considerable interest is his adaptation of Seneca's *De clementia*.[50] He included many of the traditional commonplaces about human nature, robbing them of their original profundity and freshness and clothing them in bizarre sophistication. In his preoccupation with style and parade of learning he failed to acquire the critical judgement of a historian, and the results of his efforts to manipulate valuable, undated information into an annalistic scheme are tantalizingly absurd.

13 It is entirely appropriate that Thucydides should have made his last appearance in Greek at the fall of Byzantium. The Greek historian, Turkish official, Critobulus[51] is the most obvious example extant. In his speeches he tried to 'improve' on Thucydides, as so many had tried in the previous 1,850 years; his narrative is nearer to the Byzantine Greek of his day, the immediate ancestor of modern 'demotic'. This divergence in style is not altogether surprising in its period: the great English dramatists of the next century, after all, alternated happily, from scene to scene, the common speech of the working population with the polished rhetoric of educated renaissance society.

14 Only fifty years after Critobulus published his history, Erasmus produced (1516) his Greek edition of the New Testament, thus riveting the Reformation to the Renaissance. Erasmus was a close friend of John Colet, who was bold

50. Millar, loc. cit., pp. 78–9; Syme *The Roman Revolution*, p. 414 (index wrong in 1st ed.).

51. The most accessible text of Critobulus is in Müller, *Fragmenta historicorum*, v (Paris, 1883). His preface is strongly reminiscent of Thuc. I. In Book I. 34 he describes a siege with a strong flavour of the siege of Plataea, Ch. 40 a naval battle which suggests Thuc. Book VII. Critobulus played a big part in the events, becoming ruler of Imbros in 1456 and of Lemnos as well in 1459. He finished his history in 1470 in Constantinople. He was an eye-witness of the plague in 1467. Müller's summary of him is apt and worthy of Quintilian's school: 'ceterum a pressa Thucydidis dictione longe abest Critobulae verbositas, tanto molestior illa quum variare loquendi formulas non satis auctor noverit.' See excerpt in Section II.

enough to introduce Greek into the curriculum of St Paul's, London. The 'new' subject survived the vicissitudes of Tudor England, and a century later (1628) Thomas Hobbes brought Thucydides to the ordinary English reader in translation.[52] His place in English thought and letters is best illustrated by Lowes Dickinson's remarkable words: 'It is not fanciful to say that the Peloponnesian War which ravaged Greece is a close parallel to the war of 1914. The mere scale is irrelevant. Essentially the facts are the same . . .' Thucydides *might* have forgiven this interpretation of κτῆμα ἐς αἰεί.[53]

## II. Historical Models

15 In the passages which follow some idea can be gained of the variety of the ways in which the ancient historians used models and of their motives for selecting the ones they did.[54] The examples have been grouped into separate sections according to theme.

## A. 'Beware of the Tyrant'

16 In Hist. I. 55. §24 Sallust adapted Demosthenes on Philip when writing an anti-Sullan speech. At first sight Philip and Sulla do not have much in common, but historical parallels used in the law courts could be far more far-fetched, and (see Quintilian II. 4, §§18–22) were well practised at school. There would be no harm in Sallust's reminding his readers of the most famous treasury of abuse in the ancient world. When rewriting the speech actually delivered by Cato the younger in 63 B.C. to rouse the Roman Senate against another threat of tyranny

52. His preface expresses so much more neatly the sentiments of the long-winded Polybius, e.g. p. xx – 'In *truth* consisteth the *soul*, and in *elocution* the *body* of history. The latter without the former, is but a picture of history; and the former without the latter, unapt to instruct' – and p. vii.

53. Vd. Thuc. I. 23.

54. See n. 47 above and R. M. Ogilvie's edition of Livy I–V for more examples of Livy's use of Thucydides. Livy is leaning heavily on his sources in these passages, so they may all be second-hand borrowings. Cf. Seneca, *Contra*, IX, decl. I. D.H. *de Thuc.* 25 is evidence that one of Livy's sources imitated Thucydides. But VII. 30–1, modelled on Thuc. I. 32 f., is the work of Valerius Antias.

Sallust again had recourse to Demosthenes. *Cf*. Dem. Phil. III. 35 with Cat. 52 §28.

## B. Patriotic Appeals and Exhortations before Battle

17 Thuc. I. 61 §1 leads to Sall. *Or. Lep*. 9–10 and *B.J*. 31 §22 [55]

    Thuc. II. 62 §3 – *B.J*. 31 §17

    Thuc. II. 62 §4–63 §2 – *Or. Lep*. 7 – Tac. *Hist*. II. 38.

    Thuc. II. 89 – *B.J*. 49 §§2–3

    Thuc. III. 12 §1 – *B.J*. 10, 14, *Ep. Mithr*. 17, *Cat*. 11, 58 §18
    and the Sallust leads to Tac. *Agr*. 30–3 extensively; the
    Thucydides also leads to Dio LXII. 3.

The most remarkable development of this 'patriotic' theme, with a conscious attempt to recall and elaborate on Thucydides, comes in the History written by Critobulus:

*Excerpt* 1

"Ἄνδρες φίλοι καὶ τῆς ἡμετέρας ἀρχῆς, ὅτι μὲν οἱ ἡμέτεροι πρόγονοι τὴν ἀρχὴν τήνδε ἣν ἔχομεν, μετὰ πολλῶν ἀγώνων τε καὶ κινδύνων τῶν μεγίστων ἐκτήσαντο καὶ ἐς δεῦρο διαδοχῇ τῇ σφῶν αὐτῶν διασώσαντες, παῖς παρὰ πατρὸς ἐκδεχόμενοι, παρέπεμψαν ἐς ἐμέ, πάντες ἴστε δήπου καλῶς, οἱ μὲν ὑμῶν καὶ κοινωνοὶ ἐνίων ἔργων ἐν μέρει γεγονότες ἐκείνοις, ὅσοιπερ ἐν τῇδε τῇ νῦν μάλιστα καθεστηκυίᾳ ἡλικίᾳ τυγχάνετε πρεσβύτατοι ὄντες, οἱ δὲ καὶ παρὰ τῶν πατέρων ἀκοῇ παρειληφότες, ὅσοι νέοι ἐστέ· οὐδὲ γάρ εἰσι τῶν πάνυ παλαιῶν, οὐδ' οἷα καὶ διὰ χρόνου πλῆθος λανθάνειν, ἀλλ' ὄψις ταῦτα μαρτυρεῖ τῶν λεγόντων μᾶλλον ἢ τῶν ὁρώντων ἀκοὴ βεβαιοῖ, χθὲς καὶ πρώην γεγενημένα. . . .

*Allies and subjects of our Empire, our ancestors won this Empire which we hold with many a struggle, oft in the greatest peril, and passed it on to me, handing it on continuously from father to son in an unbroken succession to this very hour: you know it, all of you I expect, well; some of you even shared in some of the triumphs, playing your part with them, and you will now be the oldest present, having reached that most settled time of life; others, and you will be the youth of our nation, heard it relayed by your fathers. These events I speak of are not in the very distant past nor the*

55. For otium cum libertate see C. Wirszubski: 'Cicero's cum Dignitate Otium', *J.R.S*., XLIV, pp. 1–13; *Ep ad Att*. 1 19 §6–8, *pro Sest*. 98 (mistranslated in this article).

*sort of thing forgotten in the lapse of time by most; on the contrary, those who speak of them saw them happen and can vouch for them rather than merely assure you of them because they heard them from those who saw them, and they happened only yesterday or the day before . . .*[56]

*Crit.* I. 14

18 It is impossible to reproduce all the sophistication of the original in a translation, only the verbosity. Critobulus has used Thuc. I. 73 §2 and II. 36 in some detail, and he has also adapted an idiom which comes in II. 62 §3 and another from III. 38 §2. From this last chapter (38) in section 4, comes the conceit θεαταὶ τῶν λόγων (the speaker being Cleon, characterized by his excessive use of the 'new' rhetoric of the 420s introduced by Gorgias) with its antithesis ἀκροαταὶ τῶν ἔργων. It seemed to Critobulus that he was paying Mechemet, an absolute, barbarian ruler, the greatest possible compliment by giving him the language of the Greek champion of the free society, Pericles. It is worth comparing the meaningless rhetorical flourishes of the Critobulus, the common-places fairly falling over one another, with the concentration of meaning in Thuc. II. 36 conveyed by pointed alliteration, subtle word-order, and the accumulation of associations of ideas. Critobulus evidently knew the speeches in Thucydides very well, and thought he could do better! One of the chapters pillaged by Critobulus (III. 38) had a long history before it. Plutarch used it in a rhetorical exercise devoted to proving that Thucydides only made his name because he was fortunate in his choice of subject (Excerpt 2). In the original, Cleon had been complaining that the Athenians were turning the Assembly into a theatre; Plutarch uses his words to compliment Thucydides on his one redeeming feature – his gift of making scenes (the dramatic analogy is important, because Plutarch had in mind the 'messenger speech' in a tragedy) come alive to the audience. By Plutarch's time[57] the words have become a commonplace,

56. For Procopius, another Byzantine imitation, Bury, *Later Roman Empire*, Vol. II, pp. 63–4, 419–30.

57. He adapts Thucydides' own words to pay him a handsome compliment in an exercise otherwise designed to demonstrate the Athenians' superiority in war as opposed to literature. 'ἂν γὰρ ἀνέλῃς τοὺς πράττοντας οὐχ ἕξεις τοὺς γράφοντας.'

and perhaps that was why, centuries later, the Byzantine tried to improve on them. The end of the road can be seen in Excerpt 3, Hobbes's enthusiastic preface to his translation of Thucydides. Ironically he uses the words of Thucydides' detractor with which to compliment him – he must have known them.

*Excerpt 2*

Πλὴν ὁ Σιμωνίδης τὴν μὲν ζωγραφίαν ποίησιν σιωπῶσαν προσαγορεύει, τὴν δὲ ποίησιν ζωγραφίαν λαλοῦσαν. ἃς γὰρ οἱ ζωγράφοι πράξεις ὡς γιγνομένας δεικνύουσι, ταύτας οἱ λόγοι γεγενημένας διηγοῦνται καὶ συγγράφουσιν. εἰ δ' οἱ μὲν χρώμασι καὶ σχήμασιν, οἱ δ' ὀνόμασι καὶ λέξεσι ταὐτὰ δηλοῦσιν, ὕλῃ καὶ τρόποις μιμήσεως διαφέρουσι, τέλος δ' ἀμφοτέροις ἓν ὑπόκειται, καὶ τῶν ἱστορικῶν κράτιστος ὁ τὴν διήγησιν ὥσπερ γραφὴν πάθεσι καὶ προσώποις εἰδωλοποιήσας. ὁ δ' οὖν Θουκυδίδης ἀεὶ τῷ λόγῳ πρὸς ταύτην ἁμιλλᾶται τὴν ἐνάργειαν, οἷον θεατὴν ποιῆσαι τὸν ἀκροατὴν καὶ τὰ γιγνόμενα περὶ τοὺς ὁρῶντας ἐκπληκτικὰ καὶ ταρακτικὰ πάθη τοῖς ἀναγιγνώσκουσιν ἐνεργάσασθαι λιχνευόμενος. ὁ γὰρ παρὰ τὴν ῥαχίαν αὐτὴν τῆς Πύλου παρατάττων τοὺς Ἀθηναίους Δημοσθένης, καὶ ὁ τὸν κυβερνήτην ἐπισπέρχων Βρασίδας ἐξοκέλλειν καὶ χωρῶν ἐπὶ τὴν ἀποβάθραν καὶ τραυματιζόμενος καὶ λιποψυχῶν καὶ ἀποκλίνων εἰς τὴν παρεξειρεσίαν, καὶ οἱ πεζομαχοῦντες μὲν ἐκ θαλάττης Λακεδαιμόνιοι, ναυμαχοῦντες δ' ἀπὸ γῆς Ἀθηναῖοι· καὶ πάλιν. . . . τῇ διαθέσει καὶ τῇ διατυπώσει τῶν γιγνομένων γραφικῆς ἐναργείας ἐστίν. ὥστ' εἰ τοὺς ζωγραφοῦντας οὐκ ἄξιον παραβάλλειν τοῖς στρατηγοῖς, μηδὲ τοὺς ἱστοροῦντας παραβάλλωμεν.

*Simonides, however, calls painting inarticulate poetry and poetry articulate painting: for the actions which painters portray as taking place at the moment literature narrates and records after they have taken place. Even though artists with colour and design, and writers with words and phrases, represent the same subjects, they differ in the material and the manner of their imitation; and yet the underlying end and aim of both is one and the same; the most effective historian is he who, by a vivid representation of emotions and characters, makes his narration like a painting. Assuredly Thucydides is always striving for this vividness in his writing, since it is his desire to make the reader a spectator, as it were, and to produce vividly in the minds of those who peruse his narrative the emotions of amazement and consternation which were experienced by those who beheld them. For he tells how Demosthenes is drawing up the Athenians at the very edge of the breakwater at Pylos, and Brasidas is urging on his pilot to beach the ship, and is hurrying to the landing-plank, and is wounded and falls fainting on the forward-deck; and the Spartans are fighting an infantry engagement from the sea, while the Athenians wage a naval battle from the land. Again . . .* (there follows a quotation from the scene on the shore of the Great Harbour of Syracuse, a favourite among the Roman writers. Thuc. VII. 71.) . . . Plut. *Mor.* 346 F–347, Loeb

### Excerpt 3

He setteth his reader in the assemblies of the people and in the senate, at their debating; in the streets, at their seditions; and in the field, at their battles. So that look how much a man of understanding might have added to his experience, if he had then lived a beholder of their proceedings, and familiar with the men and business of the time: so much almost may he profit now, by attentive reading of the same here written. He may from the narrations draw out lessons to himself, and of himself be able to trace the drifts and counsels of the actors to their seat.

Hobbes, I. viii

19 Finally, there are the well-known words of Nicias in VII. 69 §2. They had a long subsequent career: Sall. *B.J.* 49 §4, *Cat.* 59 §2 and Tac. *Hist.* I. 23. It is *possible* that Caesar had the occasion in mind when he wrote *B.G.* II. 25; it is more probable that he actually was that kind of soldier!

## 20 C. The Football Crowd

In the passage quoted above (Excerpt 2) Plutarch praises Thucydides' description of the naval battle in the Great Harbour. The picture of the spectators, swaying with the fortunes of the battle, was frequently singled out in the schools for repetition. It was the inspiration of:

### Excerpt 4

Τὸ δ' ἐκ τῆς πόλεως πλῆθος ἠθροισμένον ἐπὶ τὰ τείχη πᾶν ἅμα μὲν ἠγωνία τὸ συμβησόμενον, ἅμα δ' ἐπὶ τῷ παραδόξῳ τῆς ἐλπίδος ὑπερχαρὲς ὑπάρχον μετὰ κρότου καὶ κραυγῆς παρεκάλει τοὺς εἰσπλέοντας.

*The whole population had assembled on the walls in an agony of suspense on the one hand as to what would happen, and at the same time so over-*

*joyed at the unexpected prospect of succour that they kept on encouraging the fleet as it sailed in by cheers and clapping of hands.*

Pol. I. 44 §5, Loeb

21 The scene is at Lilybaeum, in the First Punic War. Livy, describing incidents in the Second Punic War at Carthage, uses Polybius twice (in Book XXX) – once in Ch. 10 and once in Ch. 25 §7. The echoes of the same battle of the harbour can still be heard in Tacitus' brilliant description of the silent crowd which watched the last struggle of Galba and Otho in Rome, battling for the Principate in A.D. 69 (*Hist.* I. 40). On each occasion an empire was at stake, as Tacitus knew very well.

## D. Great Deeds Require Great Authors

22 Cicero knew this (*Ep ad Fam.* V. 12, especially §7). Plutarch (Excerpt 2) maintained that great deeds make little men into great authors; Cicero was modest, or wise, enough not to say the same. By his day it was a commonplace of thought, and he had his examples ready – Alexander was one of them! The parentage of this idea can be traced to Pericles: little men don't believe tales of great men, the implication being that it is up to the orator to convince them. (Thuc. II. 35). Sallust tried this one in his *Catiline* (3 §2). Was Homer the ancestor of this one, in his prayers for inspiration? Cicero seemed to think so, for one (loc. cit.).

## E. How Does a Nation Win Friends?

23 Pericles: Thuc. II. 40 4–5. Sallust, *Catiline* 6 4–5. Dio – vd. the following:

*Excerpt 5*

> οὐ γὰρ τὸν αὐτὸν τρόπον πρός τε τοὺς λυπήσαντάς τινες καὶ πρὸς τοὺς εὐεργετήσαντας διατίθενται, ἀλλὰ τῆς μὲν ὀργῆς καὶ ἄκοντες μνημονεύουσι, τῆς δὲ δὴ χάριτος καὶ ἑκόντες ἐπιλανθάνονται, τὸ μέν τι ἀπαξιοῦντες εὖ πεπονθέναι δοκεῖν ὑπό τινων, ὡς καὶ ἀσθενέστεροί σφων δόξοντες εἶναι, τὸ δὲ ἀγανακτοῦντες εἴπερ ἀνατὶ κεκακῶσθαι νομισθήσονται πρός τινος, ὡς καὶ ἀνανδρίαν ὀφλήσοντες. . . . οἱ μὲν γὰρ εὖ

πράξαντες καὶ εὔβουλοι καὶ φιλοπόλιδες ἐνομίσθησαν, οἱ δὲ δὴ πταίσαντες καὶ πολέμιοι τῆς πατρίδος καὶ ἀλιτήριοι ὠνομάσθησαν.

*For men do not feel the same way towards those who have injured them and toward their benefactors, but whereas they remember their anger even against their will, yet they willingly forget their gratitude. This is because, on the one hand, they deprecate giving the impression that they have received benefits from others, since they will seem weaker than they, and, on the other hand, they are annoyed to have it thought that they have been injured by anybody with impunity, since that will imply cowardice on their part . . . For those who were successful were considered shrewd and patriotic, while the defeated were called enemies of their country and accursed.* Dio XLVI. 34, Loeb

24 Evidently Dio knew the Thucydidean vice of brevity. The passage does not come in a speech, but in a discussion of the proscriptions of 43 B.C. Dio wants his readers to know that the proscriptions were the fault of the senators who suffered in them, not of Octavian. Since the occasion is one of civil strife, by the way, he must bring in another Thucydidean echo (see H *infra*.).

## 25 F. Tyranny Makes a Bad Conscience

Thuc. II. 63 §2 – Sall. *Or Lep.* 7.

## 26 G. To the Intelligent, Calculation Can Give Courage

Thuc. II. 40 §3 – Sall. *B.J.* 7 §5.

## 27 H. Thucydides Was Fascinated by the Ravages of Civil War

Thuc. III. 81–3.

No passage was more widely used. Sallust used it at least fourteen times: *Cat.* 10 §3–4, 38 §§3–4, 39 §§2–3 (whence Tac. *Ann.* II. 33), *B.J.* 41 §5, §9, 42 §4, are among the most obvious.

It was natural that Tacitus should employ it in describing the horrors of A.D. 69, a year of unending civil strife: *Hist.* I. 21, 53, 54, probably using Thucydides direct for the only certain occasion in the surviving books of his works.

One notorious commonplace arose from that passage (82 §4): Truth is war's first casualty.

So Sallust: *Cat.* 52 §11, *B.J.* 31 §15, *Hist.* III. 48 §13, *Ep.* 1 5 §5, *Hist.* I. 12; and Tacitus: *Hist.* IV. 17, 73; I. 37–8, *Agr.* 30 §5; and (inevitably) Dio, cramming it alongside another gem (see E above).

## I. Fortune

28 Polybius I. 4 gives a glimpse of the importance of Τύχη. The variations on this theme are many and difficult; Polybius, for example, is sometimes aping Thucydides, sometimes making theological pronouncements (which Thucydides never did), and sometimes being vague and often inconsistent.

Thuc. IV. 62 §§3–4 is an important base camp for many of these literary adventures; Sallust uses it twice at least, *Cat.* 8; *Ep. ad Caes* 1. Dio carefully preserves the words of the Thucydides, giving them to Cicero among other ideas he had gleaned from Cicero's own Philippics:

*Excerpt 6*

οὔτε γὰρ τὸ πλεονεκτούμενον ἔν τινι πάντως εὐτυχεῖ, διότι καὶ ἀδικεῖται, οὔτε τὸ δυνάμει ἀλλ' ἀμφότερα ἀπὸ τῆς ἴσης καὶ τῷ παραλόγῳ τοῦ ἀνθρωπίνου καὶ τῷ ἀσταθμήτῳ τῆς τύχης ὑποκείμενα, καὶ τὴν ῥοπὴν πολλάκις οὐ πρὸς τὸ σφέτερον εὔελπι ἀλλὰ πρὸς τὸ ἐκείνων ἀδόκητον λαμβάνει.

*For the one who is overreached in any transaction is not bound to be fortunate just because he is wronged, nor is the one who has the greater power bound to be successful just because he surpasses, but both are equally subject to the perversity of human affairs and to the instability of fortune, and the turn of the scales often corresponds, not to their own hopefulness, but to the unexpected play of these other factors.*   Dio XLIV. 27 §2

## J. Don't Trust Traitors

29 Their help might be useful, but can you be sure that they won't turn again? There seems to have been a standard opinion on this in the time of Thucydides:

Thuc. III. 9 §1. Compare: Dem. XVIII. 47 Liv. XXVII. 17 Tac. *Ann.* I. 58; and Plutarch's *Coriolanus* suggests an obvious parallel. (See Ch. 23 and Russell on his sources, quoted in the Bibliography under Plutarch.)

## K. Apparent Causes Can Be Misleading

30 It is as well to go back to Hippocrates for an idea of what medical terms were in vogue in the fifth century B.C. for 'cause'.

*Excerpt 7*

διὰ ταύτας ἐμοὶ δοκεῖ τὰς προφάσιας ἄναλκες εἶναι τὸ γένος τὸ Ἀσιηνὸν καὶ προσέτι διὰ τοὺς νόμους. τῆς γὰρ Ἀσίης τὰ πολλὰ βασιλεύεται. ὅκου δὲ μὴ αὐτοὶ ἑωυτῶν εἰσι καρτεροὶ οἱ ἄνθρωποι μηδὲ αὐτόνομοι, ἀλλὰ δεσπόζονται, οὐ περὶ τούτου αὐτοῖσιν ὁ λόγος ἐστίν, ὅκως τὰ πολέμια ἀσκήσωσιν, ἀλλ᾽ ὅκως μὴ δόξωσι μάχιμοι εἶναι. οἱ γὰρ κίνδυνοι οὐχ ὁμοῖοί εἰσι. τοὺς μὲν γὰρ στρατεύεσθαι εἰκὸς καὶ ταλαιπωρεῖν καὶ ἀποθνήσκειν ἐξ ἀνάγκης ὑπὲρ τῶν δεσποτέων ἀπό τε παιδίων καὶ γυναικὸς ἐόντας καὶ τῶν λοιπῶν φίλων. καὶ ὁκόσα μὲν ἂν χρηστὰ καὶ ἀνδρεῖα ἐργάσωνται, οἱ δεσπόται ἀπ᾽ αὐτῶν αὔξονταί τε καὶ ἐκφύονται, τοὺς δὲ κινδύνους καὶ θανάτους αὐτοὶ καρποῦνται . . . μέγα δὲ τεκμήριον τούτων· ὁκόσοι γὰρ ἐν τῇ Ἀσίῃ Ἕλληνες ἢ βάρβαροι μὴ δεσπόζονται, ἀλλ᾽ αὐτόνομοί εἰσι καὶ ἑωυτοῖσι ταλαιπωρεῦσιν, οὗτοι μαχιμώτατοί εἰσι πάντων· τοὺς γὰρ κινδύνους ἑωυτῶν πέρι κινδυνεύουσι, καὶ τῆς ἀνδρείης αὐτοὶ τὰ ἆθλα φέρονται καὶ τῆς δειλίης τὴν ζημίην ὡσαύτως. εὑρήσεις δὲ καὶ τοὺς Ἀσιηνοὺς διαφέροντας αὐτοὺς ἑωυτῶν, τοὺς μὲν βελτίονας, τοὺς δὲ φαυλοτέρους ἐόντας. τούτων δὲ αἱ μεταβολαὶ αἴτιαι τῶν ὡρέων, ὥσπερ μοι εἴρηται ἐν τοῖς προτέροισι.

*For these reasons, I think, Asiatics are feeble. Their institutions are a contributory cause, the greater part of Asia being governed by kings. Now where men are not their own masters and independent, but are ruled by despots, they are not keen on military efficiency but on not appearing warlike. For the risks they run are not similar. Subjects are likely to be forced to undergo military service, fatigue and death, in order to benefit their masters, and to be parted from their wives, their children and their friends. All their worthy, brave deeds merely serve to aggrandize and raise up their lords, while the harvest they themselves reap is danger and death. Moreover, the land of men like these must be desert . . . (text uncertain) . . . Whereof I can give a clear proof. All the inhabitants of Asia, whether Greek or non-Greek, who are not ruled by despots, but are*

319

*independent, toiling for their own advantage, are the most warlike of men.
For it is for their own sakes that they run their risks, and in their own
persons do they receive the prizes of their valour as likewise the penalty of
their cowardice. You will find that Asiatics also differ from one another,
some being superior, others inferior. The reason for this, as I have said
above, is the changes of the seasons.*

Hippocrates, Airs, Waters, Places 16, Loeb

31 The famous passage on this subject of cause is Thuc. 1. 23,
where he draws a distinction between αἰτία and πρόφασις. To
these Polybius adds a third, ἀρχή.

*Excerpt 8*

ἀλλ' ἔστιν ἀνθρώπων τὰ τοιαῦτα μὴ διειληφότων ἀρχὴ τί
διαφέρει καὶ πόσον διέστηκεν αἰτίας καὶ προφάσεως, καὶ
διότι τὰ μὲν ἐστι πρῶτα τῶν ἀπάντων, ἡ δ' ἀρχὴ τελευταῖον
τῶν εἰρημένων. ἐγὼ δὲ παντὸς ἀρχὰς μὲν εἶναί φημι τὰς
πρώτας ἐπιβολὰς καὶ πράξεις τῶν ἤδη κεκριμένων, αἰτίας δὲ
τὰς προκαθηγομένας τῶν κρίσεων καὶ διαλήψεων· λέγω δ'
ἐπινοίας καὶ διαθέσεις καὶ τοὺς περὶ ταῦτα συλλογισμοὺς καὶ
δι' ὧν ἐπὶ τὸ κρῖναί τι καὶ προθέσθαι παραγινόμεθα.

*These are pronouncements of men who are unable to see the great and
essential distinction between a beginning and a cause or purpose, these
being the first origin of all, and the beginning coming last. By the beginning
of everything I mean the first attempt to execute and put in action plans
on which we have decided, by its causes what is most initiatory in our
judgements and opinions, that is to say our notions of things, our state of
mind, our reasoning about these things, and everything through which we
reach decisions and projects.* Pol. III. 6 §6, Loeb

32 Illuminating! Collingwood was not the first man to talk
about a philosophy of history. This is, of course, heavily
influenced by Aristotelian philosophy. Did Polybius use any
of these words with the same connotation as either Hippocrates
or Thucydides?

## L. The Doctrine of the Unchanging Human Heart

33 This is one of the reasons for the continuing popularity of
the famous Στάσις chapter in Thucydides (III. 82 §2). Dio
used it without intermediary. Livy seems to have had it in

mind in IV. 49 §10, perhaps having found it in Polybius. The phrasing of Tac. *Agr.* 12 §6 is forcefully reminiscent of the Livy, and since 'avaritia' is the theme of both passages, it is likely that Tacitus is in Livy's debt for the idea. Few of Tacitus' epigrams are more well known.

*Excerpt 9*

Λέξω δὲ ἤδη καὶ τὰ κατὰ τοῦτον πῶς ἐγένετο. οἱ καταποντίσται ἐλύπουν μὲν ἀεὶ τοὺς πλέοντας, ὥσπερ καὶ τοὺς ἐν τῇ γῇ οἰκοῦντας οἱ τὰς λῃστείας ποιούμενοι· οὐ γὰρ ἔστιν ὅτε ταῦτ' οὐκ ἐγένετο, οὐδ' ἂν παύσαιτό ποτε ἕως δ' ἂν ἡ αὐτὴ φύσις ἀνθρώπων ᾖ.

*I will now relate the progress of Pompey's career. Pirates always used to harass those who sailed the sea, even as brigands did those who dwelt on land. There was never a time when these practices were unknown, nor will they ever cease probably so long as human nature remains the same.*

Dio, XXXVI. 20, Loeb

## Imitation Could also Take Other Forms

34 1. IMITATION OF VOCABULARY AND IDIOM REGARDLESS OF THE IDEAS EXPRESSED

At a simple level (no doubt transmitted by Polybius):

Thuc. I. 142 §1; Liv. IV. 57 §4.

A simple idiom undergoing transformation in its passage:

Thuc. II. 3 §2; *B.J.* 84 §3–100 §4; Livy, XXI. 50 §10; Tac. *Agr.* 18.

The most interesting of all the verbal borrowings (in this case a 'calque') is the shift from the use of φιλεῖ in

Thuc. $\begin{cases} \text{III. 81 §5 'οἷον φιλεῖ ἐν τῷ τοιούτῳ γίγνεσθαι'} \\ \text{II. 65 §4 'ὅπερ φιλεῖ ὅμιλος ποιεῖν'} \\ \text{IV. 28 §3 'οἷον ὄχλος φιλεῖ ποιεῖν'} \end{cases}$ to

Sallust, *B.J.* 34 §1: '*multitudo* quae in contione aderat vehementer accensa terrebat eum clamore, voltu, *saepe* impetu atque aliis omnibus *quae ira fieri amat.*', on which Quintilian, IX. 3 §17, quoting from memory, writes: 'Ex Graeco vero translata vel

Sallustii plurima, quale est, "vulgus amat fieri".' Then it is developed further by Tacitus, *Ann.* iv. 9,: 'plerisque additis, ut ferme amat posterior adulatio.' He drops the infinitive on the assumption that 'fieri amat' is sufficiently common an idiom to be intelligible without it.

35 2. IMITATION OF DESIGN

Prefaces soon became canonical:

Hecataeus, *Fr.* 1; Hdt. 1. 1; Thuc. 1. 1–23, closely and re-peatedly followed in detail by Polybius, e.g. Excerpt I. 4 (quoted above). Dionysius of Halicarnassus fell in line on this point, and, of course, Dio did. Unfortunately Dio's preface is variously quoted in fragments and does not survive intact. Sallust expands on Thucydides and Polybius, e.g. *Cat.* 1–13 (almost a quarter of the whole monograph!). The other great Latin historians are also aware of tradition when they write theirs.

36 On most occasions the writer set out his intentions, the use he proposed to make of speeches, he reminded his readers of the size of the task he was undertaking, gave his reasons for choosing this particular subject, commented on the function of history, explained his chronological system, and made some promises about the design of the work. Invariably the preface bore little relation to its sequel, and is more interesting as a type of literary exercise in which every writer tried to do better than his predecessors.

37 Digressions were a common feature from the days of Hecataeus onwards. Herodotus used them for diversion and relief; but when antiquarian research became popular they became a canonical requirement. Geographical digressions occur in Ephorus (Diodorus Siculus xiv. 11 §§1–4), Polybius (frequently), Sallust (*B.J.* 17), and in the works of Tacitus, e.g. *Agricola* 10 (modelled largely on the Sallust).

38 There is an unusual digression in Polybius on the desir-ability of training future generals in mathematics to help them

count bricks in sieges and to prevent them panicking in an eclipse.[58] Polybius is using his philosophical training to help him in a commentary on Thucydides. See Plato's *Republic* 522 c-d, where Socrates urges 'mathematics for the generals'.

## III. The Frontiers of History

### A. Epic Poetry

39 History was studied at Rome because orators needed the factual knowledge,[59] because it fitted a man for life, filling him with all the right ideas,[60] and because the standard authors used the language of oratory.[61] In the schools' curriculum as material for the art of literary criticism it followed the poets; they had been the staple diet of secondary education since Hellenistic times. History, as a literary art, had originally evolved from epic poetry. It is hardly surprising, therefore, that the historians, when choosing heroic themes, should employ the language of epic poetry. Critics discussed the relationship of poetry to history in every generation. See Aristotle (*Poetics* 9). Cicero was always insistent on a wide education for orators (*de Or.* 1. 67, 69; 11. 33–8, among other passages) and regarded poets and orators as 'near neighbours':

*Excerpt* 10

Est enim finitimus oratori poeta, numeris astrictior paulo, verborum autem licentia liberior, multis vero ornandi generibus socius ac paene par.

*The poet is a near neighbour of the orator, a little more bound by metrical rules but given greater freedom in choice of words. In many types of embellishment they are brothers-in-arms.*　　　　Cic. *de Or.* 1. 70

40 Dionysius noted (*de Thuc.* 23–4) that Herodotus used the language of poetry. Quintilian was mostly concerned with the literary aspect of history. (Cf. Book II. Chapter 4. 18–22

---

58. Pol. IX. 19 §§5–9, inspired by Thuc. II. 20 §2.
59. Cicero, *de Oratore* I. 16–18.
60. Quint. XII. 1 §30.
61. Quint. II. 7 §§2–3.

and Book X, Chapter 1 §90). Pliny the Younger showed how influential Quintilian's teaching was among the young intellectuals:

*Excerpt* 11

Habet quidem oratio et historia multa communia, sed plura diversa in his ipsis, quae communia videntur. narrat illa, narrat haec, sed aliter: huic pleraque humilia et sordida et ex medio petita, illi omnia recondita splendida excelsa conveniunt; hanc saepius ossa musculi nervi, illam tori quidam et quasi iubae decent; haec vel maxime vi amaritudine instantia, illa tractu et suavitate atque etiam dulcedine placet; postremo alia verba alius sonus alia constructio. nam plurimum refert, ut Thucydides ait, κτῆμα sit an ἀγώνισμα quorum alterum oratio, alterum historia est. his ex causis non adducor ut duo dissimilia et hoc ipso diversa, quo maxima, confundam misceamque, ne tanta quasi colluvione turbatus ibi faciam quod hic debeo; ideoque interim veniam, ut ne a meis verbis recedam, advocandi peto. tu tamen iam nunc cogita quae potissimum tempora adgrediar. vetera et scripta aliis? parata inquisitio, sed onerosa collatio.

*Admittedly oratory and history have many things in common, but more which is divergent in the very things which they appear to have in common. They both tell stories but in different ways: history tells much that is unglamorous, unattractive and familiar to our daily lives, whereas poetry is suited by anything out of the ordinary, magnificent and sublime. Bones, muscle and sinew are suitable subject matter for history, but for poetry – flesh and flowing hair. History is satisfying mostly if it is forceful, bitter and fast-moving; poetry by being leisurely, graceful and sensuous. Lastly, their vocabularies are different, the kind of sounds which suit them and the arrangement of words. It is most important, as Thucydides says, whether you are writing the treasure of a life-time or a best-seller; the second is speech-writing, the first history. . . .* Pliny, *Ep.* v. 8 §§9–11

41 Livy made use of the epic poets when writing 'heroic' narrative: e.g. (i) Horatius Cocles (II. 10 §8 and §10; Ogilvie, p. 260). Compare Ennius, *Ann.* 216v and Virgil, *Aen.* XII. 558. (ii) Lake Regillus (II. 20 §§1–3). Compare Homer, *Il.* III. 15 f.; IV. 104–54; XL. 251–74; XIV. 402– XV. 280. Livy's source was a Latin author using Homer; Livy removed the divine elements. (iii) Camillus (v. 49 §3). Cf. Ennius, *Ann.* 196v.

42 Tacitus disapproved of poetic influence, just as he disapproved of Livy:

*Excerpt* 12

> iam vero iuvenes et in ipsa studiorum incude positi, qui profectus sui causa oratores sectantur, non solum audire, sed etiam referre domum aliquid inlustre et dignum memoria volunt; traduntque in vicem ac saepe in colonias ac provincias suas scribunt, sive sensus aliquis arguta et brevi sententia effulsit, sive locus exquisito et poetico cultu enituit. exigitur enim iam ab oratore etiam poeticus decor, non Accii aut Pacuvii veterno inquinatus, sed ex Horatii et Virgilii et Lucani sacrario prolatus.

From exigitur:
*An orator is now expected to have some poetic embellishment, and not one from Accius or Pacuvius with the dust of centuries on it, but he has to do some temple-robbing of Horace, Virgil and Lucan.*

Dialogus 20 §4

43 Lucan,[62] M. Seneca's grandson and author of the epic *Civil War*, is a prize example of a rhetorically trained epic poet. He used Livy's digression on Alexander the Great (Livy, IX. 17–19) as one of his models for the denunciation of Alexander (C.B. X. ll. 20–52). In the course of his poem he describes four great storms.[63] These have an ancestry reaching back to the *Odyssey*, Tragedy (Greek and Latin),[64] and, as is best known, Virgil.[65] Livy's storms are memorable.[66] Two are known – at Delphi when the Gauls tried to sack the Sanctuary, and on the Alps when Hannibal was crossing. It must be assumed that he also described one in Book XVIII.[67] Petronius borrowed from Livy when he described Caesar's crossing of the Alps (*Satyricon* 122), and Lucan owed a line (1. 183) to Petronius.

62. See M. P. O. Morford *The Poet Lucan* (Blackwell, 1967), especially Ch. II, pp. 16–17, and Ch. III on the Storm, especially pp. 20–1.

63. IV. 48–120; V. 504–677; IX. 319–47, 445–92.

64. V. 291 ff.; XII. 403–25; Aesch. *Ag.* 649–57; Pacuvius, *Teucer* 350–65, quoted by Cicero, *de Or.* III. 157; Accius, *Clytaemnestra*, quoted by Cicero; *Topica* 61 (cf. *pro Caelio* 18).

65. Aen. I. 50–157 is the greatest. Cf. III. 548–87.

66. Book XXI. 58 §§3–11 and Book XL. 58 §§3–7.

67. The *Epitome* refers to it: 'res . . . prospere gestas deformaverunt naufragia classium'.

44 The problem with Tacitus is not to find evidence of poetic influence, but rather to decide whether, in each of the many 'poetic' passages, he received the influence direct from the poet concerned. One example (*Hist.* I. 3 §2 and Lucan *B.C.* IV. 808 f.) suggests a very close connection. However, the common attitude of the two men will account for many verbal echoes.[68] Tacitus had probably been reading Lucan shortly before writing the preface to the *Histories*.[69] Virgil's influence on his writing is much more obvious than Lucan's. (*Aen.* I. 50–157 with *Ann.* II. 23–4; *Ann.* I. 61 §1, 53 §2 with *Aen.* VI. 442.)

## B. Tragedy

45 Cornford's *Thucydides Mythistoricus* is still the most invigorating and intelligent discussion of Thucydides' thought and design which has yet been published. Brunt's criticism of his thesis should be read in its earlier version.[70] It must be remembered that Thucydides was constantly adding to his history, and his assessment of the causes of the Athenians' final defeat (II. 65) must have been one of his last. **Pattern** and **cause** are two very different matters, and Cornford was well aware of this; so were the tragic poets, and so was Thucydides.[71] Which **caused** the death of Agamemnon? The hereditary curse of the House of Atreus? The Sacrifice of Iphigeneia? The killing of a hare by an eagle? The massacre of the innocents and the sacrilege in Troy? or the ὕβρις of Agamemnon, expressed in his boastfulness or in his walk on purple? Cornford's argument[72] is that as Thucydides became more and more absorbed in the 'drama' of the War, the events took on an increasingly 'mythical', that is 'tragic', pattern; the Aeschylean moral of ὕβρις, shorn of its theology, influenced

68. See Syme *Tacitus* 143, who quotes *B.C.* VIII. 489. But cf. Tac. *Dial.* 20 §4.

69. Syme, loc. cit., 146.

70. The point he makes is more clearly stated in the earlier article in *History for Today*.

71. See, *per contra*, Page and Denniston on the *Agamemnon*, pp. xxiv–xxxi (Oxford, 1957). Yet even there the editors admit, 'It does not follow that Aeschylus absolves mankind from all responsibility' (p. xxix).

72. See especially pp. 224–36, 242–3.

him in his choice of verbal themes[73] and incident. Cornford does not claim that Thucydides set himself the task of writing a tragedy in prose. Nobody can deny the interest Thucydides showed in 'human error' and in the consequences of 'trusting one's luck'.[74] Compare III. 39, 45; IV. 55, 50, and the Melian Dialogue with IV. 22; VII. 77 and the laconic opening of Book VII. When Cornford describes the characters of Cleon and Alcibiades as possessing mythical significance he is embarking on a topic outside the present discussion.

46 Tragic design did not begin in the fifth century. When Homer selected as a theme the Wrath of Achilles he was bound to give his poem a 'tragic' pattern. When Thucydides selected the conflict between the Athenians and Spartans he could not foresee the outcome, and he seems to have started without any clear idea of design. In the Hellenistic period the 'historians' neither modelled themselves on Thucydides nor understood what his contemporaries meant by 'tragic'. To them 'tragic' history meant 'gaudily colourful' stories.[75] They ignored Aristotle's insistence that a hero's failing ($\dot{\alpha}\mu\alpha\rho\tau\dot{\iota}\alpha$) was not a moral matter, and they took the line that to be 'improving' history had to be moralistic. Polybius tried to correct the trend (cf. Bk II. 56 §§10–13; XXIX. 12 §§4–5, §§7–10; VII. 7 §6) and reinterpreted what Thucydides meant by hoping history would be useful.[76] (Bk I. 4 §11; VII. 7 §8; II. 56 §10; IX. 2 §4; III 57 §9; VI. 2 §8; X. 21 §3).

73. See especially Gomme, *M.E.* 159–60.
74. See especially I. 140; III. 45; IV. 14, 17–18, 21, 30, 32; V. 105; VII. 61–2, 64 and the frequent use of παρὰ λόγον or παράλογος: I. 65; II. 61, 91; IV. 26, 55; III. 65; VI. 33; I. 78; III. 85, 89, 16; VII. 28, 55; VIII. 24. These are taken from Steup's edition of Classen's Commentary, pp. lxiii–lxviii (Berlin/Zürich/Dublin, 1966). It is also well worth pursuing the references to πλεονεξία and its cognates: III 45; IV. 17, 21, 41, 61–2; V. 114; VI. 11, 13; VII. 47, 55, 61, 66.
75. Albin Lesky, *Greek Tragedy*, tr. by Mrs H. A. Frankfort, London, 1965, pp. 5 and 17.
76. See Walbank's *Commentary*, pp. 16–26, and his article on 'Origins of tragic history', pp. 4 *seq.*

## C. Biography

47 Herodotus told stories about men, just as Homer had sung about heroes. Character was of the utmost importance in the stories he told. Both Herodotus and Thucydides believed that character was best revealed by what men did and said. So did the tragic poets, their contemporaries. Compare the technique of Herodotus in the case of Artabanus (VII. 10–18, 46–52) or of Croesus (I. 26–59, 69–92; III. 36) with that of Thucydides on Cleon (III. 36; IV. 19–39, 122; V. 7, 16) or on Nicias (IV. 27–28, 54, 129–30; V. 16–46, 83; VI–VII, especially 86, where ἄξιος and ἀρέτη are so frequently wrongly taken in a moral sense. See Dover *ad loc.*) or Alcibiades (II. 65; VI. 12, 15, 27, 48, 60–1, 88–9; VIII. 6, 14–17, etc.). In the next generation Xenophon made excerpts from his own *Hellenica*, embellished them and published them as a life of Agesilaus. Isocrates meanwhile published the first biography of a living person on Evagoras of Cyprus *c.* 365 B.C. The Platonic and Aristotelian traditions meanwhile encouraged interest in character. So far no one had thought of ransacking other people's histories for biography. Traditionally the Peripatetic Aristoxenus, about fifteen years younger than Aristotle according to Suetonius[77] in his list of Greek and Roman biographers, was the first to publish biographies of literary worth, and presumably used historical sources. Polybius wrote a life of his friend Philopoemen, the Achaean leader and ally of the Romans. Of these lives, Xenophon's and Polybius' came to be treated as the standard models for the great biographers of the first century B.C. onwards (Cic. *ad Fam.* V. 12).

48 The story of biography in early Rome is of a tradition totally different from the Greek. Every Roman household of any standing would have a family-portrait gallery – *imagines*, or busts – with *tituli* attached giving a list of their offices. These would form the substance of epitaphs, such as that quoted by

---

77. Jerome in J. P. Migne's *Patrologiae Latinae cursus completus*, XXIII. 821. See Stuart, p. 132, and the bibliographical section in general.

Cicero on A. Atilius Calatinus.[78] These *tituli* also formed the basis of *laudationes funebres*. One or two very early examples of the *laudationes* survive:

*Excerpt* 13
*Pliny, N.H. VII, Ch.* 43, 139–40

Quintus Metellus in ea oratione, quam habuit supremis laudibus patris sui L. Metelli, pontificis, bis consulis, dictatoris, magistri equitum, quindecimviri agris dandis, qui primus elephantos primo Punico bello duxit in triumpho, scriptum reliquit: decem maximas res optimasque, in quibus quaerendis sapientes aetatem exigerent, consumasse eum. voluisse enim primarium bellatorem esse, optimum oratorem, fortissimum imperatorem, auspicio suo maximas res geri, maximo honore uti, summa sapientia esse, summum senatorem haberi, pecuniam magnam bono modo invenire, multos liberos relinquere, et clarissimum in civitate esse. haec contigisse ei, nec ulli alii post Romam conditam; longum est refellere et supervacuum, abunde uno casu refutante.

> Cf. Marrou, pp. 354–5. Speaker: Q. C. Metellus Macedonicus. Delivered in 221 on his *grand*-father.

From *decem* (the earlier part being merely a summary of his official positions): *He achieved the ten best and greatest things for philosophers to spend their lives pursuing: he wanted to be the leading warrior, the best orator, the bravest general, to have the greatest achievements sanctioned by his auspices, to hold the highest office, to be the wisest man, to be regarded as the greatest senator, to make a fortune honourably, to leave many children behind him and to be the most famous man in the state.*

*Excerpt* 14

Nec vero habeo quemquam antiquiorem, cuius quidem scripta proferenda putem, nisi quem Appi Caeci oratio haec ipsa de Pyrrho et non nullae mortuorum laudationes forte delectant. Et hercules eae quidem exstant: ipsae enim familiae sua quasi ornamenta ac monumenta servabant et ad usum, si quis eiusdem generis occidisset, et ad memoriam laudum domesticarum et ad inlustrandam nobilitatem suam. Quamquam his laudationibus

---

78. *de Sen.* 61: 'hunc unum plurimae consentiunt gentes populi primarium fuisse virum.' The whole of the lengthy epitaph was inscribed on his tomb. Cf. *C.I.L.* I. I, 6, 8 for the earliest known, 7, 9, 10, 11, 15 are expanded. Cic. *de Leg.* II. 63 gives an example of a Hellenized version.

historia rerum nostrarum est facta mendosior. Multa enim scripta sunt in eis quae facta non sunt: falsi triumphi, plures consulatus, genera etiam falsa et ad plebem transitiones, cum homines humiliores in alienum eiusdem nominis infunderentur genus; ut si ego me a M'. Tullio esse dicerem, qui patricius cum Servio Sulpicio consul anno x post exactos reges fuit. Catonis autem orationes non minus multae fere sunt quam Attici Lysiae, cuius arbitror plurimas esse . . .

*I don't know of anyone before Cato whose writings I would consider fit to quote, unless anyone would enjoy the speech Appius Claudius Caecus made about Pyrrhus and some of those funeral orations. They are extant, all right! The families used to keep copies of them as a kind of distinction on record; they would produce the speeches if somebody in the family died and found they were excellent reminders of their glorious past and means of enhancing their own nobility. Unfortunately these panegyrics have not improved the veracity of our national history. They include several fabrications – triumphs that were never held, too many consulships, fictitious pedigrees and transfers to the plebs when, for example, humbly born men might be grafted on to a family tree which happened to bear the same name though unrelated. For example, I might claim to be descended from the Manius Tullius who was a patrician consul with Servius Sulpicius in 501 B.C. However, Cato's speeches are about as numerous as the speeches of the Attic writer Lysias who, I believe, holds the record.*

Cicero, *Brutus*, 61–2[79]

49 It is not always easy to draw the line between history and biography, as the Cicero excerpt shows. Livy confirms (VIII. 40 see n.[80]) that not much reliance could be placed on the *laudationes funebres*, but he was not deterred from writing at length on the early history of Rome by that fact. Cornelius Nepos (99–24 B.C.) tried to make it clear that he was writing biography not history,[81] although he claimed with reason that he used numerous sources,[82] among others Ephorus, Thucydides (whom he translates *verbatim* in Chapter 9 of the

79. Octavian on his grandmother, Suet. Aug. 8. *C.I.L.* XIV. 3579, Hadrian on his mother-in-law.

80. Serv.: in Aen. I. 712.

81. Pelopidas 1.

82. E.g. Livy, XXXIX. 25 §10 for Cimon 2 §15, I. 46 §5 for Alcibiades 2 §38. See Tarn, Vol. II, for his Alexander and its subsequent influence, pp. 34–9.

*Themistocles*), Theopompus, Polybius, and Xenophon whom he imitates closely in the *Agesilaus* (see Excerpt 10). His preface (next excerpt) reads in the approved historical style:

*Excerpt* 15

Praef 1: Non dubito fore plerosque, Attice, qui hoc genus scripturae leve et non satis dignum summorum virorum personis iudicent, cum relatum legent, quis musicam docuerit Epaminondam, aut in eius virtutibus commemorari, saltasse eum commode scienterque tibiis cantasse, sed ii erunt fere, qui expertes litterarum Graecarum nihil rectum, nisi quod ipsorum moribus conveniat, putabunt. hi si didicerint non eadem omnibus esse honesta atque turpia, sed omnia maiorum institutis iudicari, non admirabuntur nos in Graiorum virtutibus exponendis mores eorum secutos . . . (8) sed hic plura persequi cum magnitudo voluminis prohibet, tum festinatio, ut ea explicem, quae exorsus sum.

*I am quite sure, my dear Atticus, that there will be several people who will consider this type of writing irresponsible and unworthy of the characters of distinguished men. They will find I have included who taught Epaminondas music, that I include among his virtues the fact that he danced well and was an expert on the flute. If I am right they will be the sort of people who have never read a word of Greek and think that the only definition of 'right' is what accords with their own moral principles. If these readers learn that the same things are not 'honourable' and 'dishonourable' for everybody but, rather, people base their moral judgements on the traditions of their ancestors, they will not raise their eyebrows in surprise that, in talking about the virtues of the Greeks I have used their principles . . . But I cannot pursue that topic now: this is too big a book and I must make haste to tell the story I have begun.*

50 Nepos made a greater contribution to the biographical tradition of Rome than is often acknowledged. This Preface shows his honesty, his broad-mindedness, and his shrewd estimate of his public. To the same public Cicero had to pretend he could not remember the name Polyclitus.

51 Plutarch[83] (*c.* 46–126) is well known for his parallel biographies. In him the traditions of comparisons, panegyric,

83. See A. J. Gossage, *Latin Biography*, pp. 45–77; Robert Flacelierè's introduction to the Budé (Paris, 1964) edition of the *Lives*, Vol. I, pp. ix–lxiv; Gomme, *Commentary*, Vol. I, pp. 54–84; D. A. Russell, 'Plutarch's Life of Coriolanus', *J.R.S.*, 53, pp. 21–8.

philosophy, and 'usefulness' unite. His own interests were wide (including mathematics, science, medicine, and Platonist philosophy), he travelled much, and he was wealthy enough to possess a large library. He did not write history and was not a scholar, in the strict sense, though he would pursue a historical problem if it interested him, without an expert's experience of the relative value of sources nor the imagination to understand political circumstances. He used Thucydides extensively in the Greek Lives (e.g. *Them.* 27 §1, of which he may have used a learned edition) and, like Herodotus, believed that actions reveal character. He must have used Thucydides also on *Themistocles* (see Chs. 7–9). He must have had access to collections of anecdotes and sayings. His is one of the rare cases where we can see the ancient historian at work on his sources and models, using his memory when the exact reference was too tedious to uncover.[84] His chief trouble was his inadequate Latin (*Demosth.* 2 §§2–4), which caused him to restrict his reading of Latin to the major authors and limited his influence on later Roman authors. But with the Renaissance and North's translation (1579, from the French) he was the principal source for Englishmen's knowledge of Antiquity. His impact on the early eighteenth-century moral thinking is well known.[85]

52 Plutarch's nearest rival, both for later importance and for a claim to rank as a historian, is his younger contemporary, Suetonius (*c.* 70–*c.* 130). He must have known Tacitus personally, known what he was writing, but it is anybody's guess whether he hoped to rival him or simply admired him.[86] There is no passage which can be quoted to prove the acquaintance of one of them with the other's writing. It is just possible that *Nero* 52 is a criticism of *Annals* XIV. 16 §1. His love of sensation is well illustrated by a comparison of his

84. Epaminondas 4 §6. Cf. Gossage, op. cit., p. 52.

85. Gossage, pp. 67–71.

86. Syme: *Tacitus*, pp. 689, 781–2; Appendix 76 for details of his life (pp. 778–81). G. B. Townend's chapter in *Latin Biography* (pp. 79–111) is invaluable on every aspect of Suetonius. For his sources, see Syme, op. cit., pp. 180–1, 189, 271, 388, 501–2, and Townend, p. 89.

death of Vitellius (Ch. 16) with the Tacitus version (*Hist.* III. 84–5). There is little doubt that they used the same sources in this and on many other occasions. Some of these sources must have been the collections of slanders which were rapidly made on the death of any Emperor (e.g. Tac. *Ann.* I. 1 §5, *Hist.* I. 1 §§1–2), and perhaps Nonianus and Cluvius Rufus (two 'lost' historians) bear the main responsibility. Suetonius was not a skilful historian, and when not interested happily copied conflicting sources (*Nero* 33 §1 and 40 §3, with *Claudius* 44 §2; *Nero* 38 §1 with *Nero* 43 §1 and Tac. *Ann.* xv. 38 §1). On the other hand, *Gaius* 8 is a good example of his qualities when his interest was aroused. But he had the enormous advantage over more professional historians of occupying an official position under the Emperor Hadrian, and he certainly took advantage of the access to Imperial Archives; the draught he felt when sacked after the *Augustus* is very obvious.

53 Suetonius pandered to contemporary taste in his choice of topic and model. Noticeable features of his work are his *divisiones* (tables of contents, an orator's habit), the chapter headings contained in them, and the recurring details in his accounts: lists of campaigns, of treaties and buildings, family details, personal appearance and habits, survey of religion, lists of omens portending death. All these were constantly imitated. The most remarkable imitation is that of Einhard's *Life of Charlemagne*. In the Carolingian Cross in Aachen Cathedral is a medallion of the head of Augustus. The message was understood by Alcuin, and the right biographer[87] was found. Later, the biographer of the first Norman King of England, anxious to demonstrate the importance of his subject, decided to copy great sections of Einhard's *Vita Caroli*. In these copies (Einhard's is not unscholarly, and certainly shows that he knew more than just the *Augustus*) the most extraordinary trait is the repetition of personal habits and appearance. It seems that the

87. See David Knowles, *The Evolution of Medieval Thought*, p. 76, Longman's, 1962, *Latin Biography*, p. 98. For later influence of Suetonius and Einhard (especially of the latter on William of Malmesbury) see R. W. Southern, *St Anselm and his Biographer*, pp. 325–7, Cambridge, 1963.

biographers had two functions: they had to recall the man closely enough to be credible, but they also had to explain to posterity what rank he held among the great. The practice is familiar to Londoners, who have seen James II listening to the demonstrations in Trafalgar Square dressed in a Roman toga.

54 Biography, history, poetry, funeral orations, and letters of condolence or commemoration, the frontiers were never sharp; how could they be when those who wrote them all received the same ingredients in their education and prided themselves on their versatility? The oddest, and greatest, of the bunch is the *Vita Agricolae*. Of this Professor Syme has said, 'It is best left to be defined in its own terms.'[88]

## IV. Conclusion

55 If the question is put 'Why did the Romans use Greek models when writing history?' the simple answer is 'Because they were told to' – by Cicero, Dionysius, Horace, Quintilian, and Lucian, to mention but a few. Literary renown depended on showing a good literary pedigree. Posterity might be assured still further if the work could be proved to be useful. But the answer is not a simple one. For all his verbosity and sententiousness, Polybius did the greatest possible service to Roman history: he broke the monopoly of Hellenistic rhetoric, and Cicero then proved that the baldness of Cato's *Origines* was not the only alternative to it in Roman prose literature. Polybius pointed back to the great originals, and he did so at a time when, after conquering Greece, the Romans were ready to believe in their great destiny as a nation and to yearn for a great national literature. But history and oratory were inseparable in their public lives and in their education; so, since they were taught the art of oratory ('rhetoric') in Greek with a solid basis of literary criticism, it was inevitable that the first

88. Op. cit., p. 125; Stuart, op. cit., p. 253; and Ogilvie and Richmond, pp. 11–21, who accept its own definition as biography with a flavour of the 'exitus illustrium virorum'.

Latin historians should use Greek authors as their models. The later historians were thus given Latin as well as Greek models. The problem then arises: are traces of Greek influence evidence for direct borrowing from the Greeks or merely for the use of Latin copiers of the Greeks? In the case of a historian like Tacitus the problem has no easy solution. A much more important question, however, suggests itself to the historian: are traces of excessive use of Greek models evidence for a rhetorical conception of history? If Sallust borrowed Philip from Demosthenes when portraying Sulla, how far can we trust his portrait?

56 A survey of the passages in which the traces of Greek originals are unmistakable shows that the selection made by the Latin historians was restricted to a limited number of favourites. That selection very soon became traditional. A study of the ancient critics supplies the reason for the narrowness of choice: Sallust and his followers chose from school text-books, compiled for 'repetition' and analysis and classified by style. It must not be forgotten that for many Hellenistic and Roman writers historiography was a literary, and not a historical, exercise. Since Homer started it all, why not?

# Bibliography

This is divided as follows:
    A. *Select*. Works which are essential and readable, arranged alphabetically by author.
    B. *Research*. Works which are worth reading or using for further illumination, arranged in three sections:
        I. General works on history, historians, and biography.
        II. General books on literature, literary criticism and education in antiquity.
        III. Ancient authors, arranged alphabetically by author.
            Texts, if not available in standard editions, are listed in III.

## A. Select

BRUNT, P. A. *Introduction to Thucydides*, tr. by Jowett and abridged by the editor, N.E.L., The Great Histories, 1966.

BURY, J. B. *The Ancient Greek Historians*, 1st ed., 1908, New York, 1958. (Abbreviated: *A.G.H.*)

CORNFORD, F. M. *Thucydides Mythistoricus*, London, 1907.

DOREY, T. A. (Ed.), *Latin Biography*, London, 1967.
(Nepos, Q. Curtius, Plutarch, Suetonius, Einhard, Historia Augusta, William of Poitiers, William of Malmesbury, Lives of St Francis)
*Latin Historians*, London, 1966.
(Early Historians, Polybius, Caesar, Sallust, Livy, Marcellinus, and Bede)

FORREST, W. G. G. *Introduction to Herodotus*, tr. by Rawlinson and abridged by the editor. N.E.L., The Great Histories, 1966.

GLOVER, T. R. *Herodotus* (Sather Classical Lectures, Vol. 3), California, 1924.

GOMME, A. W. *A Historical Commentary on Thucydides* (3 vols.), covering Book I to Book V 24. Oxford, 1945 and 1956. (The remaining volumes, edited by Professors Dover and Andrewes, are expected shortly.)

HOW, W. W., and WELLS, J. *Commentary on Herodotus* (2 vols.), Oxford, 1928.

LLOYD-JONES, HUGH, *Introduction to Tacitus*, tr. by Church and Brodribb and abridged by the editor, N.E.L., The Great Histories, 1966.

MARROU, H. I. *Histoire de l'education dans l'antiquité*, Paris 1948, 1955. Idem, tr. into English by Lamb, London, 1956.

OGILVIE, R. M. *A Commentary on Livy*, Books I–V (1 vol.), Oxford, 1965.

OGILVIE, R. M., and the late SIR IAN RICHMOND, *Cornelii Taciti de Vita Agricolae*, edited, Oxford, 1967.

SYME, SIR RONALD, *Tacitus*, (2 vols), Oxford, 1958.
*Sallust* (Sather Lectures 3), California, 1964.

## B. Research

I. General Historical

BALSDON, J. P. V. D. 'Some questions about historical writing in the second century, B.C.', *C.Q.*, 1953, pp. 158–64.

COLLINGWOOD, R. G. *The Idea of History*, ed. T. M. Knox, Oxford, 1946 hard, 1961 paper.

GOMME, A. W. *Essays in Greek History and Literature*, Oxford, 1937.
*More Essays in Greek History etc.*, David Campbell, Oxford, 1962.

JACOBY, FELIX, *Atthis* (The local Chronicles of Ancient Athens), Oxford, 1949.
*Fragmente der griechischen Historiker*, Vols. I, II, Berlin, 1923–30; Vol. III, A, Leyden, 1940. (*F.Gr.H.*)

LIVINGSTONE, R. W. *The Greek Genius and its Meaning to us*, 2nd ed., Oxford, 1915.

MOMIGLIANO, A. D. *Studies in Historiography*, London, 1966.

MULLER C. and TH. *Fragmenta Historicorum Graecorum*, 5 vols., Paris, 1841–85.

MYRES, J. L. *The Political Ideas of the Greeks*, London, 1927.

STUART, D. R. *Epochs of Greek and Roman Biography* (Sather Lectures 4), Berkeley, 1928.

WALBANK, F. W. *Speeches in Greek Historians* (3rd J. L. Myres Memorial Lecture), Oxford, undated (since 1964).

## II. General Literary

KNOWLES, DAVID, *The Evolution of Medieval Thought*, London, 1962.

LESKY, ALBIN, *Greek Tragedy*, tr. Mrs H. A. Frankfort, London, 1965.
*A History of Greek Literature*, London, 1966.

NETTLESHIP, HENRY, 'Literary criticism in antiquity', *Journ. Phil.*, Vol. 18 (1890), pp. 225–70.

OGILVIE, R. M. *Latin and Greek*, London, 1964.

SCULLARD, H. H. 'Two Halicarnassians and a Lydian', in *Ancient Society and Institutions* (studies presented to Victor Ehrenberg), Oxford, 1966.

## III. Ancient Authors

CASSIUS DIO COCCEIANUS, *v.* Dio.

CICERO, *Brutus*, ed. A. E. Douglas, Oxford, 1966.
Rambaud, M. *Ciceron et l'histoire romaine*, Paris, 1953.

CORNELIUS NEPOS, *v.* Nepos.

CRITOBULUS, for text see Muller, *F.H.G.*, Vol. V, Paris, 1883.
Pears, *The Destruction of the Greek Empire*, pp. x–xi.
Runciman, S. *The Fall of Constantinople*, 1453, Cambridge, 1965, pp. 127–8, 194.

Q. CURTIUS RUFUS:

McQueen, E. I., Ch. II in *Latin Biography* (*v.* Dorey, A.).
Tarn, W. W. *Alexander the Great*, Vol. II, Cambridge, 1949.

DIO:

Millar, Fergus, *A Study of Cassius Dio*, Oxford, 1964.

DIONYSIUS OF HALICARNASSUS (D. H.), for texts:

Cary, E. (Ed.), *The Roman Antiquities*, with introduction, Loeb, 1937.
Reiske *et al.*, *Opera Omnia Graece et Latine*, Leipzig, 1777.
Roberts, W. Rhys, *The Three Literary Letters of D. H.* with introduction, Cambridge, 1901.
*D.H. on Literary Composition*, London, 1910.
Usener, H. *D.H. Librorum de Imitatione Reliquiae Epistulaeque Criticae Duae*, Bonn, 1889.

EADMER:

Southern, R. W. (Ed.), *The Life of St. Anselm by Eadmer*, London, 1962.
Southern, R. W. *St. Anselm and his Biographer*, Cambridge, 1963.

EINHARD:

*Text of de Vita Caroli Magni*, in O. Hodder-Egger, *Scriptores Rerum Germanicarum in usum scholarum* (*S.R.G.S.*), 1911.
Painter, Sidney, *The Life of Charlemagne by Einhard*, tr. with foreword, Michigan, 1960 (paper).
Cantor, N. F. (Ed.), *The Medieval World*, 300–1300, London, 1963.
Duckett, E. S. *Carolingian Portraits*, Michigan, 1962.

EPHORUS:

*Athenian Studies*, presented to W. S. Ferguson, *Harv. Stud.* Supplement I (1940).
Barber, G. L. *The Historian Ephorus*, Cambridge, 1935.
Bury, J. B. (*A.G.H.*), pp. 162–5, 198–9.
Gomme, A. W. (*Commentary*), I, pp. 44–6, 52–4, 59, 65–6, 70.

HERODOTUS:

Myres, J. L. *Herodotus and Anthropology*, Lecture 5 in *Anthropology and the Classics*, ed. R. R. Marett, Oxford, 1908.

Myres, J. L. *Herodotus the Tragedian*, in *A Miscellany presented to J. M. Mackay*, ed. O. Elton, Liverpool, 1914.

LIVY:

Walsh, P. F. *Livy. His historical aims and methods*, Cambridge, 1963.

See *Latin Historians* (Dorey).

LUCAN:

Morford, M. P. O. *The Poet Lucan; Studies in Rhetorical Epic*, Oxford, 1967.

LUCIAN:

Text: Teubner ed. Opera; Vol. II includes the *De Compositione*, Leipzig, 1887.

Translation: Fowler, H. W. and F. G.: *Works*. Vol. II for same treatise, Oxford, 1905.

NEPOS:

Jenkinson, Edna in *Latin Biography* (Dorey).

PLUTARCH:

Flaceliere, Robert (Ed.), *Vies*, with introduction, Paris, Bude, 1964.

Gossage, A. J., in *Latin Biography*, Ch. III.

Russell, D. A. 'Plutarch's life of Coriolanus', *J.R.S.*, 53 (1963), pp. 21-8.

Smith, R. E. 'Plutarch's biographical sources in the Roman lives', *C.Q.*, 34 (1940), pp. 1-10.

Spencer, T. J. B. (Ed.), *Shakespeare's Plutarch*, London, 1964; p. 20 for further bibliography.

POLYBIUS:

Walbank, F. W. *A Historical Commentary on Polybius*, Vol. I, Oxford, 1957.

'Origins of tragic history', *Bulletin of the London Institute of Classical Studies*, 2 (1955), pp. 4 ff.

'Polemic in Polybius', *J.R.S.*, 52 (1962), pp. 1-12.

*Polybius and Rome's Eastern Policy*, *J.R.S.*, 53, pp. 1-13.

z

QUINTILIAN:

Colson, F. H. (Ed.), Book I of *Institutio Oratoria*, Cambridge, 1924.
Peterson, W. ed. Book 10, Oxford, 1891.
Austin, R. G. ed. Book 12, Oxford, revised ed., 1965.

SALLUST:

Büchner, F. W. K. *Sallust*, 1960.
Latte, K. *Sallust*, in *Neue Wege zur Antike*, II, 4, 1935.
Perrochat, P. *Les Modeles grecs de Salluste*, 1949.

*Scriptores Historiae Augustae (S.H.A.)*:

Birley, A. R. in *Latin* (Dorey), Ch. 5.
Momigliano, A. D. (*v.* B I), Ch. 9: *An unsolved problem of historical Forgery* (See further, index in Millar: *Dio* supra).

SENECA, M. (L?) ANNAEUS (*rhetor*) – *Oratorum Sententiae Divisiones Colores.*

(1) Text, with introduction and English translation, ed. W. A. Edwards, of the *Suasoriae*, Oxford, 1928.

(2) Text of the *Controversiae* (and *Suas.*), Elsevire, Amsterdam, 1672.

SUETONIUS:

Syme, Sir Ronald, *Tacitus* (q.v.A), Appendices 36, 76, 77.
Townend, G. B. in *Latin Biography* (Dorey), Ch. 4.
Townend, G. B. 'The sources of the Greek in Suetonius', *Hermes*, 88 (1960), pp. 98–120.

TACITUS:

Balsdon, J. P. V. D. '*Review of D. M. Pippidi's* Author de Tibere', *J.R.S.*, 36 (1946), pp. 168–71.
Boissier, G. *Tacitus and other Roman Studies*, tr. from the French by W. G. Hutchison, London, 1906.
Furneaux and Anderson (Eds.), *Agricola*, Oxford, 1922. (The Ogilvie and Richmond ed. is a revision of this, but many articles on the *Agricola* only have access to the 1922 ed.)
Walker, B. *Annals of Tacitus*, 1952.

THEOPOMPUS:

Bloch, in *Athenian Studies* (*v.* sub Ephorus, *supra*).
Bury, J. B., *A.G.H.*, p. 167.
Gomme, A. W. *Commentary*, I, pp. 46–9, 65, 69–70.

THUCYDIDES:

Adcock, F. E. *Thucydides and his History*, Cambridge, 1963.
Brunt, P. A. 'The compassionate scientist', *History Today*, 1957.
Classen, J. (ed. J. Steup), *Commentary*, Berlin/Zürich/Dublin, 1966.
Cochrane, C. N. *Thucydides and the Science of History*, Oxford, 1929.
Finley, J. H. 'The origins of Thucydides' style', *Harv. Stud.*, 50 (1939), pp. 35–84.
'Euripides and Thucydides', *Harv. Stud.*, 49 (1938), pp. 23–68.
Grundy, G. B. *Thucydides and the History of his Age*, London, 1911.
N. G. L. Hammond, Criticism (much needed) of the above, *C.Q.*, 34, pp. 46 ff.
Syme, Sir Ronald, 'Thucydides – Lecture on a Master Mind', *Proc. Brit. Acad.*, Vol. 48 (1960), pp. 39–56.

WILLIAM OF JUMIEGES:

*de Obitu Willelmi*, in *Gesta Normannorum Ducum*, ed. Jean Marx, Paris, 1914, p. 147.

XENOPHON:

Bury, J. B., *A.G.H.*, *see* n. 35.
Lesky, Albin, *History of Greek Literature*, (B II), pp. 616–24.

# XI

# Oratory
*Stephen Usher*

1 Eloquence was an esteemed accomplishment from earliest times. Homer's regal heroes, though nominally enjoying absolute power, had to persuade their warriors to fight well, and their fellow-princes to adopt a common plan for their mutual benefit. The *Iliad*, and to a lesser extent the *Odyssey*, contain many formal speeches belonging to these two categories, hortatory and deliberative. In Book II of the *Iliad* the fate of the expedition depends upon oratory, and the hortatory speeches of Agamemnon, Odysseus, and Nestor persuade the host to stay and fight. It is Nestor too, in Book X (ll. 204–17), who suggests to the council of chiefs that a spy should be sent into Troy in order to discover the enemy's plans. This aged king of Pylos is the prime exemplar of the power and importance of eloquence in Homer's epic: no longer the equal of the other heroes in military prowess, he was nevertheless assured of a place of honour in their councils because 'his voice flowed from his tongue more sweetly than honey'. Odysseus is a scarcely less accomplished orator, whose 'many wiles' often depend for their success upon his ability to persuade others to co-operate in their execution. And even Achilles, who usually chooses more robust methods of working his will, was educated by his mentor Phoenix 'to be a ῥητήρ ("speaker") and a doer of deeds'.[1]

1. *Iliad* IX. 443.

2 The existence of a form of forensic oratory in the heroic age is also attested in one of the scenes wrought by Hephaestus on the shield of Achilles.[2] It is the market-place of a city of 'articulate men' (μερόπων ἀνθρώπων). Two citizens are disputing over the compensation to be paid for a man who has been slain. They agree to accept the verdict of an arbitrator, who apparently arrives at his decision after listening to a panel of the city's elders, each of whom gives his interpretation of the case. A crowd is also present, cheering on the two disputants; but they play no direct part in the proceedings. The elder whose interpretation is adopted by the arbitrator receives a prize of two talents. If this payment seems excessive, at least it will be admitted that these earliest jurors worked for an uncertain reward, unlike the fifth-century Athenian juror, who received a sure two obols a day for merely sitting and dozing in the sun.

3 But for all its exuberance, power, and pathos, Homeric oratory does not meet the claim of the later opponents of rhetoric, who sought to discredit the new art by finding all its essential elements in the oldest extant literature. Homer's speeches lack systematic arrangement: they were not composed in accordance with any rules, but proceeded on the wings of poetic inspiration. The speakers themselves were, moreover, free aristocratic princes, secure in their power and not dependent upon favourable verdicts.[3] Formalization, by which oratory became a technique as well as an art, came only when and where equality and competition entered into political life, and every citizen, not only the wealthiest or the noblest, could address an assembly of his fellow-citizens and expect to be heard out. A change to this condition was set in motion at Athens by the democratic reforms of Cleisthenes (508 B.C.), and completed by the socially levelling effects of the Persian Wars. The ablest man to take advantage of this change was

2. *Iliad* XVIII. 497–508.

3. Hesiod, *Theogony*, 81 ff., says that a king should have the power to lead on his people by persuasive speech; but 'persuasion' in the epic period, when applied to the relationship between king and subject, usually meant exhortation to carry out a decision in which the subject had had no part.

Themistocles, who, with no special qualifications of birth, climbed to power over the wreckage of several aristocratic reputations. Plutarch the biographer says that he received instruction in oratory from a sophist named Mnesiphilus.[4] Whether we accept this isolated testimony or not, there is no doubt that Themistocles cultivated his powers and used them to great effect. His most spectacular political achievement was his successful advocation of a naval policy, which he was able to press to its logical consummation at the battle of Salamis. On the eve of this battle, according to Herodotus,[5] he made his most crucial speech to the wavering Greek fleet, in which he contrasted the better with the worse in man's nature, and urged them to choose the better. If such was his theme, this speech is a direct forerunner of the many extant Athenian speeches that are constructed in the so-called antithetical style, and provides strong grounds for conferring upon Themistocles the title of 'Father of Attic Oratory'.

4 The democratic movement gained momentum in the post-war years, and culminated in the reforms of Pericles and Ephialtes in 462 B.C. Whereas the growth of deliberative or political oratory is to be seen as a gradual process, forensic oratory in the form in which it later flourished owes its inception to a specific reform. Previously, law-suits had been heard by single magistrates or by elders of the Areopagus. The democrats assigned the majority of these to the newly created Popular Courts (δικαστήρια), which comprised 201 ordinary critizens chosen by lot from a body of 6,000, and paid two obols a day by the State for their services. From being a simple, undramatic hearing before a bench of unimpressionable senior citizens whose sole interest was in the correct application of the law, a law-suit now became a contest in the art of winning over a multitude of plastic but by no means uncritical minds. But in spite of the consequences of this change, no corresponding alteration was made to the old law that every citizen should conduct his own case. Unlike the citizen who spoke in the Assembly, the man who became involved in

4. *Life of Themistocles*, 2.                    5. VIII. 83.

litigation became an orator from necessity. This placed the less talented or more retiring citizen at a considerable disadvantage. He needed help.

5 In obedience to the law of demand and supply, help was not long in coming. Though no exact date can be fixed for its arrival, its provenance can be asserted with some degree of certainty. Handbooks on rhetoric were written in Sicily by Corax and his pupil Tisias in response to a local demand which arose through a somewhat similar political revolution to that experienced at Athens. The tyrants were expelled from the island between 466 and 461 B.C. Corax is reputed to have taught his countrymen to use their newly found freedom by writing a handbook on public speaking, in which he laid down a tripartite division of a speech into introduction, argument, and conclusion. But the most lasting contribution of Sicilian rhetoric is concerned with forensic oratory, and is probably the invention of Tisias. The revolution in Sicily was followed immediately by a large number of law-suits in which citizens reclaimed property which the tyrants had confiscated over a period of years. Direct evidence, removed or obscured by the passage of time, was scarce or unreliable; so that claims were difficult to establish or to refute. Tisias found a substitute for it in argument from probability (εἰκός). In addition to meeting local Sicilian needs, this form of argument had the universal advantage that it depended not upon witnesses as to fact, who could be corrupted, but upon the common sense of a jury, which could not. Those statements which the litigant needed to confirm or refute were subjected to the test of human experience. A puny man accused of assaulting a big man would argue: 'I am clearly weak and he is strong: it is therefore unlikely, according to the probabilities of human behaviour, that I should have assaulted him.' This form of argument, with its two premises and conclusion, is the rhetorical counterpart of the logical syllogism, and was called an *enthymeme*. Enthymemes might take a more condensed form, and make greater demands upon the jury's estimation of probability,

like the one given by the rhetorician Hermagoras of Temnos: 'Atalanta is not a virgin because she strolls through the woods with young men.' Here the unexpressed premiss is that girls who stroll through the woods with young men are unlikely to be virgins; but most judges would want to know more about Atalanta before committing themselves to an opinion. As the technique of εἰκός argument developed, increasing attention was centred upon character and motivation. But Tisias's contribution was fundamental if he only invented the form of argument, because this invention not only dictated the future form of the proof but also distinguished it as a section separate from the narration of facts, giving four main sections to the classical forensic oration: introduction (προοίμιον, exordium); narration (διήγησις, narratio); proof (πίστις, probatio); conclusion (ἐπίλογος, peroratio).

6 Public speaking also came within the scope of the sophists. It served two main purposes in their educative programme, one practical, the other more purely academic. Firstly, they undertook to equip their pupils for a political career, for which oratorical ability was essential. The sophists supplied much of the teaching material upon which fifth-century deliberative oratory was based. They saw it as a readily divisible medium, and used three main topics of argument: justice, expediency, and possibility. Lack of space forbids closer analysis, but the intelligent reader will find these topics pursued with masterly invention in the speeches of the Corcyreans and the Corinthians to the Athenians in Book I of Thucydides. The sophists also taught the more narrowly linguistic technique of μακρολογία or amplification, which enabled a speaker to dwell at greater length on an argument in order to drive it home. To this they applied their academic interest in language, which was centred mainly upon the precise use of words (ὀρθοέπεια) and refinement of vocabulary, and created a distinctive genre of prose in which synonyms and figures of language were used to emphasize and to prolong arguments, and, in the hands of certain exponents, purely for purposes of display.

7 The most famous and extreme early innovator in the field of display (or *epideictic*) oratory was Gorgias of Leontini. This kind of oratory was already used for state funerals: the first recorded example of an *epitaphios* is a speech delivered over the fallen at the battle of Plataea in 479 B.C. Gorgias's compositions included funeral orations; also *encomia*, or laudatory essays, like the extant *Helen*, and quasi-forensic speeches on other mythological topics, like the *Palamedes*, his only other surviving work. These two examples of Gorgias's art contain sufficient to enable us to discern his main characteristics. Basing his structure upon antithesis (which was natural to Greek and not novel), he sought quantitative parallelism also, by making corresponding clauses equal in length (i.e. having equal numbers of syllables) (*parisosis*). He also sought correspondence in sound (*paromoeosis*), both in support of the structure, by giving the same endings to parallel clauses (*homoeoteleuton*), and for additional effect by allowing the same syllables to occur in close proximity (*paronomasia*), either in pairs of words with similar roots (*etymological figure*) or in words that have no such relationship (*parechesis*). By employing these devices in profusion, Gorgias created a style that was a medley of puns, jingles, and assonances, and an impossible vehicle for serious oratory. If the tradition is representative his influence on forensic oratory was slight; but he left his mark on epideictic oratory, as we shall see when we come to examine Isocrates. Two other names should be mentioned before we turn to the surviving practitioners. Thrasymachus of Chalcedon tried to devise a distinctive style for oratory, steering a middle course between archaic and poetic diction and that of everyday speech, a course which admitted rhythmic patterns and may have included the first attempts at periodic structure. He also paid attention to emotional appeal, and devised *loci communes* ('commonplaces', or standard arguments) for the excitement of anger or pity. Finally, Theodorus of Byzantium both taught oratory and wrote forensic speeches, in which he made subdivisions of the parts laid down by the Sicilian rhetoricians. Both these men were contemporaries of Gorgias.

8 The first of the Attic orators was Antiphon (*c.* 480–411 B.C.). He was a confirmed oligarch, living in a democracy but ever working for its dissolution. He kept out of public life, however, preferring private negotiation with men of similar persuasion, and waiting for the democracy to discredit itself. His was the main inspiration behind the short-lived oligarchic revolution of 411, and he was executed when democracy was restored. His activities as a writer of speeches (λογόγραφος) may be connected with his political activities: some, at least, of his clients were either men of oligarchic sympathy or victims of democratic misrule. In the latter category was the Mytilenean Euxitheus, the defendant in the longest and most interesting of Antiphon's surviving speeches, *On the Murder of Herodes*. The dead man, an Athenian, was a passenger on the same ship as Euxitheus on a voyage from Mytilene which was interrupted by foul weather off Northern Lesbos. The ship put in at a remote haven, the passengers took to their cups, Herodes left the ship and was never seen again, dead or alive. Subsequently the relatives of the dead man brought a charge of murder against Euxitheus. Lacking direct evidence, including the *corpus delicti* itself, they examined the slaves present under torture, which they were permitted to do by law. They obtained some of the answers they wanted and fabricated some evidence of their own, including a letter alleged to have been written by Euxitheus to an accomplice.

9 The speech displays Antiphon's methods and characteristics in a number of ways. The chief interest is the central importance and elaborateness of the proof, to the virtual exclusion of continuous narrative. The test of probability is applied not only to the immediate circumstances of Herodes' death, but to the whole case for the prosecution, and even to the latter's behaviour in the preliminaries to the trial, which the orator discusses at length (8–19) before turning to the case itself in order to imply their general dishonesty and lack of scruple. The narrative, short as it is (20–4), is interrupted by deductions (22) denying premeditation and trickery, and stress

is laid on the complete absence of any suspicious behaviour on the defendant's part. The proof, which occupies two-thirds of the speech, divides into refutation (25–56) and confirmation (57–84). The refutation begins with an exposure of inconsistencies and improbabilities in the prosecution's version of the facts, and is therefore well placed close to the narrative. The sequel to this is equally logical: lacking a convincing story, the prosecution resort to witnesses. Antiphon proceeds to show that the evidence thus obtained, using slaves, who under torture will say whatever their tormentors desire, is unreliable: moreover, the prosecution killed one of the slaves before he could be cross-questioned. Appeal is made throughout to probability: the proof begins with the sentence: 'Those are the facts; now consider the probabilities arising from them'; and the defendant returns again and again to this criterion, with such formulae as 'if we are to judge from probability' (37), 'probability is my ally' (σύμμαχον) (43), 'would you think it likely?' (45), and 'what are the fair and probable conclusions to be drawn?' (49). But if the refutation is forceful and convincing, the confirmation is marginally more interesting by reason of its invention and variety. It begins (57–9) with a thorough examination of the defendant's possible motives: enmity, favour to a friend, fear, mercenary reasons. Here he has to content himself with mere denial of these motives, and fails to establish that Lycinus, his alleged associate in the murder, had no reason for wanting Herodes dead. But probability again comes to the rescue when Euxitheus says that Lycinus had no money and was not his close friend (63), thus ruling out the motives of favour and payment. After this there is a more general probability – that it is innocent people and not criminals who fail to cover their tracks – and this serves as a bridge to broader topics. (This widening of interest as a speech progresses is found in most of the longer Attic orations.) The first is that of the exaction of the death penalty on inconclusive evidence. Antiphon gives historical examples (another device which became a permanent feature) and stresses the irreversibility of this sentence. Next he defends his father's career,

349

mentioning the revolt of Mytilene against the Athenian democracy in 428 and arguing at length (74–80) that he had merely shared in the common error. The presence of this topic here and in many later Attic speeches reminds us that all oratory was in some degree political, since the speaker's standing as a citizen affected the attitude of the jury, which was itself a body of citizens. The final piece of confirmatory evidence seems even more irrelevant to the modern reader. Euxitheus affirms that since Herodes' death he has been present at many sacrifices and on shipboard, without causing divine indignation. This presumptive evidence of divine favour, and therefore innocence, is also adduced by Andocides (*On the Mysteries*, 137–8), but is not used by subsequent orators: it may therefore be regarded as an early feature which was judged to be out of harmony with the spirit of the fourth century.

10 Both the introduction and the conclusion contain features which are also confined to Antiphon and Andocides. Most obvious is their length: those of Lysias are less than half as long. Much of the length is taken up with repetition and amplification, but a number of commonplaces may be noted which recur in other orators: the plea of inexperience, the danger of his position, the advantages enjoyed by the prosecution and their vexatiousness, confidence in the fairness of the jury. Whereas later orators use one or two of these, it seems characteristic of early oratory to introduce as many of them as possible. Several of these *loci communes* may well owe their origin to the need to cover up the artificiality of the professionally composed speech.

11 Turning finally to Antiphon's style, we encounter a majority of characteristics which place him firmly in his fifth-century context. Like Thucydides, who admired him greatly both as a man and as an orator, his tone is uniformly serious, even grave; it is also dignified, never permitting him to indulge in scurrility. His inclusion of a number of archaic, poetic, and compound words in his vocabulary appears to aim at the same effect of grandeur and remoteness from common speech. A

further characteristic of his style is the use of substantives and the substantival forms of adjectives and verbs in preference to finite verbs, as in the following passage:

κρεῖσσον δὲ χρὴ γίγνεσθαι ἀεὶ τὸ ὑμέτερον δυνάμενον ἐμὲ δικαίως σῴζειν ἢ τὸ τῶν ἐχθρῶν βουλόμενον ἀδίκως με ἀπολλύναι. ἐν μὲν γὰρ τῷ ἐπισχεῖν ἔστι καὶ τὰ δεινὰ ταῦτα ποιῆσαι ἃ οὗτοι κελεύουσιν· ἐν δὲ τῷ παραχρῆμα οὐκ ἔστιν ἀρχὴν ὀρθῶς βουλεύεσθαι·

*You must never let your power to satisfy justice by saving my life be over-ridden by my enemies' desire to outrage it by putting me to death. A delay will still allow you to take the awful step which the prosecution urge upon you; whereas haste will make a fair consideration of the case quite impossible.*

Here the articular infinitive τῷ ἐπισχεῖν and the substantival expression τῷ παραχρῆμα are doing the work of conditional clauses with finite verbs. Antiphon also likes to minimize finite verbs by making one suffice for several clauses (e.g. *Herodes* 71–3), by using expressions like ἀνάγκη with ellipsis of ἐστί (e.g. *Choreutes* 18–19), and by creating new substantives from verbs (e.g. ὀπτήρ, γνωριστής). This tendency, allied to that of rhetorical amplification and a taste for unusual words, gives Antiphon's style a characteristic combination of fulsomeness and weightiness, which later critics described as 'grand' (ἁδρός – a word used to describe well-grown animals and swollen rivers). The distinctiveness of his style will emerge further as we examine those of his successors.

12 Antiphon's contemporary Andocides was also an oligarch, but was more flamboyant and less discreet in his political activities. He was involved in the scandal of the mutilated Hermae, and spent twelve years (415–403 B.C.) in exile. As an orator he was strictly an amateur, composing speeches only for his own use and not undergoing any formal training in rhetoric. (We may fancifully imagine that, with his family claiming descent from Hermes, the god of rhetoric, he felt himself divinely endowed with inborn talent.) Two of his three extant speeches, the *De Reditu* and the *De Mysteriis*, were

attempts (the second being successful) to secure his recall. The third, the *De Pace* (392 B.C.), on the subject of peace with Sparta, led to unsuccessful negotiations which caused his final exile. Thus Andocides is a political orator whose personal fate is closely bound up in the debates with which he is concerned.

13 Our interest in Andocides is thus threefold: as an early exemplar of Athenian political oratory; as an orator who initially thought he could manage without theoretical knowledge, but later decided that he could not; and as a man speaking solely on his own behalf, with everything to gain or lose by his words. The second of these aspects merits the closest examination. His failure to secure his recall with his speech *De Reditu* is attributable as much to bad (or unconventional) oratory as to an unfavourable political climate in 408, the probable year of its delivery. The most obvious fault is a lack of orderly arrangement and partition, and in particular the absence of a well-defined introduction containing the necessary plea for pity and flattery of the jury. Indeed, the tone of much of the speech is haughty and reproachful, the speaker implying that he deserves gratitude rather than punishment. This failure to woo the audience's goodwill is not counterbalanced by any positive attempt to stir them in his favour, or to divert them with the rough, sarcastic wit or the talent for narrative which he displays in the *De Mysteriis*. This speech is an altogether different proposition. Although there are still signs of uncertainty in the matter of arrangement, and occasional loosely constructed sentences (e.g. 57), there is clear evidence of fruitful lucubrations with rhetorical handbooks. The introduction contains several commonplaces, and so resembles that of Lysias' nineteenth speech that they may have a common source. But the special character of Andocides' oratory is not to be sought so much in the degree to which he adapted himself to existing theory as in his discovery of natural talents which added to the effectiveness of his oratory. He excels as a raconteur, and also takes every opportunity of enlivening his narratives with live speech (*diatyposis*) (e.g. 4, 41–2, 49, 51, 63,

101). The value of graphic narrative is especially great in the *De Mysteriis*, because it perforce contains much legal argument. His narratives add variety and relief, and themselves vary in their effect, some being exciting (e.g. the story told by Diocleides 38–40), others full of pathos (e.g. 49–50), and others capped by sarcastic humour (e.g. 129). Finally, we may observe in his ability (natural or, more likely, cultivated) to write in the grand style in passages like 29–33 and 146–50, and his use of historical examples, further evidence of a study of rhetoric. The process of learning seems to have gone a stage further in the *De Pace*, which complies with the rules for deliberative speeches by dealing with the topics of necessity (13), practicability (15), honour (17), expediency (17), and justice (18). But this formal accomplishment was achieved at a considerable loss of freshness and vigour, qualities which the oratory of Andocides, if it was to compete with that of others more completely equipped with the purely technical skills, could not afford to abandon.

14 Lysias, who was almost exclusively a forensic speech writer, became a professional by accident. Born at Athens around 458 B.C., he spent about thirty years of his life in Sicily and South Italy, returning to Athens around the year 415. With his brother Polemarchus he built up a successful business as a shield-maker, but this was ruined by the Thirty Tyrants in 404, who murdered Polemarchus and narrowly missed murdering Lysias. After the restoration of the democracy Lysias brought an action against Eratosthenes, one of the Thirty. In his speech he made full use of a thorough knowledge of rhetoric which he had acquired as a pupil of Tisias while in Sicily, and made such an impression on the jury that he decided to become a professional speech-writer. Thirty-five accredited speeches have survived, representing perhaps one-sixth of his total output.

15 Lysias' contribution to the development of oratory lies in two main aspects. Firstly, he refined the language by banishing archaism and poetic expressions, and in doing so made a break with the past which was never subsequently repaired. His

language is a pure literary Attic, in which simplicity and directness of expression are never allowed to degenerate into vulgarity or colloquialism, even when he is placing words in the
mouths of men of humble birth. The importance of this principle is seen when it conflicts with characterization, the second
individual aspect of Lysias' art. The spoken words of the rustic
defendant in the first speech (18, 21, 26) seem stiff and formal,
and leave us to guess what this outraged farmer actually said on
these occasions.

16 The portrayal of character in a forensic speech can serve as
an extended argument from probability. When used effectively
by a defendant, it may lead a jury to believe that a person of
such a character would be unlikely to do such a crime; and con-
versely, a skilful prosecutor might convince his audience that
the crime of which the defendant is accused is in accordance with
his character. Lysias uses characterization mainly in weak cases,
like the thirteenth and twenty-fourth speeches, and those in
which popular prejudice against the crime itself is liable to
affect the jury's verdict, as in the first, third, and seventh
speeches. The first speech contains Lysias' finest characterization. The defendant Euphiletus caught his wife's adulterer *in
flagrante delicto* and slayed him. This he was entitled to do by
Athenian law, but most wronged husbands preferred to accept
monetary compensation. The relatives of the adulterer
Eratosthenes (not the tyrant accused in the twelfth speech)
based their case on alleged entrapment, claiming that Euphiletus lured him into the bed-chamber on the fatal night. To meet
this Lysias devoted half the speech to narrative (the best
medium for the portrayal of character), in which Euphiletus is
depicted, through a detailed but lucid description of his actions
and words, going back to his marriage and his early relation
with his wife, as a simple, trusting husband who did not see
through his wife's deceit. His emotions likewise lack subtlety,
so that when he at last discovers the truth his reactions are
predictably violent. This portrayal admirably suits the needs of
the case: it discredits the prosecution's imputation of a planned

murder by showing the defendant to be incapable of guile; and it enables the jury to understand why Euphiletus could not have accepted any 'civilized' settlement with the adulterer. A man cannot help his character: Euphiletus could not have been expected to act in any other way, and deserves sympathy rather than punishment. The long narrative of this speech (6–28) also includes the facts vital to his argument: his normal behaviour on the night of the homicide, when he dined with a friend, who later departed; and the fact that he had to arouse his neighbours in order to have witnesses. Both these facts are subjected to the test of probability in the proof section of the speeches: as to the first, his dining with his friend in the house should have been expected to discourage the adulterer from entering; and again, if Euphiletus had been expecting Eratosthenes his most likely course would have been to detain his guest rather than let him go and face the adulterer alone (40). As to the second point, if the murder had been planned as it happened, with his neighbours as witnesses, these would have been apprised beforehand, and not have to be aroused from sleep. But Euphiletus was not the scheming kind. Thus character and fact become the servants of proof; action over a period becomes a guide to likely action in a given set of circumstances; and the sympathy of the jury is won for a man who acts according to his nature and yet finds himself in the toils of the law.

17 The degree of individuality in the characterization of Euphiletus is striking. It owes its lifelike quality to its admission of venial flaws, and renders Lysias unique among orators and superior to the later theorists, to whom 'ethopoeia' meant no more than a portrayal of good character, with an emphasis on the gentler virtues. Individual characterization is discernible in the third and seventh speeches, in which the defendants are both well-to-do, but the former is bolder and more aggressive, exhibiting these qualities by means of abundant correlatives (e.g. 7, 10, 25, 29) and rhetorical amplifications (e.g. 7, 15–17, 26, 28); while the defendant in the seventh speech is more timorous, but also more punctilious in marshalling his argu-

ments. Mantitheus, who defends his right to stand for state office in the sixteenth speech, is dashing and gallant, but ingenuous and respectful, qualities natural to his youth. One of Lysias' most interesting characters is the disabled ex-soldier in the twenty-fourth speech, whose claim to continued receipt of a state pension of three obols a day is disputed on the grounds that his property exceeds the stipulated minimum of three *minae*. He has a busy shop near the market-place, so the prosecution may well have been justified. Lysias therefore avoids the main argument completely, and dwells instead on his client's lameness as a means of exciting sympathy, and gives him a clown-like combination of dignity (portrayed by occasional outbursts of elevated style (e.g. 10, 16–18, 22–4)) and jocosity heavily underlined by sarcasm (e.g. 2, 12, 14). Here characterization is used to divert and entertain, with the purpose of persuading the audience of the unimportance of the facts of the case: the very opposite of the use made of characterization in the first speech.

18 Detailed characterization is less appropriate to a prosecutor than to a defendant: he merely has to show that he is honest himself and that his opponent is a scoundrel. In his own speech against Eratosthenes, his most powerful prosecution speech, Lysias makes judicious use of his narrative powers, but not primarily for the purpose of characterization. The narrative is used not simply to record facts but to explain motives to the speaker's advantage. Here the recurrent theme is the greed of the Thirty and his own misfortune in possessing wealth. The proof, when it begins (25), is, as in the first speech, no more than deduction from the facts, and the speaker is left with time to expatiate in more general terms on the misdeeds of the oligarchic regime. Eratosthenes, far from emerging as an individual, is but one of several criminals. The degree of individual characterization in Lysias thus depends on the nature of the case and the standpoint of the speaker.

19 Lysias' place in the development of prose style is no less important than his contribution to Attic Oratory. He is the

first successful exponent of the plain style, which is characterized by simple clausal structure, and is associated by the later
critics with narrative, the prime virtue of which was thought
to be clarity. The narratives of the first and twelfth speeches
may be read as perfect examples of the plain style, with their
use of common words, running, paratactic clausal structure
rather than hypotactic and periodic; swift action and clever use
of tense variation, short sentences, and a minimum of rhetorical
amplification. The appearance of naturalness should not lead
us to assume a lack of skill: Lysias' style was a conscious
reaction against the prevalent prose style. Being new, it required thought. The greatest danger he had to avoid was that
in achieving plainness his style would lose all literary quality.
We must not be deceived by Plutarch's story of a client of
Lysias who, on complaining that the speech he had written
for him did not stand up very well to repeated reading, received
the derisive reply that the jury would hear it only once.[6] Like
most other orators, Lysias wrote with an eye to publication,
which was the most effective way of advertising his skill. His
concern for artistic simplicity, as opposed to the reproduction
of the common colloquial language of the semi-literate, is seen
most clearly in his passages of live speech, but is present
throughout his oratory; so that he is one of those writers to
whom the axiom 'ars est celare artem' might be most appropriately applied.

20 Isaeus was the natural successor to Lysias in his taste for
Attic purity and economy, but requires separate study for two
reasons. Firstly, he was a specialist in the law of inheritance,
and his eleven surviving speeches are all concerned with this
difficult branch of the law. Secondly, he is known to have
acted as the private tutor of Demosthenes, whose first speeches
were directed against rapacious relatives. Whether or not a man
died intestate, the disposition of his property might be disputed, and its final destination might depend upon who could
claim the closest ties of affection. Emotions could therefore run

6. Plutarch, *De Garrulitate*, 4.

high in such cases. Accusation and recrimination played an important part, and Isaeus was very strong in this department of his proofs. His characteristic style included frequent repetitions, schemes of question and answer, and other figures of language and thought that increased the forcefulness, pungency, and earnestness of his argument. A full study of figures of speech in Isaeus[7] has shown that he resembles Demosthenes rather than Lysias in his use of those which promote these qualities. Characterization, in so far as it comes into play at all, is typical rather than individual. Isaeus is, like Antiphon, chiefly interested in technical (ἔντεχνος) rather than factual (ἄτεχνος) proof. Moreover, he uses the elaborated logical proof, or epichireme (an example of which is the argument in 7, 19–20), rather than the incomplete rhetorical syllogism favoured by Lysias. This is a further example of the thoroughness and intellectualism which brought him his reputation, and provided him with the most famous of oratorical pupils.

21 Demosthenes (c. 384–323 B.C.) overshadowed all other Greek orators in the estimation of later antiquity, and consigned them to an undeserved obscurity. His renown rested to a large extent upon the fact that the greatest oratory is that which is spoken in protest, and that the particular lost cause which he championed was one of perennial appeal – democracy against tyranny, freedom against slavery. Reason as well as economy therefore justifies confinement to his political speeches. But first we shall do well to examine some important details of his career. He was attracted to oratory during his adolescent years, but lacked the natural endowments of a strong voice, good articulation, and good wind. But unlike Isocrates, he resolved to overcome these weaknesses, and his determination is attested by the various exercises and devices he employed to improve his delivery: we read that he hung a dagger from the ceiling in order to keep one of his shoulders from twitching, practised his enunciation with pebbles in his mouth, and went down to the seashore at Phalerum and spoke

7. W. W. Baden, 'The Principal Figures of Language and Figures of Thought in the Speeches of Isaeus', Dissertation, Baltimore, 1906.

to the waves as a preparation for competition with the noise of
the assembly. He brought the same painstaking perfectionism
to the actual composition of his speeches, backed by four years
of intensive theoretical learning at the hands of Isaeus. From
these facts it will be plain that his style was the product of
Herculean labours, and a triumph of application over physical
disabilities.

22 The most immediately striking characteristic of Demosthenes' style is the richness and freedom of his vocabulary.
'Richness' can be induced by two means: the use of existing
words in a metaphorical sense, and the introduction of new
words and expressions to accommodate the greater complica-
tion and wealth of thought. Freedom of vocabulary implies an
extension of this procedure to words which previous writers
have excluded because they considered them to be poetical or
colloquial. These categories will be examined separately.

23 Demosthenes is a bold coiner of metaphors, the inventor
of the now hackneyed expression 'drunk with success', which
he applied in a double sense to his arch-enemy Philip II, the
convivial king of Macedon, in his 1st *Philippic* oration (49).
Additional colour is extracted from metaphor by means such
as this, and also by a more general relevance of a word's
original context to that in which it is being used. Hence, since
Demosthenes is usually advocating an offensive policy, military
metaphors form a large proportion of those employed.
'Philip,' he says,[8] 'does not wish the freedom which we foster
to lie in wait (ἐνεδρεύειν) upon his moments of peril.' 'Philip',
again,[9] 'has set a tyranny in siege (ἐπετείχισεν) over Attica'.
The related activities of wrestling and hunting are also represented, and this group is completed by a list of words which
represent violence, as when the city's traitors have 'mutilated'
her (ἠκρωτηριασμένοι),[10] or Demosthenes' opponents 'burst
themselves' (διαρράγωσι)[11] with their own lies, and a further

8. *On the Chersonnese*, 42.
9. *Phil.* 4. 8.
10. *De Corona*, 296.
11. *De Corona*, 87.

list consisting of derogatory metaphors, like καταπτύω, 'I abhor' (lit. 'I spit upon'),[12] τυρεύειν, 'to make a mess' (lit. 'to make a cheese'),[13] τετύφωμαι, 'I am demented' (lit. 'I am enveloped in smoke').[14] The other main group is that of health, growth, and decay. The most famous of these is his statement that 'Greece was sick' (νενόσηκεν ἡ Ἑλλάς[15] and αἱ δὲ πόλεις ἐνόσουν).[16] Elsewhere there are references to 'deafness' (κωφότητα),[17] of 'growing evil' (φυομένου κακοῦ),[18] of 'reaping the harvest' (καρποῦσθαι),[19] and the expression 'He who produces the seed is responsible for the fruit' (ὁ γὰρ τὸ σπέρμα παρασχὼν οὗτος τῶν φύντων αἴτιος).[20] With these examples enough has been said about metaphor in Demosthenes to illustrate the freedom and imagination with which he employed it.

24 Demosthenes felt the constricting effect of Attic purity more acutely than his predecessors, and frequently transgresses its limits. Actual colloquialism (i.e. the use of words which belong exclusively to familiar speech) is difficult to isolate, since many such words found their way into literature, especially through the comic poets. Thus σπερμόλογος[21] ('gossip'), περίτριμμα[22] ('pettifogger'), and κίναδος[23] ('puppy') are all found in Aristophanes. But neologisms are to be found in Demosthenes in plenty. Here we shall mention the best known: the verb φιλιππίζειν,[24] and the adjectives he used to abuse his political rival Aeschines, ἰαμβειόφαγος,[25] ('mouther of iambs'), referring to his career as a tragic actor, and γραμματοκύφων[26] ('scribbler').

25 Demosthenes' methods of increasing his powers of exact expression are perhaps even more important than those of achieving added colour. Once again we may refer first to superficial devices: his employment of a wide range of new nouns, especially those derived from verbs (a procedure the

12. *De Corona*, 200.
13. *Fals. Leg.* 295.
14. *Phil.* 3. 20.
15. *Phil.* 3. 39.
16. *De Corona*, 45.
17. *Fals. Leg.* 226.
18. *De Corona*, 62.
19. *Chers.* 63–4.
20. *De Corona*, 159.
21. *De Corona*, 127.
22. Ibid.
23. Idem, 162.
24. Idem, 176.
25. Idem, 139.
26. Idem, 209.

beginnings of which we saw in Antiphon); and neuter adjectives with the article, which especially assist in abstract expression. But more important than examples of lexical wealth of this kind is his bold use of attribution, which I shall illustrate without more ado:

ὁ γὰρ τότε ἐνστὰς πόλεμος ἄνευ τοῦ καλὴν δόξαν ἐνεγκεῖν ἐν πᾶσι τοῖς κατὰ τὸν βίον ἀφθονωτέροις καὶ εὐωνοτέροις διῆγεν ὑμᾶς τῆς νῦν εἰρήνης, ἣν οὗτοι κατὰ τῆς πατρίδος τηροῦσιν οἱ χρηστοὶ ἐπὶ ταῖς μελλούσαις ἐλπίσιν, ὧν διαμάρτοιεν, καὶ μετάσχοιεν ὧν ὑμεῖς οἱ τὰ βέλτιστα βουλόμενοι τοὺς θεοὺς αἰτεῖτε, μὴ μεταδοῖεν ὑμῖν ὧν αὐτοὶ προῄρηνται.[27]

*The war which broke out at that time, besides bringing you glory, saw you supplied with all the necessities of life in greater abundance and at lower cost than the present peace, which these fine patriots are maintaining against the state's interests and in hope of future gain. May they fail in these hopes, and may they rather share with you men of good intent in the blessings you are praying for, lest they should involve you in the disastrous results of their policy.*

The flow of the sentence is not greatly swollen by amplifications and synonyms, and yet it is quite long. The reason for this is that nearly every substantival unit is in some way expanded, and not merely by the attribution of an adjective: these units almost become clauses:

ὁ γὰρ τότε ἐνστὰς πόλεμος, ἄνευ τοῦ καλὴν δόξαν ἐνεγκεῖν, ἐν πᾶσι τοῖς κατὰ τὸν βίον ἀφθονωτέροις, ὑμεῖς οἱ τὰ βέλτιστα βουλόμενοι.

These attributive complexes are artistically relieved towards the end by clauses containing finite verbs. In this concentrated, precise manner of expression the definite article plays a vital part. He also uses it with the infinitive, a device to which he has recourse more frequently than any other Greek author, and which has provided him with a means of exact expression that is more effective than neologism or colloquialism.

26 Although this taste for attribution represents what is peculiarly Demosthenic, we should be far from showing the

27. Idem, 89.

full measure of his greatness if we left matters there. Demosthenes mastered all the rhetorical devices and styles which his predecessors were able only singly to master. There is no more effective antithesis than the famous climactic one in which he summarily contrasts his career with that of Aeschines:

ἐδίδασκες γράμματα, ἐγὼ δ᾿ ἐφοίτων. ἐτέλεις, ἐγὼ δ᾿ ἐτελούμην. ἐγραμμάτευες, ἐγὼ δ᾿ ἠκκλησίαζον. ἐτριταγωνίστεις, ἐγὼ δ᾿ ἐθεώρουν. ἐξέπιπτες, ἐγὼ δ᾿ ἐσύριττον. ὑπερ τῶν ἐχθρῶν πεπολίτευσαι πάντα, ἐγὼ δ᾿ ὑπερ τῆς πατρίδος.

*You were a teacher, I a pupil; you were an initiator in the Mysteries, I an initiate; you were a clerk in the Assembly, I attended it; you were a third-rate actor, I a spectator; you were hissed off the stage, I did the hissing; all your politics have favoured our enemies, mine my country.*

Demosthenes is an unsurpassed exponent of the various forms of question, which he employs for refutation, explanation of policy, and even for exhortation (e.g. Phil. 1. 44). And hyperbaton, or the separation of grammatically connected words, is employed more effectively by him than by any other Greek writer (e.g. *De Corona*, 18, ἄκριτος . . . ταραχή; cf. *Symmories*, 16).

27 For an example of the grand style we need to look no further than the introduction to his finest oration, the *De Corona*. This passage, with its solemn invocation of the gods, its predominance of long syllables, amplification (πᾶσι καὶ πάσαις, εὐσεβείας τε καὶ δόξης, τοὺς νόμους καὶ τὸν ὅρκον), and use of correlatives (ὅσην . . . τοσαύτην) has the weighty, measured quality required of this style and of the occasion, his defence of his entire public career.

28 His mastery of the plain style is best demonstrated in narrative. He does not often allow a narrative to proceed for long without interruption in the form of comment, but in the short time he allows himself he manages to paint a picture full of atmosphere and emotion. The most famous of these rapid-fire narratives is his account of the arrival at Athens of the news of the capture of Elateia by Philip.[28] Confused, nervous action is

28. *De Corona*, 169–70.

portrayed, first by the repetition of indifferent constructions, then by the tumbling participles, ἐξαναστάντες μεταξὺ δειπνοῦντες, aorist followed by present, further tense variations in the finite verbs ἐξεῖργον and ἐνεπίμπρασαν, and finally by the repeated καί. Then, as the story reaches its climax, the herald's call and after a pause (παρῄει δ' οὐδείς.) the appearance of Demosthenes alone of those present, the structure becomes heavy with a string of genitive absolutes, underlining the full import of the situation and the part played in it by the speaker.

29 The comparative rarity of the middle style, which is characterized by balance and smoothness, and which we shall see when we come to Isocrates, is not without significance. This style was devised primarily to give pleasure and edification: and Demosthenes was conspicuous among the political orators of his day in that he never tried to ingratiate himself to his audiences, but on the contrary, often reproved and berated them in his efforts to goad them into action. It is this quality of urgent admonition that informs his finest political speeches, the first three *Philippics*, the *Olynthiacs*, the speech *On the Chersonese*, and above all the *De Corona*. Few politicians can have vindicated, as Demosthenes did in this speech, a career which, if judged purely on results was a failure, to the extent that his opponent failed to obtain one-fifth of the votes. It is to the eternal credit of the Athenians that they rated patriotism higher than success.

30 Four of Demosthenes' contemporaries attained sufficient fame to merit passing notice. They are Aeschines, Lycurgus, Hyperides, and Dinarchus. Aeschines became a political speaker after an unsuccessful career as a tragic actor. Demosthenes envied his commanding presence and his fine voice, but had no cause to envy his oratory or his political acumen. The best of his three surviving speeches is *On the False Embassy*, in which he reveals qualities which have caused critics to compare him with Andocides – rough humour (e.g. 34–7) (a quality lacking in Demosthenes), and a taste for narrative – to which he adds a personal penchant for quotation from the

poets, natural in one professionally acquainted with their works. He is also an effective exponent of the letter of the law, as he shows in his speech *Against Ctesiphon*. But he cannot match the deeply felt patriotism of Demosthenes, and admirably illustrates the fact that there is no substitute for sincerity in an orator. He has nothing to compare with Demosthenes' broad general arguments on the subject of the position of Athens in the Greek world. Lycurgus was a brilliant financier with an impressive record of public service when he wrote his only surviving speech, *Against Leocrates*. By attacking a man whose sole crime was a failure in patriotism, it portrays the quality which earned for its author comparison with the Elder Cato. Like the earlier orators, he does not indulge in scurrility; but the lofty sentiments expressed do not compensate for the Isocratean monotony of his style. The loss of all but one complete speech and some fragments of the speeches of Hyperides is probably the worst blow to the student of Attic oratory, if the opinion of later antiquity is any guide. His forensic technique seems to have consisted in lulling the audience into docility by his informality in the prooemium and narrative, and then subjecting his opponents to rigorous and destructive logic in the proof. But his best speech was perhaps the *Epitaphios*, which was spoken over the fallen in the Lamian War (323 B.C.). This expressive and moving speech, which survives in fragments, represents the summit of the Greek achievement in that genre. Dinarchus was probably the least distinguished of the four. Interesting from the fact that he belonged to the generation following the others, and lived into the third century, he was a professional speech-writer, but had no original methods; indeed, his efforts to imitate Demosthenes earned him some uncomplimentary names at the hands of later critics. We have to wait for another age and another language for a rival to Demosthenes.

31 Discussion of Isocrates has been postponed in defiance of chronology because of his importance for the subsequent development of oratory. Although he began his career as a

forensic speech-writer, he soon turned his back on this lowly trade and gave his attention to higher things – to politics and education. Sharing Demosthenes' natural disabilities, he chose not to conquer them and become an active public speaker, but to influence opinion through the written word. The names of the sophists Prodicus and Gorgias, the rhetorician Tisias, the moderate democrat Theramenes, and Socrates are mentioned by our sources among his teachers; so that he was not lacking in theoretical training on a variety of cultural topics. He spent the last fifty years of his long life (he was 98 when he died in 338 B.C.) teaching in the school which he founded in Athens around 392 B.C. and writing political essays. In domestic politics he favoured parliamentary rather than pure democracy, having witnessed the latter's effects in the Peloponnesian War. In foreign policy he was a fervent advocate of aggressive Panhellenism, with Persia as the enemy. The influence of his political pamphlets was considerable; but his educational theories and methods had a far more permanent influence.

32 Isocrates agreed with Plato that the pursuit of knowledge ('philosophia') should be man's main preoccupation, but disagreed with him as to the nature of knowledge. He considered that absolute knowledge ($\epsilon\pi\iota\sigma\tau\eta\mu\eta$) is beyond human attainment, an argument which is confirmed by the many theories that had by then been propounded concerning the nature of the universe. The most that man can attain to in fundamental matters is opinion ($\delta\delta\xi\alpha$), which because of its uncertainty can be influenced by argument. From this comes the special importance of rhetoric; but this word must be completely divested of its derogatory associations before we can understand Isocrates. He believed that men who learn to compose noble speeches on lofty subjects acquire a wisdom above the mere craft of a forensic pleader, and deserve a place in the highest councils of the State. Noble thoughts can be conceived only by a noble nature, which can be inculcated by stimulating the faculty of reason in suitable subjects (Isocrates admits that his pupils must possess natural gifts and, quite as important,

the capacity for hard work). Thoughts must then be expressed in words, and Isocrates undertook to teach his pupils both what to say and how to say it. The two processes were inseparable: the word λόγος can mean both 'reason' and 'eloquence' in Isocrates' discussions.

33 There is little doubt that belief in the power of words themselves, artistically arranged, was central to his teaching, and that his pupils were encouraged to model their style upon that of the master. He discussed his own works with them, composing and titivating them at leisure. The result was a style that was recognized early as being more suited to private reading than declamation. Its most obvious characteristic is the length and structural complexity of its sentences. Two main principles govern its composition, the first of which is designed to create tension, the second to relieve it. The term 'period' applied by later critics to this sentence is a metaphor, the original word meaning 'race-track', around which competitors run, returning to the point from which they started. Applied to a sentence, the words are the runners, but we are concerned not with their 'return' but with the completion of the sense which they have built up on their journey. A true period is not complete in its meaning until the last word or group of words has been uttered. The reader or listener is thus kept in suspense with (it is hoped) his attention riveted. But this tension may be relieved to some extent by not postponing for too long the elements which introduce the main action. Following this principle, Isocrates regularly gives a central position in his period to the main predicate. But at this point an example is needed, and the opening sentence of the *Panegyricus*, arguably his best work, admirably suits our purpose.

Πολλάκις ἐθαύμασα τῶν τὰς πανηγύρεις συναγαγόντων καὶ τοὺς γυμνικοὺς ἀγῶνας καταστησάντων, ὅτι τὰς μὲν τῶν σωμάτων εὐτυχίας οὕτω μεγάλων δωρεῶν ἠξίωσαν, τοῖς δ' ὑπὲρ τῶν κοινῶν ἰδίᾳ πονήσασι καὶ τὰς ἑαυτῶν ψυχὰς οὕτω παρασκευάσασιν ὥστε καὶ τοὺς ἄλλους ὠφελεῖν δύνασθαι, τούτοις δ' οὐδεμίαν τιμὴν ἀπένειμαν· ὧν εἰκὸς ἦν αὐτοὺς

μᾶλλον ποιήσασθαι πρόνοιαν· τῶν μὲν γὰρ ἀθλητῶν δὶς
τοσαύτην ῥώμην λαβόντων οὐδὲν ἂν πλέον γένοιτο τοῖς
ἄλλοις, ἑνὸς δὲ ἀνδρὸς εὖ φρονήσαντος ἅπαντες ἂν ἀπολαύσειαν
οἱ βουλόμενοι κοινωνεῖν τῆς ἐκείνου διανοίας.

*Many times have I wondered at those who first convoked the national assem-
blies and established the athletic games, amazed that they should have
thought the prowess of men's bodies to be deserving of so great bounties,
while to those who had toiled in private for the public good and trained
their own minds so as to be able to help also their fellow-men they appor-
tioned no reward whatsoever, when, in all reason, they ought rather to have
made provision for the latter; for if all the athletes should acquire twice
the strength which they now possess the rest of the world would be no better
off; but let a single man attain to wisdom, and all men will reap the
benefit who are willing to share his insight.*

In strict grammatical terms the main verb is ἐθαύμασα, but the
heart of the action, and therefore of the period, is the antithesis
between the honour accorded to physical prowess and the
obscurity suffered by men of intelligence, i.e. the predicates
μεγάλων δωρεῶν ἠξίωσαν and οὐδεμίαν τιμὴν ἀπένειμαν. What
follows explains this central statement: Isocratean periods
regularly conclude with explanatory or causal clauses, frequently, as here, with γάρ. The final word διανοίας reasserts the
superiority of brain over brawn, and the word-order in the
final clause has been arranged so that it should come last.
Thus is the overall periodic effect achieved, by building up a
tension which is partially relieved in the centre, but is resumed
and finally dissolved by the last word. But this is only one of a
variety of forms of a complex organism which, in the hands of
a master like Isocrates, can be almost infinite. For example,
when the central antithesis is in the form οὐκ . . . ἀλλά as it
commonly is, it is natural for the chief interest to lie in the
second limb, thus often postponing the main action until
almost the end.[29] Again, on occasion, and especially in passages
of narrative, tension is built up by a long series of subordinate
clauses, and then the period comes to a close with a quick

29. E.g. *Areopagiticus*, 13.

succession of main verbs, relieving the suspense with swift action.[30]

34 The special importance of the end of the period gave rise to the idea that it should be invested with certain rhythmic properties, which would heighten its impact by momentarily giving it the character of poetry. These *clausulae*, which may have been originally adumbrated in the fifth century by Thrasymachus or Theodorus, appear to have been composed not to any regular metrical pattern but according to certain preconceived ideas of the character of individual feet. The least dignified feet were the iambus ($\cup$ –), the trochee (– $\cup$), and the tribrach ($\cup \cup \cup$); the most dignified the dactyl (– $\cup \cup$), the anapaest ($\cup \cup$ –), the spondee (– –), and the cretic (– $\cup$ –). The difficulty of knowing how prose was resolved into feet, and uncertainty as to the part played by *stress*, render informed examination of the problem impossible. Nevertheless, two rules seem to hold good in most of the clausulae of Isocrates: that one of the last two feet must be long, and schemes of rhythm that are predominantly iambic or trochaic are avoided. It is also possible to demonstrate the achievement of certain effects, but one example will have to suffice:

.... τὴν αὐτὴν τροφὸν καὶ πατρίδα καὶ μητέρα καλέσαι προσήκει.

The high tone of the words themselves is enhanced by the relative frequency of short syllables in the last seven words, which contrasts with the predominance of long syllables in the preceding words; but most important is the need to end with weight, here seen in the two final long syllables.

35 The effectiveness of periodic structure depends as much upon the writer's sense of when *not* to use it as upon his mastery of the art itself. In his best orations Isocrates varies the length of his periods greatly, and alternates periodic with simpler structure, choosing each according to the subject-matter. In a passage discussing the successes of Athens against

30. E.g. *Panegyricus*, 28–9; *Archidamus*, 45–6.

enemies in the past his description of early wars is simple and uneventful;[31] but when he comes to the Persian Wars the structure becomes more elaborate, beginning with a string of genitive absolute constructions.[32] Thereafter period follows upon period as Athenian virtue is extolled, until the tone strongly resembles that of a funeral speech.[33]

36 The style of Isocrates, especially as exemplified in the last passage, places him in direct succession to Gorgias, the one the pioneer, the other the perfector of *epideictic* or display oratory. Isocrates' contribution to its development consisted in his removal of its more puerile elements, especially the obsession with the various forms of *paronomasia* (puns, rhymes, and jingles), and the introduction of the principle of smoothness. He avoids *hiatus* (the clashing of a vowel ending a word with a vowel beginning the next word) altogether and likes to effect smooth transitions by employing relative pronouns. But he retained the Gorgianic usage of antithesis, extensively employing *parisosis* and *paromoeosis*, and adapted it to the period, thus creating a new medium of artistic prose which was widely imitated, both by his immediate pupils, who included the historians Ephorus and Theopompus and the orators Hyperides and Lycurgus, and by later prose writers. The central theme of his teaching, that the power of rhetoric could and should be employed in every medium in which thought, argument, and persuasion participate, obtained wide acceptance, and formed the basis of subsequent education in both the Greek and the Roman world.

37 The decline of oratory in Greece and its rise in Rome is separated by a period of some 150 years. During that time a great deal of scholarly work was done, mostly by Greek rhetoricians, including the most famous and important ancient treatise on rhetoric, the *Rhetoric* of Aristotle. Only one other complete treatise from this fruitful period survives, the *Rhetorica ad Alexandrum*, attributed to Anaximenes of Lampsacus; but some skilful reconstruction work has been done on

31. *Panegyricus*, 68–70.     32. Idem, 71.     33. Idem, 75–7.

the teachings of Theophrastus, Hermagoras of Temnos, and
Philodemus of Gadara. In a short chapter on oratory the
temptation to digress into literary criticism must be strenu-
ously resisted. It must therefore suffice to have mentioned the
chief names, and to observe their influence when we return to
practical oratory.

38 Our information about early Roman oratory is fragmentary. The Senate and the Popular Assembly no doubt
heard many men of considerable natural gifts forcefully attempting to guide their counsels in times of crisis. But from the
two centuries separating the earliest Roman orator of whom we
have record – the blind Appius Claudius, whose stern eloquence dissuaded the Senate in 278 B.C. from treating with
King Pyrrhus – to Cicero, only a handful of names has survived to which it is possible to attribute any oratorical personality. The second century is the turning-point. Two things
then conspired to stimulate the study of oratory: the growth of
Greek influence and the increasing instability of the political
situation. In their first dealings with the Greek world the
Romans saw themselves as friends and liberators, and the more
enlightened among them embraced Hellenic culture. Greek
rhetoric, with its clear and practical systematization, had
especial attractions for the Roman man of state. Greek rhetoricians found many eager pupils at Rome, and seemed assured of a secure place in her society. But on the political front
relations became strained. Roman elation at the liberation of
Greece from the tyranny of Philip V of Macedon and his successors was soon replaced by disillusionment. Greece remained
in tumult, and the more Rome became involved, the more
remote seemed a settlement. More and more Romans became
disgusted at the Greek inability to achieve the degree of internal harmony which Rome herself had achieved, with the
result that the opponents of Hellenism were heard with growing sympathy. In 161 B.C. a law was passed empowering Roman
magistrates at their discretion to expel Greek rhetoricians
and philosophers. But this was only a temporary reaction,

accomplished through sheer force of personality on the part of vehement Mishellenists like the Elder Cato. But this doughty figure himself demonstrated the insidious power of Greek culture, for while constantly voicing his disapproval of rhetoric (one of his precepts was 'rem tene, verba sequentur' – 'master your subject-matter: the words will come'), he obviously believed that oratory could be taught, and further found when he came to practise it himself that the Greeks had discovered the most effective techniques and devices. These he used in his own oratory, thus compelling our admiration for his practical sense, if not for his consistency. The following passage illustrates his adaptation of Latin to rhetorical form:

dixit a decemviris parum bene sibi cibaria curata esse. iussit vestimenta detrahi atque flagro caedi. decemviros Bruttiani verberavere, videre multi mortales. quis hanc contumeliam, quis hoc imperium, quis hanc servitutem ferre potest? nemo hoc rex ausus est facere: eane fieri bonis, bono genere gnatis, boni consultis? ubi societas? ubi fides maiorum? insignitas iniurias, plagas, verbera, vibices, eos dolores atque carnificinas per dedecus atque maximam contumeliam, inspectantibus popularibus suis atque multis mortalibus, te facere ausum esse? set quantum luctum, quantum gemitum, quid lacrimarum, quantum fletum factum audivi! servi iniurias nimis aegre ferunt: quid illos, bono genere gnatos, magna virtute praeditos, opinamini animi habuisse atque habituros, dum vivent?

*He said that his provisions had not been satisfactorily attended to by the decemvirs. He ordered them to be stripped and scourged. The Bruttiani scourged the decemvirs, many men saw it done. Who could endure such an insult, such tyranny, such slavery? No king has ever dared to act thus; shall such outrages be inflicted upon good men, born of a good family, and of good intentions? Where is the protection of our allies, where is the honour of our forefathers? To think that you have dared to inflict signal wrongs, blows, lashes, stripes, these pains and tortures, accompanied by disgrace and extreme ignominy, while their fellow-citizens and many other men looked on! But amid how great grief, what groans, what tears, what lamentations have I heard that this was done! Even slaves bitterly resent injustice; what feeling do you think that such men, sprung from good families, endowed with such high character, had and will have so long as they live?*

Loeb translation

The first difference from Greek is its *asyndeton*, or absence of connective particles. The initial effect of abruptness created by this is enhanced by the relative brevity of the sentences. There is also little effort to achieve clausal balance, with the sole and startling exception of the *chiasmus* 'decemviros Bruttiani verberavere, videre multi mortales' (chiasmus is rarely found in Greek, perhaps because it was regarded as too precious!). But there is a great amount of amplification ('copia'); rhetorical questions figure throughout; there is also *anaphora* ('ubi . . .? ubi . . .?') and etymological figure ('eane fieri *bonis, bono* genere gnatis, *boni* consultis . . . *habuisse* atque *habituros'*). The overall effect is one of singular force, achieved mostly by the devices of the grand style, the medium of vehemence, chosen with a remarkable linguistic feeling for what could be adapted from one language to another.

39 The years 133–121 B.C. witnessed political revolution at Rome. After Tiberius Gracchus had lost his life while trying to push through quite moderate social reforms his younger brother Gaius attacked the senatorial establishment on a much broader front, backed by a political alliance with the business class and, more relevant to the present discussion, with the popular assembly, which he held in allegiance by his oratory. Vehemence was his chief characteristic also, and was backed by a simple directness of thought. Thus his oratory became more of a spectacle for the assembly than a mental exercise. But even as such it contained an element of calculation, if we are to believe Plutarch,[34] who says that he posted a slave with a tuning instrument near the rostrum, with instructions to signal to him when his voice became too shrill. His gestures were, we may surmise, similarly calculated and rehearsed, while in the composition of the speeches themselves he is said to have supplemented a thorough acquaintance with Greek models by *ad hoc* assistance from the rhetorician Menelaus of Marathus. Among his fragments is a piece of introduction and a piece of narrative that are Lysianic in their balanced directness. There

34. *Life of Tiberius Gracchus*, 2. 6.

are also fragments containing the more forceful figures of thought, including *climax*[35] and *hypophora*.[36] Gaius presents a picture of a politician with a thorough grounding in the transmitted theory of oratory, who used these resources eclectically with an eye to a particular audience.

40 The lesson of Gaius's success, however transient, was not lost on his senatorial opponents, the self-styled *optimates*. The next two names are senatorial: M. Antonius (consul in 99 B.C.) and L. Licinius Crassus (consul in 95 B.C.). With these two Roman oratory seems to have attained a new maturity. Antonius published none of his speeches, perhaps because he wished to stress the *ex tempore* virtuosity of his art. With little evidence on which to rely, Cicero finds most to praise in his arrangement and inventiveness, but, anachronistically adopting Attic standards of purity, finds his diction less than completely satisfactory. Crassus appears to have been Antony's counterpart, his strength lying in his knowledge of the law and his interpretation of it, through which qualities he appealed to the mind rather than the emotions.

41 At the height of the careers of Crassus and Antony the first national school of Roman oratory was founded in 92 B.C. by a certain L. Plotius Gallus. The origin of this attempt to break away from Greek influence was political: Hellenism was an aristocratic cult, and certain popular leaders had already expressed their contempt for things Greek. The new school was to serve as a breeding-ground for a new generation of popular orators with a ready-made appeal to their Roman audiences. Crassus, as censor in 82 B.C., headed the aristocratic

35. *Oratorum Romanorum Fragmenta*, ed. Malcovati, p. 187: pueritia tua adulescentiae tuae inhonestamentum fuit, adulescentia senectuti dedecoramentum, senectus rei publicae flagitium.

*Your childhood was a disgrace to your adolescence, your adolescence a shame to your old age, your old age an affront to the State.*

36. Idem, p. 196: quo me miser conferam? quo vortam? in Capitoliumne? at fratris sanguine redundat. an domum? matrem ut miseram lamentantem videam et abiectam?

*Whither shall I take myself in my unhappy state? Whither shall I turn? To the Capitol? But it is flowing with my brother's blood. To my house? To see my mother in downcast mourning?*

opposition. He closed the school on the grounds that its founders were themselves inadequately equipped, so that their pupils would leave it in virtual ignorance of rhetoric, and possessing only an empty arrogance based on false confidence.

42 The last orator of any stature before Cicero was Q. Hortensius Hortalus, who was eight years older than Cicero and consul in 69 B.C. His style, of which we have no original specimen, was said to have been modelled not upon those of Lysias and Hyperides, the favourite models of Roman orators up to his time, but upon the so-called *Asiatic* style of the Hellenistic period. Of this style it is difficult to isolate any clear characteristics. Its chief exponent, Hegesias of Magnesia (in Asia Minor, hence the name Asiatic), was said to have avoided the nobler rhythms and the period, and to have written in a disjointed style dominated by iambs and trochees. Cicero's description of the style of Hortensius does not suggest these characteristics, but rather excessive floridity and extravagance of gesture.[37] He provides a partial explanation of this apparent discrepancy: he says that there were two kinds of Asianism, the one pithy ('sententiosus') and pointed ('argutus'), its sentiments expressed with neatness and elegance rather than force; and the other 'borne along with words in rapid flight' ('verbis volucre atque incitatum'), which implies, in its extreme form, excessive verbiage. Hortensius was prone to excess in both these aspects of Asianism, which did not matter so much when he was younger; but when it became necessary to invest his seniority with a certain dignity (*gravitas*) he was ill served by the conceits and the bombast of Asianism, and yet did not abandon them.

43 So much for Cicero's judgement of his greatest rival as an orator. It is commendably moderate and restrained, but it raises certain doubts as to the degree of accuracy attainable in prose-style criticism in this period of controversy. Cicero himself was later accused of *Asianism* by purists who found the same faults in his style as those which he censures in Hortens-

37. Cicero, *Brutus* 320, 325–7.

ius. It must therefore be concluded that, whatever narrow definitions were assigned to the term Asianism when it was first used, it later came to mean any style which departed from the usage of the approved Attic models. Such a strait-jacket might fit lesser orators like Calvus and Brutus, but was too constricting for Cicero; so that their criticisms, if based on such narrow criteria, may well have been valid. But it is also clear that the term was widely applied to successful orators by their less successful rivals, so that in less responsible hands 'Asiatic' was merely a term of opprobrium.

44 We know more about Cicero than any other figure in antiquity. His fifty-eight surviving speeches, which cover the period from 82 to 43 B.C., the year of his death at the age of 63, are nearly all political in character. Their volume and their author's constant obtrusion of his personality give an altogether exaggerated impression of Cicero's part in the shaping of events in this momentous epoch. But in the history of prose style their importance is incontestably great; and their author has added significantly to their interest by writing elsewhere, and at length, on the theory and practice of oratory. We may therefore conveniently begin our examination with Cicero's own choice of the qualifications of the ideal orator, which with characteristic self-effacement he denies to all his Roman predecessors. The passage runs as follows:[38]

> I shall say nothing of myself: I shall speak only of other orators, none of whom gave the impression of having studied literature more deeply than the common run of men, literature, which is the fountain-head of eloquence; no one who had embraced philosophy, the mother of all good deeds and good words; no one who had learnt civil law, a subject most necessary for private cases and essential to the orator's good judgement; no one who had at his command the traditions of Rome, from which if occasion demanded he could call up trustworthy witnesses from the dead; no one who, by rapid and neat mockery of his opponent could unbend the minds of the jurymen and turn them awhile from solemnity to smiling and laughter; no one who could widen

38. Cicero, *Brutus*, 322.

the issue and draw his speech away from a limited dispute referring to a particular person or time to a general question of universal application; no one who could delight by a temporary digression from the issue, or move the judge to violent anger or tears,
or, in fact – and this is the special quality of the orator, could turn
his feelings whichsoever way the occasion demanded.

Cicero's patent intention that his readers should recognize
these qualities in himself makes doubly interesting the examination of their occurrence in his speeches. Of the eight attributes
listed, three may be subsumed under the general heading of
*humanitas* (or, for want of a better word, 'culture'). Cicero's
ideal orator is a man of wide education and cultural interests,
with a general knowledge of literature; he has also studied
philosophy, which enables him to reason clearly and understand moral issues, and history, which furnishes him with
*exempla*. Two of the remaining attributes must depend largely
on this cultural background: all three aspects of it may come
into play when an issue is widened into a universal question;
and for his digressions the orator will draw on his knowledge of
history and literature, or a marriage of the two in the form of
mythology.

45 Of the three remaining attributes we may dismiss knowledge of the law with some dispatch. This is not because Cicero
was deficient in it, but because, in spite of his protestations to
the contrary,[39] he was less interested in the legal technicalities
of his cases than in a broad rhetorical exposition of their wider
implications. This is proved by the fact that he preferred to
speak second, or even third, after the legal arguments had been
thoroughly expounded by an earlier speaker. Nevertheless,
some of his speeches display formidable expertise in legal
argument, notably the *Pro Cluentio* and the *Pro Balbo*, and he
had the scholar's and the antiquarian's interest in ancient law.

46 Wit and humour, and the power to arouse the emotions are
primarily matters of style in the narrower sense. It will be
convenient at this point to add to them a list of other stylistic

39. *De Oratore*, 1. 166 ff., 173, 184; *Orator*, 120.

qualities, culled from Cicero's *De Oratore*,[40] in order to complete his portrait of the ideal orator. They are choice of words, sentence composition, speed in repartee, gesture, and memory. The last three of these are concerned with the impromptu element of oratory; the first two come under the heading of 'prose style', and will be dealt with when we come to that subject.

47 We turn now from theory to practice, and look first at Cicero's *humanitas*. The speech *Pro Archia* displays this quality in its purest form. Archias was a Greek poet whose claims to Roman citizenship Cicero is supporting, both for personal reasons, because he was hoping that Archias might compose an encomium on the subject of his consulship, and for political reasons, because Archias was in some way connected with Pompey, whom Cicero wished to cultivate. In his speech Cicero swiftly demolishes his opponent's case (which, as second speaker, he no longer has to refute in detail), and devotes most of the speech to an *extra causam* praise of literature, and in particular its power to immortalize the deeds of men. Turning to literary allusion, we find some of the best examples in the *Pro Caelio*. This was a case of alleged bribery at an election, and Caelius had a highly impeachable past record of irresponsibility. Like Lysias in his twenty-fourth speech, Cicero seeks to distract the jury from the ready-made probability argument against the character of Caelius by means of humour, but it is humour on an altogether higher plane than that accorded the Old Pensioner. It is diverting, urbane, and erudite: except for moments of earnest pleading, chiefly in the peroration, the jury is treated to a feast of polished oratory in the middle style, garnished with wit, more or less barbed, and seasoned, for the taste of the more learned, with quotations from Ennius, Terence, and Caecilius. Why does Cicero defend Caelius in this way? Plainly it would have been a perilous procedure if he had had to cope with damaging factual evidence; and in cases where this exists, like the *Pro Cluentio*

40. I. 17–18.

and the *Pro Milone*, literary allusion has no place. But the evidence against Caelius was based very largely on character,[41] and Cicero answers it in a similar way, making Clodia, Caelius's chief antagonist, the main object of attack. Two possible reasons may underlie the literary flavour of the speech in addition to the nature of the evidence: the fact that Caelius himself had pretensions as a wit and a lampoonist, and Cicero was trying to show him the way to a refinement of his taste; and the fact that the trial was held on a holiday, so that the jury were disgruntled at having to attend, and Cicero felt that they would appreciate a little entertainment for their trouble.

48 Cicero's interest in philosophy, attested by his considerable literary output on the subject, had a strong practical and political bias. It was no accident that, like many other Romans, he was more attracted to Stoicism than to Epicureanism, for the former embraced politics wholeheartedly, the latter advocated withdrawal. It is further natural that he should have put his knowledge to practical use in his speeches, especially since philosophy was very popular among educated Romans. Opportunities were many, though some were more inviting than others: his criticisms of the Stoicism practised by the Younger Cato in the *Pro Murena*[42] are authoritative enough; but those of the brand of Epicureanism practised by Piso in the *In Pisonem*[43] are less well informed. But of more general importance is the philosophical tone which he likes to inject into discussions of more immediate relevance to his cases. These are mostly concerned with legal and historical questions. In the *Pro Roscio Amerino*[44] he explains the reasoning behind the special arrangements made for the punishment of parricides; in the *Pro Sestio*[45] there is a discussion of the origin of society, which is relevant in a speech which is largely taken up with a description of the Roman political scene and Cicero's own position in it. There are also references to specific historical

41. See Austin's edition (Oxford, 1933), Appendix V.
42. 60 *seqq.*
43. 42, 59, 65.
44. 72.
45. 91-2.

situations: in the *Pro Flacco*[46] he ascribes the downfall of Greece to the excesses of its democratic assemblies; while the *De Imperio Gnaei Pompei*[47] contains a more detailed discussion of the careers of the naval powers of the Eastern Mediterranean. Nothing could have been more to the taste of a Roman audience than the interest in precedent, whether for imitation or avoidance, aroused by such discussions as these.

49 Digression which reflects a more general cultural interest is also to be found. In the *Verrine Orations* there are two ingredients which encourage such dilations: first Sicily herself, the scene of Verres' crimes, a magical island, full of mythical associations, draws from Cicero a noble encomium[48] and a version of the story of the Rape of Proserpine, and secondly, art treasures, of which Cicero considered himself a connoisseur. His description of the statues taken by Verres from the temple of Heius shows no deep knowledge[49] (it has been suggested that Verres knew more about art than Cicero at the time of these orations;[50] he had certainly had more opportunities for investigation); but is that of a cultivated man who was interested in a wide range of humane studies.

50 From these various manifestations of Cicero's *humanitas* we turn to the narrower subject of his oratorical style. This style developed considerably, and we shall not draw our examples from his earliest speeches. Nevertheless, the characteristics which some of these speeches exhibit to an excess which he himself describes as *iuvenilis redundantia* ('youthful prolixity')[51] remain permanent and almost ubiquitous. The idea of *copia*, or 'full treatment', as we might say under Transatlantic influence, is applied equally when the object is to excite emotions and when a milder, more contemplative reaction is sought. Take the impassioned opening of the *First Catilinarian*, that most

46. 16.
47. 54.
48. 4. 106–7.
49. 4. 5.
50. See F. H. Cowles, *Gaius Verres: an historical study*. Cornell Studies in Classical Philology, xx, 1917, 207 pp.
51. *Orator*, 107.

famous of apostrophes: six rhetorical questions follow one upon the other, the fourth of which contains six anaphoric subject-phrases ('nihil . . .'). Scarcely less lavishly wrought is the passage in the *Second Philippic* in which Cicero deplores Antony's purchase of the dead Pompey's house:[52]

O audaciam immanem! tu etiam ingredi illam domus ausus es? tu illud sanctissimum limen intrare? tu illarum aedium dis penatibus os impurissimum ostendere? quam domum aliquamdiu nemo adspicere poterat, nemo sine lacrimis praeterire, hac te in domo tam diu deversari non pudet? in qua, quamvis nihil sapias, tamen nihil tibi potest esse iucundum.

*What monstrous temerity! Did you actually dare to enter that house? You, to cross that most hallowed threshold? You, to show your face most vile to the household gods of that dwelling? Does it cause you no shame to tarry so long in a house which nobody could bear to behold for so long, and nobody pass by without shedding some tears? A house in which, though you may be without sensitivity, can have nothing congenial to offer you.*

Here, too, *amplificatio* is all-embracing: the first anaphoric tricolon, 'tu . . . ausus es', 'tu . . . intrare', 'tu . . . ostendere', says the same thing in three different ways, and the following sentence repeats the sentiment with the addition of emotional colour. Subsequently we find 'sine mente, sine sensu', 'te et tua et tuos', and 'neque vigilantem neque in somnis' in the next sentence is picked up again in the following sentence, which also contains 'violentus et furens'. This use of a swollen, inflated style in passages of fierce invective such as these is peculiarly to Cicero among Roman orators, and establishes his debt to the exponents of μακρολογία and especially Isocrates, who, however, has no passages of invective for Cicero to use as direct models. And the debt to Isocrates does not end there. Cicero makes wide use of the Isocratean period, an example[53] of which we shall quote in full for purposes of comparison:

Sed ne cui vestrum mirum esse videatur, me in quaestione legitima et in iudicio publico, cum res agatur apud praetorem populi

52. 68.
53. Cicero, *Pro Archia*, 3.

Romani, rectissimum virum, et apud severissimos iudices, tanto conventu hominum ac frequentia hoc uti genere dicendi, quod non modo a consuetudine iudiciorum, verum etiam a forensi sermone abhorreat, quaeso a vobis ut in hac caussa mihi detis hanc veniam, accommodatam huic reo, vobis, quem ad modum spero, non molestam, ut me pro summo poeta atque eruditissimo homine dicentem, hoc concursu hominum litteratissimorum, hac vestra humanitate, hoc denique praetore exercente iudicium, patiamini de studiis humanitatis ac litterarum paulo loqui liberius et in eius modi persona, quae propter otium ac studium minime in iudiciis periculisque tractata est, uti prope novo quodam et inusitato genere dicendi.

*It may, however, be a matter for surprise in some quarters that in an enquiry dealing with statute law, in a public trial held before a specially selected praetor of the Roman people, and a jury of high dignity, in the presence of a crowded audience of citizens, my speech should be made in a style out of keeping not merely with the conventions of the bar, but also with forensic language. But I beg for your indulgence, an indulgence which will, I trust, cause you no inconvenience, and which is peculiarly applicable to the nature of my client's case; and I would ask you to allow me, speaking as I am on behalf of a distinguished poet and a consummate scholar, before a cultivated audience, and the praetor whom we see occupying the tribunal, to enlarge somewhat upon enlightened and cultivated pursuits, and to employ what is perhaps a novel and unconventional line of defence to suit the character of one whose studious seclusion has made him a stranger to the anxious perils of the courts.* Loeb translation

The characteristics are by now familiar, and it will suffice to draw attention to the overall structure. It hinges on the centrally placed main verb 'quaeso', which is preceded by six subordinate clauses, bolstered by amplifications and appositions, and followed by eight further clauses, similarly padded, concluding with the object of his plea, without which the period is incomplete – that he be allowed to use 'novo quodam et inusitato genere dicendi'. This example of the Ciceronian period certainly exaggerates its qualities: the speaker himself is aware of them. But if he matches, and even exceeds, Isocrates here in amplification he is significantly less prone to antithesis, which is absent. Elsewhere Cicero achieves balance through the use of correlative constructions (tantus . . .

quantus, ita ... ut, cum ... tum, etc.), rather than with a Latin equivalent of οὐκ ... ἀλλὰ, and still less of μὲν ... δὲ. The Ciceronian period usually derives its length not from the balancing and the opposition of clauses, as is the case in Isocrates, nor by the accumulation of verbal or substantival complexes, as in Demosthenes, but from simple exuberance of ideas, which gives rise to an abundance of amplification, with synonyms and antonyms, and apposition, by which descriptive phrases are attributed to important nouns. That is why the commonest figure of language in Cicero is *anaphora*, the repetition of a word at the beginning of successive clauses or phrases.

51 But there is another side to the coin: Cicero was versatile. Of the three published speeches which he made during Caesar's dictatorship, the first, the *Pro Marcello*, exemplifies all that we have said about the Ciceronian period, and is composed mainly in that style (see especially 5, 6, 8, 22). But the same speech also contains passages of trenchant brevity (e.g. 30–2) when the subject demands; and in the second speech of the trio, the *Pro Ligario*, this economic style predominates. The penultimate sentence of this speech perhaps offers a clue: 'Longiorem orationem causa forsitan postulet, tua certe natura breviorem'; especially when Plutarch tells us [54] that the speech caused Caesar to colour and tremble. This forceful style, founded on brevity, the native Latin asyndeton, and the use of the more dynamic figures of speech, like exclamation and rhetorical question, was to be his chief weapon in his most violent Philippics. It will be appropriate to leave Cicero with another quotation from the speech that was most admired by his contemporaries, and which largely brought about his death, the *Second Philippic*:[55]

ut igitur in seminibus est causa arborum et stirpium, sic huius luctuosissimi belli semen tu fuisti. doletis tres exercitus populi Romani interfectos: interfecit Antonius. desideratis clarissimos cives: eos quoque nobis eripuit Antonius. auctoritas huius ordinis

54. *Life of Cicero*, 39, 7.
55. 55.

afflicta est: afflixit Antonius. omnia denique, quae postea vidimus
– quid autem mali non vidimus? – si recte ratiocinabimur, uni
accepta referemus Antonio. ut Helena Troianis, sic iste huic rei
publicae belli causa, causa pestis atque exitii fuit. reliquae partes
tribunatus principii similes. omnia perfecit, quae senatus salva re
publica ne fieri possent perfecerat. cuius tamen scelus in scelere
cognoscite. restituebat multos calamitosos: in iis patrui nulla
mentio. si severus, cur non in omnes? si misericors, cur non in
suos?

*Just as seeds are the origin of trees and their roots, so have you been the
seed of this lamentable war. You men grieve at the slaughter of three
Roman armies: Antony slew them. You long for the famous men taken
away: these too were taken away by Antony. The prestige of this senatorial
order has been damaged: Antony damaged it. In fine, all that we have
since seen – and what evil have we not seen? – if we judge the matter rightly
we shall ascribe to Antony, and to him alone. Just as Helen brought war
upon the republic, and was the cause of our pestilence and our destruction.
The latter part of his tribunate was like the beginning. He did all those
things which the senate had succeeded in preventing when the republic was
intact. But you have experience of his crime in its actuality. He restored to
power many dangerous men, but among these his own uncle was not included.
If he was to be harsh, why not equally to all? But if indulgent, why not
towards his own relatives?*

52 The first Roman emperor, Augustus, brought peace and
centralized government, and set about the task of reconstruction with measured skill and moderation. As the bringer of
peace after a generation of war, he found most Romans prepared to sacrifice their sovereign freedom for the sake of
ordered government, provided that the sacrifice was painless
and devoid of insult. His success in this delicate task, which
was due to his feeling for traditional Roman values, won him
the genuine gratitude of his people; but in the new state he
created there was no place for the vehement expression of
individual views, and oratory suffered as a result. The mood of
the age was typified by the oratory of Augustus himself, who
spoke with cool precision, avoiding alike obscurity and artificiality and maintaining an even tone.

53 But if the general mood was thus characterized there were
other channels through which eloquence might flow. Rhetoric

was the main instrument of Roman education under the Republic, and remained so under the empire, but with a change of emphasis and a change of scope. The Romans, prompted by their Greek mentors, regarded oratory as a branch of acting, and the word *declamatio* itself was applied equally to the theatre and to the rostrum. Under the empire, with the removal of the political application of the art, its potential as a medium of entertainment was realized to the full. The rhetorical schools assumed a more general cultural function in society (a development which Cicero and his predecessor Isocrates would surely have applauded): the rhetorican catered for a wider public, and offered his art as a more humane alternative to the Colosseum, with perhaps more success than modern musical performances compete with football matches.

54 Declamatory performances took two forms, called *controversiae* and *suasoriae*. In so far as both were discourses on set themes, which were highly debatable and open to a number of interpretations, they both owe much to the philosophical debates on nature, law, and the human condition found in such treatises as Aristotle's *Topics*, and ultimately derive their form from the epideictic fictions of Gorgias, the *Helen* and the *Palamedes*. *Controversiae* are concerned with imaginary forensic cases which expose ambiguities in the law or conflicts between two laws. The purpose is not to ridicule the law but to lay the chosen subject open to debate and individual interpretation. The following is a typical theme:

> The law concerning rape allows the victim to demand either death or marriage of the seducer. A man raped two women in one night; one demanded his death, the other marriage.

Leaving aside the question of which fate would be worse for the unfortunate seducer, this theme admits of a number of treatments. One speaker may ask which woman was raped first, and make his judgement accordingly, another may suggest that both women's demands be satisfied; and a third may dwell on the danger to society (the 'universal question' again), and question whether the woman demanding marriage can thus guarantee the safety of the rest of her kind.

55 The law here cited is imaginary, and even though most themes of *controversiae* had some basis in existing law, they had a fictional flavour. Violence figured prominently: tyranny, piracy, rape, and murder were favourite themes, and the declaimer became to some extent a purveyor of melodrama. But his impact as such was to some extent impaired by the stylistic aspects of his art, which divided the audience's interest and diluted the effect of each of the two sides of his performance. Stylistically four factors governed composition: *color*, *divisio*, *descriptio*, and *sententiae*. *Color* was the particular line or 'slant' of argument adopted. It depended on the speaker's interpretation of the case. Thus a murder might be represented as an act of revenge, or greed, or mercy, depending either upon how the speaker genuinely viewed the act or upon which line of argument offered the most promising rhetorical possibilities. Cause and consequence, either real or contrived, of the deed under indictment: this was what *color* was concerned with. *Divisio* is the process of asking certain questions concerning the deed, and distinguishing the arguments accordingly. The questions asked included whether it was permissible by law ('an liceat'), and if not, whether it was justifiable by accepted standards of morality ('an oportuerit', 'an aequum sit'). This provided a balance, satisfying to the Roman mind, between consideration of the law and discussion of ethical questions, and formed the basis for the composition of Roman forensic oratory under the empire.

56 The *sententia* was the characteristic mode of expression. Its essential quality was that of a self-contained, memorable utterance, designed to express the points at issue, or their implications, in a novel, clever, and summary way. Thus a speaker in the case quoted above could aptly say

perieras, raptor, nisi bis perire meruisses;[56]

*You would have died, seducer, had you not twice deserved death.*

56. Seneca, *Controversia.* 1.5.2.

and the audience would have 'something to take away with them'.[57] Paradox, as displayed in the above *sententia*, was a favourite ingredient, but 'gnomic' flavour was its original and essential characteristic, and the one which met the prime requirement of the *sententia*, memorability.

57 The *descriptio* was a digression, introduced for added entertainment and display, and contributing little or nothing to the main argument. It could be on moral issues connected with the case, like the effects of poverty, greed, and lust, or simply geographical or ethnological descriptions. They added considerably to the length, but not much to the content.

58 The immediate ancestry of the *suasoria* is to be traced to deliberative rather than forensic oratory. In it a general question of conduct is predicated to a historical or mythical character, thus giving rise to such subjects as 'Should Cato marry?' or 'Should Alexander navigate the sea?' Treatment of such subjects as these might include a great diversity of historical and biographical material, which rendered the *suasoria* the more interesting of the two forms of declamation, both to us and to the Romans. A set of seven *suasoriae* has survived among the works of the Elder Seneca, the finest of which is the sixth, entitled 'Should Cicero beg Antony for his life?' Like the other six, it is a collection of the opinions of a variety of speakers, rhetoricians, and other public men, first represented as addressed to Cicero himself, and later the judgements passed on Cicero by his surviving contemporaries. These two parts are separated by a discussion of how the *divisio* was handled by the various rhetoricians. Here the old deliberative themes of honour, justice, expediency, and necessity reappear. Hardly any rhetorician argued positively: most urged Cicero to die with the republic. It is easy to imagine the outlet that such themes afforded to republican sentiment, and also the danger which the more sensitive emperors like Nero discerned in them. But if Cicero was a ghost from the past, which was

57. Tacitus, *Dialogus De Oratoribus*, 22, 3.

politically embarrassing, his influence upon imperial oratory was restricted to its interest in past history, literature, and law. The new style, with its antithesis and its pointed brevity, was a negation of his ample periods, and served different ends.

59 The influence of the *suasoria*, both in style and content, upon the whole range of Silver Age Latin literature was so great as to become one of its distinguishing characteristics. In particular, epic and elegiac poetry, whose subjects were mythological or historical, became the second home for the pointed, epigrammatic phrase. Many poets were practising declaimers, among them Ovid. His *Heroidum Epistolae*, though primarily examples of pathetic *prosopopoeia*, in which the plight of various mythological heroines is portrayed, nevertheless contain several recognizable *sententiae*.[58] The *Amores* are an even richer source of *sententiae*, the subject being especially suited to their occasional irony, and to the tone of oracular didacticism which Ovid likes to assume on the subject.[59] But he also wrote extended pieces which have the form and content of *suasoriae*. Two examples will suffice here: the speeches of Ajax and Ulysses in Book XIII of the *Metamorphoses*, and the whole of the second book of the *Tristia*.

60 An even more enthusiastic declaimer was the poet Lucan, a Spaniard who shared the passion of his countrymen, the Senecae, father and son, for the art, and incurred the envy of Nero through his prowess. Given a historical subject such as the Civil War, the theme of his *Pharsalia*, we may be prepared for rhetorical pyrotechnics; and we get them. *Sententiae* abound:[60] so does a taste for amplification, exaggeration,

58. E.g. Res est solliciti plena timoris amor (1. 12). *Love is a thing fraught with anxious fear.*

59. E.g. Casta est quam nemo rogavit (1. 8. 43). *Pure is she whom no man has wooed.*

60. E.g. Audendo magnus tegitur timor (4. 702), *Bravado can conceal great fear*; quicquid multis peccatur inultum est (5. 260), *A crime shared by many goes unpunished*; and, applied to characters: victrix causa deis placuit sed victa Catoni (1. 128), *The gods preferred a victorious cause, Cato a lost one*; nec quemquam iam ferre potest Caesarve priorem Pompeiusve parem (1. 125), *Caesar could not now tolerate anyone as his superior, and Pompey could tolerate no equal.*

digression,[61] and gruesome detail.[62] The influence of declamatory technique is so great as to affect the whole character of the poem.

61 Among prose authors the influence of the new style was no less profound. Velleius Paterculus was the first historian to embrace it, adapting it quite skilfully to the epitomizing character of his History of Greece and Rome. Tacitus, after studying and imitating Cicero in his *Dialogus de Oratoribus*, settled for a pregnant, intense style which, though extremely individual, traced its ancestry from Sallust through the pointed style of the declaimers. The same influence is also to be found in the prose of Valerius Maximus, Curtius Rufus, and Florus.

62 The oratory of the early Empire had many contemporary critics, who proclaimed in various ways what was itself a rhetorical commonplace – that the best was in the past. It is perhaps significant, however, that this *convicium saeculi* was voiced by men who had practised and accepted the new style. The Elder Seneca records several criticisms by authorities whose views would otherwise be unknown to us, like Asinius Pollio, Cassius Severus, and Votienus Montanus. The gravamen of their complaints against declamation was its artificiality and remoteness from reality, a characteristically Roman criticism. But there is an aspect of Roman oratory which did not apply to Greek in its period of original creativity: the fact that it was subject from its inception to minutely drawn rules and systems, which satisfied the same Roman passion for order that made them into the world's greatest lawgivers and soldiers. That was why rhetoric became more and more elaborate in Roman hands; and the Silver Age critics probably realized that they were participating in an inevitable process which drew its impetus less from political forces than from their own national character.

61. E.g. 7. 385–455.
62. E.g. 7. 617–46.

# Bibliography

ADAMS, C. D. *Demosthenes*, New York, 1927.

BONNER, R. J. and SMITH, G. *The Administration of Justice from Homer to Aristotle*, Chicago, 1930–8.

BONNER, S. F. *Roman Declamation*, Liverpool, 1948.

CLARKE, D. L. *Rhetoric in Greco-Roman Education*, Columbia, 1957.

CLARKE, M. L. *Rhetoric at Rome*, London, 1966.

CLOCHÉ, P. *Isocrate et son Temps*, Paris, 1963.

DOBSON, J. F. *The Greek Orators*, London, 1919.

DOREY, T. A. (Ed.), *Cicero* (in the series 'Studies in Latin Literature and its Influence'), London, 1965.

FREEMAN, K. *The Murder of Herodes*, London, 1946

GOMPERZ, H. *Sophistik und Rhetorik*, Leipzig, 1912.

HARRISON, A. W. *The Law of Athens*, Oxford, 1968.

HINKS, D. A. G. *Corax and Tisias*, C.Q., 1940.

HUDSON-WILLIAMS, H. L. *Isocrates*, G. & R., 1940.

HUDSON-WILLIAMS, H. L. 'Political and forensic oratory', C.Q., 1951.

HUDSON-WILLIAMS, H. L. 'Thucydides, Isocrates and the rhetorical method of composition', C.Q., 1948.

JAEGER, W. *Demosthenes*, Berkeley, 1938.

JAEGER, W. *Paideia*, Vol. III, Oxford, 1961.

JEBB, R. C. *The Attic Orators from Antiphon to Isaeus*, London, 1888.

KENNEDY, G. *The Art of Persuasion in Greece*, London, 1963.

LEEMAN, A. D. *Orationis Ratio*, Amsterdam, 1963.

LAVENCY, M. *Aspects de la Logographie Judiciaire Attique*, Louvain, 1964.

ROBERTS, W. R. *Greek Rhetoric and Literary Criticism*, New York, 1963.

RONNET, G. *Etude sur le style de Demosthene*, Paris, 1951.

SMETHURST, S. E. *Cicero and Isocrates*, T.A.P.A., 1953.

USHER, S., *Individual Characterisation in Lysias*, Eranos, 1965.

# *Index*

Roman figures refer to chapter numbers; Arabic figures refer to paragraph numbers.